THE STRUCTURE OF WORLD HISTORY

KOJIN KARATANI

THE STRUCTURE OF WORLD HISTORY

FROM MODES OF PRODUCTION
TO MODES OF EXCHANGE

Translated by Michael K. Bourdaghs

Duke University Press Durham and London 2014

Printed in the United States of America on acid-free paper ∞
Interior designed by Courtney Leigh Baker
Typeset in Arno Pro by Westchester Publishing Services

Library of Congress Cataloging-in-Publication Data
Karatani, Kojin, 1941–
The structure of World history : from modes of production to modes
of exchange / Kojin Karatani ; translated by Michael K. Bourdaghs.
pages cm
Includes bibliographical references and index.
ISBN 978-0-8223-5665-3 (cloth : alk. paper)
ISBN 978-0-8223-5676-9 (pbk. : alk. paper)
1. Exchange—Social aspects. 2. Capital. 3. Economics—Sociological
aspects. I. Bourdaghs, Michael K. II. Title.
HM548.k37 2014
330.9—dc23   2013041879

CONTENTS

TRANSLATOR'S NOTE

This translation is based on the first edition of *Sekaishi no kōzō*, which was published by Iwanami Shoten in 2010, but it also incorporates substantial revisions and additions that the author prepared for a future revised edition of the book. Japanese personal names are given in the Western order—that is, given name first and family name second, including in the bibliography. Finally, I would like to acknowledge the research assistance that I received from Scott Aalgaard in preparing this translation.

AUTHOR'S PREFACE TO THE ENGLISH TRANSLATION

This book is an attempt to rethink the history of social formations from the perspective of *modes of exchange*. Until now, in Marxism this has been taken up from the perspective of *modes of production*—from, that is, the perspective of who owns the means of production. Modes of production have been regarded as the "economic base," while the political, religious, and cultural have been considered the ideological superstructure. In the way it splits the economic from the political, this view is grounded in capitalist society. Accordingly, the view runs into difficulties in trying to explain precapitalist societies: in Asiatic or feudal societies, to say nothing of the clan societies that preceded these, there is no split between political control and economic control. Moreover, even in the case of contemporary capitalist societies, viewing the state and nation as simply ideological superstructures has led to difficulties, because the state and nation function as active agents on their own. Marxists believed that ideological superstructures such as the state or nation would naturally wither away when the capitalist economy was abolished, but reality betrayed their expectation, and they were tripped up in their attempts to deal with the state and nation.

As a result, Marxists began to stress the *relative autonomy* of the ideological superstructure. In concrete terms, this meant supplementing the theory of economic determinism with knowledge derived from such fields as psychoanalysis, sociology, and political science. This, however, resulted in a tendency to underestimate the importance of the *economic base*. Many social scientists and historians rejected economic determinism and asserted the autonomy of other dimensions. Even as it led to increased disciplinary specialization, this stance became increasingly widespread and accepted as legitimate. But it resulted in the loss of any totalizing, systematic perspective for comprehending the structures in which politics, religion, philosophy, and other dimensions are interrelated, as well as the abandonment of any attempt to find a way to supersede existing conditions.

In this book, I turn anew to the dimension of the *economic*. But I define the economic not in terms of modes of production but rather in terms of modes of exchange. There are four types of mode of exchange: mode A, which consists of the reciprocity of the gift; mode B, which consists of ruling and protection; mode C, which consists of commodity exchange; and mode D, which transcends the other three. These four types coexist in all social formations. They differ only on which of the modes is dominant. For example, in capitalist society mode of exchange C is dominant. In *Capital*, Marx considered the capitalist economy not only in terms of modes of production but also in terms of commodity exchange—he theorized how the ideological superstructure could be produced from mode of exchange C. Particularly in volume 3 of *Capital*, he took on the task of explicating how a capitalist economy is above all a system of credit and therefore always harbors the possibility of crisis.

But Marx paid only scant attention to the problems of precapitalist societies. It would be foolish to criticize him on this though. Our time and energy would be better spent in explaining how ideological superstructures are produced through modes of exchange A and B, in the same way that Marx did for mode of exchange C. That is what I have attempted in this book. One other question I take up is how a society in which mode of exchange A is dominant emerged in the first place.

Since Marcel Mauss, it has been generally accepted that mode of exchange A (the reciprocity of the gift) is the dominant principle governing archaic societies. But this principle did not exist in the band societies of nomadic hunter-gatherers that had existed since the earliest times. In these societies, it was not possible to stockpile goods, and so they were pooled, distributed equally. This was a pure gift, one that did not require a reciprocal countergift. In addition, the power of the group to regulate individual members was weak, and marriage ties were not permanent. In sum, it was a society characterized by an equality that derived from the free mobility of its individual members. Clan society, grounded in the principle of reciprocity, arose only after nomadic bands took up fixed settlement. Fixed settlement made possible an increased population; it also gave rise to conflict with outsiders. Moreover, because it made the accumulation of wealth possible, it inevitably led to disparities in wealth and power. Clan society contained this danger by imposing the obligations of gift-countergift. Of course, this was not something that clan society intentionally planned. Mode of exchange A appeared in the form of a compulsion, as Freud's "return of the repressed." This, however, led to a shortcoming for clan society: its members were equal but they were no longer free (that is, freely mobile). In other words, the constraints binding individuals to the collective were strengthened.

Accordingly, the distinction between the stage of nomadic peoples and that of fixed settlement is crucial. As is well-known, Marx hypothesized a "primitive communism" existing in ancient times and saw the emergence of a future communist society as that primitive communism's restoration after the advancement of capitalism. Today this stance is widely rejected as a quasi-religious historical viewpoint. Moreover, if we rely on anthropological studies of currently existing primitive societies, we are forced to reject this idea of primitive communism. We cannot, however, dismiss the idea simply because it cannot be found empirically—nor should we. But Marxists have largely ducked this question.

The problem here is, first of all, that Marx and Engels located their model of primitive communism in Lewis H. Morgan's version of clan society. In my view, they should have looked not to clan society but to the nomadic societies that preceded it. Why did Marx and Engels overlook the difference between nomadic and clan societies? This was closely related to their viewing the history of social formations in terms of mode of production. In other words, when seen from the perspective of their shared ownership of the means of production, there is no difference between nomadic and clan societies. When we view them in terms of modes of exchange, however, we see a decisive difference—the difference, for example, between the pure gift and the gift based on reciprocity.

Second, when seen from the perspective of modes of exchange, we are able to understand why communism is not simply a matter of economic development nor of utopianism, but why it should be considered instead the return of primitive communism. Of course, what returns is not the communism of clan society but that of nomadic society. I call this mode of exchange D. It marks the return of repressed mode of exchange A at the stages where modes of exchange B and C are dominant. It is important to note, though, that clan society and its governing principle mode of exchange A themselves already constitute the return of the repressed: in fixed settlement society, they represented attempts to preserve the equality that existed under nomadism. Naturally, this did not arrive as the result of people's desire or intention: it came as a compulsory duty that offered no choice.

Mode of exchange D is not simply the restoration of mode A—it is not, that is, the restoration of community. Mode of exchange D, as the restoration of A in a higher dimension, is in fact only possible with the negation of A. D is, in sum, the restoration of nomadic society. Yet this too does not appear as the result of human desire or intention, but rather emerges as a duty issued by God or heaven or as a *regulative idea*. In concrete terms, D arrives in the form of universal religion, which negates religions grounded in magic or reciprocity.

But there is no need for mode of exchange D to take religious form. There are cases where mode of exchange D appeared without religious trappings—in, for example, Ionia from the seventh to the sixth centuries BCE, or Iceland from the tenth through the twelfth centuries CE, or the eastern part of North America in the eighteenth century. What these share in common is that all were poleis formed by colonialists: covenant communities established by persons who had become independent from their original states or communities. In them, if land became scarce, rather than perform wage labor on another person's land, people would move to another town. For this reason, disparities in landed property did not arise. Because people were nomadic (free), they were equal. In Ionia, this was called *isonomia*. This meant not simply formal political equality but actual economic equality. Of course, these communities were all short-lived: they ended when they reached the limits of the space available for colonization. These examples show that communism depends less on shared ownership of the means of production than on the return of nomadism.

But in actuality, all around the world socialist movements that aimed to bring about mode of exchange D were generally carried out under the guise of universal religions. In the latter half of the nineteenth century, socialism became "scientific" and lost its religious hue. But the key question here is not whether socialism is religious; it is whether socialism intends mode of exchange D. Socialism in the twentieth century was only able to realize societies dominated by modes of exchange B and C, and as a result it lost its appeal. But so long as modes of exchange B and C remain dominant, the drive to transcend them will never disappear. In some form or another, mode of exchange D will emerge. Whether or not this takes religious form is unimportant. This drive is fundamentally rooted in that which has been repressed from nomadic society. It has persisted throughout world history, and will not disappear in the future—even if we are unable to predict the form in which it will appear.

Kojin Karatani
April 20, 2012

PREFACE

This book marks an attempt to move beyond the present-day Capital-Nation-State system by rethinking the history of social formations from the perspective of modes of exchange. I first raised this prospect in an earlier book, *Transcritique: On Kant and Marx* (2001; English translation, 2003). My goal here is to develop that idea in depth. Accordingly, to explain the project of the present book, I would like to start by reviewing the argument I made in *Transcritique*.

I give the name *transcritique* to the task of reading Marx by way of Kant and Kant by way of Marx. This does not mean, of course, a simple comparison or synthesis of the two. In fact, another philosopher stands between these two: Hegel. To read Marx by way of Kant and Kant by way of Marx is also to read Hegel by way of these two philosophers, who precede and follow him. In other words, it means to undertake a new critique of Hegel.

I began to feel the urgent need for such an undertaking around 1990, in the period that began with the revolutions in Eastern Europe and ended with the dismantling of the Soviet Union. Around that time the expression "the end of history" as used by Frances Fukuyama, an official in the U.S. State Department, achieved wide currency. In fact, the origins of this expression can be traced back beyond Fukuyama to the French Hegelian philosopher Alexandre Kojève. Kojève provided a variety of interpretations of Hegel's view of "the end of history."[1] But Fukuyama used the concept to signify the collapse of the communist order and the ultimate victory of America. He maintained that history had ended because the 1989 East European revolutions signaled the final victory of liberal democracy, after which there could be no subsequent fundamental revolutions.

There were many who ridiculed Fukuyama's views, but in a sense he was correct. But if he were claiming that what occurred in 1990 was the final victory of the United States, he was mistaken. Even if it appeared that American hegemony was established and that globalization and neoliberalism had triumphed, it is clear today, some twenty years later, that these led to their own breakdown. As a result we see in every country to a greater or lesser extent the adoption of state-capitalistic or social-democratic policies. We see this, for example, in what President Obama calls "change." Yet this transformation does not somehow overturn "the end of history": rather, the transformation serves as proof of the end of history's arrival.

In *Transcritique* I argued as follows. What is called the nation-state is the joining together of two heterogeneous entities, state and nation, by means of a hyphen. But to understand modern social formations, we have to add to this the capitalist economy. In short, we have to see it in terms of Capital-Nation-State. This is a mutually complementary apparatus. For example, a capitalist economy allowed to take its own course will inevitably result in economic inequality and conflict. But the nation, as something that intends communality and equality, will seek to resolve the various contradictions and inequalities introduced by the capitalist system. The state in turn realizes this intention through such measures as taxation, redistribution, and various regulations. Capital, nation, and state are distinct entities, each operating according to its own principles, but like a Borromean knot, they are linked in such a manner that all will fall apart if any of the three is missing. I have called this Capital-Nation-State.

In my view, the situation that Fukuyama called "the end of history" means that once this Capital-Nation-State form is realized, any subsequent fundamental revolution is impossible. The change we see proclaimed recently around the world is not evidence that Capital-Nation-State has broken down, but rather that its mechanisms are functioning only too well. The Capital-Nation-State circuit is perfectly stable. Because people are not even aware that they are trapped within its circuit, they mistakenly believe that they are making historical progress when in fact they are simply spinning around in circles within it. In *Transcritique* I described the situation:

> One often hears the prediction that, thanks to the globalization of capital, the nation-state will disappear. It is certain that economic policies within nation-states do not work as effectively as before, because of the growing network of international economic reliance on foreign trade. But, no matter how international relations are reorganized and intensified, the state and nation won't disappear. When individual national economies are threatened by the global market (neoliberalism), they de-

mand the protection (redistribution) of the state and / or bloc economy, at the same time as appealing to national cultural identity. So it is that any counteraction to capital must also be one targeted against the state and nation (community). The capitalist nation-state is fearless because of its trinity. The denial of one ends up being reabsorbed in the ring of the trinity by the power of the other two. This is because each of them, though appearing to be illusory, is based upon different principles of exchange. Therefore, when we take capitalism into consideration, we always have to include nation and state. And the counteraction against capitalism also has to be against nation-state. In this light, social democracy does nothing to overcome the capitalist economy but is the last resort for the capitalist nation-state's survival.[2]

I wrote these words in the 1990s, and they can stand without revision even today. Capital-Nation-State is truly an ingenious system. My purpose here, however, is not to praise it but to transcend it. On this point, my thought since 2001 has changed considerably from what it was in the 1990s when I wrote *Transcritique*. I was compelled to undertake a comprehensive reconsideration of the structure of world history by the situation that has emerged since 2001.

In the 1990s, I was intrigued by the possibility of a new global movement of resistance toward capital and the state. While I didn't have a clearly defined vision, I did have the vague sense that such a movement would naturally develop into a transnational alliance. This sort of atmosphere could be found everywhere at the time, as symbolized by the 1999 antiglobalization protests in Seattle. For example, Jacques Derrida proposed a "New International," while Antonio Negri and Michael Hardt called for simultaneous global rebellion by the "multitude." Sharing a similar perspective, I launched a praxis-oriented political movement.

That sort of optimism, however, was crushed by the situation that emerged after 9/11 in 2001—right around the time I published *Transcritique*. In the events of that time, what might appear to be a conflict between religions was in reality a baring of the deep fissures that existed between North and South. Moreover, what emerged was not simply conflict between various states but rather fissures within movements of resistance to capital and the state. At the time I became even more acutely aware that state and nation were not merely elements of the "superstructure" but instead functioned as active agents on their own. Countermovements against capital and the state inevitably splinter once they reach a certain level. That has been the case until now, and it will remain the case for the foreseeable future. I realized that I needed to rethink and expand the argument I had made in *Transcritique*.

That is when I came upon the idea of a comprehensive rethinking of the history of social formations from the perspective of modes of exchange. This idea was originally proposed by Marx. But to carry it out fully required a rejection of conventional Marxist formulas. Nor would it be sufficient, I realized, to simply reinterpret Marx's texts. Until 2001, I was at heart a literary critic and theorist, so my readings of Marx or Kant took the form of textual criticism. In other words, even when I was presenting my own views, I presented them only in the form of meanings that could be derived from the given texts. But this sort of textual reading was inherently limited. My own views often conflicted with theirs, and there were many domains and problems that they never considered. Accordingly, in taking up the problem of the structure of world history, I felt the need to construct my own theoretical system. I have always disliked systematic undertakings and was never particularly good at them. Nonetheless, I am now for the first time in my life venturing to construct a theoretical system. This is because the problem I am wrestling with here can only be explicated systematically.

My task was in one sense a revisiting of Marx's critique of Hegel. This is because it was Hegel, in his *Philosophy of Right*, who first explicated capital, nation, and state as a mutually interrelated system. He grasped Capital-Nation-State dialectically as a triplex system, a totality in which the presence of each was a necessity. It was also the unity formed by the three mottos of the French Revolution: liberty, equality, fraternity. Marx launched his own work from a critique of Hegel's *Philosophy of Right*. But in doing so Marx regarded the capitalist economy as constituting the base structure, while he took nation and state to be part of the ideological superstructure. Because of this, he was never able to grasp the complex social formation that is Capital-Nation-State. This led him to the view that state and nation would naturally wither away once the capitalist system was abolished. As a result, Marxist movements have always stumbled badly in the face of problems of the state and nation.

The reasons for this lie in Marx's failure to see that state and nation, like capital, have their own real bases and hence cannot be dissolved simply through acts of enlightenment, as well as in his failure to see that they exist in a structure of interrelationship. If we want to sublate capital, state, nation, and religion, we must first understand what they are. Simply rejecting them will get us nowhere: in the end, we would be forced to acknowledge their actuality and ultimately would reach the stage of cynically sneering at any *idée* that promised to transcend them. This is precisely the condition of postmodernism.

Accordingly, to revisit Marx's critique of Hegel requires us to take up the modern social formation and the "world history" that led to it—a world history that Hegel grasped, albeit in the mode of idealism—and to turn them on their head the way Marx did via a materialist approach, while not losing sight of Hegel's Capital-Nation-State trinity. To achieve this, it is crucial that we view world history not from the perspective of modes of production but rather of modes of exchange. Historically, all social formations exist as combinations of multiple modes of exchange. Social formations differ only in the question of which mode of exchange is dominant. A capitalist social formation is one in which commodity exchange is the dominant mode, a situation that also leads to modifications in the other modes of exchange. The result is the formation of Capital-Nation-State.

Taking this position does not require us to abandon Marx. As I discussed in *Transcritique*, Marx provided a brilliant explication in *Capital* of the world formed by the mode of exchange known as commodity exchange. To do so, he had to bracket off the questions of nation and state, so that inevitably his consideration of those questions was inadequate. I wrote then that, rather than merely criticize him for this, it made more sense to take up the methods Marx adopted in *Capital* and extend them to the state and nation. The present book represents my attempt to carry this out.

But simply to demonstrate the historical necessity of Capital-Nation-State would be to stop where Hegel stopped. My task here is to clarify the necessity of its being transcended. To explore this requires us to return once more to Marx's critique of Hegel. Marx's critique of Hegel was a materialist inverting or turning on its head of Hegel's idealist speculations, which is commonly imagined as an up-down inversion (between the sensible or material and the ideal). But it is most important to see how it was an inversion between before and after.

According to Hegel, the essence of something only becomes apparent in its effects. That is, he viewed things *ex post facto*, "after the fact." Kant, on the other hand, viewed things *ex ante facto*, "before the fact." With regard to the future, we can only make predictions, not draw positive conclusions. For this reason, Kant held that ideas are illusions. But they are *transcendental illusions*. This means that, unlike illusions that arise from our sense perception, we cannot eliminate them by way of reason, because they are illusions that are necessary to reason itself. In plain language, without these illusions we would lapse into schizophrenia.

For example, with regard to world history, Kant says that looking at developments up until now, we can regard them as gradually progressing toward the "kingdom of ends" (a world in which moral law is realized). He calls this sort of idea a "regulative idea." This is distinct from a "constructive idea" in that, while it can never be realized, it perseveres as an indicator that we strive to approach.[3] By contrast, for Hegel, ideas were not, à la Kant, something oriented toward future realization but that would never go beyond the stage of illusion. For Hegel, ideas were not illusions; they were real: reality itself was ideal. For Hegel, history by definition was over.

When he turned Hegel on his head, Marx saw history not as something that had ended, but as something that must be realized in the future. This represents a switch from an after-the-fact to a before-the-fact standpoint. Yet the sort of necessity that can be elucidated from an after-the-fact standpoint cannot be assumed before the fact. Here necessity can exist only as an illusion (idea). In sum, to adopt a before-the-fact standpoint means in a sense to return to Kant's position. Though he largely ignored Kant, Marx was unable to avoid the problems that necessarily arise whenever one adopts a before-the-fact standpoint. For example, it becomes impossible to assert the historical necessity of communism.

I would like to cite the case of another post-Hegelian philosopher, Kierkegaard. He critiqued Hegel, arguing that while speculation is by its nature backward looking, ethics were forward looking. Backward looking here means the after-the-fact standpoint, whereas forward looking means to adopt a before-the-fact standpoint. The latter requires a *salto mortale* (fatal leap). Like Marx, Kierkegaard largely ignored Kant. Nonetheless, Kierkegaard also clearly returned to a before-the-fact standpoint, just as had Marx. In sum, the key issue here is not a choice between Hegel or Kant. Anyone who adopts a before-the-fact standpoint will be confronted with the same problems.

Ernst Bloch called Marx's philosophy the "Philosophy of the Future." It attempts to see the "Not-Yet-Conscious"; it is "forward dreaming."[4] This is correct, yet we must also note that Marx consistently refused to make any conclusive statements about the future. For example, in the *German Ideology*, Marx writes, "Communism is for us not a state of affairs which is to be established, an ideal to which reality [will] have to adjust itself. We call communism the real movement which abolishes the present state of things. The conditions of this movement result from the now existing premise."[5] Here Marx refuses to define the end (or ending) of history. In this, he is not only negating Hegel but also rejecting Kant.

In fact, what Marx called communism hardly differs from what Kant called "the kingdom of ends." It is, in other words, a society in which you treat any other "always at the same time as an end and never merely as a means to an end."[6] Kant's morality was not a question of good and evil but of freedom (spontaneous self-determination). To treat the other as an end is to treat the other as a free being. In the absence of this kind of morality, there can be no communism. Yet Marx refused to take up morality directly. Insofar as one begins from morality, communism will end up as "an *ideal* to which reality [will] have to adjust itself." In contrast, Marx argued that real material processes in themselves contain the "premises" that necessarily lead to communism.

The problem is, insofar as you look at material processes or economic substructures from the perspective of modes of production, you will never find the moral moment. For this reason, the moral moment must be sought not in economic structure but in the idealistic dimension. In fact, Kantian Marxists, Sartre, and others have attempted to supplement the economically deterministic forms of Marxism by introducing an existential, moral moment. But in my view this is unnecessary. If we rethink the economic base from the perspective of exchange, broadly defined, then there is no need to posit a moral dimension exterior to "economy." The moral moment is included within the modes of exchange. For example, seen from the perspective of mode of exchange, communism consists precisely of the realization of mode of exchange D. This is surely a process that is in equal measures economic and moral. Moreover, mode of exchange D is the return in a higher dimension of the primal mode of exchange A (reciprocity). This comes about not as a result of people's desires or ideas, but rather is inevitable, like Freud's "returned of the repressed."

What becomes clear from the perspective of "the structure of world history" is that Capital-Nation-State is a product of the world system, not of any one nation. Accordingly, its sublation cannot occur within a single nation. For example, if a socialist revolution occurs in one country, other countries will immediately interfere or otherwise take advantage of the situation. Marx of course already took this into account: "Empirically, communism is only possible as the act of the dominant peoples 'all at once' and simultaneously, which presupposes the universal development of productive forces and the world intercourse bound up with them."[7] It was for this reason that Marx was opposed to the outbreak of the Paris Commune— even if once the uprising got under way, he became a passionate supporter. This was because the Paris Commune was limited to a single city, or at most to one nation, France. Accordingly, the Paris Commune would inevitably end in failure, and even if it were able to sustain itself, it would fall into a reign of terror, just as had the French Revolution. Proof of this was subsequently provided by the Russian Revolution.

Since then the slogan "simultaneous world revolution" has been continuously bandied about, but it has remained little more than a slogan. No one has directly confronted Marx's position that a socialist revolution is possible only as a simultaneous world revolution. The mythic vision of a simultaneous world revolution remains today—the image of a global revolt by the multitude is one example. But the end result that this will lead to is already obvious. What I want to propose here, however, is not the abandonment of the concept. I want instead to think of simultaneous world revolution in a different form. In this lies the only real possibility for sublating Capital-Nation-State.

As I noted, in the situation that has unfolded since 2001, I have felt an urgent need to rethink the problems harbored in countermovements against global capital and the state. During this time I found myself returning to Kant and Hegel. In a very interesting way, the Iraq War abruptly resurrected the classical philosophical problems of Kant and Hegel, normally of concern only to specialists in philosophy, within the context of contemporary politics. For example, while France and Germany supported the United Nations, ideologues of U.S. neoconservatism derided it as a Kantian delusion. In doing so, they were taking up the position of "Hegel," though they did not specifically invoke his name. On the other hand, European social democrats, such as Jürgen Habermas, who opposed the U.S. war in Iraq, countered with "Kant." I opposed the former, naturally, but I was also unable to support the latter.

In the midst of this process, I began to reconsider Kant, in particular what he called the problem of "perpetual peace." One reason for this was the radical situation that emerged with the Japanese state's decision to send troops to Iraq despite the postwar constitution's explicit renunciation of the right to make war. The Kantian origins of that constitution are clear. My rereading of Kant, however, is not simply concerned with peace but also with the sublation of state and capital. What Kant calls "perpetual peace" is not simply the absence of war, but rather the abolition of all antagonism between states—meaning, that is, the abolition of the state itself.

Instead of rereading Kant's notion of a world federation of nations from the perspective of pacifism, I tried to reread from that of the sublation of state and capital. I realized then that Kant too had been thinking about simultaneous world revolution. He supported a Rousseau-style bourgeois revolution, but he also saw that it could not succeed if it took place in only one country—other countries would inevitably interfere or invade. This is why Kant conceptualized a world federation of nations even before the French Revolution. This was not for the sake of abolishing war; it was for making the bourgeois revolution into a simultaneous world revolution.

Just as Kant feared, when a bourgeois revolution did take place in the single nation of France, the surrounding absolutist monarchies immediately intervened, and the fear provoked by this external terror resulted in an internal (reign of) terror. Additionally, the war to defend the revolution from the exterior transformed into Napoleon's European war of conquest. In the midst of this Kant published "Perpetual Peace: A Philosophical Sketch" (1795), calling for the establishment of a federation of nations. Consequently, the proposal has always been considered an instance of pacifism. What Kant aimed at was not peace as the simple absence of war, however, but rather the simultaneous global realization of a bourgeois revolution that would sublate state and capital. The federation of nations was to be the first step toward this. On this point, we find an utterly unexpected encounter between Kant's and Marx's thoughts.

Kant did not believe that the federation of nations would be realized through humanity's good will; instead it would be realized through war— that is, by means of irresistible force. In fact, his idea was realized only after two world wars: the League of Nations and the United Nations. These were, of course, inadequate in form. That the sole pathway toward overcoming Capital-Nation-State lies in this direction, however, is something beyond doubt.

INTRODUCTION **ON MODES OF EXCHANGE**

Marx's Critique of Hegel

Today's advanced capitalist nations are characterized by a triplex system, the Capital-Nation-State trinity. In its structure, there is first of all a capitalist market economy. If left to its own devices, however, this will inevitably result in economic disparities and class conflict. To counter this, the nation, which is characterized by an intention toward communality and equality, seeks to resolve the various contradictions brought about by the capitalist economy. The state then fulfills this task through such measures as taxation and redistribution or regulations. Capital, nation, and state all differ from one another, with each being grounded in its own distinct set of principles, but here they are joined together in a mutually supplementary manner. They are linked in the manner of a Borromean knot, in which the whole system will fail if one of the three is missing.

No one has yet adequately comprehended this structure. But in a sense, we can say that G. W. F. Hegel in his *Philosophy of Right* attempted to grasp it. But Hegel regarded Capital-Nation-State as the ultimate social form and never considered the possibility of its being transcended. Having said that, if we wish to transcend Capital-Nation-State, we must first be able to see it. Accordingly, we must begin with a thorough critique (investigation) of Hegel's *Philosophy of Right*.

In his youth, Karl Marx launched his intellectual career with a critique of Hegel's philosophy of right. At that time, in contrast to Hegel's system that posited the nation-state in the final position,

Marx maintained that state and nation were part of the ideological super-structure and that it was really bourgeois society (the capitalist economy) that formed the fundamental base structure. Moreover, he applied this view to the totality of world history. For example, Marx writes:

> The general conclusion at which I arrived and which, once reached, be-came the guiding principle of my studies can be summarised as follows. In the social production of their existence, men inevitably enter into defi-nite relations, which are independent of their will, namely relations of production appropriate to a given stage in the development of their ma-terial forces of production. The totality of these relations of production constitutes the economic structure of society, the real foundation, on which arises a legal and political superstructure and to which corre-spond definite forms of social consciousness. The mode of production of material life conditions the general process of social, political and intel-lectual life. It is not the consciousness of men that determines their exis-tence, but their social existence that determines their consciousness. . . . The changes in the economic foundation lead sooner or later to the trans-formation of the whole immense superstructure. In studying such transformations it is always necessary to distinguish between the mate-rial transformation of the economic conditions of production, which can be determined with the precision of natural science, and the legal, politi-cal, religious, artistic or philosophic—in short, ideological forms in which men become conscious of this conflict and fight it out. . . . In broad outline, the Asiatic, ancient, feudal and modern bourgeois modes of pro-duction may be designated as epochs marking progress in the economic development of society. The bourgeois relations of production are the last antagonistic form of the social process of production—antagonistic not in the sense of individual antagonism but of an antagonism that ema-nates from the individuals' social conditions of existence—but the pro-ductive forces developing within bourgeois society create also the mate-rial conditions for a solution of this antagonism. The prehistory of human society accordingly closes with this social formation.[1]

Frederick Engels and later Marxists would subsequently call this view his-torical materialism. The problem here is that this view takes the state and nation to be part of the ideological superstructure, on par with art or phi-losophy. This represents a criticism of Hegel, who regarded the state as an active agent (subject), since this Marxist view regards the state as a mere ideological phenomenon that is determined by bourgeois society. This led in turn to the conclusion that if the economic structure were transformed, the state and nation would automatically disappear. This neglect of the active agency of state and nation would lead to various missteps by Marxist movements. On the one hand, among Marxists it brought about state socialism (Stalinism); on the other hand, it helped lead to the victory of those who opposed Marxism in the name of National Socialism (fascism). In other words, far from dissolving the state or nation, movements to transcend capitalism ended up strengthening them to an unprecedented degree.

This experience became an important lesson for Marxists. In response, they began to stress the *relative autonomy* of the superstructure. For example, some Marxists—including, for example, the Frankfurt School—began introducing elements from Max Weber's sociology or Sigmund Freud's psychoanalysis. Of course, in doing so they were not abandoning the concept of determination by the economic base. Yet in reality they tended to shelve the question of the economic base without giving it serious consideration.[2] Moreover, this tendency led to assertions of the autonomy of other domains such as literature or philosophy, as well as of the *ultimate indeterminacy* of textual interpretation, and it hence became one of the sources for postmodernism. But such claims for the *relative autonomy of the superstructure* led to the belief that state and nation were simply representations that had been created historically and that they could be dissolved through enlightenment. This view overlooks the fact that state and nation have their own roots in the base structure and therefore possess active agency.

Previously, historical materialism has faced critical questioning from those branches of scholarship that explore precapitalist forms of society. Marx's division of economic base from political superstructure is a view grounded in modern capitalist society. For this reason, it doesn't work as well when applied to the case of precapitalist societies. To begin with, in primitive societies (tribal communities) there is no state, nor any distinction between economic and political structure. As Marcel Mauss pointed out, these societies are characterized by reciprocal exchanges. This cannot be explained in terms of a *mode of production*. The anthropologist Marshall Sahlins, who persisted in using the concept of mode of production, devised the concept of a "domestic mode of production," one characterized by underproduction.[3] But this underproduction can be better explained through reciprocal exchange: because surplus products are not allowed to accumulate and are instead given away to others, production necessarily remains underproduction.

In the case of the *Asiatic mode of production*, the state apparatuses (the military, bureaucracy, policing mechanisms, and so on) do not somehow stand above economic relations of production. Rather, political relations between emperors or kings and the layers of bureaucracy that support them and the ruled classes are in themselves already economic relations. No distinction exists between economic and political structures here. It is the same in classical antiquity. The unique political systems of Greece and Rome, distinct from those of the Asiatic states, cannot be adequately explained through the slave-system mode of production. Slaves were simply indispensable in securing the freedom and equality of citizens.

Accordingly, if we posit that economic base equals mode of production, we are unable to explain precapitalist societies. Worse, we remain unable to understand even capitalist economies. The capitalist economy is itself dependent on its 'ideological superstructure': to wit, its vast system based on money and credit. In order to explain this, in *Capital* Marx began his inquiry not from mode of production but rather from the dimension of commodity exchange. The capitalist mode of production—in other words, the relation between capital and labor—is organized through the relations between money and commodity (mode of exchange). But Marxists who advocated historical materialism failed to read *Capital* with sufficient care and ended up trumpeting only the concept of mode of production time and time again.

For these reasons, we should abandon the belief that mode of production equals economic base. This does not in any way mean, however, that we should abandon the concept of economic base in general.[4] We simply need to launch our investigation from the mode of exchange rather than from the mode of production. If exchange is an economic concept, then all modes of exchange must be economic in nature. In short, if we take the term *economic* in a broad sense, then nothing prevents us from saying that the social formation is determined by its economic base. For example, the state and nation originate in their own distinct modes of exchange (economic bases). It would be foolish to distinguish these from the economic base and regard them as ideological superstructure. The inability to dissolve state and nation through enlightenment is due to their being rooted in specific modes of exchange. They also, it is true, take on idealistic forms. But we can say the same thing about the capitalist economy, with its base in commodity exchange. Far from being materialistic, the capitalist system is an idealistic world based on credit. It is for precisely this reason that it always harbors the possibility of crisis.

The Types of Mode of Exchange

When we speak about exchange, we automatically think of commodity exchange. Insofar as we live in a capitalist society in which commodity exchange is the dominant mode, this is only natural. But there are also other types of exchange, beginning with gift-countergift reciprocity. Mauss located the principles for the social formation in archaic societies in the gift-countergift reciprocal system, under which various items are given and reciprocated, including food, property, women, land, service, labor, and rituals. This is not something limited to archaic societies; it exists in general in many kinds of communities. Strictly speaking, however, this mode of exchange A is not a principle that arises from within the interior of a community.

Marx repeatedly stresses that commodity exchange (mode of exchange C) begins with exchanges between two communities: "The exchange of commodities begins where communities have their boundaries, at their points of contact with other communities, or with members of the latter."[5] Even if it appears that these exchanges take place between individuals, in fact those individuals are acting as representatives of families or tribes. Marx emphasized this point in order to criticize the views of Adam Smith, who believed that the origins of exchange lay in exchanges between individuals, a view that Marx thought was simply a projection of the contemporary market economy onto the past. But we must not forget that the other types of exchange also arose in exchanges between communities. In other words, reciprocity is something that arose between communities.

In this sense, reciprocity has to be distinguished from the pooling that occurs within a household. For example, in a hunting-and-gathering band formed by several households, captured spoils are pooled and equally redistributed. This pooling or redistribution derives from a principle that exists only within the interior of a household or within a band formed by several households. In contrast, reciprocity arises when one household or band establishes lasting amicable relations with another household or band. In other words, it is through reciprocity that a higher-order collective that transcends the individual household takes form. Accordingly, reciprocity is not so much a principle of community as it is a principle for forming larger, stratified communities.

Mode of exchange B also arises between communities. It begins when one community plunders another. Plunder in itself is not a kind of exchange. How, then, does plunder get transformed into a mode of exchange?

If a community wants to engage in continuous plunder, the dominant community cannot simply carry out acts of plunder but must also give something to its targets: it must protect the dominated community from other aggressors, as well as foster it through public works, such as irrigation systems. Herein lies the prototype for the state. Weber argued that the essence of the state was its monopoly on violence. This does not simply mean that the state is founded on violence. The state protects its constituent peoples by prohibiting nonstate actors from engaging in violence. In other words, the establishment of the state represents a kind of exchange in that the ruled are granted peace and order in return for their obedience. This is mode of exchange B.

There is one other point I should note here. When the economic anthropologist Karl Polanyi lists the crucial unifying forms of human economy in general, in addition to reciprocity and exchange, he includes "redistribution."[6] He regards redistribution as something that has always existed, from archaic societies to the contemporary welfare state. But the redistribution occurring in archaic societies was of a different nature from that occurring under a state. For example, in a chiefdom society, it appears as if each household is subjected to taxes by the chief. But this is always a form of pooling carried out according to a compulsory reciprocity. In other words, the chief does not hold absolute power. In a state, on the other hand, plunder precedes redistribution. It is precisely in order to be able to plunder continuously that redistribution is instituted. Redistribution by the state historically takes place in the form of public policies—irrigation systems, social welfare, or public order. As a result, the state takes on the appearance of an authority acting on behalf of the "public." The state (monarchy) is not simply an extension of tribal society's chiefdom. It instead originates in mode of exchange B—that is, in plunder and redistribution. To find redistribution in an identical form in all societies as Polanyi does is to overlook the unique dimension that distinguishes the state.[7]

Next we have mode of exchange C, or commodity exchange, which is grounded in mutual consent. This arises when exchange is neither constrained by the obligations inherent in gift giving, as in mode of exchange A, nor imposed through violence, as in the pillaging of mode of exchange B. In sum, commodity exchange is established only when the participants mutually recognize each other as free beings. Accordingly, when commodity exchange develops, it tends to free individuals from the primary communal constraints that arise from the principle of gift exchange. The city takes form through this sort of free association between individuals. Of course, as a secondary community the city also functions as a kind of constraint on its members, but this is of a different nature from the primary community.

What is crucial in the case of commodity exchange is that its premise of mutual freedom does not mean mutual equality. When we speak of commodity exchange, it may appear that products or services are being directly exchanged, but in fact this takes place as an exchange between money and commodity. In this case, money and commodity and their respective bearers occupy different positions. As Marx wrote, money possesses the power of universal exchangeability. A person who has money can acquire the products or employ the labor of another without resorting to violent coercion. For this reason, the person who has money and the person who has a commodity—in other words, the creditor and the debtor—are not in positions of equality. The person who possesses money attempts to accumulate more money by engaging in commodity exchange. This is the activity of capital in the form of the movement of self-valorization of money. The accumulation of capital takes place not through physical coercion of the other but through exchanges grounded in mutual consent. This is possible through the difference (surplus value) that is realized through exchanges across different systems of value. This is not to say that such exchanges do not generate differences between rich and poor; of course they do. In this way, mode of exchange C (commodity exchange) brings about relations of *class*, which are of a different nature from the relations of *status* that are generated by mode of exchange B, even though these two are often connected.

In addition to these, I must also describe mode of exchange D. This represents not only the rejection of the state that was generated through mode of exchange B but also a transcending of the class divisions produced in mode of exchange C; we might think of mode of exchange D as representing the return of mode of exchange A in a higher dimension. It is a mode of exchange that is simultaneously free and mutual. Unlike the other three modes, mode of exchange D does not exist in actuality. It is the imaginary return of the moment of reciprocity that has been repressed under modes of exchange B and C. Accordingly, it originally appeared in the form of religious movements.

There is one more point I should add here with regard to the distinctions between modes of exchange. In trying to find in "the political" a relatively autonomous, unique domain, Carl Schmitt writes: "Let us assume that in the realm of morality the final distinctions are between good and evil, in aesthetics beautiful and ugly, in economics profitable and unprofitable."[8] In the same way, Schmitt argues, the final distinction unique to the political is that between friend and enemy. But, in my view, this is a characteristic of mode of exchange B. Accordingly, the unique domain of the political must originate in the economic base, broadly defined.[9]

It is just as true that there is no unique domain of the moral separate from the mode of exchange. Usually, the domain of morality is thought of as being separate from the economic realm, but morality is in fact not unrelated to modes of exchange. For example, Friedrich Nietzsche argues that the consciousness of guilt originates in a sense of debt. This suggests how deeply the moral or religious is connected to modes of exchange. Accordingly, if we see economic base in terms not of modes of production but of modes of exchange, we can understand morality in terms of economic base.

Let us take the example of mode of exchange A (reciprocity). In a tribal society this is the dominant mode of exchange. Here no one is permitted to monopolize wealth or power. Once a state society—in other words, a class society—emerges, mode of exchange A is subordinated, and mode of exchange B becomes dominant. Mode of exchange C develops under it, but remains in a subordinate role. It is with capitalist society that mode of exchange C becomes dominant. In this process, mode of exchange A is repressed but never eliminated. It is finally restored as "the return of the repressed," to borrow Freud's expression. This is mode of exchange D. Mode of exchange D represents the return of mode of exchange A in a higher dimension.

Mode of exchange D was first discovered at the stage of the ancient empires as something that would transcend the domination of modes of exchange B and C. Mode of exchange D was also something that would transcend the religious constraints of the traditional community that was the foundation of the ancient empires. For this reason, mode of exchange D was not a simple return to mode of exchange A but rather a negation of it that restored it in a higher dimension. The most direct instances of mode of exchange D are found in the communistic groups that existed in the earliest stages of universal religions such as Christianity and Buddhism. In subsequent periods, too, socialist movements have taken a religious form.

Since the latter half of the nineteenth century, socialism has lost its religious hue. But the crucial point here is that socialism at its root marks the return in a higher dimension of mode of exchange A. For example, Hannah Arendt points out that in cases of council communism, the councils (soviets or Räte) appear not as the end result of revolutionary tradition or theory: "What is more, they never came into being as a result of a conscious revolutionary tradition or theory, but entirely spontaneously, each time as though

TABLE 1 Modes-of-Exchange Matrix

B: Plunder and redistribution (Domination and protection)	A: Reciprocity (Gift and countergift)
C: Commodity Exchange (Money and commodities)	D: X

TABLE 2 The Modern-Social-Formation Matrix

B: State	A: Nation
C: Capital	D: X

there had never been anything of the sort before."[10] This suggests that the spontaneously arising council communism represents the return of mode of exchange A in a higher dimension.

Mode of exchange D and the social formation that originates in it can be called by many names—for example, socialism, communism, anarchism, council communism, associationism. But because historically a variety of meanings have been attached to these concepts, we are likely to invite misunderstanding and confusion no matter which one we use. For this reason, here I will simply call it X. The name doesn't matter; what is important here is to understand the phase to which it belongs.

To sum up, modes of exchange can be broadly divided into four types: reciprocity, plunder and redistribution, commodity exchange, and X. These are shown in the matrix given in table 1, where the horizontal rows indicate degree of equality or inequality and the vertical columns indicate degree of coercion or freedom. Table 2 situates the forms that historically have derived from these: capital, nation, state, and X.

The next important point to make is that actual social formations consist of complex combinations of these modes of exchange. To jump to my conclusion, historical social formations have included all of these modes. The formations differ simply in terms of which mode takes the leading role. In tribal societies reciprocal mode of exchange A is dominant. This does not mean the modes B or C are nonexistent—they exist, for example, in wars or in trading. But because the moments for B and C are here subordinated to the principle of reciprocity, the kind of society in which B is dominant—a state society—does not develop. On the other hand, in a society in which mode B is dominant, mode A continues to exist—for example, in farming communities. We also find the development of mode C—for example, in cities. In precapitalist social formations, however, these elements are administered or coopted from above by the state. This is what we mean when we say that mode of exchange B is dominant.

When mode of exchange C is dominant, we have a capitalist society. In Marx's thought, a capitalist social formation is a society defined by the capitalist mode of production. But what is it that distinguishes capitalist production? We will not find it in such forms as the division and combination of labor, or again in the employment of machinery. After all, these can all be found in slavery systems as well. Nor can we simply equate capitalist production with the production of commodities in general: both slavery and serfdom systems developed as forms of commodity production. Capitalist production is different from slavery or serfdom production in that it is commodity production that relies on *the labor power commodity*. In a slavery system, human beings become commodities. Accordingly, only in a society where it is not human beings themselves but rather human labor power that is commodified can we say there is capitalist production. Moreover, it exists only when commodity exchange permeates the entire society, including the commodification of land. For these reasons, capitalist production can only be understood if we look at it in terms of mode of exchange—not in terms of mode of production.

In a capitalist society, commodity exchange is the dominant mode of exchange. This does not mean, however, that the other modes of exchange and their derivatives completely vanish. Those other elements continue to exist but in altered form: the state becomes a modern state and the community becomes a nation. In other words, as commodity exchange becomes the dominant mode, precapitalist social formations are transformed into the Capital-Nation-State complex. Only in this way can we materialistically rethink the trinity system that Hegel grasped in his *Philosophy of Right*—as well as how it might be sublated.

Marxists regarded state and nation as parts of the ideological superstructure. But the autonomy of state and nation, an autonomy that cannot be explained in terms of the capitalist economic base, does not arise because of the so-called relative autonomy of the ideological superstructure. The autonomy of state and nation arises instead because each is rooted in its own distinct economic base—its own distinct mode of exchange. The world that Marx himself tried to explicate was that formed by the mode of commodity exchange. This is the world we find in his *Capital*. But this bracketed off the worlds formed by the other modes of exchange, namely the state and nation. Here I want to try to think about the different worlds formed by the different modes of exchange, to examine the historical vicissitudes of the social formations that arose as complex combinations of these, and finally to ascertain the possibilities that exist for sublating those formations.

Types of Power

I would like next to consider the various types of power produced by the different modes of exchange. Power is the ability to compel others to obey through given communal norms. There are roughly speaking three kinds of communal norms. First, there are the laws of the community. We can call these rules. They are almost never explicitly stipulated, nor are they enforced through penal codes. Nonetheless, violation of these rules leads to ostracism or expulsion, and so violations are rare. Second, we have the laws of the state. We can think of these as laws that exist between communities or within societies that include multiple communities. In spaces in which communal rules no longer hold sway, laws of the state arise as shared norms. Third, we have international law: laws that govern relations between states. In other words, these laws are shared norms that apply in spaces where laws of the state do not hold sway.

The relevant types of power differ depending on which of these shared norms is at issue. The important point here is that these shared norms do not bring about power. To the contrary, these shared norms cannot function in the absence of some power. Ordinarily, power is thought to be based in violence. In reality, however, this is true only in the case of the shared norms (laws) of the state. For example, within the interior of a community in which rules are effective, there is no need to resort to violence to ensure the functioning of shared norms. This is because another coercive force, one of a different nature from violence, is operational. Let's call this the power of the gift. Mauss describes the self-destructive gift giving known as potlatch in the following terms:

> But the reason for these gifts and frenetic acts of wealth consumption is in no way disinterested, particularly in societies that practice the potlatch. Between chiefs and their vassals, between vassals and their tenants, through such gifts a hierarchy is established. To give is to show one's superiority, to be more, to be higher in rank, *magister*. To accept without

giving in return, or without giving more back, is to become client and servant, to become small, to fall lower (*minister*).[11]

To make a gift is to gain sway over the recipient, because the failure to make a return gift means falling into the status of a dependent. This occurs without the use of violence. If anything, it appears at first glance to be an utterly gratuitous act of benevolence. Nonetheless, it results in the exertion of a control over the other that is even more effective than violent coercion. Mauss believed that "the things exchanged . . . also possess a special intrinsic power, which causes them to be given and above all to be reciprocated."[12] The aboriginal Maori people of New Zealand called this power *hau*. I will discuss this again, but what is important to note for present purposes is that the reciprocal mode of exchange is accompanied by its own type of power.

For example, in a potlatch ceremony the recipients attempt to overpower their rivals by giving back even more than they have received. Potlatch is not itself warfare, but resembles warfare in that the motive behind it is to gain supremacy over one's rivals. There are also cases of gift giving that seem not to follow this tendency. For example, membership in a community is something bestowed as a gift as soon as one is born. Each member bears an obligation to reciprocate for this. The force by which the community constrains each of its members is the force of this sort of reciprocity. For this reason, within the community there is no particular need to impose penalties in cases where a member violates the norms (rules). Once it is known to the community at large that a member has violated the norms, that is the end: to be abandoned by the community is equivalent to death.

In the second instance, occurring outside the domain of a community or in situations in which more than one community exists, the rules of a single community do not apply. Accordingly, the need arises for shared norms (laws) that transcend the community. In order for these to function, however, there must be some force of compulsion. This is actual force (violence). Weber argues that state power is rooted in the monopolization of violence. But not all violence is capable of becoming a force that polices communal norms. In actual practice, the state is established when one community comes to dominate another community through violence. In order to transform this from a single act of plunder into a permanent situation, this domination must be grounded in a set of shared norms that transcends any one community—one that, in other words, must be equally obeyed by the rulers or ruling communities. The state comes into existence at such times. While the power of the state is backed up by violence, that power is always mediated by laws.

Just as the force that imposes the rules of a community is rooted in the reciprocal mode of exchange, so too is the force that imposes laws of state rooted in a specific form of exchange. Thomas Hobbes was the first to discover this. He saw the basis for the state in a covenant "entered into by fear," "a contract, wherein one receiveth the benefit of life" or "money" or "service."[13] This means that the power of the state is something established not solely through violent coercion, but more importantly also through (free) consent. If it were only based on violent coercion, its power could not survive for any extended period. Accordingly, what is important here is that the power of the state is rooted in a specific mode of exchange.

Third, we have the question of how there come to be laws between states—that is, shared norms existing in realms beyond the reach of state law. Hobbes argues that relations between states exist in a "Natural Condition," a state of nature over which no law can exist. Yet in reality trade is carried out between communities, and laws are born of the actual practice of this trade. These are so-called natural laws. They are not merely abstract concepts: any state that needs to conduct trade cannot afford to ignore them. These are sustained not by the power of the community or state but rather by a power that is born of commodity exchanges: in concrete terms, the power of money.

As Marx stresses, commodity exchange is something that arises between two communities. What took form in this were exchanges carried out through a universal equivalent form (money). This was the result of what Marx calls "the joint contribution of the whole world of commodities."[14] We might also call it the social contract between commodities. The state has no hand in this. In reality, if there were no laws of the state, commodity exchange could not take place. In other words, this contract could not be implemented. But the state is unable to produce the sort of power that is generated by money. Money is minted by the state, but its currency is not dependent on the state's authority. Money's currency depends instead on a power that takes form within the world of commodities (and their possessors). The role of the state or empire (supranational state) extends only to guaranteeing the metallic content of the currency. But the power of money extends beyond the domain of any single empire.

Commodity exchange is a form of exchange that takes place by free mutual consent. On this point, commodity exchange differs from the situation of the community or state. But this is also how it produces a form of domination that differs from the state. The power of money is a right that money (and its owner) holds vis-à-vis a commodity (and its owner). Money is a privileged "pledge" than can be exchanged at any time for any commodity. As a result, unlike commodities themselves, money can be accumulated. The accumulation of wealth begins not in the storing up of products but in the accumulation of money. By contrast, a commodity that is never exchanged for money in many cases ceases to be a commodity: it is discarded. Because a commodity has no guarantee that it will enter into an exchange, the owner of money enjoys an overwhelmingly superior position. Herein lies the reason for the desire to accumulate money, as well as for its active implementation—that is, for the birth of capital. The power of money is different from the power that is based in gift exchanges or violence. Without having to resort to physical or mental coercion of the other, this power is exercised through exchanges based on mutual consent. Hence, for example, forcing a slave to work is different from making a laborer work through wages. But this power of money also brings about a kind of class domination that differs from the class (status) domination that was grounded in violence.

It should be clear now that every mode of exchange produces its own unique form of power, and moreover that types of power differ in accordance with differences in modes of exchange. The three types of power discussed exist in various combinations in every social formation just as all social formations are combinations of the three modes of exchange. Finally, we must add a fourth power in addition to the three already mentioned. This would be the form of power that corresponds to mode of exchange D. In my view, this type was first manifested in universal religions in the form of the "power of God." Modes of exchange A, B, and C, as well as the types of power that derive from them, will stubbornly continue to survive. It is impossible to resist them. It is for this reason that mode of exchange D appears—not so much as something deriving from human desires or free will, but in the form of a categorical imperative that transcends them.

The Concept of Intercourse

My rethinking of history from the perspective of modes of exchange rather than modes of production clearly represents a departure from the common wisdom of Marxism. However, it is not necessarily a departure from Marx. I am taking *exchange* in a broad sense—just as the early Marx used the concept of intercourse (*Verkher*) in a broad sense. For example, in *The German Ideology* we find the word *intercourse* used in the following four passages:

With money every form of intercourse, and intercourse itself, becomes fortuitous for the individuals. Thus money implies that all intercourse up till now was only intercourse of individuals under particular conditions, not of individuals as individuals.

The next extension of the division of labour was the separation of production and intercourse, the formation of a special class of merchants.

The form of intercourse determined by the existing productive forces at all previous historical stages, and in its turn determining these, is *civil society*. The latter, as is clear from what we have said above, has as its premise and basis the simple family and the multiple, called the tribe, and the more precise definition of this society is given in our remarks above.

With the conquering barbarian people war itself is still, as indicated above, a regular form of intercourse.[15]

As these examples show, the concept of intercourse here includes occurrences within a given community, such as a family or tribe, as well as trade taking place between communities, and even war. This is what it means to take exchange in a broad sense.

Moses Hess was the first to put forward this concept of intercourse. Slightly older than Marx, he was a philosopher of the Young Hegelian school (the Left Hegelians); Hess was the first to transform and expand Ludwig Feuerbach's critique of religion (theory of self-alienation) into a critique of state and capital. In Hess's book *On the Essence of Money* (1845), he proposed the concept of intercourse, using it to grasp the relations between man and nature and between man and man. Hess first argues that "life is the exchange of productive life-activities." He continues:

The intercourse of men is the human workshop wherein individual men are able to realise and manifest their life or powers. The more vigorous their intercourse the stronger also their productive power and so far as their intercourse is restricted their productive power is restricted likewise. Without their life-medium, without the exchange of their particular powers, individuals do not *live*. The intercourse of men does not originate from their essence; it *is* their real essence.[16]

In Hess's view, the relation of man and nature is intercourse. More concretely, it is metabolism (*Stoffwechsel*), or material exchange. In German, *Wechsel* literally means "exchange," so that the relation of humans to nature is one of intercourse or exchange. This is an important point when we consider

Marx's "natural history" perspective—as well as when we consider environmental problems.

Hess next points out that this sort of relation between man and nature necessarily takes place by way of a certain kind of social relation between people. This too consists of a kind of intercourse. In this case, Hess cites as modes of intercourse plunder ("murder-for-gain"), slavery, and the traffic in commodities.[17] In his view, as traffic in commodities expands, this mode replaces plunder and slavery (that is, the use of violence to steal the products of others or to force them to labor), yet in the end this amounts to carrying them out in another form, through the means of money. This is because a person who possesses money is able to coerce others. In this, the various capabilities of people are alienated from them in the form of money. Moreover, the division and coordination of people's labor come to be organized by capital, regardless of their intention.

Hess believed that a truly communal form of intercourse would become possible only after the passing of the capitalist economy. Since in a capitalist system people carry out cooperative enterprises under the sway of capital, they need to abolish the capital that is their own self-alienation and manage their cooperative production according to their own wills in order to see the realization of an "organic community." This is another name for what Pierre-Joseph Proudhon proposed as "Associations," or cooperative production. In a sense, Marx too held to this view throughout his life.

That Marx at the stage of the *Economic and Philosophical Manuscripts* (1844) was influenced by Hess's theory of intercourse is obvious, and as the quoted passages show, this carried over into *The German Ideology* as well. But after this, as Marx plunged deeply into the specialized study of economics, he began to limit his use of the word *intercourse* to its ordinary meaning. This cannot be detached from the fact that in *Capital* he focused exclusively on research into one form of intercourse, that of the capitalist economy that was established with the expansion of trade (commodity exchanges) between communities. Most likely, this is what led him to give only secondary consideration to the domains of state, community, and nation. But rather than criticize Marx for this, we should devote ourselves to the task of extending the work Marx carried out in *Capital* into the domains of state and nation.

Beginning from its foundational mode of exchange, commodity exchange, Marx explicated the totality of the complexities of the capitalist economic system. Far from being the material base, this capitalist economic system, woven out of money and credit, is something more akin to a religious world whose existence is based on faith—in other words, credit. It is not something that can be explained solely through the capitalistic mode of production. The same is true for state and nation. They may appear to be merely ideological or abstract, but they are rooted in fundamental modes of exchange, just as is the capitalist system—the state in mode of exchange B and the nation in mode of exchange A. These are not simply ideological or representations. The modern capitalist economy, state, and nation historically took shape through the combination and subsequent modification of the fundamental modes of exchange.

"Exchange" between Man and Nature

In order to deal with state, nation, and capital comprehensively, we must rethink them, starting from *exchange*, broadly defined—that is, from the concept of intercourse. Moreover, replacing the concept of production with that of exchange has special significance today. As I noted, Marx's emphasis on the concept of production arose because his fundamental understanding of humanity situated it within its relation to nature. This is something he learned from Hess, seeing it as metabolism—in other words, as exchange. Why is this of importance? For example, when we produce something, we modify raw materials, but at the same time we also generate unnecessary waste products and waste heat. Seen from the perspective of metabolism, these sorts of waste products must be reprocessed. When microorganisms in the soil reprocess waste products and make them reusable, for example, we have the sort of ecosystem found in the natural world.

More fundamentally, the earth's environment is a cyclical system that circulates air and water and finally exports entropy into outer space in the form of waste heat. If this circulation were blocked, there would be an accumulation of waste products or of entropy. The material exchanges (Stoffwechsel) between man and nature are one link within the material exchanges that form the total earth system. Human activity is sustainable when it relies on this sort of natural circulation to obtain its resources and recycle its waste products.[18] Until the beginning of capitalist industrial production, human production did not result in any major disruption of the natural ecosystem. Waste products generated by people were processed by nature, a system of material exchanges (metabolism) between man and nature.

In general, however, when we consider production, we tend to forget about its waste products.[19] Only its creativity is considered. The production we find in the work of philosophers such as Hegel follows this pattern. Even

Marxists who attacked this sort of Hegelian thought as idealism failed to see production in materialist terms. They failed to think of production as something inevitably accompanied by the generation of waste products and waste heat. As a result, they could only think of production as something positive and believed that any evil in it must be the result of human exploitation or of class domination.[20]

As a result, Marxists in general have been naively positive in their view of progress in productive power and scientific technology. Accordingly, criticisms of Marxists made by ecologists are not off the mark. But we cannot say the same for Marx himself. In *Capital* he points out that capitalist agriculture "disturbs the metabolic interaction between man and the earth, i.e. it prevents the return to the soil of its constituent elements consumed by man in the form of food and clothing; hence it hinders the operation of the eternal natural condition for the lasting fertility of the soil."[21] His source here was the German chemist Justus von Liebig, the originator of chemical fertilizer agriculture as well as its first critic: he was the first to advocate a return to a circulation-based system of agriculture. Marx writes,

> Moreover, all progress in capitalist agriculture is a progress in the art, not only of robbing the worker, but of robbing the soil; all progress in increasing the fertility of the soil for a given time is progress towards ruining the more long-lasting sources of that fertility. The more a country proceeds from large-scale industry as the background of its development, as in the case of the United States, the more rapid is this process of destruction. Capitalist production, therefore, only develops the techniques and the degree of combination of the social process of production by simultaneously undermining the original sources of all wealth—the soil and the worker.[22]

Here Marx criticized not only capitalism's exploitation of workers but also its exploitation of nature, which destroys the natural balance of soil and humans. He moreover argues that the "moral of the tale, which can also be extracted from other discussions of agriculture, is that the capitalist system runs counter to a rational agriculture, or that a rational agriculture is incompatible with the capitalist system (even if the latter promotes technical development in agriculture) and needs either small farmers working for themselves or the control of the associated producers."[23] What he has in mind here is neither large-scale capitalist superfarms nor large state-run collective farms. Marx is arguing that the management of agriculture should be carried out by associations (federations) of small-scale producers.

Seen from this perspective, Marx's thesis in "Critique of the Gotha Program" should be clear. The Gotha Program was adopted as party platform upon the inauguration of the German Social Democratic Party, with the support of both the Marx and Lassalle factions. Upon reading it though, Marx privately mounted a biting critique. One of the platform's key points lay in the assertion, based on Ferdinand Lassalle's thought, that labor was the source of all wealth and civilization. Marx rebuts this: "Labour is *not the source* of all wealth. *Nature* is just as much the source of use values (and it is surely of such that material wealth consists!) as labour, which itself is only the manifestation of a force of nature, human labour power."[24] Identifying human labor as the ultimate source of value is precisely the view of industrial capitalism. Marx is critical here of the view that puts industrial production at the center (a view shared not only by Lassalle but also by most members of the Marx faction at the time). In this we see the continuing relevance of the "natural history" perspective that sees man and nature in terms of metabolism, which had been part of Marx's thought since the beginning. In addition, Marx rejects the Lassalle faction's proposal to have the state promote producer cooperatives. In Marx's view, the point was not to have the state foster associations but rather to have the development of associations lead to the disappearance of the state. In reality though, when Marxists have seized power they have generally organized producer cooperatives through the state, whether in the form of collective farms or of people's communes.

Widespread awareness of the significance of this "metabolism" and "material exchange" arose only after the adoption of fossil fuels, especially oil. The use of these fuels meant that metabolism was no longer a problem limited to the realms of agriculture and land. Oil is the raw material for detergents, fertilizers, and other chemical products, in addition to being an energy source. The industrial waste products generated in these uses have unleashed global (worldwide) environmental problems. As I noted, the global environment is a kind of heat engine. A cyclical system is maintained by using the processes of atmospheric and water circulation, with entropy finally exported to outer space in the form of waste heat. Disruptions in this cycle will unavoidably lead to environmental crises such as climate change and desertification, and, ultimately, accumulated entropy will lead the global environment to "heat death."

This situation is brought about by man's exploitation of nature. But to see this solely as a relation of man and nature, that is, as a problem of technology or civilization, is deceptive. Such a view conceals the relations of exchange between people that lie behind the exchange relationship between people and nature. In fact, the first environmental crisis in world history was produced by Mesopotamian irrigation agriculture, which resulted in desertification. The same phenomenon was seen in the Indus and Yellow River civilizations. These were the earliest examples of institutions (states) that simultaneously exploited people and nature (the soil). In our industrial capitalist society, we now see this being carried out on a global scale. If we fail to grasp the problems of the exchange relations between people and the Capital-Nation-State form that these bring about, we will never be able to respond to these environmental problems.

The History of Social Formations

I have said that I will rethink the history of social formations from the perspective of modes of exchange. The historical stages of development of social formations discussed in Marx's "Forms Preceding Capitalist Formations" (*Grundrisse*)—the primitive clan, Asiatic, ancient classical slave system, Germanic, and capitalist modes of production—are my point of departure for this.[25] With some additional qualifications, this classification system is still valid today.[26]

The first qualification is to remove Marx's geographical specifications. For example, what Marx calls the Asiatic social formation is not limited to Asia in any strict sense. It can also be found in Russia, the Americas (the Incas, Mayans, Aztecs), and Africa (Ghana, Mali, Dahomey). Similarly, the feudal mode is not limited to Germania—we see a similar phenomenon in Japan, after all. For these reasons, we must remove the geographical specifications in order to see social formations structurally.

The second qualification is that we should not regard these formations as marking the successive stages of a linear historical development. Originally, Marx's historical stages came about as a materialist rephrasing of Hegel's *The Philosophy of History*. Hegel regarded world history as the process of realization of universal freedom. It started from Africa, passed through Asia (China, Indian, Egypt, Persia), then onto Greece and Rome, from there to Germanic society, and finally to modern Europe. It was a development from a stage in which no one was free to a stage in which only one person was free, then one in which a minority were free, and finally a stage in which all were free. Marx dismissed this as an idealistic approach and rethought world history from the perspective of modes of production, that is, of who owned the means of production. In this way, he arrived at an ordering that began with the primitive-communism mode of production, followed by the Asiatic mode of

TABLE 3

Political Superstructure	Stateless	Asiatic state	Ancient classic state	Feudal state	Modern state
Economic Base (Mode of Production)	Clan society	King / vassals (agricultural community)	Citizen / slave	Feudal lord / serfs	Capital / proletariat

production in which the king owns everything, the Greek and Roman slavery system, and then the Germanic feudal system. Table 3 presents the schema of Marx's historical stages as defined by mode of production.

According to Marx, the Asiatic agricultural community was the first formation to develop from clan society, and it constituted the economic base for the Asiatic state. But in fact the Asiatic agrarian community was not something that developed as an extension of clan society; it was instead established by the Asiatic state. For example, large-scale irrigation agriculture was organized by the state and subsequently gave shape to the agrarian community. While it may appear as if it were something that developed out of clan society, this was not the case. We actually see stronger continuity with earlier clan societies in the cases of Greek and German societies.

It is a mistake to see the Asiatic state as the primary stage of development. The Asiatic state as it appeared in Sumer and Egypt was characterized by bureaucratic structures and standing armies with a remarkably high degree of development—a level that would take states in other areas many years to reach, in some cases taking until the modern period. These centralized states took form through rivalries among multiple city-states. In Greece, on the other hand, the city-states remained independent and were never unified. This was not due to Greek civilization being more advanced; to the contrary, it was because the principles of reciprocity persisting since the period of clan societies retained a strong influence. This is one of the causal factors that led to the rise of democracy in Greece.

These problems cannot be explained through modes of production. That perspective remains blind to, for example, the epochal significance of Greek and Rome in terms of historical stages. It is absurd to try to explain Greek democracy and the culture linked to it through the slavery-system mode of production. The Greek slavery system was necessary only to secure the democracy of the city-state—that is, to preserve the freedom and equality of citizens. For this reason, the first question to ask here is how this freedom and equality developed. To answer this, we need to employ the perspective of modes of exchange.

It is crucial to realize that the various social formations—clan, Asiatic, ancient classical, and Germanic—are not successive linear historical stages but instead exist simultaneously and in mutual interrelationship. Because each social formation exists in a world of mutual interrelationships, none can be considered in isolation. On this point, my thinking is in agreement with the "world systems" theory proposed by Immanuel Wallerstein and Christopher Chase-Dunn, among others.[27] The latter distinguishes between very small systems (what Wallerstein calls mini-systems) in which no state exists, world-empires that are ruled by a single state, and world-economies in which multiple states engage in competition without being unified politically. When we view these distinctions in terms of modes of exchange, we obtain the following results.

Mini-systems—in other words, world systems that exist prior to the rise of the state—are grounded in the principle of reciprocity. Next, in the case of world-empires, we have a world system in which mode of exchange B is dominant, while in world-economies we have one in which mode of exchange C is dominant. What I want to emphasize here, though, is that these distinctions are not based on scale or size. A world system grounded in principles of reciprocity is generally small, yet if we look at the Iroquois Confederation of tribes, we realize that it is possible for such a system to extend across a vast space. This also explains the secret of the vast empire built up by the nomad tribes of Mongol. Locally, each country in the empire was an instance of Asiatic despotism, but mutual relations in the community formed by the rulers of these countries were based on the reciprocity of a tribal confederation. By comparison, other world-empires, including the Roman Empire, were local.

Marx's Asiatic social formation is characterized by a system in which one community gains ascendance over another and mandates compulsory service or tribute payments. In other words, it is a system in which mode of exchange B is dominant. Of course, there are various kinds of systems in which mode of exchange B is dominant, including feudal and slavery systems. They differ in whether the principle of reciprocity still remains intact within the ruling community. If it remains, it is difficult to establish a centralized order: establishing a centralized order requires abolishing reciprocity among the ruling classes. Only then are a central authority and the organization of a bureaucratic system possible.

This does not mean, however, that the other modes of exchange do not exist within an Asiatic social formation. For example, excepting the tribute payments and compulsory service that are imposed on it, a local agrarian community under Asiatic despotism remains self-governing in internal matters and is grounded in an economy based on reciprocity. Which is to say that mode of exchange A maintains a strong presence. Yet such agricultural communities are largely created through irrigation projects or acts of conquest organized by the state, meaning they are dependents of the state (monarchy). On the other hand, mode of exchange C also exists in Asiatic social formations: in them, we find both trade and cities. Their cities are frequently on a very large scale, but they are usually under the control of a centralized state. In this sense, in Asiatic social formations, modes of exchange A and C exist, yet mode of exchange B is dominant.

Next, Marx argues that what he calls the ancient classical and Germanic social formations were grounded in slavery and serfdom systems, respectively. This means that these formations' primary principle lies in mode of exchange B. Accordingly, Samir Amin regards feudal systems as being a variation of the tribute system state. In this aspect the Greco-Roman and Germanic social formations were clearly similar to the Asiatic social formation, but they were quite different in other aspects. This becomes apparent when we look at the degree to which reciprocal mode of exchange A persisted within the ruling community. In Greece and Rome, centralized bureaucratic systems were rejected. For this reason, they never established centralized orders capable of unified rule over multiple communities and states. They became world-empires only when they adopted the form of the Asiatic world-empire, as happened under Alexander III (Alexander the Great). In Europe world-empire existed only nominally; the reality was continuous struggle among feudal lords. Because no powerful political center capable of controlling trade existed, marketplaces and cities tended to have autonomy. This explains why the so-called world-economy developed there.

Wallerstein maintains that the world-economy appeared first in sixteenth-century Europe. But world-empire and world-economy do not necessarily form stages in a linear historical development. As Fernand Braudel notes, world-economy existed before this—in, for example, ancient classical societies.[28] In these we find trade and markets not under state control. This is a decisive difference from the Asiatic world-empire. Still, these world-economies did not exist in isolation. While receiving the benefits of this world-empire, they existed on the *submargin*, where they were buffered from military or political subjugation.

Taking the example of western Asia, when Mesopotamian and Egyptian societies developed into vast world-empires, the tribal communities on their peripheries were either destroyed or absorbed. Yet at the same time, the Greek cities and Rome were able to develop into city-states. These imported the civilization of western Asia—namely, its writing systems, weapons, and religions, among other things—but they did not adopt the model of a centralized political system and instead revived the direct democracy that had existed since the days of clan society. This option for dealing with the center was possible, however, only because they were situated at a certain distance from it. Karl Wittfogel called this sort of region a "submargin."[29] If regions were too close to the core, as in the case of the "margin," they would have been dominated by or absorbed into the despotic state. If they were too far away, on the other hand, they would likely remain untouched by either state or civilization.

If we say that Greece and Rome were established on the submargin of the Oriental empires, then we can also say that feudalism (the feudal social formation) was established in Germanic tribal societies, which were on the submargin of the Roman Empire. More precisely, they were situated on the submargin of the Islamic empire, which reestablished the west Asian world-empire in the wake of the fall of the Roman Empire. Europe's inheritance of Greek and Roman culture took place through the Islamic world. In that sense, the Hegelian notion of a linear development from Greece and Rome to Germany is nothing more than a Eurocentric fiction.

What more than anything distinguishes feudalism from a despotic tribute-based state is the persistence or lack of the principle of reciprocity within the ruling-class community. A feudal order is established through a bilateral (reciprocal) agreement between the lord and his retainers. The lord grants feudal domains to his retainers, or he provides them with direct support. In return, the vassals offer loyalty and military service to the lord. Because this agreement is bilateral, if the lord fails to fulfill his obligations, retainers may abrogate their allegiance to him. This is not something that developed from Greece or Rome. It arose instead from the principle of reciprocity that had persisted since clan society, a principle that had vanished in Greece and Rome and that did not permit the king or chief to assume an absolute position. The Germanic peoples inherited the civilizations of the Roman and Islamic empires but rejected the bureaucratic hierarchies of the despotic state. As I have already noted, this is a stance possible only on the submargin of a world-empire. It is, moreover, not something limited to western Europe (Germania): in the Far East, Japan too had a feudal system. The Japanese actively imported China's civilization in all areas, but they

TABLE 4

Social Formation	Dominant Mode of Exchange	World System
Clan	Reciprocity	Mini-system
Asiatic	Plunder and redistribution (B1)	World-empire
Ancient classical	Plunder and redistribution (B2)	
Feudal	Plunder and redistribution (B3)	
Capitalism	Commodity Exchange	World-economy

implemented only the surface trappings of the Asiatic despotic state and its attendant ideologies.

In feudal systems that refused the establishment of a centralized state, trade and cities were able to develop outside of state control. In concrete terms, western European cities took advantage of ongoing struggles between the pope and kings and between feudal lords to establish their own independence. In agricultural communities too, we see the transformation of land into private property and the rise of commodity production. In this sense, the feudal order led to the rise of a world-economy system that was not unified politically. Herein lies the reason for why the capitalist world system arose from Europe. This schema can be seen in table 4.

The Modern World System

Finally, the capitalist social formation is a society in which mode of exchange C (commodity exchange) is dominant. We must approach this not from within a single social formation but rather through the interrelationship of social formations—that is, as part of a world system. Seen from the perspective of world systems, once the world-economy that developed from sixteenth-century Europe began to cover the entire world, the previously existing structure of world-empires, along with their margins and submargins, became untenable. As Wallerstein notes, what took its place was the world-economy structure consisting of core, semiperiphery, and periphery. In this, the previous world-empires found themselves situated in the periphery.

Just as it is impossible to understand the economy of a single nation without reference to the world system, so too is it impossible to understand any single state in isolation, without reference to the world system. The modern state is a sovereign nation, but this is not something that appeared within the boundaries of a single, isolated nation. In western Europe, the sovereign nation was established under the interstate system of mutually recognized sovereignty. What forced this to happen was the world-economy. Expanding European domination then forced a similar transformation on the rest of the world. Among the previous world-empires, those such as the Incas or Aztecs that consisted of loose tribal confederations underwent dissolution into tribal societies and colonization. Moreover, many tribal societies that existed on the margins of these former world-empires were also colonized by the European powers. But the old world-empires were not easily colonized. In the end, they were divided up into multiple nation-states, as was the case with the Ottoman Empire. Those such as Russia or China that escaped this fate established a new world system through socialist revolution and thereby seceded from the world-economy.

Next let us examine this transformation from within a single social formation. The rise to dominance of mode of exchange C does not mean the extinction of the other modes of exchange. For example, while it may appear that the previously dominant plunder-redistribution mode of exchange B has disappeared, in fact it has merely changed form: mode B has become the modern state. In western Europe, this was first manifested in the form of the absolute monarch. The monarch allied with the bourgeoisie to bring about the fall of the other feudal lords. The absolute monarchy brought about the state equipped with a standing army and bureaucratic structure. In a sense, this was the delayed realization of something that had long existed in the Asiatic empires. Under the absolute monarchy, feudal land rent transformed into land taxes. The aristocracy (feudal lords) who had lost their feudal privileges at the hands of the absolute monarch became state bureaucrats who received the redistribution of these land taxes. At the same time, the absolute monarchy, by engaging in this redistribution of taxes, took on the garb of a kind of welfare state. In this way, the plunder-redistribution mode of exchange lives on at the core of the modern state.

The absolute monarchy was overthrown by the bourgeois revolution. But the bourgeois revolution actually strengthened the centralization of power by toppling the "intermediate powers" (Montesquieu) that were capable of resistance under the absolutist order, such as the nobility and the church.[30] In this way, a society emerged in which the principle of commodity exchange was universally affirmed. Yet this does not mean that the previously existing modes of exchange were abolished. The plunder-redistribution mode persisted; now, however, it took on the form of state taxation and redistribution. Moreover, the "people," having replaced the king in the position of sovereign, were subordinated to the politicians and bureaucratic structures that were supposed to be their representatives. In this sense, the modern state is virtually unchanged from earlier states. In the previously existing states, whether Asiatic or feudal, mode of exchange B was dominant, but the modern state takes on the guise of the now dominant mode of exchange C.

And what is the fate of reciprocal mode of exchange A in the capitalist social formation? Under it, the penetration of the commodity economy dismantles the agricultural community and the religious community that corresponded to it. But these return in a new form: the nation. The nation is an "imagined community" (Benedict Anderson) based on reciprocal relations. It brings about in imaginary form a communality that transcends the class conflict and contradictions caused by the capitalist system. In this way, the capitalist social formation is a union (Borromean knot) of three forms, Capital-Nation-State.

So far we have revised the social formations that Marx described in terms of modes of exchange. But this alone is insufficient. We must also take up one more instance: mode of exchange D. Previously I said that this would be the return of mode of exchange A in a higher dimension and that it would take the form of an X that transcends Capital-Nation-State (see tables 1 and 2). But this argument took up mode D only within the terms of a single social formation. Social formations always exist in relation to other social formations. In other words, they exist within world systems. Accordingly, mode of exchange D should be thought of at the level of a world system that includes multiple interrelated social formations. More precisely, it cannot be thought of in terms of a single isolated social formation. The sublation of Capital-Nation-State can be realized only in the form of a new world system.

To recapitulate, world mini-systems came into being through mode of exchange A, world-empires through mode of exchange B, and world-economy (the modern world system) through mode of exchange C. If we understand this, we can also understand how a world system X that supersedes these would be possible. It will come into being as the return of mode of exchange A in a higher dimension. In concrete terms, world system X will come into being not through the power of military force or money but through the power of the gift. In my view, what Immanuel Kant called "a world republic" was the ideal of this sort of world system. Table 5 diagrams this.

In the following chapters, I explore these fundamental modes of exchange. I will try to clarify how the social formations that take shape as combinations

TABLE 5 World Systems

World-empire	Mini-world system
World-economy	World republic
(modern world system)	

of these and the world systems ended up taking the form of Capital-Nation-State and how it might be possible to supersede this. First, however, I would like to note several things. I treat these four primary modes of exchange as separate entities. In reality, they are interrelated and cannot be taken up in isolation from one another. Nonetheless, in order to see their relationships, we must first clarify the phase in which each exists. As I have already argued, in *Capital* Marx bracketed off the other modes of exchange in order to explain the system formed by commodity exchange. I will carry out a similar procedure with regard to the state and nation. This will provide the basis for seeing how state, capital, and nation are related to one another—how, in other words, these fundamental modes of exchange are related historically. In order to do this, I will distinguish four separate stages: world mini-systems that have existed since before the rise of the state, the world-empires that arose before capitalism, the world-economy that has emerged since the rise of capitalism, and finally the present and future.

Finally, to avoid any misunderstandings, let me make one last observation. I am not trying to write here the sort of world history that is ordinarily taken up by historians. What I am aiming at is a transcendental critique of the relationships between the various basic modes of exchange. This means to explicate structurally three great *shifts* that have occurred in world history. To do this is to set us on the trail to a fourth great shift: the shift to a world republic.

PART ONE　**MINI WORLD SYSTEMS**

So-called primitive societies come in a wide variety of forms, ranging from small nomadic bands of hunter-gatherers to clan or tribal societies that engage in fishing, simple rain-fed agriculture, or slash-and-burn farming. Among clan or tribal societies, we also find many variations, ranging from chiefdoms that exist largely in name only to those that possess power similar to that of a kingship. Here, though, I will distinguish primarily between the societies of nomadic hunter-gatherer peoples and those of hunter-gatherer peoples with fixed settlements: I see a great leap in the history of social formations in the shift from the former to the latter. This is the problem I take up in part I.

In the history of social formations, shifts in dominant mode of exchange are crucial; they produce radical change. First, there is the shift to the social formation in which mode A is dominant; second, the shift to the social formation in which mode B is dominant; and third, the shift to the social formation in which mode C is dominant. To put this in other words, these shifts lead to the establishment of clan society, state society, and industrial capitalist society, respectively. Until now, most attention has been focused on the last two shifts, and there has been little or no attention paid to the shift to clan society. But when we look at the history of social formations from the perspective of modes of exchange, this first shift is of crucial importance. If the shifts to state society or capitalist society mark radical leaps, then surely the appearance of clan society also involved a similarly radical shift.

For example, Marcel Mauss pointed out that it was the principle of reciprocity (mutuality) that held together primitive societies. This does not apply, however, to the society of nomadic bands. Accordingly, the social formation that realized the principle of reciprocity must have been born of the shift away from this form. This cannot be positively proven, because today's so-called primitive societies do not provide sufficient evidence to allow us to resolve this problem. Today's (rapidly disappearing) nomadic bands have not existed in their current societal form since ancient times. There is the possibility, after all, that they were once fixed settlers engaged in simple farming and herding who, pressured by the incursion of the state and civilization, "regressed" into being nomadic bands. For example, the Bushmen, a hunter-gatherer people of the Kalahari Desert, seem well adapted to life in the desert, but it is believed that they did not originate there but rather migrated to it under pressure from other tribes. It is simply unclear if most nomadic hunter-gatherer peoples have existed in the same form since ancient times.

For this reason, the question of what sort of societies existed in nomadic bands before the rise of clan society is not a problem that can be solved empirically; it must be approached as a kind of thought experiment, an imaginary problem. All we can do is extrapolate from the societies found in currently existing nomadic bands. Nomadic bands tend to form through the assembling of multiple monogamous families, sometimes including cases of polygamy. The cohesiveness of the band is maintained through such means as pooling resources and communal meals. But the bonds holding the band together are not rigid: members can leave at any time. These are generally small groupings consisting of about fifteen to fifty people. This number does not increase above the level at which pooling (equal distribution) of foodstuffs is possible, nor does it decrease to below the minimum level required to engage in communal hunting. In addition, the band as a whole is not a fixed entity, and neither are the bonds of individual families. If the husband or wife breaks away from shared life, the marriage between them is regarded as being dissolved. Bonds joining together different families are even more unstable. Consequently, the structure of family relations remains undeveloped, and no higher structure transcending the band emerges.

Clan society presents a striking contrast to this. It is a stratified society grounded in lineage, featuring a complex organization. Clan society is of course different from state society. But if we are going to stress this difference—if we are going to stress the significance of the Neolithic revolution that brought it about—then we should also stress the significance of the difference between nomadic band society and clan society and the transformations that it brought about. This is because the latter transformation represented a greater breakthrough. In clan society, we already find early stages of agriculture and livestock herding, as well as political structures such as chiefdoms. The elements that would develop into the state already existed within clan society. By contrast, in societies that precede the emergence of clan society, we find only small bands or camps gathering together—at best several families. Moreover, their form of collective life was continuous with what had existed for millions of years in species that preceded *Homo sapiens*, including primates. This is why the establishment of clan society was such an epochal development.

In considering prehistoric times, we must call into question one commonly accepted notion. We find a representative version of it in the concept of a Neolithic Revolution grounded in the cultivation of crops and livestock, as proposed by Vere Gordon Childe.[1] According to this view, people first began to engage in farming and livestock herding, and then they began to live in fixed settlements. As productive capacity increased, cities developed, class divisions emerged, and finally the state was born. The first problem with this view is its assumption that agriculture led to fixed settlements; in fact, the appearance of fixed settlements preceded the appearance of agriculture. Many hunter-gatherer peoples lived in fixed settlements. Furthermore, many engaged in simple crop or livestock production. In other words, they did not adopt fixed settlements for that purpose. Rather, crop and livestock production emerged naturally as a result of hunter-gatherers having taken up fixed settlements. The real breakthrough came with the adoption of fixed settlements, which preceded the appearance of agriculture.

The anthropologist Alain Testart distinguishes between nomadic and sedentary hunter-gatherer peoples. He maintains that in the former, the booty of the hunt is distributed equally, while in the latter inequalities emerge.[2] This is because the storing up of products becomes possible with fixed settlement. Therefore, he locates the origins of human inequality here. I share a similar view, but I want to focus on why the inequalities arising from this storage capacity did not result in a class society or the state. There was some system in place that inhibited inequalities and kept the appearance of the state in check. That system was none other than clan society itself.

In general, the emergence of the state is celebrated as a major breakthrough in human history. If anything, however, what was important was the creation of a system capable of preventing the rise of inequalities and the state once these became possible with the emergence of fixed settlements and their capacity for storing up. The principle behind this was reciprocity. In this sense, clan society was not a primitive society; rather, it was a highly developed social system.[3]

The impetus behind the shift from small band society to clan society was clearly the adoption of fixed settlement. That being the case, how did fixed settlements come about? How did a world system, albeit a very small one, emerge from band society? Before we pursue these questions, however, we must first clarify the differences between the society of a small band and clan society. What this boils down to is the difference between pooling and reciprocity.

ONE THE SEDENTARY REVOLUTION

Pooling and Reciprocity

Since Marcel Mauss, anthropologists have studied how primitive societies are based on the principle of reciprocity. But an ambiguity remains with regard to reciprocity: should gift giving (redistribution) taking place within a single household be regarded as constituting reciprocity? In other words, how should we distinguish between reciprocity and the pooling of resources? For example, within the household, the basic unit of clan society, we find pooling and redistribution, but these cannot properly be called reciprocal. Even if these constitute a kind of gift giving, they are not carried out with the expectation of receiving a countergift. Accordingly, Bronisław Malinowski, who researched the Trobriand Islands, distinguished transactions on the basis of motive, differentiating between those that were carried out for self-interest and those that were disinterested. In other words, he distinguished between reciprocal and pure forms of gift giving. Gift giving within households or small clan communities are instances of pure giving, characterized by an absence of the principle of reciprocity. But Mauss believed that even instances of what appeared to be pure gift giving were actually governed by reciprocity. If the donor feels a sense of satisfaction, then that in itself constitutes a kind of reciprocity, just as it does when the recipient feels a certain sense of obligation.

In clan societies it is difficult to distinguish between pure and reciprocal gift giving, between pooling and reciprocity. Marshall Sahlins, however, tries to draw a clear distinction between them:

he argues that pooling is an activity occurring within a single household, whereas reciprocity occurs between households:

Pooling abolishes the differentiation of the parts in favor of the coherence of the whole; it is the constituting activity of a group. On the other hand, the household is thereby distinguished forever from others of its kind. With these other houses, a given group might eventually entertain reciprocal relations. But reciprocity is always a "between" relation: however solidary, it can only perpetuate the separate economic identities of those who so exchange

Lewis Henry Morgan called the program of the domestic economy "communism in living." The name seems apposite, for householding is the highest form of economic sociability: "from each according to his abilities and to each according to his needs"—from the adults that with which they are charged by the division of labor; to them, but also to the elders, the children, the incapacitated, regardless of their contributions, that which they require. The sociological precipitate is a group with an interest and destiny apart from those outside and a prior claim on the sentiments and resources of those within. Pooling closes the domestic circle; the circumference becomes a line of social and economic demarcation. Sociologists call it a "primary group"; people call it "home."[1]

What Morgan discovered as "communism in living" and what Marx called "primitive communism" can only exist in band societies, consisting of a limited number of households. Pooling that exists in clan societies is already under the sway of the principle of reciprocity. This is why Sahlins acknowledges that the principle of reciprocity penetrates into the household.[2] Yet it is important that we retain the distinction between pooling and reciprocity.

It is also important to distinguish between the reciprocity of the gift and trade. For this purpose, Sahlins defines two extreme poles in order to explain how reciprocal exchanges are of a completely different nature from trade. At one extreme, reciprocity takes the form of pure gift giving, and at the other extreme, it takes the form of something like a war of reprisal. Moreover, he attempts to see how the character of reciprocity is spatially defined within the community. In other words, he thinks that the character of reciprocity displays different aspects depending on whether it is positioned in the core or on the periphery of the community. It can be differentiated into three levels, depending on relative kinship distance from the core household (family).[3]

1 Core (the family): generalized reciprocity / the pole of solidarity (within a lineage)
2 Within a settlement: balanced reciprocity / the midpoint (within the sphere of a tribe)
3 Between tribes: negative reciprocity / the pole of asociality

Generalized reciprocity, the first item, is the kind of reciprocity found within a household (family). But it appears to be a kind of pure gift giving. Accordingly, insofar as we confine ourselves to looking within the core of the community, reciprocity gives the impression of being purely altruistic, filled with good will. We have to keep in mind, however, that there are two kinds of reciprocity: positive and negative. The negative form of reciprocity appears in the third example, between tribes. As examples of this, Sahlins discusses haggling, chicanery, and theft, and we could also more broadly include here the kind of reciprocity found in a vendetta. Even reciprocity that appears at first glance to be positive in fact harbors antagonism. For example, in a potlatch ceremony one subjugates others by showering gifts on them that they are unable to reciprocate.

In relation to these two extremes, the second example, which takes place within the sphere of a single settlement, represents the midpoint. If it approaches the first type, reciprocity takes on a positive form and even approaches the state of nonreciprocal pure giving. But if it approaches the third type, it becomes negative and antisocial. It is at the midpoint between these two that balanced reciprocity appears. Hence, we can conclude that reciprocity has different functions depending on its spatial deployment. In this case, the space of tribal society is not simply a space that spreads out horizontally from its core. Tribal society is stratified: its clans are composed of individual households, the tribe itself of clans, and above those we have confederations composed of tribes. Seen from this perspective, it is clear that the core is positioned near the lowest stratum, while the sphere between tribes is positioned near the highest stratum.

At any rate, it seems that we should think of the characteristics of reciprocity not so much in terms of the second type (balanced reciprocity) but rather of the first and third types—that is, in terms of the reciprocity that exists within communities on the scale of a single household and the reciprocity that exists in relations with other communities. In the first type, it is clear that reciprocity can lead to pooling or equalization. Consequently, it is easy to confuse reciprocity and pooling. In the third type, we see how reciprocity in gift giving can create amicable relations between previously

hostile communities. Moreover, we see how reciprocity provides the principle for expansion of the community.

Trade and War

I would like to examine the nature of the third type, reciprocity in the form
of a relation to the exterior. Clan societies do not exist in isolation from other
groups. This is because they need to engage in trade of various goods. But
economic exchanges between clans are possible only in cases where they
belong to some higher-order collective or, absent that, when mutually amicable relations exist between them. Both of these situations are produced
through acts of gift giving.

We can see one example of this in the *kula* exchanges from the Trobriand
Islands, as reported by Malinowski in his *Argonauts of the Western Pacific*.[4]
Kula is a mode of exchange carried out between a large number of clans
who live within a wide sphere enclosed by a ring of islands. Kula is carefully
distinguished from what is called *gimwali*, a purely economic exchange of
useful goods. That is to say, kula is not carried out for profit or to fill actual
needs. A kind of currency called *veigun* is used in conducting kula. When
people are given veigun, they are obligated to then give it away to someone
else. In this way, veigun circulate from island to island. As a result, "socia-
ble" relations between peoples living on the various islands, ordinarily isolated from one another, are reconfirmed.

It goes without saying that kula is of a different nature from economic
exchange. It is a competitive ritual of ostentatious displays of generosity in
the form of gift giving. But what is important here is that kula is followed by
bartering for material necessities. In other words, it is not the case that economic exchanges are looked down on in this society. It is precisely because
they are necessary that the need arises to establish relationships that will
render them possible. Kula occurs within the sphere of a higher-order community that links together the various islands. This ritual of gift giving re-
confirms and reactivates the already existing confederation of tribes.

There are also cases of gift giving being used to open up exchanges with
previously unknown others—for example, the practice of silent trade. In it,
one places some article in an already-established place, gives a signal, and
then hides—whereupon the other party appears, places an article thought
to be of equal value next to the first article, and then departs. If the two parties are both satisfied with the article supplied by the other, they take it home
and a trade is realized. In this way, useful goods are exchanged, but contact

between the two parties is avoided. This is different from the reciprocity of gift giving, but it partakes of the same mode: the exchange of useful goods (commodity exchange) is executed in a reciprocal form. Accordingly, silent trade shows how trade (commodity exchange) is made possible.

Next let us examine the wars that are another possible outcome in encounters between different tribes or clans. Claude Lévi-Strauss believed that peaceful relations between communities were established through gift giving, whereas a failure in this led to war. But Pierre Clastres has criticized this view, arguing that it overlooks how primitive societies have changed due to interference and influence from the contemporary West.[5] As a rule, the earliest folkloric records show that such societies were in fact extremely belligerent. Clastres points out that the Yanomami tribe of the Amazonian backcountry, which has had no contact with the outside world, engages in endless warfare; he asserts that war is not simply caused by a failure in exchange but rather is the reigning presumption. Exchange (gift giving) is carried out, if anything, for the sake of establishing alliances that are useful in waging war. In his view, war brings about decentralization within the interior of the community. Thanks to this warfare, the formation of a centralized state is rendered impossible. It is precisely the ceaseless warfare between tribes that explains why such communities do not transform into states.

But the warfare that Clastres sees in the Yanomami tribe occurs within a higher-dimension community. It is of a different nature from war waged against the outside world. The wars that Lévi-Strauss described as arising from a failure to secure peace through gift giving pertained to encounters between a higher-order community and its exterior. Accordingly, the existence of warfare within the tribal community does not amount to a negation of the principle of reciprocity: this sort of warfare is in fact a kind of reciprocity. In many ways it resembles vendetta or potlatch. By waging war the tribes are attempting to vanquish their rivals, and there are even cases of extermination. But this is not done for the purpose of subordinating those rivals. War is carried out for the sake of one's "honor"; it is a kind of sacrifice. It helps build a sense of cohesion and identity for each of the participating clan communities and does not lead to the conquest of other clans. Accordingly, just as is the case in vendettas, warfare here is carried out endlessly. This sort of war exists because there is no transcendent power capable of towering over the various clans and tribes—in other words, because there is no state—just as this war is what renders the establishment of such a state impossible.

Reciprocity impedes the formation of the state through its positive character (amicability), but even more so through its negative character (war). Reciprocity impedes the concentration of power, the formation of a higher stratum. Reciprocal gift giving generates close bonds between communities and a higher-order community—in other words, reciprocal gift giving leads to the stratification of communities. But this is not at all hierarchical. Reciprocity does not recognize one community (clan or tribe) as standing in a higher position, nor does it recognize one chief as standing in a position superior to other chiefs. It does not permit the establishment of a state.

Stratification

Through the reciprocity of the gift, the community leaves behind the "state of nature" in its relation with another community, producing instead the condition of peace. The state likewise represents an overcoming of the natural condition, but the peace obtained through gift giving is of a fundamentally different nature. A higher-order community is established through gift giving, one different in nature from the agrarian community organized under the state. Sahlins describes the role filled by the gift:

> The gift, however, would not organize society in a corporate sense, only in a segmentary sense. Reciprocity is a "between" relation. It does not dissolve the separate parties within a higher unity, but on the contrary, in correlating their opposition, perpetuates it. Neither does the gift specify a third party standing over and above the separate interests of those who contract. . . . The gift is no sacrifice of equality and never of liberty. The groups allied by exchange each retain their strength, if not the inclination to use it.[6]

Unlike the agrarian community that is organized by and subordinated to the state, the higher-order community formed through gift giving neither unites nor subordinates the lower-order communities. In tribal societies, even if a higher-order community is established, the independence of the lower-order communities does not disappear. In that sense, antagonism continues to exist within the interior of the tribe. As a result, while gift giving builds amicable relations with other communities, it also frequently becomes aggressively competitive. In potlatch, for example, the goal is to overwhelm one's rivals by giving in such excess that they are unable to reciprocate. Of course, this is not done for the sake of ruling over others. It is carried out for the sake of defending the independence (honor) of the community—in other words, of liberating it from the threat posed by other communities. It is also for the sake of strengthening the sense of identity within the community.

In this sense, vendetta is also an instance of reciprocity. For example, when a member of one community is murdered by a member of another community, revenge (reciprocation) is pursued. The "obligation" for reciprocation here strongly resembles the "obligation" of gift-countergift. When a member of the community is killed, it is a loss to the community and hence can only be repaid by imposing a similar loss on the perpetrator's community. But once a vendetta is initiated and revenge obtained, this in turn must be reciprocated, so that the process continues without end. The gift exchanges of a potlatch sometimes continue until both communities completely exhaust their resources, and it is the same with vendetta. Vendetta is abolished only when a higher-order structure capable of sitting in judgment of crime arises: the state. This shows, in reverse, how the existence of vendetta impedes the formation of a state. This is because vendetta restores the independence of each community from the higher-order structure.

The reciprocity of the gift, as the trade in kula shows, establishes a federation among multiple communities—a kind of world system. This kind of league is not stable and always harbors much internal chaos, meaning that it must from time to time be reconfirmed through additional reciprocal acts of gift giving. The unity of the community established through reciprocity is segmentary in nature. To wit, it does not become a structure capable of governing from above—a state. Most likely, we can situate the form of chiefdom as a further extension of this sort of tribal confederation. This represents the stage just before the emergence of the state. Even here, however, the principle of reciprocity that resists the state remains in effect. The state will only emerge after a nonreciprocal mode of exchange becomes dominant.

The Sedentary Revolution

Sahlins takes up reciprocity as a question of spatial distribution, with pooling located at the core and negative reciprocity at the periphery. What happens, though, if we reposition reciprocity along an axis of temporal development? In that case, bands engaged in pooling would appear first, and then these bands would establish mutual bonds of reciprocity, expanding their society in a stratified manner. But first we have to deal with a more basic problem: why would such a change come about?

Band society is based on pooling—in other words, on the principle of equality achieved through redistribution. This is inseparable from the nomadism of these hunter-gatherer peoples. Because they are continuously on the move, they are unable to store up the spoils of their activities. It makes no sense to treat those spoils as private property, so they are distributed out equally among members and sometimes even to outsider guests. This is pure gift giving, with no obligation for reciprocity. To never store up supplies is to never have any thought for tomorrow—or, for that matter, any memory of yesterday. In nomadic band society, nomadism (freedom) in and of itself brings about equality. Alain Testart argues:

> In hunter-gatherer peoples, the flexibility, divisibility and fluidity of the social structure did not permit exploitation beyond the limits of what was tolerable to all. If such did arise, the exploited parties would simply move on to live in another place and the band would split. Accordingly, collective decisions had to be reached through unanimous agreement. Under conditions of fixed settlement, the structures of fixed residence and storage become factors inhibiting the free movement of people. Because those who are dissatisfied can no longer simply leave, exploitation intensifies. Taking up fixed settlement is the first step toward the development of political coercion, which is a necessary precondition for the development of new forms of exploitation.[7]

Why then would these peoples choose to adopt fixed settlement? When we consider this, we must first rid ourselves of one common bias: the unfounded belief that human beings are essentially sedentary dwellers, that they will naturally settle down in one place if conditions allow. In fact, even today, even when state coercion is employed, it is not easy to force nomadic peoples to adopt fixed residence. This was all the more true for hunter-gatherer peoples. Their pursuit of a nomadic lifestyle did not necessarily come about because they needed to follow their prey. If that were true, then, for example, they would settle down in one location if it provided sufficient food. But we find that this is not the case. That alone was not sufficient to cause them to abandon the nomadic mode of life that had persisted since the primate stage. It seems clear that they disliked fixed settlement because it produced a variety of difficulties.[8]

First, it leads to personal conflict and discord within and without the band. In a nomadic life, if things get bad people simply move on. If the population grows too big, for example, members can leave. This accounts for the flexibility seen in band society. But once a band takes up sedentary settlement, it has to come up with ways of dealing with the conflicts and discord that increase in frequency as the population grows. It becomes necessary either to unify in segmentary fashion multiple clans or tribes through the establishment of a higher-order community or to impose rigid constraints directly on the various members. Second, the personal conflicts that arise are not limited to the living: fixed settlement makes the disposal of the dead more difficult. In animism, the dead are generally believed to resent the living. In the case of a nomadic lifestyle, all you need to do is bury the dead and then move on. But in the case of fixed settlements, you must coexist with the dead, who are always nearby. This transforms the view of the dead, as well as the fundamental concept of death. A community that takes up sedentary settlement is reorganized into a structure based on lineage that worships the dead as ancestral gods. The principle on which this sort of community is established is reciprocal exchange.

Sedentary settlement requires direct confrontation with various difficulties that were previously avoided through constant movement. Why in the world did hunter-and-gatherer peoples adopt fixed settlement? Basically, the reason was climate change. During the Ice Age, the human race advanced to cover an area stretching from the tropics to the midlatitudes, and in the late Paleolithic age, tens of thousands of years ago, it further expanded into the subarctic regions of the midlatitudes. Large-game hunting was the central occupation during this period. But with the warming that followed the end of the Ice Age, temperate areas of the midlatitudes saw increasing forestation and a concomitant disappearance of large-game animal stocks. Foraging too was affected by the increasingly pronounced seasonal variations. In this period, human beings adopted fishing. Unlike hunting, fishing requires the use of equipment that cannot be easily transported. As a result, it became necessary to take up sedentary settlement. Most likely the very first fixed settlements were located at the mouths of rivers.

Even today we can observe many examples of societies that occupy fixed settlements in order to pursue fishing. Peoples who occupy fixed settlements and engage in fishing can be found across a geographical band that stretches from California in North America to Siberia and Hokkaido. Testart attaches great importance to the acquisition of techniques for smoking fish, which in turn enabled stockpiling: according to him, this is the origin of "inequality." But the ability to smoke fish isn't the only thing that made stockpiling possible. More fundamentally, it was sedentary settlement itself. The very ability to stockpile smoked fish presupposes fixed residence.

Sedentary life brought about other unintended results. For example, simple crop cultivation and livestock herding arose almost as a matter of course once sedentary settlement was adopted. This is because, taking for example the case of cultivation, the very fact of people taking up residence in a fixed space leads to a change in the vegetation of the surrounding primeval forest, as seeds from the plants the people eat take root and grow. Just as fixed settlement leads to the development of cultivation as an extension of gathering activities, so too does herding of livestock develop as an extension of hunting. In this sense, the adoption of sedentary settlement precedes the rise of agriculture and livestock herding. This kind of cultivation and livestock rearing was not connected to the Neolithic Revolution. Yet fixed residence did bring about a change more important than the Neolithic Revolution: the emergence of clan society grounded in the principle of reciprocity.

Fixed residence made stockpiling possible, just as it also led to inequality and warfare. Left to its own devices, it would likely have led to the establishment of a state. In other words, sedentary settlement would have led to the Neolithic Revolution. Clan society was formed so as to prevent this. For nomadic bands, pooling was a natural necessity. But in a society in which numerous households take up fixed residence collectively, pooling takes on the form of an abstract norm. For each household pooling takes the form of the obligations of the gift.

The adoption of fixed settlements also created problems with regard to the status of women. When a hunter-gatherer people took up fixed settlement, in actual practice it pursued its livelihood through fishing or simple cultivation and herding, but it preserved the lifestyle that had existed in the hunter-gatherer phase. In sum, a division of labor persisted in which men engaged in hunting and women carried out foraging. But in reality the men's hunting became a largely ritual activity. With the adoption of sedentary settlement, the necessary production was increasingly carried out by women. Yet it is important to note that this change led not to an elevation but to a lowering in the status of women. The males, who produced nothing directly but only engaged in symbolic production or supervision, stood in the superior position.

Following Morgan and Johann Jakob Bachofen, Frederick Engels posited the existence of matriarchy at the oldest stages of human history and thought that the status of women rose with the development of cultivation. The Marxist anthropologist Morris Bloch has criticized this. First of all, there is no reason to believe that matriarchy forms the oldest stage of history. Second, we have to distinguish between the practice of matrilineality and actual matriarchy. There are many examples of matrilineal societies in which women have a subordinate status. The important thing is not the distinction between patrilineal or matrilineal but rather the structuring of society according to lineage in general. Bloch furthermore argues:

> As Engels noted, women contribute differentially to the processes of production in different types of society but the contribution of women in the production of the most important goods of the society does not necessarily give them a high status as he thought. Among the pastoralists of East Africa women produce most of the foodstuffs through agriculture, but only cattle, cared for by men, are defined as the really important and noble product, and in fact women's dominant productive contribution is given as an excuse for their social devaluation as low creatures unconcerned with the aesthetic and political value of pastoralism. Again in the New Guinea Highlands, women are the main agents in producing both agricultural products and the most valuable possession—pigs—but then, in the view of these people, what really matters is not production, but large-scale, ceremonial exchanges and the significance of women's role in production is once more ideologically denied.[9]

While the status of women declined with the appearance of sedentary settlement, it is no mistake to assert that the status of women in clan societies was relatively high. The decisive decline in status came with the establishment of the state and the beginning of agricultural civilization. After this, production was carried out by women and by conquered subordinate peoples. On the other hand, clan society also had a functioning system for dissolving the inequalities of wealth and the hierarchies of power it incessantly generated, one that preserved the equality that had prevailed in nomadic society even in the society at the stage of fixed settlement, where it was no longer practically possible: a system of reciprocity. Following Masaki Nishida, I would like to call this the *sedentary revolution*, to distinguish it from the Neolithic Revolution that produced the state.[10]

In clan societies there was a chief who took charge of pooling and redistribution. But this chief did not possess absolute power, precisely because the principle of reciprocity prevented it. For example, the position of chief was obtained by giving away acquired wealth through treating others without reserve to feasts—but this is also how the chief lost wealth and, eventually, the position as chief. The principle of reciprocity blocked the emergence of class differences and the establishment of a state. In this sense, it is not true that fixed residence immediately led to class society or the state. To the contrary: fixed residence led to the rise of a system that rejected class society and the state.

The Social Contract

I would like to consider the process by which clan society took shape, especially in comparison to the rise of the state. As a thought experiment, we have already considered a situation in which a hunter-gatherer people takes up some sort of fixed settlement, coexisting with many other bands and households. What sort of situation was this? Even before adopting sedentary settlement, the nomadic band would have been in contact with other bands. In other words, the possibility for trade, war, and gift giving with others had already existed. For example, as Lévi-Strauss writes,

> The small nomadic bands of the Nambikwara Indians of western Brazil are in constant fear of each other and avoid each other. But at the same time they desire contact, because it is the only way in which they are able to exchange, and thus to obtain products or articles that they lack. There is a link, a continuity, between hostile relations and the provision of reciprocal prestations. Exchanges are peacefully resolved wars, and wars are the result of unsuccessful transactions.[11]

They live in mutual fear, and yet at the same time they must somehow come into contact and carry out exchanges with each other. To achieve this they must first exchange in gift giving and thereby create amicable relations. But in the case of nomadic bands such as the ones Lévi-Strauss discusses, lasting relations with other bands are not established, because they quickly move on to new locations. For this reason, reciprocal exchanges will not lead to the formation of a higher-order community. No structure beyond the family can emerge.

But the example that Lévi-Strauss offers also suggests that gift giving offers a possible way out from the fearful state of nature that exists between bands. Thomas Hobbes saw the state as a social contract that led to peace by leaving behind the state of nature, but Sahlins argues that we can see another form of social contract in the gift.[12] Of course, this is of a different nature from the social contract that Hobbes saw as the basis of the state (in which each individual transfers away his or her natural rights). In this version of the social contrast, natural rights are not transferred away; they are instead *given*. In this case, the donor retains the power of the gift. In other words, the recipient of the gift acquires the right to act as the agent of the donor, but at the same time, the recipient is also bound by the donor. Their relationship is bilateral, which is to say reciprocal.

Both sides of this are worth noting. In band society, the household (family) belongs to the band but is not subordinated to it. This also means that the binding force of the household is relatively weak: the husband-wife relation is easily dissolved. People come together to form a community, but the possibility always exists for them to leave that community. Even after the rise of clan society, the nomadism that characterized band society remains basically unchanged. For example, if the population increases or if there is an outbreak of discord within it, people are free to emigrate. This leads to the foundation of a new independent clan, albeit one that remains allied with the original clan. This kind of alliance, based on the principle of reciprocity, extends from the clan to the tribe and from the tribe to the confederation of tribes. But this kind of alliance never becomes a hierarchical order. While the lower-level groups are in some sense subordinated to the higher-level group, this is not a total subordination; they preserve their independence. This is a defining characteristic of mini world systems, which are grounded in the principle of reciprocity.

The key point here is that insofar as it is grounded in the principle of reciprocity, the community can organize itself into a higher-level community, but this can never become a state—which is to say, it can never become an absolute, centralized power. For example, in the case of the Iroquois nation, the highest organ of government was the council of chiefs, but, as Marx wrote, "decision [was] given by the Council. Unanimity was a fundamental law of its action among the Iroquois. Military questions [were] usually left to the action of the voluntary principle. Theoretically each tribe [was] at war with every other tribe with which it had not formed a treaty of peace. Any person [was] at liberty to organize a war-party and conduct an expedition wohin er wollte [wherever he wanted to]."[13]

The Obligations of the Gift

Band societies engage in pooling—all things are owned in common. But once band societies take up sedentary settlement and each household begins stockpiling goods, inequalities and competition arise. The reciprocity of the gift is the method adopted to dissolve these outcomes. According to Mauss, reciprocity is sustained by three obligations: the obligation to give, the obligation to accept a gift, and the obligation to make a countergift. It is through these obligations of the gift that strong bonds are born between groups that were originally hostile or distant. It is also through the gift that the principle of equality that originated within the household is expanded to encompass the entirety of a larger community. Clan society always includes elements that will generate inequalities of wealth and power, but at the same time it always holds these in check through the obligations of the gift.

There are many kinds of obligations of the gift. For example, the incest taboo cannot be separated from the obligations of the gift. Scientists who study anthropoids have shown that incest is almost unknown among them.[14] The avoidance of incest, then, is not unique to humans. The incest prohibition seen in primitive societies must not be a simple avoidance, but rather something born of a different purpose. Emile Durkheim was the first to propose that incest was prohibited for the sake of exogamy, but he tried to explain this in terms of such factors as impurity of blood.[15] It was his nephew Mauss who linked the relation of the incest taboo and exogamy to the reciprocity of the gift. Exogamy is a system of reciprocity in which the household or clan gives away a daughter or son, and then receives in turn.[16] This is precisely why incest must be prohibited. The incest taboo is the renunciation of the "right to use" within the household or clan. But when daughters or sons are given away to some external group, they still belong to the original household or clan. In this sense, this represents not a transfer of ownership but a gift.

The obligations of the gift apply even in cases where spouses are obtained through kidnapping, which at least on the surface would seem to go against this. According to Lévi-Strauss, "even marriage by capture does not contradict the rule of reciprocity. Rather it is one of the possible legal ways of putting it into practice. The bride's abduction dramatically expresses the obligation upon any group holding girls to give them up."[17] Abduction of brides is permitted because the group from which the girl is stolen from the start was under an obligation to give away its daughters. In this way, even marriage by abduction helps create social bonds.

It is in clan society that exogamy forms an order based on reciprocity. Band society also practices exogamy. We see this in, for example, the Bushmen and Nambikwara peoples, who practice cross-cousin marriage. But here marriage practices are not reciprocal. This is because in these groups neither the band nor the family takes a fixed form. Accordingly, they have not acquired the sort of kinship structure found in clan society. In other words, their families (households) are not organized according to lineage, nor do they belong to higher-order groups such as clans. In band society, the family is an independent unit. Consequently, the incest taboo found in clan society means that the family, which until then had retained its independence even as it participated in the band, has been subordinated to a higher-level group. The clan community is structured through reciprocal exogamy, which also leads to the establishment of a higher-order community (tribe or tribal confederation) that links together various clans. In this sense, kin-based societies are based not in relations of blood but in social bonds created through the power of the gift. We need to consider this a problem that is not limited to kinship structure; more broadly it is a problem of reciprocal exchange in general.

TWO **THE GIFT AND MAGIC**

The Power of the Gift

We have been considering reciprocal exchange not as a system existing within a single community, but as an activity by which a community creates a state of peace with another community. As a result of this sort of reciprocal exchange, a larger community with a
segmentary form is established. In this process, reciprocal exchange
becomes institutionalized—in other words, it becomes an obligation imposed by the community. But this obligation does not function with regard to other communities. That being the case, how
does the gift come to have the power to transform antagonistic relations between communities?

Marcel Mauss, following the beliefs of the aboriginal Maori tribe,
thought that *hau* (magic power) resided in the gift-object. Even
among those who accept Mauss's theory of the gift, this has been a
target of criticism. For example, Claude Lévi-Strauss complained
that this view adhered too closely to the beliefs of the primitives
Mauss was studying, while in science, "once the indigenous conception has been isolated, it must be reduced by an objective critique so as to reach the underlying reality." The gift creates a cycle
not because of the hau that resides in the gift object, Lévi-Strauss
maintained, but rather because the gift is like "an indeterminate
value of signification," a floating signifier akin to an algebraic symbol in a mathematical structure.[1]

But Lévi-Strauss was able to reject Mauss's thought only because
Lévi-Strauss limited his understanding of reciprocal relations to

those existing within an already-established community. In the end, a structure is nothing but a system that functions within a given community. But if we want to see the process by which one community creates anew, or actively renews, a sense of communality with another community through the reciprocity of the gift, we cannot ignore the power of the gift. This is what Mauss sought.

The Marxist anthropologist Maurice Godelier reevaluates Mauss's fascination with hau from this perspective—Lévi-Strauss's critique notwithstanding. Godelier draws an analogy between capitalist commodity exchange and gift exchange, concluding that "in each case the real relations people entertain with the objects they produce, exchange (or keep) have vanished, disappeared from their consciousness, and other forces, other, this time imaginary, actors have replaced the human beings who originally produced them."[2] Godelier believes that the power residing in a gift-object arises because actual social relations are reified in it. He contrasts this with the case of capitalist society, in which social relations are reified and thereby obfuscated through the money-commodity exchange relationship.[3]

In my view, however, we don't need to rely on the theory of reification to explain this. In commodity exchange, one specific commodity—gold, for example—possesses the power of being exchangeable for all other commodities. We call this money. Without considering how it comes to possess this power by being situated as the universal equivalent form, people tend to think that the power dwells within this object itself. This resembles the belief in reciprocal exchanges that holds that hau dwells in the gift-object itself.

The difference between these two forms, however, is more important than their resemblance—the difference, that is, between commodity exchange and reciprocal exchange. In commodity exchange, right of ownership is transferred from one party to the other. Accordingly, to possess money is to possess the right to acquire ownership over other things. For this reason, the desire to accumulate money arises—the perverse desire (fetishism) for money instead of things. This does not happen with the gift. In the gift, rights of usage are handed over, but not rights of ownership. The gift-object functions as a kind of money, but unlike actual money, the gift-object does not possess the right to own other things: to the contrary, it brings with it the obligation to give things away (the obligation to make a countergift). In sum, whereas money promotes stockpiling and expanding possession, hau functions as a force that rejects ownership and desire.

Magic and Reciprocity

Mauss employed the Maori concept of hau to explain the power of the gift. This amounted to explicating reciprocity through the religious beliefs of a clan society: this was the target of Lévi-Strauss's criticism. But the problem with Mauss does not rest on the fact that he tried to explain reciprocity through magic. If anything, he should have tried to explain magic through reciprocal exchange, but of course he didn't. Magic is the attempt to control or manipulate nature or other people by means of the gift (sacrifice). In other words, magic in itself already includes reciprocity. Like the reciprocity system, magic is not something that existed from the start. At the stage of nomadic bands, magic had yet to develop. Its development began with the adoption of sedentary settlement.[4]

Animism precedes and forms a precondition for the appearance of magic. Animism is a belief system that regards all things, whether created by nature or humans, as being animate (possessing life spirit). It already exists at the stage of the nomadic band: the practice of burying the dead proves this. Yet while animism is the foundation of magic, it does not itself bring about magic. Magic appears only when a relation of reciprocal exchange is established with this *anima* (spirits). This development occurs only after the nomadic band takes up fixed settlement and a clan society is established.

Freud drew an analogy between animism and the stage of infantile narcissism.[5] Lévi-Strauss was critical of this position. In his view, primitive societies have their own infantile children and neurotics: "The most primitive culture is still an adult culture, and as such is incompatible with infantile manifestations in even the most highly developed civilization. Likewise, psychopathological phenomena in the adult remain an adult fact with nothing in common with the normal thinking of the child. In our opinion, the examples of 'regression' to which psychoanalysis has given so much attention must be considered in a new light."[6]

Still, it is possible for us to approach the world of animism without resorting to analogies with the infantile or psychopathological. Animism consists of an attitude that sees all objects as being anima. This is not especially difficult to understand; we can understand it by way of a phenomenological approach. The key to this can be found in Martin Buber's *I and Thou*. He divides human attitudes toward the world into two types: the "I-Thou" relation and the "I-It" relation. The *It* in the latter is not limited to things: we could just as well use *he* or *she*. Whether a person or a thing, it can be found whenever something is objectified as *It*. At that moment, *Thou* disappears. The reverse is also true: if we adopt the attitude of I-Thou, even a material thing can become Thou.

On the other hand, the I in the I-Thou attitude is of a different nature from the I in the I-It attitude. In the latter, I is a subject in relation to an object. Accordingly, in the I-Thou relation, Thou is not an object, nor is I a subject: "When *Thou* is spoken, the speaker has no *thing*; he has indeed nothing. But he takes his stand in relation."[7] When we take up the I-Thou attitude, both humans and nature are Thou, and they seem to harbor anima. We can call this way of thinking animism.

Animism is thus the taking up of an I-Thou stance toward the world. This is not a characteristic limited to primitive peoples. For example, Buber describes his experience of exchanging gazes with a cat. For a fleeting moment, it seemed as if they had encountered one another as Thou. But, Buber writes, "the rotation of the world which introduced the relational event had been followed almost immediately by the other which ended it. The world of *It* surrounded the animal and myself, for the space of a glance the world of *Thou* had shone out from the depths, to be at once extinguished and put back into the world of *It*."[8] In short, Buber concludes, modern man is already living in a world of an I-It relation, making it exceedingly difficult to bracket this and encounter the world or others as Thou.

Hunter-gatherer peoples faced the opposite difficulty. Freud tried to explain animism and magic from a child's feeling of omnipotence, but "adult" primitives could not live exclusively in an I-Thou world: they were not "children." The adults could not imbibe the sense of omnipotence that arises from the environment of a child, who needs only to cry to get its mother to tend to its needs. As a matter of practical reality, adults had to live in an I-It world. But in order to do so, they needed to bracket the I-Thou relation and treat natural objects and people as if they were merely It. For example, as hunters they had to kill animals, but an anima dwelled in each animal. To be able to engage in hunting, these adults had to transform their attitude toward the world from I-Thou to I-It. This transformation was carried out by means of what we call sacrifices.

Sacrifices are gifts that impose a debt on nature, thereby sealing off the anima of nature and transforming it into an It. The same is true for magic. It is a mistake to think that magic consists of manipulating the natural world by means of spells or rituals. Magic made it possible to objectify nature as an It by despiritualizing it by means of the gift. For this reason, we can say that magicians were the first scientists.[9]

But, as I have already suggested, magic was rarely practiced in the society of nomadic hunter-gatherer peoples, precisely because they were nomadic. They had little need, for example, to fear the spirits of the dead: all they had to do was bury them and move on. The same was true for the victims of their hunting. One of the difficulties that arose with fixed settlement was the need to coexist not only with other people but also with the dead. People offered gifts in order to keep the spirits of the dead in check. This took the form of funeral rites, as well as ancestor worship. The dead became the ancestral gods who were responsible for unifying clan society.

From the perspective of nomadic hunter-gatherer peoples, a purely objectified It does not exist: everything is Thou. Things are equated with spirits. In sedentary clan society, however, an I-It attitude again emerges. It is for this reason that magic develops and the social status of the magician-priest rises. But there is a limit to this: the principle of reciprocity itself bars the magician-priest from assuming a transcendental status. This is similar to the way the status of a chief in clan society may be bolstered, but the chief never acquires the kind of absolute authority enjoyed by kings. But in the state societies that appear after the rise of clan society, the anima of Thou is rendered absolute in the form of God, while nature and other people become It, objects to be manipulated.

The Problem of Migration

I have described how the shift from nomadic band to clan society began with the adoption of sedentary settlement. The question is not why fixed settlement led to state society, but rather why it led to clan society. In other words, why did fixed settlement lead down the road to peace, equality, and a segmentarily organized society instead of war, class society, and centralized authority? There was no necessity for adopting this particular course: it only came to seem necessary after it had been adopted. If anything, it was more likely that the adoption of fixed settlement would have led to class society and, eventually, the rise of the state. Accordingly, we should regard the establishment of clan society not as a preliminary stage leading toward state formation but rather as the first attempt to sidestep the path that led from fixed settlement to state society. In this regard, clan society is not primitive; instead it discloses to us a possibility for the future.

In considering this problem, I think we need to return to a text that is today entirely ignored by anthropologists: Freud's *Totem and Taboo* (1912). He was concerned not so much with totem as with the problem of how within primitive society the bonds of brotherhood were established and maintained. To summarize, Freud was interested in how tribal society produced the equality and independence that characterized clans. He sought the causes for this in the foundational event of a murder of the patriarch by his sons. Needless to say, this represents the application of the psychoanalytic concept of the Oedipal complex to the history of the human race. In doing so, Freud referred to the views of the leading scholars of his day, borrowing in particular from the theories of Charles Darwin, James J. Atkinson, and William Robertson Smith. In Freud's own words:

> From Darwin I borrowed the hypothesis that human beings originally lived in small hordes, each of which was under the despotic rule of an older male who appropriated all the females and castigated or disposed of the younger males, including his sons. From Atkinson I took, in continuation of this account, the idea that this patriarchal system ended in a rebellion by the sons, who banded together against their father, overcame him and devoured him in common. Basing myself on Robertson Smith's totem theory, I assumed that subsequently the father-horde gave place to the totemic brother-clan. In order to be able to live in peace with one another, the victorious brothers renounced the women on whose account they had, after all, killed their father, and instituted exogamy. The power of fathers was broken and the families were organized as a matriarchy. The ambivalent emotional attitude of the sons to their father remained in force during the whole of later development. A particular animal was set up in the father's place as a totem. It was regarded as ancestor and protective spirit and might not be injured or killed. But once a year the whole male community came together to a ceremonial meal at which the totem animal (worshipped at all other times) was torn to pieces and devoured in common. No one might absent himself from this meal: it was the ceremonial repetition of the killing of the father, with which social order, moral laws and religion had taken their start.[10]

Today's anthropologists completely reject this theory. There was no such "ur-father" in ancient times: rather than resembling the dominant males of gorilla bands, Freud's version seems more like a projection back onto clan society of the figure of the patriarch or king that emerged only after the rise of the absolute-monarchy states. This does not, however, render meaningless Freud's understanding of the murder of the primal father and of its subsequent ritual repetition. Freud's real interest lay with the question of how the brotherhood system was maintained.

In nomadic band society, there was no primal ur-father. To the contrary, the bonds uniting the band and family were fragile. In this sense, the theories that Freud relied on were mistaken. Yet the adoption of fixed settlement meant that the appearance of inequalities and war—that is, the rise of a state or ur-father—was now possible. Clan society, the brotherhood, was established by suppressing this possibility. Considered in this light, Freud's explanation remains valid: it explains why clan society did not transform into a state. It is as if clan society perpetually killed off in advance the ur-father that would inevitably appear if matters were left to their own devices. Even if the primal murder of the father never occurred empirically, it was nonetheless the cause that sustained the structure produced through reciprocity.

The egalitarianism existing in clan societies is quite powerful: it permits no uneven distribution or disparities in wealth or power. But this egalitarianism cannot be explained in terms of personal jealousy or some kind of nostalgic idealism: it is compulsory. Freud explains its compulsory nature in terms of "the return of the repressed." In his view, when that which has been repressed and forgotten returns, it appears not simply as a memory but as a threat.[11] In Freud's theory of clan society, what returned was the murdered father. But in my view, what came back in this "return of the repressed" was the nomadism (freedom)—since equality came with nomadism—that was abandoned with the adoption of fixed settlement. This explains why the principle of reciprocity functioned with the force of a threat.

Marx took up the history of social formations from the perspective of modes of production. To see this history in terms of modes of production is to see it from the perspective of who owned the means of production. In Marx's vision, primitive communism was characterized by communal ownership, class society by class struggle between the dominant class that owned the means of production and the class that did not, and the final stage by the return of communal ownership in a higher dimension. But this view fails to distinguish between the nomadic stage and the fixed-settlement stage of clan society. Moreover, while this view places great weight on the equality that existed in the first stage, it ignores the nomadism (freedom) that made this possible in the first place. In short, it is apt to see communism only in terms of equality of wealth, and not in terms of nomadism (freedom). We can overcome these errors by rethinking the problem from the perspective of modes of exchange.

PART TWO WORLD-EMPIRE

I n part I we examined the first epochal shift in the history of social formations: the establishment of the social formation in which mode of exchange A is dominant—clan society. In part II I explore the subsequent shift to a social formation in which mode of exchange B is dominant—the emergence of state society. To understand this we must first reject one widely accepted dogma: the concept, to cite one representative version, of a Neolithic Revolution (Agricultural Revolution) grounded in crop cultivation and herding, as propounded by V. Gordon Childe. According to this view, people first undertook agriculture and livestock herding and then adopted fixed settlement, and with the resulting expansion of production powers came the development of cities and the emergence of class divisions, all ultimately leading to the rise of the state.

I have already criticized this dogma. The adoption of fixed settlement preceded the rise of agriculture: crop cultivation and livestock herding were natural developments that followed from the adoption of sedentary settlement. The development of crop cultivation and livestock herding do not constitute a so-called agricultural revolution that results in the appearance of the state. Why? Because people do not entirely abandon the practices of the hunter-gatherer life even after they adopt fixed settlement. Moreover, through the principle of reciprocity they held in check the class divisions and accumulation of wealth that fixed settlement and stockpiling threatened to produce. The tribes and tribal confederations that emerged were characterized by a segementary, stratified structure, so that even when these expanded in scale they could never become anything more than simple chiefdoms. Before the shift to a state proper could occur, another causal factor had to be introduced, because even with the spread of precipitation-based and irrigation-based forms of agriculture, people did not fundamentally abandon the lifestyles and principle of reciprocity that had persisted since the period of hunting and gathering. Therefore, we cannot conclude that the state form arose out of agriculture. If anything, the reverse is true: agriculture began from the state.

Childe himself was a Marxist, but the reason his views won wide acceptance among non-Marxists was that there was very little that was Marxian about them. For example, the phrases *Neolithic Revolution* and *Agricultural*

Revolution derive from an analogy with the Industrial Revolution. But any claim that industrial capitalism or the contemporary state were produced by the Industrial Revolution would be a manifest confusion of causes and effects. The invention of the spinning machine and the steam engine were clearly epochal, but their widespread adoption could only take place under the domain of a mercantile state and capitalist manufactures who were competing in a world market. Accordingly, the Industrial Revolution cannot serve as an explanation for the state or capital. To the contrary, in order to explain the Industrial Revolution, we must first take into consideration the roles of the state and capital. This is precisely what Marx did.

In *Capital* Marx begins his exploration of capitalist production not from the invention or deployment of machines but rather from the manufactures—that is, from the organization of labor that he called the division and combination of labor.[1] Machines had already long existed, but their practical widespread deployment came only with the development of manufactures. What this means is that, even more important than the machine itself was the way it fragmented and then recombined human labor—in other words, the way the machine transformed human labor into something machinelike. This meant the creation of a new kind of laborer, one unlike the earlier guild artisan, one who was capable of enduring the division and combination of labor. This was not easily accomplished, and it cannot be understood by solely looking at technologies of production.

The same thing can be said with regard to the Neolithic Revolution. It likewise cannot be explained solely through reference to the invention of the plow or other technologies of production. As Marshall Sahlins notes: "Extrapolating from ethnography to prehistory, one may say as much for the neolithic as John Stuart Mill said of all labor-saving devices, that never was one invented that saved anyone a minute's labor. The neolithic saw no particular improvement over the paleolithic in the amount of time required per capita for the production of subsistence: probably with the advent of agriculture, people had to work harder."[2] Sahlins is correct in this. But it is probably incorrect to claim that production power was increased solely by forcing people to work longer hours. It is a fact that labor-saving technologies were invented during this period: technologies for the organization of labor. In irrigation agriculture, the construction of irrigation channels is more important than agricultural labor. The labor required for this is of a different nature—not only from hunting and gathering but also from crop cultivation and farming. As Karl Wittfogel noted, this labor is closer to that of heavy industry.[3] It requires discipline and a system of division and combination of labor that is capable of organizing large numbers of people. The Agricultural Revolution was brought about not by machines but rather by what Lewis Mumford calls the "mega-machine." As Mumford notes, military organization and labor organization are at heart nearly identical.[4]

In the terms of the relationship between technology and nature, the innovations achieved by ancient civilizations had little impact. But they were epochal in terms of the techniques for ruling over human beings. The archaeological distinction between the implements of the Bronze Age and the Iron Age was developed not so much in relation to means of production as it was to means of warfare (weapons) employed by the state. Moreover, by far the most important technology for ruling over people was the bureaucratic system. It is what frees people from personal relations and from relations of reciprocity. Likewise, an army becomes much stronger when it is organized into a chain-of-command system through the adoption of a bureaucratic order. This was also what made large-scale irrigation agriculture possible.

The technologies for ruling people don't rely on naked compulsion: instead, they install forms of discipline that make people voluntarily follow rules and work. In this regard, religion is of utmost importance. In *The Protestant Ethic and the Spirit of Capitalism*, Max Weber linked the work ethic to the Reformation, but we see something similar in ancient civilization. As Sahlins argues, people in hunter-gatherer societies spent few hours engaged in productive labor. If you want to take such people and mobilize them for public works or agricultural labor, simple compulsion alone will not suffice. What is needed is a voluntary sense of diligence. This transformation in work ethic took religious form. People were not simply coerced; they voluntarily undertook to work for the sake of their king-priest. Their industriousness was motivated not by force but by religious faith. Moreover, this was not a matter of empty words: the king-priest provided the farming population with military protection, while also compensating them through acts of redistribution.

To rethink this transformation in work ethic from the perspective of religion does not require us to abandon the perspective of modes of exchange. This is because what historians of religion call the development from animism to religion corresponds to what we have called the shift from reciprocal mode of exchange A to mode of exchange B. The gods of animism were not transcendental: they were *anima* (spirits) immanent within each thing or person. But with the establishment of the state, the gods acquired transcendental status. This implied at the same time an increase in the power of the chief-priest. A new agrarian community took form. This community was of a fundamentally different nature from the community of the clan or tribe, which admitted no transcendental chief-priest and which preserved the mutual independence of households and clans.

I will return to this problem in more detail. For present purposes, I would like to stress that it is not easy to transform persons who carry on the traditions of hunter-gatherer peoples into an agricultural people.[5] Even after the adoption of rainfall agriculture and livestock herding, people did not abandon the traditions of nomadic life. They continued to hunt and forage even as they engaged in crop cultivation, just as they continued to be warriors at the same time as they were farmers. The existence of subordinate farming peoples and the agrarian community were the result of large-scale irrigation farming initiated by the state. As I will discuss, it was not the Asiatic community that gave birth to the Asiatic despotic state, but rather vice versa.

On the other hand, the warrior-farmer lifestyle persisted in societies based on rainfall agriculture that were located on the periphery of civilizations. Moreover, as agriculture and fixed settlement advanced, there were also nomadic herding peoples who rejected these developments. On this point, these nomadic herders resembled hunter-gatherer peoples. But they differed from hunter-gatherer peoples in that they adopted livestock-herding practices originally invented in protocities and states. Nomadic herders lived in an arm's-length relation to sedentary settlers. Even as nomadic herders rejected the agrarian community, they established through covenants a community that was of a different nature from the clan community. This was because "contracts" between tribes that regulated the use of grazing lands, water springs, and wells were essential. This sort of community by covenant was not hierarchical. As a result, it was difficult for these to transform into states, and such instances were in fact rare. Nomadic herders established states only in cases where they pillaged or conquered previously existing core states. In other words, they did not create states on their own, but rather assumed control over already-existing state structures. For this reason, nomadic herders were not significant players in the creation of the state, but they were an indispensable factor in the establishment of multiregional states—that is, of empires.

The Protocity as State

The state did not arise as a result of the Agricultural Revolution: to the contrary, the Agricultural Revolution was a consequence of the rise of the state. For this reason, we cannot look to the Agricultural Revolution for answers if we want to know how the state came about. But we can fruitfully look at the fascinating writings of the urban-planning critic Jane Jacobs, who expressed strong doubts about the orthodox dogma that development of agriculture led to the rise of the city.[1] In *The Wealth of Nations*, Adam Smith maintains that while agriculture advances in countries where industry is developed, the opposite is not true. Nonetheless, Jacobs writes, with regard to primitive history, Smith believed that agriculture began with the establishment of the community and that this then led to the development of cities and states. She notes that Smith's view subsequently became dogma, accepted even by Karl Marx. Jacobs boldly sets out to overturn this view. She thought that the origins of agriculture lay not in the agricultural village but rather in the city, where goods and information from many communities accumulated and where persons possessing technical skills gathered. She calls this the *protocity*. It was there that various crop-cultivation techniques and new products were developed, and it was there that various animals were domesticated and selective breeding introduced. She argues that agriculture and livestock herding began in the city and only later spread to the peripheries.

I basically agree with this view. But I also have to note that Jacobs's views are distorted by another bias, one that originated with the classical economists: the belief that the economy exists independently of politics (the state). This is nothing more than an ideology of capitalist societies. In reality, even in capitalist societies the state is not some mere ideological superstructure ultimately determined by economic processes. Without the initiative of the mercantile state, manufactures and the Industrial Revolution would never have appeared—not just in late-developing capitalist nations but even in Britain. The Industrial Revolution was premised on the existence of a world market; moreover, it arose as a result of initiatives undertaken by states that were competing for hegemony in that world market.

When we look back at the ancient period, we see the following: Jacobs's protocities were actually proto-city-states. Starting from the historic ruins of Çatalhöyük in Turkey's Anatolia region, she carries out a thought experiment regarding the protocity that must have previously existed there. But in my view, this must have been a proto-city-state. In other words, as soon as the city came into being, so too did the state. To say that agriculture began with the city is to say that it began with the state. Otherwise agriculture could not have led to widespread trade or high-volume production. For example, the ancient states—Mesopotamia, Egypt, Indus, and China—all began in the estuaries of great rivers. This was not because these locations were particularly well suited to agriculture. To the contrary, these were areas in which continued reliance on rainfall agriculture could never lead to advanced development. Of course, they did include areas with alluvial soil capable of becoming fertile farmland given sufficient water. But to claim this as causal is to argue backward from conclusions. People first gathered in those regions not for the purpose of engaging in agriculture but rather to engage in fishing. It was only subsequently that they began to raise crops and livestock and then engage in trade. The reason cities appeared near river mouths was that they were important nodes in river transportation.

The proto-city-states began above all as places that made it possible for communities to engage in trade with other communities. Agriculture began in them and then spread to the hinterlands. It was through trading and warfare conducted among these proto-city-states that large-scale states came to be established. And, finally, it was these states that led to the development of irrigation agriculture. This was done for the purpose of expanding exports to neighboring countries, as we see in the case of Sumer. Large-scale irrigation agriculture was made possible, in short, by the "world market" that existed at the time. In other words, it began in a world system composed of multiple city-states.[2]

Various theorists of the origins of cities propose that they began as sacred centers or as fortress towns. But these amount to the same thing. Max Weber maintains that cities began as new "federations by oath" established between multiple clans and tribes.[3] Because these oaths or covenants pledged faith to a new god, in this sense the cities were sacred centers. Yet in addition to being centers of trade, these cities were at the same time fortress towns that defended against external enemies, pirates, and bandits—they were, that is, armed states. As these instances show, the rise of the city cannot be separated from the rise of the state. In other words, mode of exchange B and mode of exchange C are inseparable from one another.

In terms of the order of my argument, I will deal with mode of exchange C later, but this does not mean that C appeared only after B. Mode of exchange C existed from the earliest stages of the social formation—that is, from the stage in which A was dominant. This is because the community in a fixed settlement needs to carry out trade (commodity exchange) with other communities. But a state of war exists in the gap between two communities. Clan society creates a state of peace by establishing a higher-level community through the reciprocity of the gift. A confederation of tribes overcomes the state of war existing between communities by means of the reciprocity of the gift. This is one kind of social contract. If this expands, it takes on the form of a chiefdom. The chiefdom has its own spatial capital, which hosts meetings of the council of chiefs and also becomes the site of trade between communities. For these reasons, we can call this the primary form of the state and city. To move from this to the state proper—to move from chiefdom to monarchy—requires a great leap. This is because the state is based on a nonreciprocal principle of exchange.

Exchange and the Social Contract

In primitive societies the dominance of mode of exchange A did not mean that trade (commodity exchange) was absent; to the contrary, the former made trade possible in the first place. In short, it was precisely mode of exchange A that created the possibility for mode of exchange C. This does not, however, answer the question of how trade between communities that transcended the level of tribe or tribal confederation became possible—the question of how a state of peace became possible.

One hint for an answer comes from Thomas Hobbes. But before I turn to the relevant passage from Hobbes, I must first note one thing: he sought the origins of the state in a "social contract" in which various individuals existing in a state of war transfer their natural rights to one specific person (the sovereign). In taking the individual as his point of origin, Hobbes was in agreement with his critic, Jean-Jacques Rousseau. For example, Rousseau writes, "Society consisted at first merely of a few general conventions, which every member bound himself to observe; and for the performance of covenants the whole body went security to each individual. . . . [I]t became necessary to commit the dangerous trust of public authority to private persons, and the care of enforcing obedience to the deliberations of the people to the magistrate."[4] This is the Rousseauian social contract. But to explicate the state by starting from the individual is similar to trying to explicate commodity exchange by beginning with exchanges between individuals: it amounts to projecting onto the past a view that became seemingly self-evident only in modern society.

Today Hobbes's theory is interpreted as explaining not so much the origins of the state as the basis for majority rule—that is, the basis for why the minority must accede to decisions made by the majority. But in fact Hobbes's state of nature consisted not of conflict between individuals but rather between the king, feudal lords, church, and cities, among others. He grasped the social contract as being the process by which the king emerged as the absolute sovereign from among these competing entities. This process was not unique to the feudal societies of western Europe. The same conditions existed before the emergence of the despotic state in Mesopotamia: prior to its emergence there were a plethora of city-states existing in mutual rivalry. The Sumerian *Epic of Gilgamesh* depicts the process by which, out of this condition, one king managed to achieve dominance and concentrate power in himself. In this sense, while Hobbes's observations are in some aspects historically specific to the experiences of the early modern period, we can also say that he grasps the process of emergence of the state in universal terms.

Accordingly, when we consider the origins of the state, the social contract that Hobbes described in *Leviathan* remains valid insofar as we think of it as being something that binds communal entities instead of individuals. What deserves attention here is the nature of this contract. The contract that Hobbes describes is a covenant "extorted by fear." Ordinarily, we don't consider agreements entered into out of fear as being contracts.[5] But according to Hobbes, even these are contracts:

> Covenants extorted by fear are valid. . . . Covenants entered into by fear, in the condition of mere nature, are obligatory. For example, if I cove-

nant to pay a ransom, or service, for my life, to an enemy, I am bound by it. For it is a contract wherein one receiveth the benefit of life; the other is to receive money, or service, for it, and consequently, where no other law (as in the condition of mere nature) forbiddeth the performance, the covenant is valid.[6]

In this way, when Hobbes sees the establishment of the state (sovereign) as arising through a social contract, he means it in the sense of a covenant extorted by fear. He then divides the process of establishment of the state into two aspects:

> The attaining to this sovereign power is by two ways. One, by natural force, as when a man maketh his children to submit themselves and their children to his government, as being able to destroy them if they refuse, or by war subdueth his enemies to his will, giving them their lives on that condition. The other is when men agree amongst themselves to submit to some man, or assembly of men, voluntarily, on confidence to be protected by him against all others. This latter may be called a political commonwealth, or commonwealth by *institution*, and the former, a commonwealth by *acquisition*.[7]

At root, the state is "a commonwealth by *acquisition*." There are states (city-states) that can be described as commonwealths "by *institution*." But these arise only in cases when they neighbor a powerful state. When "some man, or assembly of men," from these communities is given the power of sovereignty, it is for the sake of resisting some other state. In that sense, even a commonwealth by institution is fundamentally based on a covenant extorted by fear. As Hobbes notes, it makes no difference if the sovereign is a monarchy, aristocracy, or a democracy. After all, the sovereign can be a single man or an assembly of men. What is important here is that the sovereign is essentially born of a covenant extorted by fear.

This covenant extorted by fear is a kind of exchange—those who submit receive something in return: "Giving them their lives on that condition." The ruler likewise takes on the obligation to carry this out. Hobbes saw that what at first glance does not appear to be an exchange was in fact an exchange: "One receiveth the benefit of life; the other is to receive money, or service for it." This is not an instance of mode of exchange C (commodity exchange); it belongs instead to mode of exchange B. Hobbes says: "It is not therefore the victory that giveth the right of dominion over the vanquished, but his own covenant. Nor is he obliged because he is conquered (that is to say, beaten, and taken or put to flight)."[8] The state emerges when the vanquished community actively consents to being governed. That is what makes this an exchange. The ruler likewise is obligated to guarantee the community's safety.

Hobbes believed that laws were possible only after the establishment of the state (sovereign). This does not mean, however, that the sovereign is free to arbitrarily establish any law. It means instead that the law will not function in the absence of some power that compels obedience, and that the sovereign holds the power to enforce legal norms. Weber defines the essence of the state as being a monopoly on violence. What this actually means is that armed force or power wielded by state no longer belongs to the category of violence. Anyone else carrying out the same acts would be punished for having committed violence. Behind the law stands armed force. Seen from another perspective, what this means is that the power of the state is always exercised through the law.

The victor (ruler) plunders the vanquished. If this were simply a matter of pillaging, however, it would not lead to the rise of the state. The establishment of the state occurs when the pillaged booty is offered up in the form of taxes (tribute): then we see the beginning of exchange. It is through this procedure that the vanquished secure their rights of ownership. They are plundered by the state in the form of taxation or forced labor, but in return are protected from pillaging by anyone other than the state. As a result, the ruled come to think of this forced labor or tribute not as something taken from them by force, but rather as countergifts (obligations) offered in return for gifts (favors) granted by the ruler. In other words, the state is established through the transformation of plunder and violent compulsion into a mode of exchange.

The Origins of the State

Prestate societies and state societies differ from each other in a number of ways. In prestate societies a higher-order community is established through the principle of reciprocity. Lower-level groupings are subordinated to higher-level groupings, but they preserve their autonomy. For this reason, it is not uncommon for decisions and regulations issued by the higher order to go unheeded. Similarly, when violent conflict breaks out between clans, the higher-level grouping lacks the power to halt it. As a result, violent conflicts are quite common. Nonetheless, they do not lead to the rise of a centralized authority. To the contrary: the existence of this sort of reciprocal conflict holds in check the possibility of centralization.

Seen in this light, it becomes clear that the state emerges when reciprocity between communities is prohibited. For example, in Babylon's Code of Hammurabi, a compilation of legal codes that had existed since Sumer, we find the famous "an eye for an eye" clause. This is not a call for engaging in "tit for tat." Instead it marks a ban on endless vendettas. It means that criminal acts or discord between communities are not to be resolved by the parties themselves but rather through judgments rendered by the state that exists over them. In terms of the history of law, "an eye for an eye" represents the beginning of *nulla poena sine lege*, the doctrine that there can be no punishment without law. Because vendetta signifies the autonomy of the community with regard to higher-level organizations, the law of "an eye for an eye" amounts to the negation of autonomy for the lower-level community. Seen from this perspective, the transformation of the Greek polis into states proper occurred at the moment when reciprocal vendettas were banned.[9]

This shift from a prestate condition to a state cannot be understood if we confine our considerations to the interior of a single community. For example, some see the state as an independent public power whose purpose is resolving class conflicts that arise within the community. In another view, it is the organ (means) by which the ruling classes control the ruled classes. Marx and Engels propose both views. Both views see the state as something that arises through developments internal to a single community. But the state could not possibly emerge through the development of a single community: a community grounded in the principle of reciprocity is capable of resolving whatever contradictions arise within it through the gift and redistribution. Moreover, in the case of chiefdom states, we find hierarchies and vassalage relations based on clientelism (patron-client relations), but these are fundamentally relations of equality (reciprocity) and hence are incapable of transforming into the kind of vassalage relations or hierarchies that characterize state bureaucracies. A sovereign possessing absolute authority could never be born from this kind of situation.

This leads us naturally to consider the following possibility: that this kind of sovereign is not born from within the community through a process of self-alienation, but rather originally comes from the outside—in other words, that the sovereign arrives as a conqueror. This view asserts that the origin of the state lies in conquest. Engels saw the cause of the end of the clan community and the beginning of the state as coming not from the interior but from the situation of ruling over other communities, citing as an example the case of Rome's ruling over the Germanic tribes:

> We know that rule over subjugated peoples is incompatible with the gentile constitution. . . . Thus, the organs of the gentile constitution had to be transformed into organs of state, and owing to the pressure of circumstances, this had to be done very quickly. The first representative of the conquering people was, however, the military commander. The securing of the conquered territory internally and externally demanded that his power be increased. The moment had arrived for transforming military leadership into kingship. This was done.[10]

But conquest does not immediately bring about the state. In many cases, conquest accomplishes nothing more than isolated acts of pillage. In still other cases, as when nomadic peoples become conquerors, it ends with the appropriation of an already existing state structure. Rousseau criticized theories that saw the origins of the state in acts of conquest by the strong:

> Because, in the first case, the right of conquest, being no right in itself, could not serve as a foundation on which to build any other; the victor and the vanquished people still remained with respect to each other in the state of war, unless the vanquished, restored to the full possession of their liberty, voluntarily made choice of the victor for their chief. For till then, whatever capitulation may have been made being founded on violence, and therefore ipso facto void, there could not have been on this hypothesis either a real society or body politic, or any law other than that of the strongest.[11]

If conquest is not able to bring about the state, then it seems that the state must come "from within." But the sovereign cannot be produced internally. Internal conflicts between clans belonging to a single community will not lead to the rise of an independent public power. In sum, we have a thesis that the state arises from within the community and an antithesis that the state does not arise from within the community. But this antinomy can be resolved when we see that the origin of the state lies in a kind of exchange carried out between ruling and ruled communities. This exchange takes the form of the conquering side offering protection to the vanquished in return for their subservience, as well as redistribution in return for the offered tribute. When this happens, the reality of conquest is disavowed by both parties.

It is true that there are some cases where a sovereign emerged from within the community even in the absence of conquest. In clan societies, for example, at times of crisis the chief can temporarily become a sovereign wielding extraordinary powers—powers that are then canceled when order is restored. Moreover, in cases where warfare is the normal condition, the chief can become sovereign on a permanent basis. In other words, when the threat of external invasion is constant, the position of the chief acquires absolute status on a permanent basis. In such cases, kingship emerges. For this reason, even when conquest does not actually take place, if the threat of it is constant, a sovereign can arise from within the interior of the community. Accordingly, even in cases where it seems to appear from within, ultimately the sovereign is something that comes from outside. In reality, once a state comes into being, the other communities around it must either submit to its rule or become states themselves. Therefore, even when a community appears to have transformed itself into a state from within, external relations with other states will always form the backdrop.

The Community-State

Hobbes locates the basis for the establishment of the state in an exchange (contract) whereby "one receiveth the benefit of life; the other is to receive money, or service for it." This is not something that takes place at the level of individual persons, but rather at the level of relations between communities: the state is established on the basis of an exchange (contract) between the ruling and ruled communities. In this exchange the ruled community submits and pays tribute to the ruling community and thereby receives security. But because this is a provisional contract, the possibility exists that it might be overturned. In order for a state to be fully established, further exchanges are necessary. In addition to levying tribute and forced labor on the ruled community, the ruling community must also redistribute the wealth it receives in the form of taxes. The state must appear as if it were the agent of redistribution for the community—in short, as if it were fulfilling a public function of the community. When this happens, the state comes to be regarded as simply an extension of the chiefdom community.

In reality, however, chiefdom society and the state are of fundamentally different natures, and the former cannot become a state simply by expanding. For example, the chief or priest of tribal society can never become the king of a state, no matter how much power this person manages to accumulate.

This is because the principles of reciprocity remain stubbornly in force. Whatever wealth or power the chief may accumulate comes by way of gifts. In order to sustain that power, the chief must in return continually give things away ungrudgingly. Failing to do so would cause him to lose his position. But it is precisely this generosity in giving that causes the chief to lose his wealth. In the end, privileged positions never survive for long. Therefore, the state will never emerge as a simple extension or expansion of the previously existing community.

As I noted, monarchy (the state) comes not from within the community but from outside. But at the same time it must appear as if it has come from the interior of the community, as if it were simply a further extension of that community. If it fails to achieve this, a monarchy (state) will not be firmly established. In this sense, just as the modern state takes the form of the nation-state, the state since antiquity has taken the form of the *community-state*.

In the formation of this community-state, the key role was played by religion. In clan and tribal communities, chiefs were simultaneously priests. The same was true at the stage of the proto-city-state that subsumed multiple tribes. For example, the temple was not simply a place for religious rituals; it was also a storehouse of wealth that was to be redistributed, and the chief who carried out this redistribution was the priest. In this sense, the priest and the political chief could not be distinguished from one another. At the stage of the proto-city-state, the chief held much greater power than at the stage of the chiefdom state, now acting as priest in the service of gods who transcended the deities (ancestral or tribal) of the various member communities. Weber thought that the city emerged as a federation by oath, but the oath in question was above all a pledge to worship the same god(s). This marked the moment of emergence of a community-state that transcended the previously existing clan communities.

The ancient state was born of conflicts between city-states. In terms of religion, what came out of this process was the rise of a god that transcended the gods worshipped by the various clans and tribes. This development signifies the establishment of a state that transcended the previously existing clan and tribe communities. To consider this in more concrete terms, let us take up the example of the Sumerian state (Ur, Uruk, and so on), the earliest known instance of a commonwealth by acquisition. The Sumerian state grew out of conflicts between multiple city-states along the Tigris and Euphrates Rivers. These conflicts dramatically accelerated processes that were already under way. As one city-state emerged victorious, its gods also triumphed. If a state became increasingly more powerful, its gods likewise became universal and transcendent. The monarch of the city-state that emerged as victorious from these wars ruled the others not simply through military force, but also became the priest serving a god that transcended all the other previously existing gods (in the case of Egypt, the pharaoh directly became a deity). This is how the monarch obtained voluntary subjection from the masses. In this way, along with the establishment of the monarchical state, a new imagined community was created that transcended the various clans and tribes. The crucial point here is that it was not the development of the community that led to the rise of the state; to the contrary, it was only after the establishment of a centralized state that a new community would emerge.

The Asiatic State and the Agricultural Community

With the rise of the state, the previously existing clan and tribe communities underwent a transformation. We can take this up in terms of both the levels of the ruling and the ruled communities. At the level of the ruling community, the existing community and its reciprocal mode of being—in positive terms, its principle of equality; in negative terms its tendency to engage in vendettas—disappeared, and a hierarchical order took shape. This did not happen all at once though. Centralization within the ruling stratum is achieved only gradually, through the overcoming of "intermediate powers" (Montesquieu), such as various chiefs (aristocrats) and priests. In the emergence of the ancient despotic state, we see something that structurally resembles the emergence of the absolutist monarchy in early modern Europe: a form in which all people give their allegiance to an absolute despot who has suppressed the aristocracy (the powerful clans).

In tandem with this increasing centralization in the ruling class, at the level of the ruled classes, the existing clan community is reorganized into an agrarian community. The agrarian community appears as if it were simply an extension of clan society. For this reason, Marx viewed the "Asiatic mode of production" and the Asiatic agrarian community as the first mode to develop out from primitive society (clan society); he then tried to use this to explain the Asiatic state. For example, taking up the remnants of the agrarian community that survived in the Punjab region of India's Indus River basin, he argues: "The simplicity of the productive organism in these self-sufficing communities which constantly reproduce themselves in the same form . . . supplies the key to the riddle of the unchangeability of Asiatic societies, which is in such striking contrast with the constant dissolution and refounding of Asiatic states, and their never-ceasing changes of dynasty."[12] In sum, he believed that the despotic state was eternal because the Asiatic community was eternally unchanging.

But this way of describing things leads to misunderstandings. The community's Asiatic mode appeared only after the establishment of the Asiatic despotic state, not the other way around. For example, in Sumer the state mobilized increasingly large numbers of people to engage in large-scale irrigation projects, granting them land in return for their work. It was thus the state that created the agrarian community. Other than requiring payment of tribute and forced labor, the despotic state did not interfere in the internal affairs of the agrarian community, in which regular systems of self-government and mutual aid existed. At first glance, these may appear to be remnants of the principle of reciprocity from clan society. But here the autonomy with regard to higher-order organizations that characterized clan societies no longer exists.

I have already pointed out how the reciprocity of clan societies was characterized not solely by positive aspects, such as mutual aid and equalization, but also by negative aspects, including the tendency to subjugate others by force. We see this, for example, in destructive competitions such as potlatch and vendettas. Reciprocity does not acknowledge any higher authority. The agrarian communities that formed under Asiatic despotism preserved reciprocity in such aspects as mutual aid and equalization. But they lost the other aspect of reciprocity: their autonomy. The people were completely subordinated to the state (monarch)—in fact, this was why the agrarian community was permitted a measure of self-governance. The community also acquired a degree of communal adhesion not found in clan societies.

Next we need to note that the formation of the Asiatic despotic state could not have taken place simply through military conquest: it required the introduction of a new principle for governance. The despotic state emerged from conflicts between numerous city-states as a territorially extensive state. In tandem with this, there emerged a society in which traditional communal norms no longer held sway. The transcendental status acquired by the gods of these supranational states was not simply a question of religion: these states that governed over vast territories needed the idea of the rule of law (ruling by means of law).

We tend to associate the idea of conflict between city-states chiefly with the Greek polis, as well as with the activities of various philosophers, including the Sophists. But there is little doubt that similar conditions existed earlier in the formation of the ancient empires, even if there are no extant records. For example, when we consider the use in the subsequent Babylonian and Assyrian empires of words that originated in Sumerian civilization, we catch a glimpse of the epochal shift that civilization represented. The principle of "an eye for an eye," which marked a decisive break with the principles of reciprocity, was not a law that just naturally came about: it had to first be expounded by philosophers.

We can see this clearly when we look at ancient China. The Warring States period (403–221 BCE), characterized by fighting among city-states, gave rise to the so-called Hundred Schools of Thought, with the appearance of many great thinkers, including Confucius, Laozi, and Han Fei. In the same manner as the Greek Sophists, they traveled from one state to another, each expounding his own school of thought. Because it was no longer possible to rule according to the customary practices and religions of clan society, the various states needed new theories. Among them, Qin emerged as a powerhouse due to the work of chancellor Shang Yang, who advocated the philosophy of legalism; Qin subsequently produced the first emperor who built the empire. This emergence of a centralized government ruling over a supranational state was made possible by Qin's theories, which advocated suppressing the hereditary aristocracy, instituting a rigorous philosophy of legalism, and standardizing the system of measures and weights. The Qin dynasty soon collapsed, but the Han dynasty that followed it took up Confucianism as its principle for governing and thereby became the prototype for subsequent empires.

The Warring States period in China with its Hundred Schools of Thought was roughly synchronous with the age of conflict between the city-states of Greece, and there is a strong resemblance between the two. In China this process of empire formation also meant the closing off of possibilities that had opened up during the Warring States period; the Asiatic despotic state remained in place after this. The important thing to remember at this point is that the Asiatic despotic state did not appear simply as a natural extension of earlier clan societies. Whether in Sumer or China, its appearance required a breaking with the traditions that had existed since clan society. Once a centralized order was established, the despotic state then tried to actively co-opt traditions dating back to clan society. This is why the agrarian community organized by the despotic state took on the appearance of being a continuation of clan society.

Marx described the Asiatic community as a "general slavery." It was neither a slavery system nor an agricultural serfdom. Each individual was a member of a self-governing community. But that community belonged to the monarch. The monarch had no need to meddle in the community's affairs. Individuals were constrained by their status as members of the community. For this reason, self-governance became the means by which the state controlled the community. Accordingly, the state and the agrarian community are entities of completely different natures, but they do not exist in isolation from one another. The agrarian community is an imagined community whose framework is provided by the despotic state—just as the modern nation cannot exist in the absence of the framework of the centralized state. Asiatic despotism existed in the form of an amalgamation of the despotic state with the agrarian community.

One common misunderstanding about Asiatic despotism confuses it with a slavery system. Under the Asiatic state, the masses were neither cruelly abused nor neglected—if anything, they were carefully safeguarded. For example, as John Maynard Keynes notes, the construction of the pyramids was carried out as a measure for dealing with unemployment and as a state policy for generating effective demand.[13] In this sense, the despotic state (patriarchal patrimonial system) was a kind of welfare state. In the same way, the Eastern Roman Empire (Byzantine) was also a welfare state.[14] This was not because it was a Christian state, but rather because it was an Asiatic despotic state—that is, a state where the emperor was also the pope. Weber argues that the emergence of welfare-state social policies in western Europe occurred under the absolute monarchies:

> Patriarchal patrimonialism is mass domination by one individual; as a rule it requires officials, whereas feudalism minimizes the demand for these. As far as it does not rely on alien patrimonial troops, it strongly depends upon the subjects' good will, which feudalism can afford to forego to a large extent. Against the dangerous aspirations of the privileged status groups, patriarchalism plays out the masses who everywhere have been its natural following. The "good king," not the hero, was the ideal glorified by mass legend. Therefore, patriarchal patrimonialism must legitimate itself as guardian of the subjects' welfare in its own and in their eyes. The "welfare state" is the legend of patrimonialism, deriving not from the free camaraderie of solemnly promised fealty, but from the authoritarian relationship of father and children. The "father of the people" (*Landesvater*) is the ideal of the patrimonial states. Patriarchalism can therefore be the carrier of a specific welfare policy, and indeed develops

it whenever it has sufficient reason to assure itself of the good will of the masses. In modern history this happened, for example, in England under the regime of the Stuarts, when they fought against the anti-authoritarian forces of the Puritan bourgeoisie and of the semi-feudal *honoratiores*: Laud's Christian welfare policies had partly clerical, partly patrimonial roots.[15]

In western Europe, it was under the absolute monarchies that the concept of the king nurturing his subjects first appeared. But this sort of welfare-state concept was quite common in Asiatic states. In China, from the Han dynasty on, despotic rule was based on Confucianism. The despot was regarded as an enlightened ruler, one who ruled not through military force but through virtue. Through his bureaucrats, the despot was expected to rule, administer, show concern for, and take care of his subjects.

Another common misunderstanding of the Asiatic despotic state views it as a rigid despotic system that reached into every corner of governance. In fact, that sort of monarchical power is always fragile and short-lived. To sustain a monarchy over the long-term requires the deployment of religion, alliances through marriage, vassalage relations with feudal lords, and bureaucratic systems. As a result of these, however, forces constantly arise to resist the monarch: priests and other religious figures, powerful clans, and patrimonial officials from private estates. On top of these, nomadic peoples from the outside spot this internal dissent and seize the opportunity to invade. In this way, dynasties fall, after which once again a new dynastic is established. The "constant dissolution and refounding of Asiatic States, and the never-ceasing changes of dynasty" (Marx) was of this nature.

It was the structure of the despotic state, more than the Asiatic agrarian community, that remained in a permanent state of stasis in the face of these "never-ceasing changes of dynasty." We should pay special attention not so much to the early stages of the state that was based in the early, undeveloped agrarian community, as to how in formal terms the mature modalities of the centralized state—in other words, the systems of bureaucratic organization and the permanent standing army—were brought about by the Asiatic state. These modalities and the processes that brought them about were subsequently repeated elsewhere. We cannot simply conclude that the unchanging nature of the agrarian community caused the despotic state to be similarly stable. Real permanence was achieved not by the agrarian community but rather by the organs of the state that governed the community from above, including the bureaucracy and standing army. Even as dynasties changed with dizzying speed, these organs carried on, fundamentally unchanged, making it possible for the agrarian community to persist in unchanged form.[16]

Why didn't the despotic state appear in Greece or Rome? I will examine this again later, but here let me sketch in the answer. It was not because Greek and Roman society were at a so-called advanced stage; to the contrary, it was because they were "backward." As Marx in his later years pointed out, it was because in the Greek and Roman city-states, among the ruling community (citizens), the principle of reciprocity from clan society remained strongly in force, resisting the emergence of a centralized state. That was why these city-states could not produce a centralized bureaucratic structure. Moreover, the market economies that developed in them were not under state control. This is also, however, connected to their inability to implement either the sort of despotic rule that could reorganize conquered communities into agrarian communities or the sort of imperial rule that would integrate multiple conquered states and communities into itself. Rome in the end did become a vast empire, but that was due if anything to its adoption of the Asiatic imperial system. For these reasons, we should regard the despotic state that emerged in Asia not simply as a primitive early stage but rather as the entity that perfected (in formal terms) the supranational state (i.e., empire).

The Bureaucratic System

Ancient civilizations arose in river-basin areas and carried out large-scale irrigation agriculture. This is why Marx linked the Asiatic despotic state to irrigation agriculture. Weber also argues as follows:

> Bureaucratization is stimulated more strongly, however, by intensive and qualitative expansion of the administrative tasks than by their extensive and quantitative increase. But the direction bureaucratization takes, and the reasons that occasion it, can vary widely. In Egypt, the oldest country of bureaucratic state administration, it was the technical necessity of a public regulation of the water economy for the whole country and from the top which created the apparatus of scribes and officials; very early it found its second realm of operation in the extraordinary, militarily organized construction activities. In most cases, as mentioned before, the bureaucratic tendency has been promoted by needs arising from the creation of standing armies, determined by power politics, and from the related

developments of public finances. But in the modern state, the increasing demands for administration also rest on the increasing complexity of civilization.[17]

Karl Wittfogel inherited Marx and Weber's view. Wittfogel thought that Oriental despotic states were established through large-scale irrigation agriculture, but he abandoned the geographical limitation of the concept, rechristening them "hydraulic societies."[18] Some have critiqued his view, arguing that there is no necessary link between the despotic state and irrigation agriculture.[19] Another possible criticism arises from cases such as Russia, where despotic states arose even in regions that did not employ irrigation agriculture. Wittfogel himself later attempted to explain how despotism could appear in nonhydraulic regions such as Russia, seeking the cause in external influences: in Russia, he argued, the Asiatic despotic state was introduced via Mongolian rule.[20]

But this in itself already demonstrates the need to think of despotism separately from irrigation agriculture. The civilization realized by hydraulic societies was not just a matter of technologies for dominating nature; more than that, it consisted of technologies for governing people—namely, state apparatuses, standing armies, bureaucratic systems, written language, and communication networks. Consequently, this civilization could be transmitted even to regions that had no irrigation agriculture, for example to nomadic peoples such as the Mongols. Technologies for governing people preceded technologies for governing nature.

How did bureaucratic systems come about? It is clear that they developed out of massive public-works projects, but an important question remains: where did the people who engaged in these projects and the bureaucrats who managed them come from? The people of clan society hated the idea of becoming subordinated farmers, as did nomadic peoples. Even when they became rulers, they despised the thought of becoming bureaucrats, and so they remained warrior-farmers. The complete absence of any development of a bureaucratic system in the Greek polis is one instance of this. In Rome, because there was no bureaucratic system, tax collection was contracted out to private parties. In sum, we have to take into consideration the fact that people do not voluntarily choose to become bureaucrats.

Weber maintains that the bureaucrats of Egypt were in reality slaves of the pharaoh, and that manorial lords of Rome relied on slaves to carry out their business.[21] The reason for this, Weber writes, was that the pharaohs and lords could employ violent force against slaves. In Assyria, many bureaucrats were eunuchs. These instances suggest the impossibility of a bureaucratic system arising among members of a community based on the principle of reciprocity. In other words, a bureaucratic system arose only after the reciprocal autonomy between monarch and retainers had been completely done away with.

According to Weber, the bureaucratic system subsequently comes to be based on a guaranteed cash salary system.[22] In that sense, he argues, the full development of a money economy is a precondition for the emergence of a bureaucratic system. Under this cash salary system, the bureaucrats begin to experience regularized opportunities for advancement, discipline, and regulations, and a status-based sense of honor. Moreover, bureaucrats became the actual ruling class in the state, in place of the frequently changing rulers (monarchy). Yet they remain fundamentally slaves, which is precisely why they become de facto masters: the despotic lord, after all, can do nothing without bureaucrats. We see here an instance of Hegel's "master-slave" dialectic.

Another basis of the bureaucratic system was written language. Writing became indispensable at the stage of empires that encompass multiple tribes or states. Written language in turn led to the creation of standardized spoken language. This was already the case in Sumer, and in Egypt the mastering of multiple complex writing systems was a necessary condition for becoming a bureaucrat. The power of the bureaucrat lay above all in the knowledge of writing. One who cannot read and write the records of past and present cannot govern a state. The unbroken continuity of the bureaucracy in China depended more than anything on its emphasis on writing and literature.

Despotism in ancient China was fully realized with the Han dynasty. In its wake came numerous invasions by nomadic peoples. The conquering dynasties, however, never abolished the existing state bureaucratic structures, choosing instead simply to take them over. These repeated conquests had the effect of cutting the intimate communal connections between the state apparatus and clans and tribes, moving that apparatus toward a position of neutrality. The civil-service-selection examination system that began in the eighth century with the Sui dynasty transformed the bureaucratic system into an independent organ that could serve any ruler (dynasty). Despite "the constant dissolution and refounding of Asiatic States, and the neverceasing changes of dynasty," with the exception of a temporary period of Mongolian rule, this system would survive into the twentieth century.[23]

FOUR **WORLD MONEY**

The State and Money

Karl Marx repeatedly stressed that commodity exchange began with exchanges between different communities. In doing so, he was critiquing a misperception that had existed since Adam Smith, who located the origins of commodity exchange in exchanges between individuals. Smith's view was nothing more than a perspectival inversion that projected a modern market economy onto the past. For example, even today it is quite rare to see commodity exchanges (buying and selling) take place within the interior of a community or, if the community has disappeared, within the family. In those situations, gift giving and pooling are the most commonly adopted forms. Trade is something only carried out between different communities.

This does not mean, however, that society (community) in its earliest stages did not have commodity exchanges. Commodity exchange did not develop out of gift giving; it existed from the start. Even hunter-gatherer peoples carried out trade. No community can be completely self-sufficient; there is always a need to obtain some goods from outside. For this reason, commodity exchange is inevitable—all the more so after fixed settlement is adopted. But in order for commodity exchanges to take place between different communities, first the state of war that exists between them must be overcome, and stable, amicable relations must be constructed. Gift giving accomplishes this purpose. For example, the famous kula trade in Melanesia takes the form of islands that have received gifts making return gifts to other islands, and it is only after these gift exchanges that exchanges of essential goods are carried out. This does not mean that trade is secondary to gift giving. Rather, trade itself is the primary goal, and gift giving is essential in making it possible.

For example, the gift-countergift cycle of silent trade takes a form that seems at first glance reciprocal. Communities that engage in silent trade are fearful of direct encounter with one another. They strongly desire to engage in trade, but want to avoid face-to-face encounters. This case plainly shows how a fear of the state of nature lies at the root of gift giving. It is not easy to establish trade between communities; it is only through gift giving that a venue for trading is opened up. Therefore, while commodity exchange has existed since the oldest periods, it was always necessarily connected to gift giving. In other words, mode of exchange C existed from the beginning, but only in the form of something incidental to mode of exchange A. As a result, it can appear as if trade was completely nonexistent in primitive societies.

To reiterate, the need for trade existed from the precivilization stage. This was why a higher-order community was established above small-scale clan communities. Proto-city-states were likewise formed in this way. The state was formed through intercourse (trade and warfare) between proto-city-states. I have already explained how the state form originates in mode of exchange B, but this does not mean that it is utterly unrelated to mode of exchange C. Rather, we can say that the state is formed in tandem with the practice of trade. Under the centralized state, in return (exchange) for its payment of taxes (tribute and forced labor), each community secures its rights of ownership. With this it becomes possible to carry out commodity exchanges—that is, the mutual transference of possessions.

When Marx in *Capital* theorizes the commodity-exchange relationship, he calls attention to the ways in which it is backed by the legal relationship between the two owners:

> In order that these objects may enter into relation with each other as commodities, their guardians must place themselves in relation to one another as persons whose will resides in those objects, and must behave in such a way that each does not appropriate the commodity of the other, and alienate his own, except through an act to which both parties consent. The guardians must therefore recognize each other as owners of private property. This juridical relation, whose form is the contract, whether as part of a developed legal system or not, is a relation between two wills which mirrors the economic relation. The content of this juridical relation (or relation of two wills) is itself determined by the economic relation.[1]

It may seem here that Marx is stressing that the juridical relationship is merely reflected in the economic relationship. But what he really means is that the economic relation of commodity exchange cannot exist in the absence of the juridical relationship. What makes commodity exchange between communities possible is the existence of the state, which punishes as legal infringements any acts of theft or failures to uphold contracts. This is grounded in mode of exchange B. There is also the matter of the credit that exists between communities, which is grounded in reciprocal mode of exchange A. Accordingly, the commodity mode of exchange C between communities can only exist when it appears in tandem with the other modes, A and B.

In this way, commodity exchange exists only with the support of the community and state. Having said that, the existence of mode of exchange C is not simply contingent. Insofar as they are unable to be fully self-sufficient, the community and state both require it. Modes of exchange A and B each have their own power: the power of the gift and the power of the state, respectively. Mode of exchange C also produces its own unique form of power. This is not something born of the state; rather, it is something that the state cannot do without. This power is, concretely, the power of money: the right to obtain some other thing directly through exchange. With money, one is able to subordinate other people not through fear but through voluntary contracts. We will look at how and why money comes into being, but the important point to keep in mind for the time being is that, just as commodity exchange requires the existence of the state, so too does the perpetuation of the state require the existence of money.

With money the state is able to hire people. This makes it possible to rule people through voluntary contracts, without having to rely on either fear or the constraints of reciprocity. For example, the power of the ancient despotic states was grounded in violence (military force), but the power of money was indispensable for this. Once the state transcended the scale of a tribal community, it needed to hire soldiers, as well as employ skilled specialists to produce weapons. For these purposes it needed money. The state acquired this through trade with distant lands, whether the state itself pursued this directly or simply imposed duty fees on trade. The large-scale irrigation agriculture that was one of the hallmarks of the ancient despotic state was aimed not so much at domestic consumption as at export.

In this way, a single social formation arises as a combination of three different modes of exchange—or the three different forms of power that derive from these, forms that are mutually in conflict yet also mutually interdependent. Even in precapitalist social formations, mode of exchange C was an important factor. No matter how it developed, however, it was fated to remain secondary to modes A and B. In other words, mode C was generally viewed negatively. For example, except for cases when they themselves became state officials, merchants were typically seen as immoral. Despite its filling an indispensable role, mode of exchange C was always placed in a position of inferiority, as seen, for example, in the case of silent trading.

In this chapter we will consider the situation of mode of exchange C in social formations where it occupies a subordinate position. Mode of exchange C undoubtedly became the dominant mode in capitalist social formations, where its characteristics are visible across the whole spectrum of social life. But all the characteristics of its power were also manifested in earlier societies. More precisely, it is in those societies that its characteristics were most explicitly revealed. Marx writes, "Interest-bearing capital, or, to describe it in its archaic form, usurer's capital, belongs together with its twin brother, merchant's capital, to the antediluvian forms of capital which long precede the capitalist mode of production and are to be found in the most diverse socio-economic formations."[2] Merchant capital and usurer's capital still exist today, but only as marginal forms. Their role is usually ignored, and in fact can be ignored, when we think about the contemporary capitalist economy. And yet the essence of capital lies precisely in merchant and usurer capital. In them the power of money, its fetish character, is most clearly revealed. Accordingly, to understand the essence of capital, we must turn our considerations back to its "antediluvian forms."

The Social Contract of the Commodity World

How was money born of commodity exchanges, and how did the power possessed by money come into being? In dealing with these questions, archaeology and anthropology are of no help to us. In a preface to *Capital*, Marx writes: "Moreover, in the analysis of economic forms neither microscopes nor chemical reagents are of assistance. The power of abstraction must replace both."[3] We are now in the same situation: in order to analyze money and capital, we must rely on the explication that Marx produced through the "power of abstraction"—that is, on the theory of value form found in the opening of *Capital*.

Marx is generally thought to have inherited the labor theory of value from Smith, David Ricardo, and the other classical economists and to have developed his theory of surplus value (exploitation) in the process of critiquing it. But this task was actually undertaken prior to Marx by English socialists of the Ricardo school. The problems that attracted Marx's attention from the start were the power of money, its religious inversion, and self-alienation. According to the classical economists, money presented no particular riddle: it was simply an indicator of the labor value borne by each commodity. From this, the Ricardo school of socialists, including Robert Owen, along with P.-J. Proudhon considered abolishing money and using instead a kind of labor voucher that would record actual hours of labor. It was Marx who criticized the excessive simplification of this approach.

The classical economists tried to explain away the problem of money by introducing the value of labor, but in fact their argument implicitly required the existence of money as its premise. For example, Smith believed that a commodity had use value and exchange value. Its exchange value consisted of its purchasing power, that is, its ability to buy other commodities. This would mean that every commodity is itself money—but this cannot be the case. Only those commodities that serve as money (gold and silver, for example) have this power. Yet commodities do not contain immanent value from the start: their value comes into being only after they are bought and sold (exchanged for money). If a product fails to sell, then no matter how much labor went into its production, it possesses no value—not even use value. It is simply discarded. A commodity only comes to have value when it is equated with some other commodity. But monetary commodities such as gold or silver certainly seem to possess an intrinsic exchange value. They appear to bestow the right to buy (to be directly exchanged for) other commodities. That being the case, how do certain commodities acquire this power? It is not because of their raw material, nor is it the result of labor expended in their production. This sort of power can only be produced through the process of exchanges of one commodity for another.

On many points, Marx carried on the thought of the classical economists. For example, he called the substance of the value of each commodity "abstracted labor" or "social labor." But in *Capital* he demonstrated that value was not something intrinsic to the commodity, that it instead was only manifested through the exchange of one commodity for another, in other words, through the value form. This means that the value of a commodity can only be understood in terms of the relationship between it and other commodities.

> Men do not therefore bring the products of their labour into relation with each other as values because they see these objects merely as the material

integuments of homogenous human labour. The reverse is true: by equating their different products to each other in exchange as values, they equate their different kinds of human labour. They do this without being aware of it. Value, therefore, does not have its description branded on its forehead; it rather transforms every product of labour into a social hieroglyphic. Later on, men try to decipher the hieroglyphic, to get behind the secret of their own social product: for the characteristic which objects of utility have of being values is as much men's social product as is their language.[4]

The abstracted, social labor that is the substance of value is bestowed only retroactively through the money (universal equivalent) that is produced through relations that equate one commodity with another. Accordingly, understanding the creation of money does not require the labor theory of value. Because Marx in *Capital* happens to discuss the labor value that inheres in the commodity prior to explaining the value form, he needlessly gave rise to much confusion. But there is no value—labor value or otherwise—intrinsic to the commodity. It acquires value only when it is equated with some other commodity. Moreover, this value is expressed in the form of the use value of that other commodity. In sum, the value of a given commodity arises from the equivalent form it locates in other commodities—in other words, from the value form.

For example, the value of commodity A is indicated by the use value of commodity B. Marx called this the simple form of value.[5] In Marx's words, at this moment commodity A is situated as the relative form of value, and commodity B as the equivalent form. In other words, commodity B is serving as money (an equivalent). But in this simple form of value, we can reverse this and buy commodity A with commodity B, in which case commodity A functions as money (equivalent). We have a situation in which any commodity can claim to be money.

In order for money proper to appear, it must be the case that only commodity B can serve as the value form. Beginning with this simple form of value, Marx theoretically explicates the development through "expanded form of value," then "general form of value form," and finally the "money-form."[6] Money appears when commodity B is situated as the value form excluded from all other commodities. When gold or silver take up the position of universal value form and all other commodities are positioned as relative value forms, then gold and silver become money. But an inversion takes place here: even though they have only become money because they are positioned in this way, gold and silver come to be thought of as possessing a special intrinsic exchange value:

> We have already seen, from the simplest expression of value, x commodity A = y commodity B, that the thing in which the magnitude of the value of another thing is represented appears to have the equivalent form independently of this relation, as a social property inherent in its nature. We followed the process by which this false semblance became firmly established, a process which was completed when the universal equivalent form became identified with the natural form of a particular commodity, and thus crystallized into the money-form. What appears to happen is not that a particular commodity becomes money because all other commodities express their values in it, but, on the contrary, that all other commodities universally express their values in a particular commodity because it is money. The movement through which this process has been mediated vanishes in its own result, leaving no trace behind. Without any initiative on their part, the commodities find their own value-configuration ready to hand, in the form of a physical commodity exiting outside but also alongside them. This physical object, gold or silver in its crude state, becomes, immediately on its emergence from the bowels of the earth, the direct incarnation of all human labour. Hence the magic of money.[7]

In Marx's words, the creation of money is "the joint contribution of the whole world of commodities."[8] We could also call this the social contract of the commodity world. The various commodities renounce their desire or right to be money, transferring it to a specific set of commodities. Because of this, the right to buy and sell is bestowed only on those commodities that are positioned as the form of value in general—the money-form. It turns out that the power of money is grounded in a social contract.

Leviathan and Capital

Seen in this way, it becomes clear that Marx's depiction in *Capital* of the creation of money resembles Thomas Hobbes's description in *Leviathan* of the emergence of the sovereign. In both, the concentration of power in a single figure is accomplished when all other actors transfer their own rights to it. In fact, Marx in discussing money actually cites the example of a king: "For instance, one man is king only because other men stand in the relation of subjects to him. They, on the other hand, imagine that they are subjects because he is king."[9]

Let's explore a little further this resemblance between money and king. Hobbes depicts the birth of the sovereign in an agreement by all members of society to transfer their own natural rights to a single person. However, we shouldn't take this to mean that all members of society got together and reached a decision through direct discussion. That could produce at best only a relatively powerful chief. Alongside the logic of this development outlined in *Leviathan*, we need to consider the actual historical processes that went into it.

The transfer by all members of society of their natural rights to one person was in reality a process in which one already relatively powerful person managed to elbow his way past all others to become even more powerful. In Europe the absolute monarchies were established when kings, who were hitherto merely leading figures, gradually managed to win supremacy over the other feudal lords and the church. Moreover, this did not lead to the establishment of an absolute sovereign. In absolute monarchies, intermediate powers such as the nobility and the church were still present. Montesquieu believed that these checked the absolute monarchy and prevented it from falling into despotism.

In France the extermination of the intermediate powers was brought about by the French Revolution that began in 1789. The bourgeois revolution did more than bring down the absolute monarchy; by destroying the intermediate powers, the revolution also established an absolute sovereign—the state in which the people are sovereign (the dictatorship of the bourgeoisie). In a sense, however, this sort of process had taken place even earlier in England with the Puritan Revolution during the seventeenth century, which toppled the absolute monarch. Accordingly, when he wrote *Leviathan*, the sovereign that Hobbes had in mind was not the absolute monarch but rather the popular sovereignty that had emerged with the execution of the king. *Sovereign* indicates a position that anyone can occupy: the monarch, the people, or any other substitute.

For this reason, Hobbes traced the emergence of the position of the sovereign in terms of its logic, rather than historically (diachronically). The same is true for the establishment of money that Marx uncovered in *Capital*. In "The Value-Form, or Exchange-Value," Marx tries to deduce the logic behind the emergence of the position that is value form as being this sort of "joint contribution of the whole world of commodities."[10] He did not attempt here to explain the actual historical creation of money. In fact, in *Capital* Marx takes up the diachronic creation of money in the chapter "The Process of Exchange," which follows after the chapter on value.

Accordingly, what is important in the theory of value form is not the actual origin of money but rather the origin of the money-form. When something becomes money, this has nothing to do with what it is made of; it happens simply because this thing has been placed in the position of money-form. According to Marx, this was the social contract of the commodity world. Why commodities and not people? It goes without saying that a social contract can only be carried out by people, not commodities. But the people in question here are people as possessors of commodities, people defined as owners under the category of commodity. For this reason, the position in which individual people are situated is of more importance than their individual wills. For example, the standpoint of someone who holds a commodity is different from that of a person who holds money. People who have money can buy things or hire people. By contrast, a person who has only a commodity (including the commodity of labor power) occupies a relatively weak position. In this way, the world created by commodity exchange, while grounded in the consent of people, acquires an objectivity that transcends human will. Herein lies the secret of the power of compulsion possessed by money; it is different from the *hau* found in the reciprocity of the gift.

In considering the actual historical creation of money, however, we must imagine a different process from this logical development. For example, so long as some thing—it makes no difference what it is—is positioned as the money-form, then it will be money. Yet not all commodities can become money. By their nature, some things have an easier time in becoming the general equivalent. Marx argues:

But with the development of exchange it fixes itself firmly and exclusively onto particular kinds of commodity, i.e. it crystallizes out into the money-form. The particular kind of commodity to which it sticks is at first a matter of accident. Nevertheless there are two circumstances which are by and large decisive. The money-form comes to be attached either to the most important articles of exchange from outside, which are in fact the primitive and spontaneous forms of manifestation of the exchange-value of local products, or to the object of utility which forms the chief element of indigenous alienable wealth, for example cattle. Nomadic peoples are the first to develop the money-form, because all their worldly possessions are in a moveable and therefore directly alienable form, and because their mode of life, by continually bringing them into contact with foreign communities, encourages the exchange of products. Men have often made man himself into the primitive material of money, in the shape of the slave, but they have never done this with the land and soil. . . . In the same proportion as exchange bursts its local bonds, and the value of commodities accordingly expands more and more into the material embodiment of human labour as such, in that proportion does the money-form become transferred to commodities which are by nature fitted to perform the social function of a universal equivalent. Those commodities are the precious metals.[11]

In reality, some materials were by their nature especially apt to serve as the equivalent. It seems likely that from among these some began to serve as general equivalents, and then from among those grew the money-form. Accordingly, it was not entirely coincidental that gold or silver became money—they filled the conditions required for a world money:

[They] are always uniform and consequently equal quantities of them have equal values. Another condition that has to be fulfilled by the commodity which is to serve as universal equivalent and that follows directly from its function of representing purely quantitative differences, is its divisibility into any desired number of parts and the possibility of combining these again, so that money of account can be represented in palpable form too. Gold and silver possess these qualities to an exceptional degree.[12]

We should not overemphasize this point, however, lest we lapse into thinking that there was some necessity for gold or silver to become money. It is important to stress that what is important here is the money-form itself, not the raw materials involved. Keeping this in mind, we can turn our thoughts to the historical rise of money.

World Money

Let's consider here what Marx called the simple, isolated, or accidental form of value. It is created through equivalence, but equivalence is not something that begins only with commodity exchange. Gifts and gift trade also involve an awareness of equivalence. The basis of this equivalence is not simply arbitrary: equivalence was determined by custom or tradition, but behind this lay the social labor time required to produce an object. The appearance that equivalence was set by custom is due to the almost imperceptibly slow rate of transformation in the natural environment and production technology. Of course, people are not conscious of this background factor. In the act of drawing equivalences, the value of one thing comes to be expressed as the use value of some other thing: "They do not know it, but they do it."[13]

Karl Polanyi in *The Livelihood of Man* stresses that equivalence is not price. From Marx's point of view, this means that price is determined only when all goods are placed in a system of interrelationship by way of a universal equivalent; equivalence can exist prior to this, but not price. In other words, with simple value form or expanded value form, there are only chains of equivalent relations. The shift from this to the general value form (or universal equivalent) requires a significant leap. What this means in actuality is the appearance of the money-form. An additional subsequent shift leads to the use of precious metals as money. At this point the system of interrelationships of commodities in all regions becomes visible through a single shared yardstick. This marks the emergence of world money, another major transformation.

This series of shifts from equivalent to world money parallels the shifts from tribal community to city-state to territorial state (empire). The earliest use of precious metals for money seems to have been the silver currency of Mesopotamia (gold was treasured in Egypt but not used as money). It is important to note here that the shift from equivalent to world money does not mean that the equivalent was completely replaced by world money. Just as multiple states and tribal communities continue to exist even after being subordinated to a supranational state (empire), multiple equivalents or universal equivalents persist even after being subordinated to world money. In practice, world money is used only for settling accounts in international trade, while within each country local equivalents or universal equivalents continue to be used. But this persistence should not mislead us into thinking that world money did not yet exist.

Polanyi writes: "Primitive money may in extreme cases employ one kind of object as means of payment, another as a standard of value, a third for storing wealth, and a fourth for exchange purposes."[14] For example, in Babylon silver was used as a yardstick for price, barley for making payments, and oils, wool, and dates for the purpose of exchanges. In this way, Polanyi stresses the multiplicity of "primitive money." But he is also careful to note that there was a fixed exchange rate of one shekel of silver to one *gur* of barley and that an elaborate system for exchanges of goods was developed. This means that silver was already a world money, even though within the country it was hardly used at all. As this example shows, even when a world money exists, other equivalents and universal equivalents are still used as money.

Precious-metal money is minted by the state. Its ability to circulate globally does not, however, derive from the power of the state: whatever the case may be within the domain covered by state power, the power of money to circulate beyond that realm does not come from the state. The state's role here is limited to determining and guaranteeing the weight of precious metal used in coins. This is, of course, a matter of utmost importance: if the amount of precious metal had to be measured anew with each exchange, trade would in effect be impossible. On the other hand, with this backing of the state, precious metals only have to be used when settling up accounts. Nonetheless, the power of precious-metal money to circulate worldwide is not something owing to the state. To the contrary, the state's ability to mint money depends on this power.[15]

This is also shown by the history of money in China. During the Warring States period, the various states flooded the market with their own currencies; the founder of the Qin dynasty attempted to carry out a unification of currencies through the power of the state, but ultimately failed. It was only the subsequent Han dynasty that was able to achieve this, and it did so by leaving things in the hands of the private economy. The Han court built up an enormous gold stockpile, but rather than mint its own money, it used this as a reserve and permitted the private minting of currency. In this way, it is said to have in a single blow expelled the tangled mixture of currencies. In sum, money became able to circulate through the combined working of state power and the power that is produced out of exchanges.[16]

Money is a commodity that has been placed in the position of the money-form. This commodity can be anything, not just gold or silver. What is crucial is that any money that will circulate internationally must be itself a commodity (use value).[17] Within the community or the state, the material used for money can be anything—even scraps of paper. But outside that sphere this will not be accepted as currency. For example, for nomadic peoples sheep served as money. They moved together with their sheep, using them both for food and as money to buy other goods. In their world, precious-metal money that was difficult to transport would not be accepted as money—to say nothing of currencies that carried only the backing of the state. This is why any money that would circulate beyond the community, beyond the state, must have use value in its raw material. Polanyi notes, "We might find, therefore, that while slaves are a means for the payment of tribute to a foreign overlord, cowrie shells function as a means of local payment."[18] Slaves are commodities (use values)—commodities, moreover, that can be transported as sheep can; therefore, slaves can circulate as external money. By contrast, cowrie shells act as a token of the equivalent and are accepted only locally.[19]

To repeat, external money (world money) must itself be a commodity (use value). Within a single value system (the relational system of commodities), this commodity serves as the yardstick of value for all other commodities. It is able to function as a yardstick of value because it fluctuates as one commodity within the total relationships of all commodities. Moreover, because this money is in itself a commodity, it is also able to enter into other commodity systems (systems of value). As a result, this commodity functions as a world money, circulating across different value systems. If we want to understand money, we need to think in terms of external money. In other words, we cannot understand money only by looking at it locally, within a single country—in the same way that we cannot understand the state if we confine ourselves to the context of a single country.

The Transformation of Money into Capital

Commodity exchange occurs by mutual consent. But it is not easily realized: it is difficult, after all, for two owners of commodities, each having what the other needs, to find one another. For this reason, in practice bartering is often carried out using customary ratios. There are also cases where one commodity fills, de facto, the role of money (equivalent). With the appearance of money, however, these difficulties are avoided. If money exists, it becomes possible to carry out exchanges of commodities that transcend limitations of time and space. But this does not completely wipe away the difficulties of exchange: the person who has money can always buy commodities, but the person who has a commodity cannot always acquire money with it. The difficulties specific to commodity exchange tend to accumulate on the side of the commodity owner.

Mode of exchange C differs from modes A and B in that it is grounded in mutual consent. This is what makes people imagine a relation of equality when they speak about commodity exchanges or the market. Yet the person who has money and the person who has a commodity are not equal. It's a question of whether the commodity will sell—if it fails to sell, it has no value. The person who has money can always exchange it for commodities: it carries the right of direct exchangeability. To own money is to possess a "social pledge" that can be directly exchanged at any time and any place for any commodity.[20] This relationship between money and commodity determines the relationship between their respective owners. Through this seemingly free and equal relation, mode of exchange C produces a kind of class domination different from that which is grounded in fear. In modern industrial capitalism, this takes the form of the relationship between money and the labor-power commodity—that is, between capitalist and proletariat. We must not confuse this with slavery or serfdom systems.[21]

In his theory of value form, Marx traces this relation between money and commodity back to the equivalent and relative forms of value. The power held by a commodity serving as money is due to its being positioned as the universal equivalent. It is a power that arises from the social contract of commodities. But once money comes into being, an inversion takes place. Money is then no longer simply the means used to carry out commodity exchange; insofar as money has the power to be exchanged at any time for any commodity, it gives rise to the desire for, and the concomitant practice of, accumulating money. This is the origin of capital. The accumulation of money has to be distinguished from the accumulation of use values. The accumulation of capital is driven less by a desire for use values (objects) than by a desire for power.

Aristotle distinguished between two forms of money making: that which is carried out from necessity and that which aims at the accumulation of money: "When the use of coin had once been discovered, out of the barter of necessary articles arose the other art of money-making, namely, retail trade."[22] Moreover, he writes, "there is no bound to the riches which spring from this art of money-making."[23] In other words, it is in the second art of money making that the transformation of money into capital takes place. Exchange is pursued to seek not use values but rather exchange values, and for this reason it is without limit. Marx, in touching upon the transformation of money into capital, refers first of all to a miser (a hoarder of money) in order to indicate the nature of inversion that takes place here:

> The hoarder therefore sacrifices the lusts of his flesh to the fetish of gold. He takes the gospel of abstinence very seriously. On the other hand, he cannot withdraw any more from circulation, in the shape of money, than he has thrown into it, in the shape of commodities. The more he produces, the more he can sell. Work, thrift and greed are therefore his three cardinal virtues, and to sell much and buy little is the sum of his political economy.[24]

A miser is one who, for the sake of accumulating this pledge, renounces actual use value. His gold lust and boundless greed do not come from any need or desire for things (use values). Ironically, the miser is without material desire—he is like the believer who renounces desire in this world precisely to store up riches in heaven. Of course, it makes no difference that misers actually existed in antiquity; what is crucial here is that the power of money unleashes an inverted drive to accumulate it.

In contrast to the miser, merchant capital aims at the self-valorization (accumulation) of money through the process of money → commodity → money + α (M-C-M′(M + ΔM)). According to Marx, "This boundless drive for enrichment, this passionate chase after value, is common to the capitalist and the miser; but while the miser is merely a capitalist gone mad, the capitalist is a rational miser. The ceaseless augmentation of value, which the miser seeks to attain by saving his money from circulation, is achieved by the more acute capitalist by means of throwing his money again and again into circulation."[25] The capitalist is a rational miser. In other words, the motivation behind the movements of merchant capital is the same as that which drives the miser's hoarding (money fetishism). As a "rational miser," the capitalist throws capital into circulation in order to see it increase: he takes on the risk of buying and selling commodities. Money carries the right to be exchanged for commodities, but commodities do not have the right to be exchanged for money. Moreover, if a commodity fails to sell (if it cannot be exchanged for money), not only does it have no value, but it also has no use value. It is simply waste to be discarded. This is why Marx called the question of whether a commodity can be exchanged for money the "fatal leap" (*salto mortale*). Our rationalist-miser capitalist who wants to propagate money through the process money → commodity → money (M-C-M′) must venture the fatal leap: commodity → money (C-M′).

The danger here is temporarily sidestepped through credit. According to Marx, this means to anticipate (C-M′) in ideal form. It takes the form of issuing a promissory note that will be settled up later. At this moment, the selling-buying relationship becomes a creditor-debtor relationship. Marx argues that this credit system emerges as a natural development with the expansion of circulation and that it in turn further expands circulation. The credit system both accelerates and extends the circuit of movement of capital, because it enables the capitalist to make additional new investments without having to wait for the completion of the M-C-M′ process.

With regard to credit, let me note that money too in a sense first appeared as a form of credit. For example, in bartering for products that have different seasonal production schedules, one first receives the other's goods and then later hands over one's own goods. In such cases, some sort of symbol is used—credit money. Even after metal coins became world currencies, in actual exchanges promissory notes were still used. Moreover, these notes themselves were used as money. Accordingly, any economic world that is based on money is a world of credit.

The problem of credit shows how intimately mode of exchange C is bound up with modes A and B. For example, Marcel Mauss saw the gift as the origin of credit trading:

> The gift necessarily entails the notion of credit. The evolution in economic law has not been from barter to sale, and from cash sale to credit sale. On the one hand, barter has arisen through a system of presents given and reciprocated according to a time limit. This was through a process of simplification, by reductions in periods of time formerly arbitrary. On the other hand, buying and selling arose in the same way, with the latter according to a fixed time limit, or by cash, as well as by lending. For we have no evidence that any of the legal systems that have evolved beyond the phase we are describing (in particular, Babylonian law) remained ignorant of the credit process that is known in every archaic society that still survives today.[26]

Credit is sustained by the idea of communality shared by parties to the exchange. The person who takes on debt must necessarily repay it. In this way, credit in mode of exchange C is sustained by mode of exchange A. At the same time, we cannot overlook how credit is also supported by the state—that is, by mode of exchange B. This is because the state provides the ultimate backing to credit through its punishment of those who default on debts. Nonetheless, the credit that is produced through mode of exchange C creates its own distinct world.

With money and credit, commodity exchanges can be carried out that transcend limitations of space and time. It was the spatial expansion of commodity exchange that made possible the activities of merchant capital. This is because exchanges that cross boundaries between different spaces generate surplus value. What is important to note here is the problem of temporality that arises from money and credit. With money and credit, it becomes possible to exchange not only with others in the shared present, but also with others who exist in the future. At least, this is what is believed. This in turns gives rise to a type of capital different from merchant capital.

For example, if a potential investment seems certain to bring a profitable return, a merchant will make it even if he or she has to borrow money to do so. In such cases, the person who lends the money is paid interest. With this we have the rise of interest-bearing capital (M-M'. . . .). In this situation, capital itself is thought to possess the power to produce interest. The "fetish character" (Marx)[27] of money reaches its maximal form in this interest-bearing capital: "In M-M' we have the irrational form of capital, the misrepresentation and objectification of the relations of production, in its highest power: the interest-bearing form, the simple form of capital, in which it is taken as logically anterior to its own reproduction process; the ability of money or a commodity to valorize its own value independent of reproduction—the capital mystification in the most flagrant form."[28] This being the case, simply to stockpile money now means to lose out on interest. In Marx's words, "it is only in usury that hoard formation becomes a reality for the first time and fulfills its dreams. What is sought from the hoard owner is not capital but rather money as money; but through interest he transforms this money hoard, as it is in itself, into capital."[29] Money in and of itself does not have the power to produce interest. It is produced rather through the movement of merchant capital (M-C-M'). Yet these are not completely separate things. The actions of merchant capital are themselves already speculative in nature: "Usurer's capital belongs together with its twin brother, merchant's capital, to the antediluvian forms of capital."[30] The existence of these forms of capital since antiquity means that the world created by mode of exchange C, far from being a materialist, rational base structure, is fundamentally a world of credit and speculation, a speculative world. In terms of form, merchant capital and usurer capital are carried on in modern capitalism: M-C-M' and M-M' continue to exist as links in the process of the accumulation of industrial capital.

Capital and State

In the process of circulation M-C-M'(M+ΔM), where does surplus value (ΔM) come from? In the words of the old adage, it comes from "buying low, selling high." Does this require unfair, unequal exchanges, as Smith maintained? Certainly, within a single value system this would be the case. But in cases of trade across multiple different value systems, even though each individual exchange is for equal value, it becomes possible to buy low and sell high. For example, let's say that in one region a certain commodity's price is expressed in terms of precious-metal money. Here price is not solely determined by the relation to precious metal, but rather by the relation to all other commodities as mediated by precious metal. In other words, price is determined within the total value system. This means that a single commodity will have different prices in different value systems. For example, tea and spices were cheap in India and China, but expensive in Europe, because they could not be produced there. If a merchant buys these up cheaply and obtains a profit by selling them in Europe, does it represent ill-begotten gain obtained through unequal exchanges? The merchant has carried out equal exchanges in each region and not engaged in any underhanded trickery. Moreover, traveling to distant lands involves risk, just as the discovery of new commodities requires talent and information. The merchant is justified in thinking that the margin obtained through trade is fair compensation for his or her own actions.

Seen from this perspective, the merchant's activity of M-C-M' consists of two equal exchanges, C-M and M-C. This is how a series of individually equal exchanges can, when carried out across different value systems, generate surplus value through buying low and selling high. If the difference between value systems is small, then the resulting margin will be small, just as a large difference will produce a large margin. This is why merchant capital emerged in the latter kind of situation—in long-distance trade. But it did not immediately lead to the emergence of private traders, because the state maintained a monopoly over trade. One reason for this was the danger involved in long-distance trade. Long-distance trade was impossible without the armed power of the state. Associations of merchants could arm themselves, but in such cases they were already operating as small-scale states.

Polanyi stressed that long-distance trade in antiquity was carried out by the state. He distinguished between that sort of trade and local markets: as a rule, trade was carried out by state officials or their equivalents. Trade was carried out at fixed prices and so could not be profitable. Accordingly, this kind of trade was driven not by a desire for profit but through a "status motive."[31] Its participants did, however, receive treasure or land from their ruler as compensation. By comparison, private trade pursued according to the "profit motive" remained small scale and impoverished, producing only minimal income and hence, according to Polanyi, it was looked down upon.

But even the state's own long-distance trade was fundamentally based on the profit motive. The fact that long-distance trade by the state was carried out according to fixed prices and the fact that it generated enormous profits are not in contradiction. Commodity prices appeared to be fixed because of the very gradual pace of changes in natural conditions and production technology. Nonetheless, price changes did occur, because the state created new export goods by pursuing irrigation agriculture, mining, and similar undertakings. These were of sufficient importance to cause the rise and fall of ancient states. But such changes were infrequent, and so trading prices in practice were roughly fixed. By engaging in trade, states were able to cheaply acquire from abroad what was expensive at home. In such cases, both trading partners benefited and thus these were regarded as equal exchanges.

Here, though, let's hypothesize the existence of private traders who repeatedly buy low in one place and sell high in another place, where they in turn buy something else inexpensively that they then again sell high elsewhere. In doing this, they are siphoning off profits that would otherwise go to the state. Consequently, the state had to regulate trade that fell outside official channels. Polanyi writes that trade driven by the status motive was regarded as an honorable activity, but when it was driven by the profit motive, it was looked down upon. Yet the state was motivated by the desire for profits, as were the bureaucrats in its service who received compensation in the form of treasure or land. The state disliked private traders only because it desired to monopolize profit. This is why the state scorned private trade, denouncing it in moralistic terms as dishonest.

When long-distance trade expands beyond the level of the state's demand, the state is forced to permit a variety of merchants to engage in trade and the transportation of goods. As compensation for permitting and patronizing this trade, the state starts to levy customs duties and tolls. Consequently, even as private trade expands and cities grow, they remain as a rule under state control. For example, in the various Chinese dynasties, markets were administered by officials, and luxury goods and fraud were strictly prohibited. Trade, on the other hand, was government administered, moving through official trade ports and often taking the form of tribute, a kind of gift trading. Merchants were treated as official envoys or missions.

For these reasons, even though it existed in fact, the practice of obtaining profits from private trade or investment—in other words, the activities of merchant and usurer capital—was viewed with scorn and hostility. By contrast, Greece and Rome had neither state-administered trade nor official supervision of markets, and no distinction was made between trade and markets. As a result, the market economy played a destructive role. Marx writes: "Usury thus works on the one hand to undermine and destroy ancient and feudal wealth, and ancient and feudal property. On the other hand it undermines and ruins small peasantry and petty-bourgeois production, in short all forms in which the producer still appears as the owner of his means of production."[32] This is why Aristotle in *Politics* regarded interest as "the most unnatural" form of getting wealth, "the most hated sort, and with the greatest reason."[33]

For Aristotle, a merchant's profiting from exchange was dishonest—yet compelling slaves to labor was honest. In the same way, in the ancient despotic states, accumulating wealth through forced labor and imposed tributes was legitimate, but doing so through circulation of goods was illegitimate.[34] But what this all means is that in this society, the dominant and legitimate mode of exchange was B. Mode of exchange C not only existed— it was indispensable, but it posed a threat to the worlds formed by modes of exchange A and B. The state needed to somehow find a way to limit and regulate it.

On this point, there was little difference in the situation among trading peoples. Since ancient times there had been tribes that earned profits through transit trade—nomadic peoples like the Bedouin and seafaring peoples like the Phoenicians. For them, profiting from long-distance trade was legitimate, and they tended to look down on sedentary agricultural production. Yet they were not private traders: they were tribal groups that formed armed merchant caravans to carry out their activities. In most cases, they operated either outside any state (empire) or as only partially subordinated elements within empires. For example, during the period from the Assyrian Empire to the Persian Empire, one trading people, the Phoenicians, were subordinated to and carried out the role of circulating goods within the world-empire, but they subsequently built their own empire (Carthage). Yet even this sort of trading people rejected the pursuit of gain, including usury, within the interior of the community. This is what Weber calls a double ethic. Because of this, the principle of commodity exchange did not penetrate into the interior of the community.[35] Under these conditions, even a highly developed practice of long-distance trade could not fundamentally alter the social formation.

In discussing the premodern period, Polanyi distinguishes between trade and market. The unification of trade and market and the operation of market mechanisms to determine prices date back only to the late eighteenth century. Before that—and especially with regard to antiquity—he maintains, we need to distinguish between the two.[36] As I've already noted, trade and market differ as follows: in the former, exchange takes place across widely different value systems, while in the latter, exchange takes place in local markets not marked by large differences. In the latter, even if differences and fluctuations arise to some degree, the margins they yield are limited. At best the merchant is permitted to obtain only handling fees that are seen as legitimate. To gain profits greater than this is perceived as fraud and not permitted over any length of time. Moreover, in ancient states, the prices of daily necessities were fixed at official rates, and necessities such as grains were subject to rationing. For this reason, such retailers were kept to a small scale. Moreover, in the market exchanges were carried out through credit: the currency used in the local market was different from that employed in external trade.

There were, however, exceptions in the ancient world: Greece and Rome. There, trade and market were one. In concrete terms, in Greece coins (including not only precious metals such as silver and gold but also base metals such as bronze and iron) were widely adopted. This meant that the external money (precious metals) used in trade and the local money (base metals) used in the market were mutually exchangeable, which meant in turn that the market and trade both belonged to a single price-setting system. Why did this occur among the Greek poleis? I will take this up in more detail in the next chapter, but to sketch in the answer briefly here, it was because in Greece there was no centralized order, no bureaucratic structure capable of regulating prices. Rather than establish a bureaucratic structure, Greece entrusted the setting of prices to the market.

This is what differentiates Greece from the other Asiatic states. Herodotus, for example, locates the difference between Persia and Greece in this point. His Cyrus the Great of Persia announces: "I have never yet been afraid of any men, who have a set place in the middle of their city, where they come together to cheat each other and forswear themselves." Herodotus himself comments: "Cyrus intended these words as a reproach against all the Greeks, because of their having market-places where they buy and sell, which is a custom unknown to the Persians, who never make purchases in open marts, and indeed have not in their whole country a single market-place."[37]

Polanyi believes that reliance on the market rather than officials to set prices was the source of Greek democracy. Letting the market set prices was politically equivalent to letting the masses decide public questions. It implied that judgments made by the masses were more reliable than those made by kings, officials, or a small number of wise leaders. This is why Plato and Aristotle opposed both democracy and the market economy. They thought that rule by a centralized state and an economy based on self-sufficiency were desirable. Their models here were Sparta and the Asiatic states.

We need to be cautious, though, about accepting the conclusions that a market economy and world-economy were established in Greece and that these led to democracy. Clearly, mode of exchange C had entered into the picture, but there was no possibility yet of it becoming the dominant mode. For example, in the various Ionian cities established by Greek colonizers, commerce and industry were highly advanced, and they produced many philosophers, scientists, and doctors. Nonetheless, the cities' glories were easily extinguished by the Persian conquest. Athens, on the other hand, defeated the Persians on the battlefield, yet never produced the kind of highly developed commerce and industry seen in Ionia. Athens became a center of international trade, but this trade was mostly left in the hands of foreigners, including resident foreigners. The citizens of Athens remained to the end warrior-farmers who scorned commerce and industry.

The penetration of a money economy damaged the civil society (the community of rulers) of the Greek city-states. This development exacerbated economic disparities and led to widespread indentured servitude among the citizens. This was a crisis not only for the polis community: it also meant a military life-or-death crisis for the state in those poleis that relied on universal military service in which all were expected to provide their own armor. The Greek poleis tried many different policies to counter this. One extreme was represented by Sparta, which banned trade and aimed at an economy of self-sufficiency. This was made possible by conquering another tribe (Messenia) and making its people into agricultural serfs (helots), but this in turn made inevitable the rise of a militaristic order, constantly on guard against possible slave revolts. The other extreme was represented by Athens. It did not reject a market economy, but instead pursued measures for resolving the class conflicts that arose among the citizens: democracy.

The move to democracy in Athens was nothing more than an attempt to preserve the existing community of rulers within the polis. This democracy led to an ever-increasing expansion of slave-system production: citizens who devoted themselves to matters military and political had no time to engage in productive labor. As this indicates, the Athenian state was grounded in mode of exchange B—albeit of a different type from that found in tribute-based states like Persia. No matter how extensively mode of exchange C might develop, it could not achieve supremacy over mode B. Under a state based in mode of exchange B, even as it rivaled that mode, mode of exchange C's continued existence depended on being subordinated to and complementing mode B. This situation would remain fundamentally unchanged until modernity.

In order for mode of exchange C to become the dominant mode in the social formation, a great leap is needed—just as was the case when mode of exchange B became dominant only with the emergence of the state.

FIVE **WORLD EMPIRES**

Asiatic Despotism and Empire

Previously, in my discussion of ancient Asiatic despotism, I focused on aspects internal to the state. The despotic state was based on forced labor and tribute systems. Through exchanges of submission for protection, the despotic state placed many neighboring communities or states under its control. That is to say, it was a social formation dominated by mode of exchange B. Seen in terms of its external aspects, however, the Asiatic despotic state is a world-empire in the form of a world system, one that subsumes multiple city-states or communities. (When I take up empires in terms of being world systems, I will call them *world-empires*; when I speak of them in terms of individual empires, I will call them *world empires*). An empire facilitates trade between communities or states, trade that was previously precarious and difficult. Empires are formed through military conquest, but in reality they have almost no need for war. The various communities and small states are quicker to welcome the establishment of an empire than to enter into a state of war. In that sense, the formation of a world-empire represents a crucial dialectical moment not only for mode of exchange B but also for mode of exchange C.

World-empires are sustained by the various principles and technologies that exist between communities. In chapter 4 I discussed the world money minted by empires. The minting of currency and the standardization of weights and measurements lead to a rapid expansion in the volume of trade carried out within the empire. Yet world-empires are not sustained by world money alone.

For example, a world-empire also needs a law that transcends its individual communities. Empires have to consider not only how to rule over the various tribes and states but also how to secure their "in-between"—in other words, how to ensure the safety of the intercourse and commerce that occur between an empire's various tribes and states. The law of an empire is in essence international law. The laws of the Roman Empire became the basis for what would be called natural law, but they were essentially international law. The same was basically true of other empires, even when not as clearly stipulated. For example, the Chinese empire recognized the status of the various tribes and states under its umbrella, so long as they offered the required tribute payments; moreover, since these tribute payments were answered with return gifts of equal or greater value, this really amounted to a form of trade. Empires do not interfere in the internal affairs of their constituent tribes and states, so long as these affairs pose no threat to the security of trade conducted within the empire. Toppled world empires always seem to get reconstituted overnight because the new conqueror, whoever it is, is actively welcomed as the new guarantor for the security of the existing order of international law and trade.

A third characteristic of empires is that they possess a world religion. World empires are formed through the unification of multiple tribes and states; for this to happen, there needs to be a universal religion that can transcend all of the local religions in those states and communities. When the Roman Empire expanded, it had to adopt as its base the religion of Christianity, which until then had been a target of imperial persecution. In the same way, when the empire of China expanded to a Eurasian scale, the philosophy of legalism (of the first Qin dynasty emperor) and Confucianism (Emperor Wu of Han) became inadequate as unifying forces. This is why Buddhism was introduced by the Tang dynasty as it pursued a dramatic territorial expansion. The world empire of the Mongols adopted Buddhism as well as Islam. These world religions also penetrated into the tribes and states located within and on the peripheries of the empire. For example, the Yamato court of Japan used Buddhism to secure its own foundation. This is because even small states, when they reached the scale of encompassing multiple tribes, needed a universal religion that could transcend the various local tribal gods. It is also noteworthy that theology in world empires tended to become rationalistic and comprehensive—as we see with Avicenna (Ibn Sīnā) in Arabia, Thomas Aquinas in Europe, and Zhu Xi in China.

A fourth characteristic of empires is world language (lingua franca). This is a written language used by multiple tribes and states—for example, Latin or the Chinese and Arabic writing systems. Countless languages (*parole*) can be spoken within the empire, but these are not regarded as true languages (*langue*)—they occupy the same position as today's dialects. Moreover, since the law, religion, and philosophy of the empire are all expressed in this world language, the distinguishing feature of empire is manifested above all in language.

These traits are shared in common by all world-empires. But world-empires also differ from one another in certain aspects. We can classify them according to the following four distinct types:

Irrigation type: western and eastern Asia, Peru, Mexico
Maritime type: Greece, Rome
Nomadic type: Mongol
Merchant type: Islam

Historically, world-empire first appeared with the irrigation type—that is, with the Asiatic despotic state. We find its prototype in Sumer. The empires that subsequently appeared in west Asia all inherited in various forms systems that had originated in Sumer, including its writing, language, religion, and bureaucracy. It was the First Persian Empire that put these all together into a more comprehensive structure. The techniques used by Darius the Great (regnant from 522–486 BCE) to unify the empire became a model for those who followed him—for example, centralized administration, administrative districts, postal systems, minting currency, the use of Aramaic as a unified official language, and religious and cultural tolerance. In East Asia, a full world-empire was finally established with the Tang dynasty, more so than with the earlier Qin and Han.

The other types of empire rose up on the periphery of the Asiatic empires and in relation to them. Karl Wittfogel's views are suggestive in this regard. As I've already noted, Wittfogel is remembered primarily for his theory of irrigation agriculture and the despotic state, but of even greater importance is the perspective he offered in taking what had been seen as historical stages of development and rethinking them in terms of a synchronous spatial structure. He saw the Oriental despotic states (hydraulic societies) as consisting of a core, around which were ranged the margin and submargin. Many have seen the world in terms of core and margin, but Wittfogel's unique contribution was to distinguish further between the margin and the submargin that lies beyond the margin.[1]

This seems to resemble the differentiation between core, semiperiphery, and periphery that Immanuel Wallerstein later proposed for the modern world system (world-economy). Wallerstein took up the theory of "dependency" that Andre Gunter Frank proposed—the theory, that is, that core exploits periphery by extracting wealth through commodity exchange—and added to it the concept of semiperiphery. This made it possible to see the core-periphery relation not as fixed but as fluidly dynamic—in, for example, the way a given region might move up into the core position or recede into the periphery.

Wallerstein seems to have been unaware that Wittfogel had earlier pointed out a similar geopolitical structure existing before the modern world system, at the stage of world-empire. The resemblance here, however, is only apparent: the core-semiperiphery-periphery structure of world-economy and the core-submargin-margin structure of world-empire are governed by completely different principles. In world-economy the dominant principle is mode of exchange C, while in world-empire it is mode of exchange B. Accordingly, the phenomena of margin and submargin in world-empire are formally quite different from their seeming counterparts in world-economy.

In world-empires, the margin was conquered and absorbed into the core. There were also cases where the margin invaded and conquered the core. In either case, the margin tended to be assimilated into the core. But submargins, unlike margins that directly bordered on an empire-civilization, were able to pick and choose which elements they would adopt from the empire-civilization. If they were too distant from the civilization, they would remain a tribal society; if they were too close to the civilization, they would likely either be conquered or absorbed. Therefore, to further clarify the argument here, I would like to add one additional category: the *out of sphere*. People who wanted to evade the control or influence of the core withdrew beyond the margin or submargin to the out of sphere, in other words to mountain or frontier regions, where hunter-gatherer society was able to survive.

The premodern world system consisted of multiple world-empires, their margins, relatively few submargins, and the out of sphere. When the modern world system (world-economy)—that is, the capitalist market—covered the globe, first, the out of sphere was enclosed by the state. Countless so-called primitive peoples were forced to "civilize." In that sense, they were assigned to the periphery of the modern world system. Second, the margins of the old world-empires became the periphery of the new world-economy. Third, the submargins of the old world-empires were situated as the semiperiphery of the new world-economy, and in a few rare cases, such as Japan, these submargins were able to move into the core. Fourth, the cores of the old world-empires were pushed into the periphery. Unlike the former margins, the old world-empire cores, with their highly developed military and bureaucratic state machineries, were not content with their new positions on the periphery of the world-economy.[2]

Margin and Submargin

The margins of world-empires were either overwhelmed or annexed by their cores. Only nomadic peoples who refused or had no need to adopt sedentary settlement were able to resist this fate. Unlike agrarian communities that were subordinated to the state, these nomadic peoples preserved the customs of hunter-gatherer and clan society. They placed great importance on "contracts" between tribes governing the use of pastureland, springs, and wells. For this purpose they established tribes and tribal confederations, but these almost never transformed into states. They did, however, from time to time join together into armed bands to invade and plunder the core, at times even seizing control over the existing state structure.

This occurred repeatedly in Mesopotamia starting in the Sumerian period. It also happened repeatedly in China from ancient times through the Qing dynasty, which was established by Manchurian invaders.[3] In general, when nomads take over as rulers of a state, they lose the spirit of being independently motivated warriors as well as their sense of solidarity and mutual aid—both rooted in the principle of reciprocity. Seeking honor, luxury, and peace, they fall prey to decline and internal corruption—whereupon they are conquered from outside by a new nomadic warrior group. The fourteenth-century Arabian philosopher Ibn Khaldun in his *Prolegomena* espied a kind of historical law in the repetition of this pattern.

There is, however, one example of a nomadic people who overcame this pattern of repeated plunder and decline and who established a sustained world-empire: the Mongol Empire. Through a grand alliance of nomadic tribes, the Mongols, with their mounted bands, were able to conquer widely and build a world empire. This was possible because at the level of the rulers, the Mongols never abandoned the principle of reciprocity. In China, for example, as the Yuan dynasty they inherited the oriental bureaucratic state apparatus, but the emperor was regarded as only one chief among others in the Mongolian tribal federation: he did not enjoy a particularly privileged status. In order to hold an election to select a new Khan, a council of chiefs gathered from across Eurasia. But the Khan too held the status of being no more than first among chiefs. The principle of reciprocity from the Mongolian tribal community was thus preserved at the level of the rulers. This is what allowed the Mongols to unify on a grand scale the various world-empires that had previously been closed off from one another.

The Mongols did not themselves actively participate in commerce, but they placed great importance on it and by unifying the previously existing world-empires were able to realize temporarily a kind of world-economy. It was there that paper money first enjoyed wide-scale circulation. Moreover, the collapse of the Mongolian empire led to the reconstruction of early modern world-empires not just in China, but in all of the regions involved, including India, Iran, and Turkey. This paralleled the global expansion of the world-economy deriving from Europe.

One other nomadic people built a world empire: the Islamic Empire. It was created through an alliance between nomadic peoples and urban merchants—more specifically, an alliance between the city merchants of Mecca and Medina and the nomadic Bedouins. This required the unifying force of the Islamic religion. Islam is an urban religion, one that affirms the value of commerce. Accordingly, the Islamic Empire was a commercial empire that extended across both desert and seas. In terms of its geography and degree of civilization, it was for all practical purposes the heir to the Roman Empire. At the peak of the Islamic Empire, western Europe was merely a submargin of the Islamic sphere. The inability of the Islamic Empire to become a modern world system was fundamentally due—just as in the case of the irrigation-type empires—to its placing of commerce and cities under state regulation. As a result, the world-empire suppressed the development of a world-economy. In other words, the independent development of mode of exchange C was held in check by mode of exchange B.

Finally, let us turn to the maritime type of empire (Greece, Rome). The key point here, if anything, is the failure of the Greeks to build an empire. Certainly, Alexander the Great built a Greek-style (Hellenistic) empire, but he did this by destroying the polis and emulating the form of the Asian empires. Rome likewise became an empire by abandoning the principles that had previously governed its city-states. Accordingly, what we need to pay attention to in the case of Greece and Rome is not so much how they constructed their empires but rather how they managed to preserve the city-state form, holding off development into a despotic state even as they bordered the sphere of Asiatic despotism and were strongly influenced by its civilization. In other words, Greece and Rome existed as submargins of the western Asian civilization-empires.

How does a submargin differ from a margin? As examples of submargins, in addition to early Greece and Rome, Wittfogel cites the Germanic tribes, Japan, and Russia prior to the Mongol conquest (the Tatar yoke). Submargins lie beyond the margins, but they are not completely outside. A submargin is not as directly connected to the core civilization as the margin, but a submargin is also not so distant as to be completely estranged from the margin. Maritime societies often fulfill the conditions that define a submargin. Through maritime trade, they are connected to the core of the empire, but since they are not connected by land, they avoid being conquered and are able to establish their own independent worlds.

In this way, a submargin is able to selectively adopt elements of the civilization system of the core. In concrete terms, submargins adopted the civilization (writing system, technology, and so on) but fundamentally rejected the centralized bureaucratic structure that existed in the core. This is because, in contrast to the way the margin is assimilated to the core, the submargin preserved to a great degree—albeit not to the same extent as the out of sphere—the principle of reciprocity (mode of exchange A), which rejected hierarchy. Even as submargins imported the civilization of the core, they did not completely submit to it and were able to develop it independently on their own terms. In them too there was little state control over exchange and redistribution, and economic matters were entrusted to the market. This is why world-economy would develop from the submargins.

Karl Marx attempted to explain the social formations of Greece and Rome in terms of a slave-system mode of production. But the slave-system mode of production cannot explain what distinguished Greece and Rome so fundamentally from the Asiatic despotic states. The Asiatic despotic states (world-empires) adopted a strategy of ruling other states and communities by imposing forced labor and tribute obligations on them, but not interfering in their internal affairs. They too had slaves, but there was no slave-system mode of production. Greece and Rome, on the other hand, never developed a tribute state model, and in them market and trade were allowed to develop free from official state control. The particular slave system that arose in Greece and Rome was a consequence of that kind of world-economy. Hence, the real question to ask here is why a world-economy developed in Greece and Rome.

To reiterate, the phenomena we see in Greece and Rome were characteristic of a submargin. For example, in the case of Greece, the preceding Mycenaean civilization was marginal—it was under the influence of the Egyptian centralized state. But the Greeks who emerged after Egypt's collapse were submarginal. They imported the technology of iron implements from western Asia and the writing system that Phoenicians had developed out of Sumerian cuneiform script, but they did not adopt the political system of the imperial core. As a result, the Greeks were unable to construct a world-empire. In the end, neither Athens nor Sparta was able to even unify the various Greek poleis.

Rome was a city-state like the poleis of Greece, but by making citizens of the leading figures of the city-states and tribes that it conquered, and by ruling through a universal law, Rome was able to expand its territory. In short, Rome was able to establish a world-empire by suppressing the exclusionary communal principles of the polis. But Rome was not able to completely abolish the principles of the polis. A clash between the principles of the polis and those of the empire continued to exist at the root of the Roman Empire. The Roman Empire was able to expand its territory beyond the scope of the First Persian Empire to become the largest empire in history, including western Europe in its domain. But that is not why the Roman Empire is of importance for our purposes: rather, it is because it displays in the clearest form this conflict in principles between polis and empire. This would recur in the modern period as a problem of the nation-state and imperialism or regionalism.

Greece

In the core areas of ancient civilizations, irrigation agriculture developed and in turn led to the establishment of regional agrarian communities. A necessary condition for this was the presence of fertile soil capable of producing grain when irrigated. In areas where this condition was lacking, only small-scale rainfall agriculture was possible, and people did not completely abandon their earlier hunter-gatherer lifestyle. In general, rainfall agriculture maintains a continuity with hunting and foraging: in it, the clan community's principle of reciprocity remained alive. For this reason, even when agriculture in such areas underwent a degree of development, these regions tended to resist the establishment of a centralized state. On the other hand, private ownership of land tended to advance under rainfall agriculture. The opening of new fields was not a massive state-sponsored project: instead it was carried out on a small scale by individuals or households. As a result, even when land was in general considered communal property, individuals who had reclaimed specific fields retained rights of usage to them. This amounted to private property. Of course, even in such cases, we cannot forget the continued existence of communal ownership and of the principle of reciprocity that was connected to it.

When we consider ancient Greece, we need to keep these conditions in mind. The Greeks settled in coastal regions along the Mediterranean. Conditions were poor for grain production, forcing the Greeks to pursue livestock herding and olive and wine production. Accordingly, with the exception of self-sufficient Sparta, the Greeks depended primarily on maritime trade. But these conditions by themselves cannot explain the unique character of Greece. For example, Greece comprised many city-states, but this was not particularly unusual: the Asiatic despotic states were also born of struggles between multiple existing city-states. The Mycenaean and Cretan civilizations that preceded Greece must have developed through a similar process; they resembled the Egyptian and Mesopotamian states, albeit on a smaller scale. If anything, this represented the most common development pattern.

Yet the Greek people who migrated south after the collapse of the Mycenaean state did not follow this pattern; they did not establish a despotic state. Instead they established numerous autonomous poleis. Why did this happen? In part, it was because these Greeks brought with them the principles of clan society. This did not simply mean they were backward. Normally, a tribal society either rejects a higher civilization or accepts it and moves toward oriental despotism. The Greeks, however, did neither, establishing instead a string of autonomous poleis. The key to solving this riddle lies in the Greeks' active pursuit of colonization between the tenth and eighth centuries BCE.

The new communities that the colonists established in this process remained independent of their previous clans and poleis. Eventually, the colonists established several thousand poleis in this manner. Their colonies were not, however, entirely unique; they shared much in common with clan society, which Lewis Henry Morgan described in the following terms: "When a village became overcrowded with numbers, a colony went up or down on the same stream and commenced a new village. Repeated at intervals of time several such villages would appear, each independent of the other and a self-governing body; but united in a league or confederacy for mutual protection."[4] Similarly, even as they continued to fight among themselves, the Greek poleis formed a loose confederation, symbolized by the Olympic Games.

Looked at in this way, it seems the distinct qualities of Greece can be explained as the result of holdovers from clan society. But we also have to keep in mind that the colonists' poleis were not simply extensions of earlier clan society: they arose out of a rejection of it. In general, the poleis were established through covenants entered into freely by individual choice. The principles of these poleis, accordingly, were unlike those of city-states that emerged as extensions of the clan community, such as Athens or Sparta; we find these principles established in Miletus and the other cities of Ionia, as well as in the cities that arose as the Ionians pursued further colonization. If these poleis seem to resemble clan society, it is not due to the persistence of that earlier form in them, but rather to its "return" in a higher dimension.[5]

When we speak of ancient Greece, Athens is usually regarded as central. The unique aspects of Greek civilizations, however, arose not in Athens but in the cities of Ionia. Commerce and industry were highly developed in them, and they were centers of overseas trade. They gathered scientific knowledge, religion, and philosophy from the whole of Asia, including Egypt, Mesopotamia, and India. But they never adopted the systems that characterized Asiatic despotism—namely, a bureaucracy and standing or mercenary army. The peoples of Ionia, early pioneers in the minting of currency, never adopted the practice of having state officials regulate prices, as was common under the Asiatic despotic states, leaving them instead up to the market. This reliance on the market rather than bureaucrats to set prices was, along with the reform of the alphabet, one causal factor that led to Greek democracy.[6] These all originated in Ionia.

Homer's epics were likewise composed and popularized in Ionia. The region is also famous for its philosophers, beginning with Thales. These are generally considered manifestations of an early stage in the Greek civilization that reached its full expression in Athens, but that view is incorrect. Rich possibilities opened up by the thinkers of Ionia were actually stunted in Athens. The same is true in the realm of politics: common wisdom has it that democracy began in Athens and then spread to the other poleis, but in fact it was originally rooted in a principle that arose first in Ionia. It was called *isonomia*, not democracy. According to Hannah Arendt:

> Freedom as a political phenomenon was coeval with the rise of the Greek city-states. Since Herodotus, it was understood as a form of political organization in which the citizens lived together under conditions of no-rule, without a division between rulers and ruled. This notion of no-rule was expressed by the word isonomy, whose outstanding characteristic among the forms of government, as the ancients had enumerated them, was that the notion of rule (the "archy" from αρχείν in monarchy and

oligarchy, or the "cracy" from κρατίν in democracy) was entirely absent
from it. The *polis* was supposed to be an isonomy, not a democracy. The
word "democracy," expressing even then majority rule, the rule of the
many, was originally coined by those who were opposed to isonomy and
who meant to say: What you say is "no-rule" is in fact only another kind
of rulership; it is the worst form of government, rule by the demos.

Hence, equality, which we, following Tocqueville's insights, frequently
see as a danger to freedom, was originally almost identical with it.[7]

Arendt seems to believe that this principle of isonomy applied to Greece in
general. But in my understanding, it originated in Ionia and then spread to
the other poleis. When it was adopted in other regions such as Athens, it
took on the form of democracy. The original principle of isonomy was found
in Ionian city-states established by colonists. There the colonists broke with
their clan and tribal traditions, abandoning both the constraints and privileges that these had entailed, to create a new community by covenant. By
contrast, Athens, Sparta, and other poleis were established as confederations (by covenant) of existing tribes and were more strongly colored by
earlier clan traditions. We see the impact of this in the forms of inequality
and class conflict that arose within these poleis.[8]

Under Athenian democracy, the impoverished majority kept the wealthy
minority in check, achieving equality through redistribution. But the principle of isonomy, as Arendt notes, associates equality with freedom. This is
possible only in situations where society is free, in other words, nomadic—
when, for example, people were free to emigrate if inequality or despotism
arose within a polis. Isonomy is premised on nomadic mobility. In this
sense, isonomy negates the constraints and bonds of clan society, but at the
same time it marks the return of the nomadic mobility that had characterized it. In other words, isonomy marks the return of clan society in a higher
dimension.

The nomadism of the Ionians can be seen in their far-flung trading and
pursuit of manufacturing. Ionia was the first society in which mode of
exchange C became dominant. Unlike Athens or Sparta, Ionia's society
rejected the closed nature of the clan community. This means that the basic
principle of isonomy, premised on the dominance of mode of exchange C,
was the return of mode of exchange A in a higher dimension—in other
words, mode of exchange D. Arendt, for example, locates the contemporary
version of isonomy in council communism.[9] In that sense, if Athenian democracy is the forerunner of today's bourgeois democracy (parliamentary

democracy), Ionian isonomy provides the key to a system that can supersede it.

But Ionian isonomy ultimately collapsed, as the region fell victim to conquest at the hands of neighboring Lydia and Persia. Ionia rose up in rebellion against this but was crushed. Greece would emerge victorious from the Persian War that followed, and the Ionian city-states again became independent, but they never recovered their original form. Politically and economically, Athens was now the center. The destruction of the Ionian poleis occurred because they lacked sufficient military power to defend themselves. But the real greatness of the Ionian city-states lay precisely in their practice of not relying on military might. Unlike democracy, isonomy is in principle incompatible with a reliance on the state and military power.

By contrast, Athens and Sparta were communities of warrior-farmers. The two never abandoned this stance. Even as a money economy penetrated into their communities, they never engaged in commerce or trade themselves. The penetration of the money economy shook many of the poleis, producing severe class divisions in Athens, Sparta, and elsewhere. Many citizens fell into indentured servitude, which immediately led to a military crisis for poleis that relied on universal conscription and citizens who supplied their own armor. Preservation of the poleis seemed to require social reform.

The measures that Sparta adopted in this situation sharply contrasted with those of Athens: Sparta banned trade and abolished the money economy. This was only possible, however, because Sparta had conquered the neighboring Messenian people and made them *helots* (slaves) and because the rich agricultural fertility of its lands made trading unnecessary. Because of this, though, Sparta constantly had to remain on guard against helot revolts, forcing it to strengthen its warrior community. This led to the birth of Spartan communism.

It was impossible for Athens, on the other hand, to abolish trade and the money economy. Accordingly, the only option open to Athens was to accept these and somehow try to resolve class difficulties by other means: democracy. Athenian democracy was adopted above all as a means to preserve the state. Athens enforced universal conscription for citizens. In particular, the phalanx tactic of heavily armed infantry that the Greeks adopted in the seventh century BCE differed radically from earlier practices, in which aristocrats were mounted and commoners served as foot soldiers. The new tactic accelerated the rise of democracy in Athens. In the Persian War, slaves served as oarsmen in Persian warships, but on the Greek side the oarsmen were citizens too poor to provide their own armor. Victory in the war led to a rising political status for these citizens.

In sum, whereas the isonomia of Ionia emerged in tandem with independent, privately owned agriculture and commerce, the democracy of Athens arose from the needs of its warrior-farmers. The first step in the process of democratizing Athens came with Solon's reforms (594 BCE). These granted suffrage to all who possessed sufficient wealth to equip themselves as soldiers. The reforms also granted relief to citizens without property, including measures to forgive debts and abolish indentured servitude. After this came the tyrants, members of the aristocracy who rose to power on a wave of popular acclaim. The tyrants, especially Peisistratus and his ilk, usurped the power of the aristocracy and tried to provide relief to impoverished citizens. One might loosely call the tyrants a manifestation of democratization. But Athenian democracy ultimately meant the repudiation of tyrants and the implementation of safeguards to prevent their reemergence. This involved a rejection of systems of representation, of the idea that some could act as representatives (agents) of others. This also meant a refusal of bureaucratic structures. Powerful public offices were now filled by rotation or lottery, and those occupying seats of power could always later be brought up before a court of impeachment.

Democracy in this strict sense of the word was realized with the reforms of Cleisthenes of Athens (508 BCE), implemented after the expulsion of the tyrants following Peisistratus's death. These reforms abolished the old tribal systems that had been the aristocracy's power base, creating instead new tribes based on place of residence. With this appeared the demos based on regional ties; rule by these demos constituted democracy. This rejected the concept of blood lineage so central to clan society, but it also represented an attempt to recover the principle of reciprocity that had defined clan society.

In this sense, the demos resembled the modern nation in being a kind of "imagined community" (Benedict Anderson).[10] Athenian democracy is inseparable from this kind of nationalism. The isonomia of the Ionian cities was fundamentally different. Whereas Athenian democracy was grounded in the exclusionary tribal consciousness of the poleis, Ionian isonomia grew out of a world that transcended tribe or polis. In Athens, foreigners could never become citizens, no matter how much wealth or land they possessed. They were given no legal protection and were subjected to high taxation. Moreover, although the citizens of Athens were ostensibly farmers, in reality they did not engage in agriculture. In order that they always be available to go to war or participate in affairs of state, they left the actual labor in the hands of slaves. A person who had land but no slaves could not perform the duties of a citizen. Slaves were a prerequisite for citizenship. For this reason, the development of democracy created an increasing need for slaves, and the citizens of Athens came to scorn manual labor as the work of slaves—a sharp contrast with the citizens of Ionia. This difference is clearly manifested in the difference between the natural philosophy of Ionia and the philosophy of Plato or Aristotle.

Ionia produced not only the natural philosophers but also such figures as the historian Herodotus and the physician Hippocrates. Plato and Aristotle claim that the Ionian natural philosophers considered only external nature and that it was only with Socrates that problems of ethics or the self came under consideration. But compared to Aristotle, who believed it was only natural for non-Greek foreigners (*barbaroi*) to be made slaves, Hippocrates and Herodotus can hardly be accused of being unethical.[11] The Ionian philosophers thought more in terms of cosmopolis than of polis, and their speculations were rooted in the principles of isonomia. In Athens, philosophers from Ionia were regarded as Sophists whose thought would promote the destruction of the social order.

With regard to Athenian philosophy, moreover, it is clear that Socrates was hardly the sort of character that Plato makes him out to be. Socrates was unmistakably critical of democracy, but unlike Plato, Socrates did not adopt the standpoint of the aristocratic faction. It is important to note that Socrates consistently tried to put into practice the command conveyed to him by his *daemon*: "He who will really fight for the right, if he would live even for a little while, must have a private station and not a public one."[12] Such conduct amounted to a rejection of the values generally accepted in Athens—of, that is, taking part as a public person (*demosios*) and becoming a political leader. In Athens, foreigners, slaves, and women could not become public persons: that in a nutshell is Athenian democracy. In contrast, Socrates insisted on remaining a private person (*idios*) in order to "fight for the right." In that sense, his position was based on the principles of isonomia. He had nothing to do with Plato's notion of the philosopher-king. Socrates's most representative followers were foreigners, beginning with the cynic Diogenes, not Plato. They were the ones who created the philosophy of the cosmopolis following the collapse of the polis.

In sum, Athenian democracy was based on the principles of a closed community. This is why it met with particular difficulties in its external relations. Thanks to its naval superiority, Athens developed into an economic center of the Mediterranean region, but the exclusionary principle of its polis doomed to failure its efforts to expand its sphere of domination. Athens resisted the First Persian Empire, for example, by creating the Delian League with other poleis through a pledge to abstain from interference in self-rule. But gradually Athens came to exploit the other poleis, extracting tribute payments from them and placing their militaries under its direction. For these reasons, it is often said that the Delian League was in fact an Athenian empire. But it lacked the principle needed to sustain an empire. The exclusionary democracy of the polis could never serve as the ruling principle for an empire encompassing multiple states and communities.

Arendt argues that because nation-states lack the principle needed for empire, when they expand, they necessarily become imperialist.[13] We can apply this insight to Athens. Pericles is remembered as a politician who devoted himself to economic equality and the social welfare of the citizens of Athens, but he achieved this by redistributing among those citizens the money acquired from other poleis through the Delian League. Imperialism and exploitation for the exterior, democracy and social welfare policies for the interior: that was Athenian democracy, making it a prototype for today's states. The result, however, was to invite enmity from the other poleis, ultimately leading to collapse when Athens was defeated in the Peloponnesian War by Sparta, acting as the representative of that enmity. But Sparta also lacked the necessary principle for empire. Empire was finally realized in Greek civilization by Alexander the Great (356–23 BCE). This empire Hellenized Asia, but at the same time it became heir to the Egyptian and Persian Empires. Alexander, for example, came to regard himself as a deity—just as had the pharaohs before him.

Rome

Rome was the most prominent city-state to emerge following Greece. As a result, it resembled the Greek city-states in a number of aspects—all the more so since the Romans deliberately copied the example of Greece in many things, beginning with the phalanx strategy of heavily armed foot soldiers. These resemblances make the differences between Rome and the Greek city-states all the more striking.

First of all, whereas Athens achieved a full democracy, Rome's was much less thorough. The Roman city-state was born, like earliest Greece, in a shift from kingship to aristocratic rule. In 509 BCE the leading chiefs (nobles) expelled the king and established aristocratic rule. These nobles (*patricii*) were something like feudal lords, retaining a large number of plebeians (*clientus*) and slaves. Actual power was held by the senate, composed of members for life drawn from the nobility. This aristocratic rule was opposed by commoners (*plebs*), primarily small- and medium-scale farmers. In 494 BCE, in a concession to the commoners' resistance, the nobles acceded to the establishment of the Plebeian Council. The aristocrats agreed to this concession out of military necessity: they required the military service of a heavily armed infantry. These soldiers were supposed to pay for their own equipment and upkeep, and so it was crucial to secure the economic base of the small- and medium-scale farmers. This is why the class divisions that were appearing within the polis could not simply be ignored.

This process resembles in some ways the process by which Athens moved from aristocratic to democratic rule. But in Rome we find no equivalent to the role played in Athens by the tyrants in toppling aristocratic rule. This was because in Rome new aristocrats (*nobiles*) emerged from among the commoners and allied themselves with the existing aristocracy. The aristocrats became wealthy by contracting to be tax collectors or participating in public-works projects, and many owned large plantations (*latifundia*) run by slaves; by contrast, small-scale farmers faced economic ruin, many of them becoming *proletaria* (citizens who had lost their land).

These class divisions among the citizens of Rome grew increasingly difficult to manage. The Gracchi brothers, for example, were tribunes who advocated a land reform in which large landholdings would be confiscated for distribution to the proletaria, but their efforts failed and they were brutally assassinated. Aristotle argued that democracy was a political form that privileged the poor, but for Rome, with its poor prospects for that kind of democratization, the solution to class problems had to be sought without instead of within. Wars of conquest were pursued in order to acquire land, slaves, and wealth that could be distributed among the proletaria. But these failed to solve the problem—in fact, the wars only further exacerbated the disparity between rich and poor, which in turn made further wars of conquest necessary.

The powerful position of consul was created in an effort to resolve Rome's deepening crisis. The consuls were supposed to ward off the rise of a dictator, which is why multiple consuls were appointed simultaneously, but in the end, this opened the way for the emergence of an emperor. For example, following a string of defeats in Rome's wars of conquest, Gaius Marius was chosen to serve as consul. He established a new military order, creating an army out of volunteer troops from among the proletaria and rewarding their service with land allotments and colonies. He was followed by Sulla, Pompey, and Caesar, and Rome was on its way to having an emperor.

Yet even as the Romans in practice abandoned the principles of the polis, they maintained its forms. For example, even after the first emperor (Augustus) appeared, he was formally subordinated to the senate— which is why imperial rule in Rome is described as a combination of republic and despotism. In fact, even after the rise of the imperial government, a system of dual rule by emperor and senate persisted, and emperors had to labor to win popular support among the citizenry by resorting to "bread and circuses." But gradually, especially after Emperor Claudius, a stable bureaucratic structure was established and the emperors themselves increasingly became the objects of deification.

There is a second point on which Rome differs from Athens. In Greece, the right of citizenship was strictly limited: citizenship was denied even to resident foreigners whose families had lived there for generations and to Greeks who lived in the colonies. Moreover, very few slaves were ever freed. As a result of this sort of exclusionary communal bond, the Greek polis had no mechanism for annexing or absorbing other communities. In contrast, Rome, with its flexible stance toward external communities, was able to build a world empire. It is important to note that the Roman Empire was formed through the expansion of the polis and not solely through military conquest. Rome first granted citizenship to the poleis of the Italian archipelago and thereafter continued to grant citizenship to leaders in the regions it conquered. Rome employed a divide-and-conquer strategy that created disparities in the treatment of conquered lands, thereby heading off the possibility of alliances and resistance arising among them.

In this way, the Roman Empire governed over multiple peoples by means of the rule of law, which is often said to represent a major difference from the First Persian Empire. Yet in reality the Roman Empire simply perfected the tribute (liturgical) state form that was common to all Asiatic empires. The world-economy that was opened up by Greece was shut down in the latter period of the Roman Empire.

Feudalism

GERMANIC FEUDALISM AND THE FREE CITIES

While the Greeks and Romans were situated as submargins in relation to Asia, the Germanic peoples existed in its out of sphere. But in the periods when Greece and Rome transformed into world-empires, the position of the Germanic tribes shifted from out of sphere to submargin. They adopted the civilization of Rome, yet at the same time rejected the political system of the Roman Empire. And it was they who ultimately brought down the Western Roman Empire.

Nonetheless, it would be foolish to claim that the Germanic peoples (Europe) were heirs to the Roman Empire after its collapse. After all, the Roman Empire continued to exist in the form of the Eastern Roman Empire (Byzantine), and in practical terms it was also was carried on by the Islamic Empires. Far from carrying on the world-empire, the Germanic peoples pursued its dismantling—what we call the Dark Ages. Of course, the authority of the emperors who succeeded the Western Roman Empire (Holy Roman Empire) and the Roman Catholic Church functioned as unifying regional principles in terms of culture and ideology. But no centralized state capable of unifying the region politically and militarily would emerge. What existed instead were independent feudal states, as well as a large number of free cities. From these emerged a world-economy that eventually became the birthplace of the capitalist economy.

If we can say that Greece and Rome rose on the submargin of the Asiatic empires, then we can also say that feudalism (the feudal social formation) rose on the submargin of the Roman Empire, namely in Germanic tribal society. To understand this, we need to look at both the ruling and the ruled communities. Among the rulers, feudalism was established through a bilateral contractual agreement between lord and vassal. The lord granted domains or provided direct support to his vassals. The vassals in turn offered the lord their allegiance and military service. Because this was a bilateral agreement, if the master failed to fulfill his duties, the vassalage relationship could be revoked.

Max Weber distinguished between various types of feudalism, among which Germanic feudalism is defined as being feudalism based on fiefs (*Lehen*, in which relationships of personal loyalty overlap with fief holding).[14] In addition, Weber discusses the category of client feudalism (*Gefolgchaft*), which existed in Japan, as a type of feudalism grounded in personal relations of loyalty but without grants of the right of manorial lordship. A distinguishing characteristic of feudal systems sustained by relations of personal loyalty is the retention of the principle of reciprocity among the ruling class. This principle of reciprocity does not allow for absolute authority on the part of the lord. Even where there was a king, he was merely first among the many feudal lords and did not possess absolute power. This resembles the position of the chief in clan societies or of the kings in early

Greece. In this sense, we can say that the traditions of the clan community were maintained in Germanic society.

In general, however, feudalism is usually aligned with serfdom systems—which is to say that it can be regarded as one variety of a forced labor and tribute system of rule. For this reason, Samir Amin regards feudalism as a special form of tribute system.[15] And yet, while reciprocity exists within the ruling classes in feudal systems, this is not the case in Asiatic tribute systems. Moreover, in a feudal system, the kind of reciprocity that exists within the ruling class also exists in a basic form between ruler and ruled. It is in this sense that serfdom systems under feudalism are different from Asiatic tribute systems (universal slavery systems). In the latter, the state (monarchy) rules over the agrarian community but does not interfere in its internal affairs. Other than the obligation to meet its quotas for providing labor and tribute, the agrarian community was self-governing.

By comparison, the serfdom system of the Germanic community was established through a "covenant . . . extorted by fear" between the individual self-supporting farmers who tilled the land and the feudal lord—in other words, through a relationship based on an exchange of protection and security for forced labor and tribute.[16] By the fourteenth century in England, for example, labor and tribute obligations were fulfilled through cash payments, so that the agrarian population's feudal obligations had been transformed into land rent paid in cash. In this way, the peasants' right to till the land was transformed into a simple leasehold. These independent farmers were known as the yeomanry. But this transformation was only possible because the relationship between feudal lord and serf was from the start a bilateral, contractual relation, one in which mutual rights of ownership were clear.

The peasantry in Europe also formed their own community. They implemented such communal regulations as the three-field system and frequently established a commons. But these measures existed because such communal regulations were necessary for agricultural production, and they remained under the control of the feudal lord. Moreover, the commons were in fact property of the feudal lord. Consequently, the Germanic community was fundamentally different from the Asiatic community, where property rights remained ambiguous, as well as from the classical ancient societies, in which private lands were divided up and owned by individual families but common lands were left in the hands of authorities to use as they pleased. In England, for example, in the process that came to be known as *enclosure*, feudal lords moved to transform the commons into pastureland for use in wool production. This was only possible because landed property rights were already clearly defined. Herein also lies the reason for the rapid collapse of the Germanic community after the introduction of a money economy, with a divide emerging between those who owned the means of production (land) and those who did not (proletaria).

One other aspect of western European feudalism that bears mention is the free city (community). These were communities founded through reciprocal covenants entered into by people who had left the feudal lord-serf relationship. Feudalism—in other words, the relative weakness of the empire—made these free cities possible. The Asiatic empires also had large cities, but these remained under state control. In Europe, by contrast, the weakness of the state led to the rise of the free cities. After the fall of the Roman Empire, the Eastern Roman Empire (Byzantine) became an Asiatic empire, its emperor became the pope, and no free cities developed under it. The Western Roman Empire, however, was composed of multiple small states (feudal states), with an emperor in name alone. As a result, the Roman Catholic Church was more powerful than either the emperor or the feudal lords.[17] The free cities in western Europe arose thanks to the special privileges they acquired by aligning themselves with the church in this three-way struggle.

In southern Europe, for example, Florence declared itself a *comune* (free city-state) in 1115. The commercial and manufacturing guilds in the textile and other industries were the main driving force behind this. In northern Europe, the archbishop of Cologne in 1112 recognized the establishment of a free community based on a covenant in which all persons residing within the city walls were citizens. This was the legal origin of the free city (commune), which had its base in the commercial and manufacturing guilds. With the establishment of the free cities, merchants and manufacturers emerged as a clearly defined status group, the bourgeoisie (Burgher). More than three thousand free cities were established across western Europe; they would become the bastions of the Reformation and the bourgeois revolutions.

The free cities were established on the basis of the principle of commodity exchange, and yet at the same time they were covenant communities. In them, the capitalistic drive for profit was countered by a second drive that arose in reaction to the economic disparities resulting from that drive for capitalist profit: a drive to restore a community based on mutual aid (commune). This is why, up through and including the Paris Commune, the cities would serve as breeding grounds for movements to supersede capitalism (communism).

Put simply, feudalism was a pluralistic situation in which no one party was able to acquire absolute superiority. Monarchs, the nobility, the church, and the cities all existed in ceaseless conflict and alliance. Accordingly, feudalism also meant an endless state of war. The anthropologist Pierre Clastres regards the perpetual warfare of primitive societies as being a measure for warding off the rise of a state, but this seems even more applicable to this case. The decentralization and polycentralism resulting from armed struggle between monarchs and feudal lords blocked the establishment of a unified state. It would only be with the absolute monarchies of the fifteenth and sixteenth centuries that kings would acquire absolute authority. Monarchs gained supremacy over their rivals, the feudal lords, and established standing armies and permanent bureaucratic structures. In a sense, this had already been achieved under Asiatic despotism. But absolute monarchies differ from the Asiatic despotic states in one important aspect: rather than trying to suppress commodity exchange (mode of exchange C), absolute monarchies assured and promoted its dominance. It was inevitable that this would ultimately lead to the bourgeois revolutions.

FEUDALISM AS SUBMARGIN

If we can say that Greece and Rome arose on the submargins of the Asiatic empires, then we can likewise say that feudalism (the feudal social formation) arose on the submargins of the Roman Empire—with, that is, Germanic tribal society. Looking at the question this way, we come to see that Marx's distinctions between Asiatic, classical, and feudal do not mark successive diachronic stages but rather positional relationships within the space of a world-empire.

Because feudalism led to the subsequent development of capitalism and the triumph of western Europe, it is often assumed that it must be something unique to western Europe. In fact, though, just as the special characteristics of Greece and Rome were the result of their being situated on the submargins of the Egyptian and Asiatic empires, the phenomenon of feudalism in western Europe arose because it was situated on the submargins of the Roman and Islamic Empires. In sum, the characteristics of feudalism are not something unique to the "Occident," but are rather the result of the relationship between core, margin, and submargin. This becomes clear when we look at an example of feudalism from East Asia: Japan.

Both Marx and Weber paid close attention to the rise of feudalism in Japan.[18] Needless to say, feudalism here means a system grounded in relationships of personal loyalty—in other words, a mutually binding contractual relationship of fief for loyalty between lord and retainers. The Annales School historians Marc Bloch and Fernand Braudel also took note of this case. But to the best of my knowledge, the only persuasive explanation for why this came about was provided by Wittfogel.[19] He argued that Japanese feudalism was the result of its being situated on the submargin of the Chinese Empire.

In Korea, situated on the margin of China, the Chinese system was imported early on, but its introduction into the island nation of Japan was delayed. The introduction of the Chinese system into Japan began with the establishment of the so-called *ritsuryō* system in the seventh and eighth centuries. Moreover, this adoption was in form only, and in reality the central state remained weak: the imported bureaucratic structure and system of state ownership of all lands and peoples never became fully functional. In areas beyond the reach of these state structures, primarily in the eastern parts of the archipelago, private property emerged with the clearing of new lands for cultivation, and a manorial system took root. The warrior-farmer community that developed there gave rise to a feudal system based on personal ties of fief for loyalty, which had a corrosive effect on the existing state structure. Rule by the warrior class would last from the thirteenth century until the latter half of the nineteenth.

During this same period, Korea saw the increasing adoption of Chinese forms; the Koryŏ court, for example, adopted a civil-service examination system for officials in the tenth century, thereby establishing the overwhelming superiority of civilian officials over military officials. This examination system remained in place into the twentieth century. In Japan, however, despite the fact that China was looked up to as the model in all things, the examination system was never introduced. The tradition of the warrior-farmer community, with its hostility to civilian authorities, remained powerful. Having said that, it is also true that the ancient imperial and ritsuryō structures remained in place, at least formally, and continued to possess some authority. This was because, instead of sweeping away the old monarchy, the feudal state chose to transform the monarchy into an object of worship, using it to secure the state's own legitimacy. This was possible in part because of the absence of any potential invaders from outside.

This appropriation of the previously existing form of authority, however, served as a check on the feudal system: it weakened the bilateral (reciprocal) ties that were at its heart. Marc Bloch argues that despite the remarkable resemblance between Japanese and European feudalisms, the relative weakness in the former of a concept of covenant that could restrain the authority was due to the fact that "outside Europe, in distant Japan, it so happened that a system of personal and territorial subordination, very similar to Western feudalism, was gradually formed over against a monarchy which, as in the West, was much older than itself. But there the two institutions coexisted without interpenetration."[20]

The Tokugawa shogunate, which seized power following the Warring States period of the sixteenth century, imported Zhu Xi's neo-Confucianism from Chosŏn Korea and attempted to establish a centralized bureaucratic structure. Moreover, the shogunate sought to legitimate itself by situating itself within the continuity of the imperial state that had existed since antiquity. As a result, in the Tokugawa period we see aspects more characteristic of a centralized state than of feudalism.[21] In reality, though, the feudal order and its culture persisted. For example, samurai were assigned the right and duty to pursue direct vendettas against enemies. In other words, alongside and distinct from the legal order of the state, personal ties of loyalty to one's master were still granted great importance. Being a warrior (samurai) was more highly valued than being a bureaucratic official. In other words, higher value was placed on the aesthetic or pragmatic than on the theoretical or systematic.

The capacity for adopting only selectively the civilization of the empire is not some quality unique to Japan, but rather a characteristic shared by all submargins. For example, even within Europe we find differences between regions that were on the margin and submargin of the Roman Empire. Whereas France and Germany displayed characteristics typical of the margin, carrying on systematically the concepts and forms of the Roman Empire, Britain lay on the submargin and hence was able to adopt a more flexible, pragmatic, unsystematic, and eclectic stance. This is why Britain, turning away from the Continent, was able to construct a maritime empire and become the center of the modern world system (world-economy).[22]

From Magic to Religion

We have so far looked at three modes of exchange and the social formations that arise as combinations of the modes. There is a fourth mode of exchange that arises out of resistance against the other three. This is the position of the fourth quadrant D in table 1 in the introduction. It has several defining characteristics. To begin with, it forms the polar opposite of mode of exchange B— that is, of the principle of the state. In the way that mode D liberates individual people from the constraining bonds of the community, it resembles a market society—in other words, mode of exchange C. And yet at the same time mode D also resembles mode of exchange A in the way that, countering the competition and class divisions of the market economy, it aims at reciprocal (mutual-aid style) exchanges, a market economy that does not lead to the accumulation of capital. This means that mode of exchange D marks the attempt to restore the reciprocal community (A) of the first quadrant on top of the market economy (C) of the third quadrant. In this situation, mode of exchange A is restored—and yet it no longer has the power to bind individuals to the community. In that sense, mode D is possible only on the condition that mode C already exists.

Mode D is further differentiated from the other three modes of exchange in that it is an ideal form that can never exist in actuality. In historical reality, it was manifested in the form of universal religions. For example, Max Weber uses the liberation from magic as the yardstick for measuring the development of religion, explicating that development by means of socioeconomic factors. He locates the development of religion in the transformation from magic to religion, or from magician to priestly class, explaining these in terms of the shift from clan society to state society.[1] In his view, the overcoming of magic is realized by modern capitalist society and modern science. I would like though to rethink this problem from the perspective of modes of exchange—because religion is itself rooted in modes of exchange.

In fact, Weber himself at times examined religion from the perspective of modes of exchange. For example, he considered magic to be a form of the gift in which one gave to the gods in order to coerce them to do something. Moreover, he believed that this continued even under salvation religions: "In these cases, religious behavior is not worship of the god [*Gottesdient*] but rather coercion of the god [*Gotteszwang*], and invocation is not prayer but rather the exercise of magical formulae."[2] He continues:

> An increasing predominance of non-magical motives is later brought about by the growing recognition of the power of a god and of his character as a personal overlord. The god becomes a great lord who may fail on occasion, and whom one cannot approach with devices of magical compulsion, but only with entreaties and gifts. But if these motives add anything new to mere wizardry, it is initially something as sober and rational as the motivation of magic itself. The pervasive and central theme is: *do ut des*. This aspect clings to the routine and the mass religious behavior of all peoples at all times and in all religions. The normal situation is that the burden of all prayers, even in the most other-worldly religions, is the aversion of the external evils of this world and the inducement of the external advantages of this world.[3]

Weber points out a kind of exchange that exists in the "prayers" of salvation religions, *do ut des* (I give so that you may give), and argues that this originates in magic. That these both involve exchanges, however, does not mean that they are the same thing: exchange in magic and exchange in prayer may bear a superficial resemblance, but they are essentially different from one another. If we overlook this difference, we will fail to understand the development from magic to religion.

Weber paid no attention to differences between modes of exchange. On this point, he was in the same boat as Friedrich Nietzsche, one of his sources. Nietzsche was the first person to take up the problems of morality and religion from the perspective of exchange. For example, he describes the sense of morality as an obligation that "originated from the very material concept of 'debt'": "The feeling of guilt, of personal responsibility originated ... in the earliest and most primordial relationship between men, in the relationship between buyer and seller, debtor and creditor." He maintains further that justice originates in the concept of economic value: "One soon arrives at the great generalization: 'Everything has its price; *everything* can be paid off'—the earliest and most naïve canon of moral *justice*, the beginning of all 'neighbourliness,' all 'fairness,' all 'good will,' all 'objectivity' on earth."[4]

Here, however, Nietzsche is committing the error of confusing debts incurred in a reciprocal exchange with those incurred in commodity exchange. The "earliest and most primordial relationship between men" is reciprocal exchange. To conflate this with commodity exchange is to commit what Nietzsche himself would call an inversion of perspective. In reality, in commodity mode of exchange C, it is precisely because a debt is created that a feeling of debt does not arise. This is if anything a liberation from the feeling of debt that originated in reciprocal relations—in other words, it is what makes it possible to conduct businesslike human relations. This is what liberated human beings from relations based in magic.

I have already taken up the development from magic to religion in terms of modes of exchange. Put simply, magic consists of the attempt to control or manipulate nature or people through gifts (sacrifices), and it is grounded in the principle of reciprocity. For this reason, magic arose and developed in the shift from the society of the nomadic band to that of sedentary clan society—in other words, magic developed in tandem with the rise of reciprocity as an organizational principle. Through this, the social position of the magician-priest was raised. There are limits to this, however, because the principle of reciprocity itself does not permit the emergence of a transcendent position. It is for the same reason that in clan society, the position of the chief was strengthened yet never acquired the absolute status of a king. But after the emergence of clan society—that is, in state society—the "thou" of spirit (*anima*) is rendered transcendent as a god, while nature and other people become simply "it," available for manipulation.

Magic is still present in state society, but its reality changes. In clan society magic functioned to maintain egalitarianism—for example, the obligations to give, receive, and make countergifts were all ways of enforcing equality. Through them magic carried out redistribution. Marcel Mauss explained this as the function of magical power (*hau*). But mode of exchange B, which is dominant in state society, is a relationship of subordination and protection. This too is a bilateral (reciprocal) relation: the rulers provide protection in return for subordination offered by the ruled. Put in religious terms, this is equivalent to prayers of supplication—when people make prayers and offerings to a god in order to receive its power. This is the beginning of religion in the narrow sense. As Weber argues, religious prayer has something in common with magic: by making a gift to a god, one attempts to extract a quid pro quo. But the bilateral nature (reciprocity) in this instance is grounded in mode of exchange B, meaning that it is of a different kind from the reciprocity of magic in mode of exchange A. Prayer differs from magic in that it is directed at a ruler king-priest—and ultimately at a transcendent god. The element of egalitarianism is absent.

There are, however, instances of magic filling an egalitarian function even in state societies: we see this in instances of the right of asylum. Under it, people are freed from social constraints. The right of asylum is universal to state societies. It possesses an ethical significance that liberates people from social constraints and limits. This does not spring up from humanism. Ortwin Henssler argues that the right of asylum originated in magic, not in some ethical significance.[5] But how could something magical in nature acquire ethical significance? In my view, the right to asylum represents the return of suppressed mode of exchange A (that of nomadic egalitarianism) during the period when clan society transformed into state society. In that sense, the right to asylum harbored an ethical significance from the start. But it was manifested in the form of a compulsion, the return of the repressed—as, in other words, a kind of magical power. State power is not able to touch people who claim asylum because they possess a kind of anima.

In general, though, the remnants of magic function to strengthen mode of exchange B rather than restore mode of exchange A. In the proto-city-state, the chief-priest is markedly more powerful than in clan society. This is because subjugating and ruling over a different clan requires more than military power; it requires a god that transcends the existing local clan gods, and with it the power of priests and other sacerdotal figures increases accordingly. That power is further strengthened through the conflicts carried out between proto-city-states. In the state that emerges through this process, the king-priest is a transcendent, centralized power. This also means that its god acquires an increasingly transcendent status. The state, through its intercourse (warfare and trade) with other states, becomes a state-empire, one that rules over a vast territory and encompasses many tribes and city-states. Through this process the god becomes increasingly centralized and transcendent, as does the king-priest.

The state is established through the military subordination of multiple city-states and tribal communities. But a stable, lasting order cannot be created solely through armed conquest and coercion. The tribute and service offered by the ruled to the ruler must be put into the form of a countergift, one offered in return for gifts received from that ruler. This is the role played by religion. For this reason, this kind of religion is a state ideological apparatus. The ruled (the agrarian community) seek aid and comfort through voluntary submission and supplication to the god. This god is in the grasp of the king-priest. In effect, prayers made to the god are prayers made to the king-priest.

This suggests that it is impossible to understand the process by which the clan community is transformed into a state without examining this religious phase. This is because religion itself is rooted in the economic dimension of exchange. Religion, in short, is indivisible from politics and economics. State-administered temples, for example, were also storehouses for stockpiling and redistributing offerings. The priestly class with its high degree of literacy was also the state's official class—just as they were also scientists who contributed to the advancement of such fields as astronomy and civil engineering. The development of magic into religion was nothing other than the development from clan society to the state. As Weber writes in this regard, magicians everywhere were first of all shamans who summoned rain, but in areas with state-organized irrigation agriculture, such as Mesopotamia, magicians lost their function. Crops were now perceived to arrive thanks to the king of the state, who created the irrigation systems that delivered water. As a result, the leader of that state acquired the status of absolute: it was he who delivered the harvest out of barren sands. Herein lays one of the origins of the god who created the world from nothing, according to Weber.[6]

This was not yet a transcendent god, however: if the god failed to answer the prayers (gifts) of the people appropriately, the people would abandon the god. More concretely, if a community or state's god failed them in war, that god was discarded. This indicates that reciprocity persisted in the relation between god and man. In this sense, magic still existed in residual form. The emergence of truly universal religion came with the appearance of a god who could not be abandoned even when prayers were left unanswered or wars were lost. How did this come about?

Empire and Monotheism

A state became a geographically extensive empire that encompassed numerous tribes and city-states through a process of intercourse (warfare and trade) with other states. In this process, the local gods of the subjugated communities and states were abandoned, while the god of the victorious country became increasingly central and transcendent, just as its king-priests acquired a more central, transcendent position. When a state brought other communities under its umbrella, naturally worship of the rulers' god was imposed on the ruled, but the local gods of the ruled were not always rejected; frequently, they were simply absorbed into the pantheon of deities and remained objects of worship. This reflected the relationship between the monarchy and the various tribal chiefs (powerful clans) that became retainers. This made it possible to encompass numerous tribes. In such cases, both the monarchy and its god remained relatively weak, roughly equal to the gods of the other tribes. On the other hand, in a more central-ized and powerful state, the monarchy's god likewise acquired transcen-dent status. This transcendent status was rooted in the transcendent status of the state (king); if the state fell, so too did its god.

In this sense, the development of religion is also the development of the state. Naturally, the establishment of an empire resulted in a high degree of transcendence for its god. The logic by which a transcendent god emerged in tandem with a transcendent monarchy and priesthood is clear enough. Nietzsche argues, "The progress of [world] empires is always the progress towards [world] divinities."[7] These "world divinities" are different from the god of a universal religion. The transcendence of god in a universal religion differs from the transcendence of a world empire or world god, and in fact is something that arises only through the negation of the latter.

The existence of empire is a necessary, but not a sufficient, condition for the emergence of universal religion. For example, monotheism is widely thought to originate in Judaism. But in fact it was not unique to Israel. Mono-theistic worship first arose in Egypt, with the Amarna reform of Pharaoh Amenhotep IV (mid-fourteenth century BCE). He abolished the existing polytheism and recognized the sun god Aten as the sole deity. Moreover, he changed his own name to Akhenaten, literally "he who serves Aten." Weber takes up the significance of this:

In Egypt, the monotheistic, and hence necessarily universalistic, transi-tion of Amenhotep IV (Ikhnaton [Akhenaten]) to the solar cult resulted from an entirely different situation. One factor was again the extensive rationalism of the priesthood, and in all likelihood of the laity as well, which was of a purely naturalistic character, in marked contrast to Israel-ite prophecy. Another factor was the practical need of a monarch at the head of a bureaucratic totalitarian state to break the power of the priests by eliminating the multiplicity of sacerdotal gods, and to restore the ancient power of the deified Pharaoh by elevating the monarch to the position of supreme solar priest.[8]

Put simply, there was constant conflict between monarch and priesthood. Concealed behind this was another conflict between the monarchy, trying to advance its own position as the supreme, centralized authority, and the local powers (nobility), subordinate yet trying to preserve a measure of autonomy. While the former worshipped a monotheistic god, the latter continued to worship various tribal clan gods. Akhenaten's introduction of monotheism signified the rise of a monarchy capable of subduing the various local gods—in other words, the various local powers.

In addition, we should not overlook another factor that pushed Akhenaten to introduce monotheism: Egypt at the time had expanded its territory to become an empire. For example, in *Moses and Monotheism*, Sigmund Freud argues that Moses was a member of the Egyptian royal family who tried to revive the monotheism that Akhenaten had created but that had subsequently been abandoned. I'll return to this hypothesis again, but for now let me note that Freud too locates the reason for Egypt's adoption of monotheism in its rise as an empire. In order to build an empire, a single omnipotent god capable of dominating the tribes and their local gods that had come under its control was indispensable. Monotheism was rejected after Akhenaten's death, vanishing without a trace. But this happened not simply because polytheistic traditions were strong: unlike the Mesopotamian Empires, Egypt was in no danger of invasion from its peripheries so long as it did not expand in scale, and so it did not require a highly centralized structure.[9]

The necessity in a world empire for a universal divinity, whether monotheistic or not, can been seen in subsequent world empires (Roman, Arabian, Mongol, and so on). Behind these universal divinities lurked the presence of a monarchy, trying to subjugate local nobilities and chiefs who were struggling to preserve autonomy. In fact, universal religions originally appeared in the form of a negation of this sort of world empire and religion. As soon as they achieved stable form, however, they found themselves appropriated into the ruling apparatus of a world empire. What we now call "world religions" rarely extended beyond the former domain of a single world empire.

Nonetheless, universal religions were at origin fundamentally hostile to the elements that composed world empires. We can explain this in terms of mode of exchange. World empires arose from situations where modes of exchange B and C had expanded spatially. Up until now, we have been considering this problem in terms of mode of exchange B—in other words, in terms of the strengthening of the state. But empires are also characterized by mode of exchange C—namely, the development of trade and markets. One of the moments that give rise to the birth of universal religions is the appearance of a world market and world money. Universal religions emerged as mode of exchange D—as a criticism of modes of exchange B and C, which were the dominant modes in world empires.

World money circulates universally, transcending any local community or state. In that sense, world money is universal money. World money appears within a world empire, yet it does not depend on the power of that world empire. It depends instead on the universal power of world money (gold or silver) itself. The empire's role is limited to minting coinage and guaranteeing its metallic content. In the absence of such a guarantee, and in the absence of guarantees for its security, trade could not develop. To that extent, we are justified in saying that world empires brought about the world market. But the power of world money is in no way dependent on the state. It is something produced through commodity exchange.

Among the various local moneys, gold and silver became world money. The worship of money is, to borrow Marx's language, a fetishism, and with the rise of world money, this fetishism became monotheistic. Under this god money, enormous transformations were wrought on society, which still preserved remnants of the older tribal community. Marx writes, "Just as in money every qualitative difference between commodities is extinguished, so too for its part, as a radical leveller, it extinguishes all distinctions.... Ancient society therefore denounced it as tending to destroy the economic and moral order."[10]

In fact, this "radical leveller" money was the downfall of the clan community. On the one hand, money freed individuals from the constraining bonds of the clan community. Individuals, who until then had been related only through their community, now directly engaged in intercourse by means of world money. These individuals, who until then were constrained by either bilateral (reciprocal) relations or ruler-subordinate hierarchies, now come into relation with one another through exchanges (contracts) mediated by money. The penetration of a money economy lessened the need to coerce others through magic or force: one could now coerce them through contracts entered into by mutual consent. In that sense, the disenchantment that Weber describes first became possible through the money economy.

Money transformed people and things into "it": money made it possible to treat people and things as measurable, quantifiable entities.

The money economy freed individuals from the constraints of the community and made them into members of the empire-cosmopolis. In addition, this "radical leveller" undermined the egalitarianism of the community—in other words, its economy and ethic of reciprocity. It also led to growing disparities in wealth. These were the two preconditions required for the emergence of universal religion. In the process of empire formation, there is a moment when, under the sway of mode of exchange B, mode of exchange C dismantles mode of exchange A; it is at this moment, and in resistance to it, that universal religion appears, taking the form of mode of exchange D.

Exemplary Prophets

The universal religions appeared independently from one another at roughly the same time in all of the regions that produced ancient civilizations. This indicates that universal religions are characteristic of a particular transitional period: the period in which city-states engage in struggle with one another and in which supranational states emerge; seen from another perspective, this is also the period in which the penetration of a money economy and the decline of the communal become pronounced. But to understand universal religions, we also need to examine their origins as critiques of the communal and state religions that preceded them, as well as the related fact that they all originated with a certain type of personality.

The personalities that originated universal religions were prophets. There are two things we need to keep in mind about prophets. First, we need to distinguish between prophets and ordinary soothsayers (fortunetellers). Soothsaying is carried out by priests and other sacerdotal officials. But a prophet does not necessarily foretell the future. In fact, the prophets of Israel stressed that they were not prophets in that sense. One of the shared attributes of universal religions is their rejection of the priestly class.

Second, and more important, we must not limit prophets only to Judaism, or to the Christianity and Islamism that derived from it. Weber distinguishes between ethical and exemplary prophets. An ethical prophet is an intermediary, charged by a god to proclaim its will and demanding compliance with the ethical obligations that are rooted in this charge—we see this in, for example, the prophets of the Old Testament, Jesus, and Mohammed. An exemplary prophet is an exemplary person, demonstrating to others the way to religious salvation through personal example—for example, the Buddha, Confucius, and Laozi.

A number of implications follow from this. First, those people who are ordinarily called philosophers should be placed in the category of religious prophets. The essence of a universal religion lies in the critique of traditional religions. That being the case, there is a clear relationship to philosophy, which first emerged as a critique of religion. For example, Frances M. Cornford sees the appearance of natural philosophy in Ionia as a shift from religion to philosophy.[11] Clearly, the natural philosophers of Ionia tried to explicate nature without resorting to religious explanations. This does not mean, however, that they rejected religion in general. While rejecting the personified gods of Olympus, they posited the concept of a new, monotheistic god: Nature. In that sense, their philosophy was connected to universal religion.

This is not limited to the Ionian philosophers. For example, Socrates of Athens fits the category of exemplary prophet. He was put to death precisely for the crime of introducing a new god into the Athens polis and thereby undermining its traditional religion. This criticism of Socrates was in a sense justified: he always obeyed the voice of his internal "daemon." In other words, his actions and words were the charges entrusted to him by a god. Of course, Socrates was a philosopher, not the preacher of a new religion. Yet it is undeniable that it was less his philosophical theories than the exemplary nature of his life and death that would subsequently move countless people. In this sense, we can consider him an exemplary prophet.

Ionia was a region developed by colonists who had separated from the community, and it developed in tandem with a global trade that extended from Asia to the Mediterranean. It was there, even before Athens, that a society rooted in the market and in discourse was nurtured. It was in this kind of society that discursive skills themselves could become commodities, as seen in classic form with the Sophists. This is why the region produced an abundance of thinkers. But we should not regard this as a unique phenomenon.

A similar situation arose in China during roughly the same period: in the Warring States period of armed conflict among the city-states, we see the emergence of the thinkers associated with the Hundred Schools of Thought, including Confucius, Laozi, Mozi, and Xun Zi. They went from country to country, preaching their philosophies, because those countries were no longer able to rely on the traditions of the clan community. For example, Confucius declared, "I would wait for one to offer the price."[12] This situation, in which the need existed for a new kind of thought, transformed thought into a commodity, leading in turn to the appearance of many philosophers. Among these, Confucius and Laozi would extend a religious influence onto subsequent generations. Neither was specifically attempting to preach a religion; it was only later that they became regarded as the founders of religions. In that sense, they clearly fall within the category of exemplary prophets.

We find the same situation in India. In the sixth century BCE, a large number of city-states existed along the Ganges River, including Kosala and Magadha. Most were kingships, although a few were aristocratic republics. Among these was the state of the Shakya people, Buddha's birthplace. During a period of warfare among these states, a large number of so-called free thinkers emerged. Their number included both materialists and radicals who rejected all forms of morality. Buddha (born circa 463 BCE) was one of these free thinkers. Buddha did not preach a new theory; instead he espoused a moral practice. He had no sense of himself as the founder of a new religion. Nonetheless, he became an exemplary prophet, one whose way of life acquired a powerful influence.

These examples demonstrate that universal religions emerged in the form of critiques of older religions and that it is thus impossible to draw a clear line dividing philosophers who critiqued religion from the founders of universal religions.

Ethical Prophets

If we look at the origin of universal religions in terms of what Weber called ethical prophets, then the earliest example was probably Zoroaster (Zarathustra) of Persia. As a prophet, he rejected the priestly class, and in making Ahura Mazda the highest god, Zoroaster denied the many gods of the Arya people, which in turn amounted to a rejection of the caste system (officials, priests, commoners). He was also the first to see society and history from the perspective not of the community or state, but as the locus of a struggle between good and evil. Here we clearly find the prototype for universal religions among nomadic societies. But because the historical record on Zoroaster is limited, I will focus my consideration of ethical prophets exclusively on Judaism.

Generally speaking, the periphery of any empire includes nomadic peoples. The origins of these nomadic peoples can be traced back to the stage of the proto-city-state. Nomadic peoples were those who, when the proto-city-state was moving toward the formation of the state and the agrarian community, rejected this emerging order. Their societies tended to be patriarchal rather than clan based, but in certain aspects they maintained the principles of hunter-gatherer clan society—in, for example, the way relations to higher-order collectives were bilateral and allowed for relative autonomy, and in the rule these peoples shared that required visitors to be welcomed with hospitality. Nomadic peoples tend to be widely dispersed from one another, but if pressure from an empire intensified, they also sometimes formed alliances to counter it.

Israel (the Jewish people) began as a covenant community among nomadic groups (the "twelve tribes"). In the Old Testament, this is narrated as a covenant with God. What this really signifies, though, is a covenant among tribes under a single god. This is not unique to the Jewish people. Whenever nomadic peoples form a city-state, it takes place by way of a covenant among tribes, a covenant entered into under a single shared god. Weber writes, "It is a universal phenomenon that the formation of a political association entails subordination to a tribal god."[13] The Greek poleis were likewise established through this sort of covenant.

In these instances, the covenant they entered into was bilateral (reciprocal). This meant that the relationship between god and man was also bilateral. The god was supposed to reward the people if they faithfully worshipped him; if it failed to do so, the god was abandoned. The rise of a state was at the same time the rise of a god, just as the fall of a state was likewise the fall of a god. In this sense, covenants between god and people were reciprocal exchange relationships. Yet the covenant between God and people in Judaism was not characterized by this sort of reciprocity. This kind of thought (Judaism) emerged during and after the captivity in Babylon, as I will discuss again in more detail. In the earliest period in Israel, this concept of God did not yet exist: at that stage, there were no notable differences between Israel and other tribal confederacies.

In fact, when the nomadic Jewish people invaded the land of Canaan and reached the stage of formation of a despotic state and agricultural community, they in practice abandoned worship of the god of their nomadic period and began to adopt the religion (worship of Baal) of the local agricultural peoples. This is the same route trod by other nomadic herding peoples who adopted fixed settlement. In Israel, the king-priest subsequently became an increasingly centralized power. The monarchy enjoyed a kind of golden age as a kind of Asiatic despotism (tribute-system state) in the period stretching from David to Solomon. Here again we see the process of development common to all Asiatic despotisms. It is clear that many prophets appeared during the age of Solomon. They criticized the high-handedness of the priestly offices, the decadence of the people, and the emergence of economic disparities and warned that the state would fail if these continued unchecked. But this sort of prophet is not particular to the Jewish religion. The criticisms of these prophets are entirely typical of what appears in general when a nomadic people is transformed into an agricultural people under a despotic state. Most likely, such prophets appeared whenever the community or state fell into crisis among formerly nomadic peoples engaged in agriculture under a despotic state. But this alone will not give rise to universal religion: it arose only after the fall of the kingdom.

In concrete terms, after the death of Solomon, the kingdom split into north and south. The northern kingdom of Israel was defeated by Assyria (722 BCE). From the perspective of Assyria, this was simply one episode in the process of its rise as a world empire. The people of the Kingdom of Israel that was vanquished at this time disappeared as a people. In other words, their god was abandoned. This is just one typical instance of the fate met by countless tribal states in the history of rising empires.

The unusual event came next, with the fall of the southern Jewish kingdom (586 BCE) at the hands not of Assyria but rather Babylonia. Many abandoned their god then—their country had perished, after all. But at this time an unprecedented event took place among the people taken away to Babylonia: even though their state had fallen, they did not abandon its god. At this moment, a new concept of God was born. The defeat of a state no longer meant the defeat of its god; it was instead interpreted as God's punishment for the people having neglected God. This meant the rejection of reciprocity between God and people. This entailed a fundamental change in the relation between God and the people—or, when seen from a different perspective, a fundamental change in the relation between people.

Among the people taken into Babylon were a relatively large number from the intellectual classes. They mainly pursued commerce—meaning that they became individuals estranged from the previous ruling structure, as well as from the agrarian community. These individuals established a new covenant community under God, one that took the form of a covenant between man and God. It was only similar to the establishment of a tribal confederation by nomadic peoples in appearance. What the prophets preached in the age of Solomon was the return to a nomadic tribal confederation—a return, that is, to the desert. The meant the return of mode of exchange A, of the community grounded in reciprocity. By contrast, what appeared in

Babylon was a federation of free and equal individuals, alienated from tribal bonds and constraints. This meant the restoration of mode of exchange A in a higher dimension, in other words, mode of exchange D.

Roughly fifty years after they were taken into captivity, the Jews were set free when the First Persian Empire destroyed Babylon, and they returned to Canaan. After that, the Jewish religious order functioned to organize the stateless people. The covenant community formed in Babylon transformed into an ethnic group governed by priests and scribes, similar to what had previously existed. The compilation of the Bible took place after this, and in this process the activities of the earlier prophets and of the myth of Moses were edited and assembled.

Judaism as a universal religion was born in Babylon. But the official version of the religion tried to portray this as the realization of earlier prophecies. This meant erasure of the historical specificity that the religion first arose in Babylon.

We can say the same thing about the myth of Moses: it was a projection of the covenant between God and people that first arose in Babylon back onto the ancient period. Historically, the Israel of the thirteenth century BCE, when Moses is supposed to have led the Israelis, was a tribal confederacy (the twelve tribes) and simply could not have sustained the kind of dictatorial leader that Moses is portrayed as. Accordingly, the Book of Exodus represents the projection of the experience of the exodus from Babylonian captivity onto the distant past.[14] This means that the origins of belief in the God of Moses are located after the period of captivity.

But even if we accept that the appearance of the God of Moses took place in this later period, the real question is why it came to carry so much significance. Freud's *Moses and Monotheism* provides an important clue here. Just as *Totem and Taboo* is dismissed by today's anthropologists, this work is generally dismissed by historians and religious studies scholars because it has no apparent grounding in historical reality. Put simply, Freud thought that Moses was a member of the Egyptian royal family who attempted to revive the monotheism of Akhenaten. In this version, Moses promised freedom to the enslaved Jews if they would accept monotheism. According to Freud, this was the covenant between God and man.

Needless to say, you will not find any specialists in the field who accept this hypothesis. But what Freud was trying to explain here was why this covenant was initiated not by people but by God. Normally, when a state is established as a tribal confederation, the resulting covenant is bilateral in nature—meaning that the god can be abandoned if it fails to keep its part of the agreement. But here we have a case where the covenant is seemingly forced on the people by God. There is nothing bilateral about it, and the people do not hold the option of abandoning it. How did such a situation come about? Those who would dismiss Freud are obligated to come up with an answer to this.

Another crucial feature of Freud's hypothesis is that after Moses led Israel out of Egypt and into the wilderness, the people killed him just before they entered the fertile land of Canaan. This is because Moses had commanded them to remain in the desert. According to Freud, amid the development of Canaanite civilization, this murdered Moses would return as the God of Moses. This, of course, is a repetition of the murder of the primal patriarch depicted in *Totem and Taboo*.

Freud's *Totem and Taboo* deals with problems that arise when a nomadic hunter-gatherer people form a clan society, while *Moses and Monotheism* takes up those problems that arise when nomadic tribes form a state society. At the stage of nomadic hunter-gatherers, the sort of despotic ur-patriarch that Freud hypothesized could not have existed, just as in nomadic herding society there is no despotic chief who rules over "our people." But such criticisms do not allow us to dismiss the significance of what Freud disclosed. The important questions here, after all, are to explain how the "brotherly" pact of clan society was possible and how the God of Moses acquired transcendent status.

Freud's answer is that Moses and his God were murdered and then subsequently reappeared as a compulsion in the form of a "return of the repressed." This view does not contradict historical reality. If we take the teachings of Moses to have been the ethics of a nomadic society—namely, independence and egalitarianism—then we can say that these were "murdered" under the despotic state (with its priestly and official establishments and its agrarian community) that developed in the land of Canaan: they were fully repressed. Of course, people did not intend to reject their own past; if anything, they wanted to defend their traditions. Yet such a situation is the mark of a total repression. Accordingly, the ethic of the nomadic age could return only in the form of the word of God as transmitted by the prophets in opposition to tradition and the priesthood, in the form of something contrary to human consciousness and will.

I have argued that in mode of exchange D, mode of exchange A is restored in a higher dimension, but in this case we should speak of a return of the repressed rather than a restoration. This is something quite different from a nostalgic restoration. In response to Freud's concept of the unconscious,

Ernst Bloch proposes the concept of the "Not-Yet-Conscious" (*das Noch-Nicht-Bewußte*).[15] This view regards Freud's return of the repressed as the nostalgic restoration of something that had existed in the past, but this is of course not the case. The return of the repressed arises precisely as what Bloch calls the "Not-Yet-Conscious." It is not and cannot be some utopian fantasy arbitrarily dreamed up by people.

The Power of God

As a tribal religion, Judaism was seemingly bound to be discarded with the fall of the kingdoms of Israel and Judah. Many of the kingdoms' people were absorbed by other states. The formation of Judaism as a universal religion, on the other hand, was the work of those who were held captive in Babylon. Their faith in Yahweh did not arise through compulsion from tribe or state: with the collapse of the state, that sort of power was no longer at work. Crucially, many of those taken into captivity came from the ranks of the ruling or intellectual classes, and in Babylon they primarily engaged in commerce. Through the experiences of losing a nation and living in a city where intercourse transcending tribal community boundaries was the normal state of affairs, a new god, Yahweh, took form among them. We could say that each individual discovered Yahweh on his or her own.

These are in fact two sides of a single phenomenon. In one aspect, God now became a universal, transcendent being that exceeded any single tribe or state. In another aspect, we see the emergence here of the relatively autonomous individual, one who is not simply a member of the community. The former meant that the "power of God" had taken on a form that transcended the power of community, state, or money. This likewise meant that mode of exchange D was invoked through the power of God as something transcending modes of exchange A, B, and C, and that it could not be invoked any other way. The latter aspect meant that mode of exchange D was premised on the existence of discrete individuals, independent from the community. These two moments cannot be isolated from one another: the existence of a god transcending the domain of any state or community corresponded to the existence of individuals who were dependent on neither state nor community.

Yet the emergence of universal religion was not simply a matter of individuals, independent of state or community, establishing a direct relation with God. Rather, through this a new kind of relation between individuals was created. Universal religions preach love and compassion. Seen from the perspective of modes of exchange, these signify a pure gift (unreciprocated gift)—in other words, mode of exchange D, which supersedes modes A, B, and C. In more concrete terms, universal religions aim at the creation of mutual-aid communities in the form of associations among individuals. As a result, universal religion aims to dismantle the state or tribal community and to reorganize these into a new kind of community. From another perspective, this also means that universal religions are formed by prophets who renounce the priestly class and organize a new body of the faithful.

Judaism was born not as the religion of an ethnic people but rather as a religious organization composed of individuals. This is particularly apparent in the case of sects like the Essenes. Of course, the sect led by Jesus was also born of Judaism. But Judaism's emergence during captivity in Babylon followed essentially the same pattern as these. Individuals who had lost their state were reorganized into a body of worshippers of Yahweh. This was a new Jewish people. In sum, Judaism should not be understood as the religion chosen by the Jewish people: to the contrary, Judaism *created* the Jewish people.[16]

After the rise to dominance of Christianity, a distorted view of Judaism arose: that it was the religion of the Jewish people and hence did not engage in proselytizing. Since the rise of Zionism, this view has come to be shared by many Jews. But Judaism historically attracted many converts—in all regions of the Roman Empire, as well as in Arabia, Africa, and Russia during the rise of Islam. It is said that Judaism became a universal religion during the Hellenistic period. But we must not forget that under Hellenism— that is, in the cosmopolis that emerged after the dissolution of polis and community—Judaism was highly attractive to many people.

Of course, when non-Jews converted to Judaism, particular tribal customs such as circumcision posed barriers. These barriers helped render visible a contradiction between the universal and the particular. Later, when this contradiction became overt within Judaism, Christianity— which opted for the universal—emerged. This did not mean that Christianity was somehow more universal. To the contrary, Christianity adapted itself to the particular—the customs of a variety of local communities and states. As a result, Christianity was able to expand, but only by becoming the religion of the community and state. For these reasons, we can conclude that universal religions do not become universal by negating the particular. Rather, they become universal through an incessant awareness of the contradiction between universality and particularity.

We can say the same thing about the transcendence and immanence of God. The god of a universal religion is transcendental and yet at the same time immanent (i.e., within the individual). If God exists externally in the form of a kind of personality, it would be nothing more than an idol. Yet if God is immanent within individual human beings, then God is entirely unnecessary: the very notion of God's existence implies that it is transcendental and therefore external. The transcendence and immanence of God forms an inseparable, paradoxical unity. If either of these two moments were to disappear, it would mean the end of universal religion.

We should neither consider Judaism a privileged example, nor should we pigeonhole Judaism as the first stage in the emergence of universal religion: these are problems that dog all universal religions. I will examine other religions, but for now there are a few points I wish to emphasize. To begin with, the prohibition on idolatry is often thought to be unique to Judaism. In fact, however, it is common to all universal religions, because a transcendent god must be unrepresentable. The existence of a god who transcends this world cannot possibly be represented in any given form, and for that reason such representation is forbidden.

In general, an idol is regarded as being the reification of some transcendent entity. Yet to regard God as a kind of personality is also a reification, as well as a kind of idolatry. For this reason, in Buddhism the transcendent being is regarded as being *mu*: nothingness. The transcendent being exists neither outside nor inside: it is nothing. In that sense, we can say that Buddhism too aims at prohibiting idolatry. In reality, though, Buddhism has subordinated itself to various states and communities and thereby lapsed into idolatry. The same is true, to a greater or lesser degree, of all universal religions.

Christianity

Jesus was a prophet of Judaism. His condemnation of the Pharisees and scribes followed the pattern of the earlier prophets' criticism of the priestly class. But Jesus's critique was more severe and thoroughgoing than those of his predecessors because he was active in a period when the Jewish people were increasingly living as individuals, separated from the traditional community under the influence of the Roman Empire and money economy. What Jesus was pointing to under these circumstances was a way of life that rejected state, traditional community, and money economy.

I have argued that universal religions appeared in the form of mode of exchange D—that is, as the negation of A, B, and C. We see this in its classic form in the teachings of Jesus—as the following examples from the New Testament show. First, there is his criticism of the Pharisees and scribes: "How well you set aside the commandment of God in order to maintain your tradition!" (Mark 7:9).[17] Then there is his rejection of family and community: "If anyone comes to me and does not hate his father and mother, wife and children, brothers and sisters, even his own life, he cannot be a disciple of mine" (Luke 14:26). Moreover, Jesus protests the inequalities of wealth and class society that are caused by the money economy and private property: "I did not come to invite virtuous people, but sinners" (Mark 2:17). "Sinners" here means not just criminals but also those who engage in supposedly impure occupations, such as tax collectors or prostitutes. Ultimately, these are all economic issues. Sin lies in private property: "So also none of you can be a disciple of mine without parting with all his possessions" (Luke 14:33).

Jesus's teachings can be summed up in two points: "Love the Lord your God with all your heart" and "love your neighbor as yourself" (Mark 12:30, 12:31). The love that Jesus speaks of is not simply a matter of the heart. It means in reality a gift without reciprocation. Jesus's sect was, as Frederick Engels and Karl Kautsky stressed, communistic. This continued after Jesus's death. For example, in Acts, we find the following passages: "Those who accepted his [Peter's] word were baptized, and some three thousand were added to their number that day. They met constantly to hear the apostles teach, and to share the common life, to break bread, and to pray" (Acts 2:41–42). "The whole body of believers was united in heart and soul. Not a man of them claimed any of his possessions as his own, but everything was held in common. . . . All who had property in land or houses sold it, brought the proceeds of the sale, and laid the money at the feet of the apostles; it was then distributed to any who stood in need" (Acts 4:32–35).

Jesus was not the first, however, to establish this kind of communism (associationism). It could be seen earlier in, for example, the Essenes. It is not the sort of thing that has to be invented by somebody. All universal religions in their early stages display this tendency, which shows that they are in fact the return of the repressed, mode of exchange A. In this way, universal religion appears in the form of something that intends a reciprocal, mutual community (association) that resists merchant capitalism, its community, and the state.

Accordingly, the distinguishing characteristics of Jesus's sect were not unique to Christianity. After all, Jesus's followers were simply one sect among many in Judaism. It was Paul who built what we know as Christianity. Followers of Judaism might have recognized Jesus as a prophet, but they could not recognize him as Christ (Messiah), because he did not bring salvation to the followers of Judaism. For this reason, it was easier for non-Jews to accept Jesus as Christ. Paul's preaching that Christ had died as a kind of sacrifice and then returned to life was in a sense universal: to wit, it shared roots with the "totem," as Freud pointed out. In addition, Paul abolished from the sect laws and customs that retained a strong flavor of Judaism. With this, the Jesus-as-Christ religion began to move beyond Judaism to penetrate into the Roman Empire (world empire).

But Christianity was transformed in this process. In the beginning, the disciples moved from place to place like a nomadic band, forming an egalitarian collective. With their success in proselytizing, however, they became something like a fixed-settlement community: a hierarchical group ruled over by priests (officiants). They came to resemble the communal structure of the Pharisee sect that they had originally rejected. At the same time, the Christian church was more than willing to curry favor with the Roman Empire. In the early stages, they believed that the "kingdom of God" would be realized on earth, as was written in the Gospels—and, moreover, that its appearance was imminent. But as this eschatological fervor abated, the kingdom of God was relocated to heaven, rendering it apolitical. Jesus's sayings and deeds acquired a new interpretation. For example, Jesus originally commanded his followers to arm themselves: "Whoever has a purse had better take it with him, and his pack too; and if he has no sword, let him sell his cloak to buy one" (Luke 22:36). But this side of the teachings now disappeared, replaced by a new emphasis on "resist not evil."

Christianity was also frequently persecuted. This was because it clashed with the religions that had existed in Rome since its establishment as a city-state. But on other social and political levels, the church did not conflict with the ruling order of the Roman Empire. For example, the church did not oppose the slavery system. The disappearance of slavery in the waning days of the Roman Empire was simply the result of a drastic rise in the price of slaves, which made slavery economically unfeasible. For these reasons, there was no problem when Rome finally adopted Christianity as its official state religion (this was done by Emperor Theodosius I in 380 CE). This contributed to the expansion of the emperor's power vis-à-vis the aristocracy and various tribal states. Christianity substituted itself for the roles previously played by various clan and agricultural gods.

In this way, when a universal religion penetrates into a state or community, it at the same time gets co-opted by it. Christianity found itself incorporated into the existing structure of king-priest under Asiatic despotism. In fact, in the Eastern Roman Empire (Byzantine), the pope was emperor. This in no way meant that Christianity was powerful. Far from it: this demonstrated the strength of the monarchy. By contrast, in the Western Roman Empire, the imperial power was weak and the church was strong. One reason for this was that in Celtic tribal society, which adopted Christianity, the priestly class had always enjoyed a dominant position. Moreover, the existing forms of tribal society would not permit the existence of a despotic power along the lines of an emperor. As a result, western Europe remained a jumble of numerous feudal lords, and the Church of Rome took on the role of preserving its identity as a world empire. So long as this was true, Christianity might be a world religion (the religion of a world empire), but it could not be a universal religion.

Heresy and Millenarianism

After the fall of the Western Roman Empire, the money economy and cities went into decline. Society took the form of agrarian communities under the control of feudal lords. Christianity penetrated throughout Europe, but in the form of the religions of local communities: new names were slapped onto existing agrarian rituals and customs, so that for example the rites marking the winter solstice and spring equinox were now called Christmas and Easter, respectively. Christianity was indispensable, however, as the sole ideology preserving the identity of the empire in the world that emerged following the collapse of the actual empire. The jumble of kingdoms and feudal fiefdoms were unified by the Church of Rome instead of by a political power. Moreover, the church itself became a landlord holding vast tracts of land—it resembled the feudal lords.

The early form of Christianity was preserved in monasteries. The monasteries dated back to the time of the Roman Empire; during the so-called Dark Ages after the fall of Rome they became the sole locus for the transmission not only of Christianity but also of ancient classical culture and learning. Because the monasteries restored the early Christian sect's principles of communal property and shared labor, they harbored elements fundamentally in conflict with the church structure. The development of production in the monasteries led to corruption, but they also ceaselessly experimented with reforms to counter this. These took the form of an insistence on returning to the ways of the early church during the time of Jesus and his disciples. In this way, Christianity always harbored within itself a movement that demanded a return to primitive Christianity.

Christianity recovered its vitality as a universal religion only when it spread beyond the monasteries—when, that is, it spread to the masses. This occurred around the twelfth century, when the money economy and cities underwent significant development. We see here how mode of exchange D is born in reaction to the ambiguous effects of mode of exchange C. The money economy severs people from the bonds of community and at the same time situates them in new class relations (between those who have money and those who don't). In other words, the money economy simultaneously brings about freedom *and* inequality. Universal religions come into existence in places where mode of exchange C has become the general rule. In places where a tightly knit agrarian community exists, a universal religion becomes simply the religion of the local community. This was the case in medieval Europe.

In the twelfth century, Christianity gained new life. It appealed to the masses of individuals liberated from the bonds of community and stirred into being new social movements. Among the features of this newly reinterpreted Christianity was, first of all, a shift to a this-worldly "City of God" in place of the otherworldly interpretations that had become dominant. This implied moreover that the City of God would be realized historically. A second feature was the rejection of church hierarchy. This led more generally to a rejection of discrimination based on status, wealth, or gender. These two features were clearly linked to popular movements that rose in opposition to the church and feudal society.

The twelfth-century Catharism and Waldensian sects were concrete examples of this kind of social movement. Catharism believed that the City of God would be realized historically in this world. It introduced the notion that this realization would take place through a struggle between good and evil. This world was created by the Jehovah-Satan of the Old Testament, and people would achieve spiritual salvation through Christ. The resemblances to Zoroastrianism and Manichaeism are obvious. Catharism also preached mysticism—the belief that God (transcendence) is imminent within all people. This led not only to a rejection of the ecclesiastical hierarchy but also to a belief in the equality of the masses and between men and women. Naturally, the church regarded this as a heresy, but the movement spread widely, becoming a threat to the feudal lords as well. In the end, Catharism was brutally exterminated by an alliance between the church and the feudal lords (the Albigensian Crusade).

The Waldensian sect, on the other hand, was a movement of lay believers founded by Peter Waldo, who advocated a life of honorable poverty in imitation of Jesus. Waldensians preached their own direct understanding of the spirit of the Gospels, but the social movement that grew out of this was declared a heresy by the church and ruthlessly suppressed. Yet the Vatican also officially recognized the religious orders of Francis of Assisi and Dominic of Osma, which originated from similar beliefs. As this shows, the church itself was obligated to attempt a revival of the original ways of the Christian church—at least to the extent that this did not threaten its own existence.

Standard narratives of religious reformation begin with Martin Luther. The reality is, however, that religious reformation began in many locations starting from the twelfth century. Moreover, reformation was inevitably linked to social movements. Luther's reformation, however, was not: he stood resolutely on the side of those who suppressed the peasant wars that erupted alongside religious reform movements. This explains the respect accorded to Luther's reformation by the church: the reformation closed off Christian belief within the interior of the individual and located the City of God in heaven. Thomas Münzer mobilized the German peasant movement that was suppressed by the feudal lords, with Luther supporting the suppression. Engels writes:

> As Münzer's religious philosophy approached atheism, so his political programme approached communism, and even on the eve of the February Revolution more than one present-day communist sect lacked as comprehensive a theoretical arsenal as was "Münzer's" in the sixteenth century. This programme, which was less a compilation of the demands of the plebeians of that day than a brilliant anticipation of the conditions for the emancipation of the proletarian element that had scarcely begun to develop among the plebeians—this programme demanded the immediate establishment of the kingdom of God on Earth, of the prophesied millennium, by restoring the church to its original status and abolishing all the institutions that conflicted with the purportedly early Christian but in fact very novel church. By the kingdom of God Münzer meant a society with no class differences, no private property

and no state authority independent of, and foreign to, the members of society.[18]

A "state of society without class differences, without private property, and without superimposed state powers opposed to the members of society": this precisely describes a social formation in which mode of exchange D is dominant. Rather than being "a genius's anticipation," what Münzer had grasped was mode of exchange D, the fundamental element of any universal religion: that which supersedes modes of exchange A, B, and C.

I have shown how mode of exchange D as disclosed by universal religions has frequently been manifested in actual social movements that took the form of religious heresies. But the influence of mode of exchange D on historical social formations can be seen in other ways as well: the state, which introduced universal religions in an attempt to shore up its own grounding, ended up engaging in a kind of self-regulation by adopting the "law" that was disclosed by universal religion.

For example, in the case of Europe, as the church became an increasingly fixed part of the state structure, church law was shaped by existing customary laws that originated in Germanic and Roman law. In turn, church law extended a powerful influence over customary law in such matters as protection of the weak (the poor, the ill, orphans, widows, travelers), humane forms of punishment, rationalization of trial procedures, suppression of private feuds (Fehde), and the preservation of peace (Pax Dei, Treuga Dei). Church law also made important contributions to theories of the ethical basis for law and state during the formation of modern national legal codes in the West, as well as to theories of international organizations and methods for peaceful resolution of international conflicts. In these ways, universal religion continues to have an enormous influence on our present-day social formation.

To see this in terms of modes of exchange, social formations, which combine modes A, B, and C, are also influenced by mode of exchange D, an influence that comes through concepts and laws originating in universal religions. Consequently, when we look at the history of social formations, we cannot ignore the moment of mode of exchange D, even though it never actually exists.

Islam, Buddhism, and Taoism

My argument is not meant to privilege Judaism or Christianity. In the processes of empire formation around the world, universal religions appeared when modes of exchange B and C reached a sufficient level of development. They were all different, but their differences were mostly the result of the historical contexts in which each arose. For example, Buddhism began as a deconstructive critique of the priestly rule and religious traditions of reincarnation and related doctrines from within which it emerged. In regions lacking this context, Buddhism produced a doctrine seemingly very similar to that which it originally set out to deconstruct: for example, Buddhism preached both reincarnation and deliverance from reincarnation. The universality of universal religions is found not in the contexts that produced them but rather in the way they deconstructed those contexts.

For example, there is a common notion that Judaism is a monotheism with an anthropomorphic God, while Buddhism is not. Certainly Zen denied the notion of a God with person-like form. Yet in reality, among many Buddhist sects (in particular Pure Land and Jōdo Shinshū), as an expedient means for the masses, the transcendent was depicted as a personified god (Amida Buddha). Shinran, the founder of Jōdo Shinshū, maintained that even though Amida Buddha did not exist, it provided an expedient means to salvation for the masses, to whom the concept of mu (nothingness) was beyond comprehension. We find this same kind of dual structure in so-called monotheistic religions. In the Judaic, Christian, and Islamic traditions, mystics scornfully rejected the idea of understanding God in terms of a kind of personhood—yet in preaching to the masses, they described God in personal terms. If they failed to do so, moreover, they risked being persecuted as heretics. Any explication of the differences between monotheism and Buddhism must take this into account.

The feature common to all universal religions is their critical stance toward kings and priests. Yet every religious group that expanded eventually found itself walking down the very road it had originally negated: it became the official religion of the state, with its clergy as part of the ruling establishment. The religion did not entirely lose its deconstructive force, however: this was revived in various local historical contexts through religious reformations, which took the form of movements to restore the practices of the primitive religious community. We see this, for example, with Islam.

The prophet Muhammad created a movement to restore the nomadic reciprocity-based community that had been lost in Judaism and Christianity. Having said that, this was fundamentally an urban religion, and the community (umma) that it proclaimed was a community on a higher dimension and hence different from the tribal community. But as Islam expanded, even as it rejected the priesthood and monarchy, it was quickly transformed into an ecclesiastic state. Following the death of Muhammad came rule by clergy-kings (caliphs). The religion's doctrine was likewise developed by the priestly class. In fact, it adopted elements of Greek philosophy, especially Aristotle, and followers of Islam became the first to take up the problem of "faith and reason," which would be carried over into medieval European Christendom.

Yet an opposing movement to restore the community (umma) also arose from within the religion, led by imams (teachers or leaders). Worship of the prophet led to enhanced authority for the clergy and monarchy, but the imams linked together in paradoxical fashion God and the individual—transcendence and immanence. Accordingly, for the masses, faith in the imams became even more important than worship of the prophet—especially in the Shia denomination, which worshiped Ali, the murdered son-in-law of Muhammad, as the first imam. Just as Paul rewrote the death of Jesus into a narrative of salvation, Shia Islam finds the key to salvation in the death of Ali. This imam faith would give rise to any number of millenarian social movements that would topple ecclesiastical states. Seen in this light, it is clear that we can apply our basic arguments about Christianity to Islam. In sum, the essence of universal religion lies in the critique of the priesthood-monarchy.[19]

We can say the same thing about Buddhism. Buddha appeared in an age characterized by a jumble of city-states and a rapidly developing money economy. It was also a period that produced a large number of free thinkers, beginning with Mahāvīra (the founder of Jainism). What Buddha carried out was the deconstruction of existing religions. This can be summed up in the rejection as illusion of the belief in an identical self that is repeatedly reincarnated—the rejection, that is, of a key ideology legitimating the caste system. This was moreover a denial of ritual and magic, as well as of the notion that one could earn deliverance from reincarnation through ascetic practice. In other words, it was a wholesale rejection of the priestly (Brahmin) class. Buddha's followers, as one would expect, formed a communistic nomadic band. Buddhism was particularly popular among merchants and women. The belief that women were of a sinful nature would later come to be associated with Buddhism, but this was simply an idea carried over from earlier religious practitioners. It was precisely because early Buddhism rejected this that it was able to win many female followers. At this stage Buddhism received the patronage of merchants and others in the ruling classes but had little connection with the agrarian population.

Buddhism became a religion of empire during the reign of the Maurya dynasty empire-builder Ashoka the Great (third century BCE). Ashoka attempted to realize politically the laws of Buddhism (dharma). Following this, Buddhism achieved a high degree of philosophical elaboration, but it still failed to penetrate into the agrarian community. As a result, when Buddhism lost its political position as official state religion, it disappeared in India. It was replaced by a popular local religion that had absorbed many elements from Buddhism—Hinduism. Buddhism's survival took place elsewhere, outside India. There, too, basically the same thing happened: wherever Buddhism spread and stabilized, it became an ideology supporting the state order, while at the same time fusing with popular local religions. In China, for example, Buddhism was adopted as the official state religion during the Tang dynasty. This was because the Tang court, unlike its predecessors, ruled over a vast empire that extended into Eurasia.

But Buddhism never completely lost the moment of negation of the clergy-monarchy. Outside of India, particularly in East and Southeast Asia, Maitreya worship—the belief that the bodhisattva Maitreya would appear in this world to realize here the Pure Land—spread, giving birth in many places to millenarian movements. In China and Korea this was linked to popular uprisings. After this, though, Buddhism lost its influence there. Aside from Southeast Asia and Tibet, Buddhism took root in Japan. But this was the result of a religious reformation. Buddhism is believed to have entered Japan in the sixth century, when it was an aid in the Yamato court's creation of a centralized power structure; after this, Buddhism was invoked as the spiritual protector of the state. Buddhism in Japan did not manifest the characteristics of a universal religion until the thirteenth century (the Kamakura era), during the transitional period in which clan society collapsed and a new agrarian community took form. In sum, Buddhism became something that appealed to individual believers only after the appearance of individuals who had cut ties with clan society.

It was in particular the Jōdo Shinshū and Nichiren sects, both of which rejected existing sects and clergy, that spread among the ordinary people. This is symbolized by the words of Shinran, who took a wife in violation of precepts that prohibited priests from marrying: "Even a virtuous man can attain Rebirth in the Pure Land, how much more easily a wicked man!"[20] Here "wicked man" does not mean a criminal, but refers instead to those who engaged in occupations that were despised and scorned by society— like the tax collectors and prostitutes of the New Testament. On the other hand "virtuous man" here refers to the wealthy and the ruling class—those who are free from having to engage in such "wicked" tasks. This sort of inversion or overturning of values bears a natural connection to the over-turning of social classes. Beginning in the fifteenth century, Jōdo Shinshū transformed into a millenarian social movement (peasant war), toppling the feudal lords and establishing a commoners' republic (Kaga) and supporting a free city (Sakai) that won autonomy from feudal lords. By the end of the sixteenth century, however, both Kaga and Sakai were annihilated by the centralized political authority that emerged under Toyotomi Hideyoshi and Tokugawa Ieyasu. After this, Buddhism became one link in the administrative apparatus of the Tokugawa shogunate, thereby losing the features that had made it a universal religion.

The founders of universal religion in China were Confucius and Laozi. As I've already described, they appeared in the Spring and Autumn and Warring States periods—that is, in the age when poleis prospered and a Hundred Schools of Thought flourished. In an age when the existing religions of the community were increasingly dysfunctional, Confucius and Laozi subjected these to a rigorous questioning. Their teachings were not presented in the form of a religion—if anything, they were presented as political philosophies, and that is indeed how they functioned. But we can say that both Confucius and Laozi introduced a new notion of God. For Confucius, this was a transcendent heaven, while for Laozi it was a foundational nature. It is unclear when Laozi lived. While it is clear that the texts known as "Laozi" were written long after Confucius's age, we also cannot dismiss the theory that Laozi was active prior to Confucius. It seems that Laozi was not a specific individual but rather several persons, or perhaps a group. For my purposes here, though, I want to stress the side of Laozi that is critical of Confucius.

Confucius's preaching can be summed up as the reconstruction of human relations on the basis of benevolence. In terms of modes of exchange, benevolence meant the pure, unreciprocated gift. The essence of Confucius's teachings (Confucianism), in other words, was the restoration of the clan community. This meant a return of the clan community in a higher dimension, not simply a restoration of tradition. This social reformist aspect of Confucius's thought was stressed in particular by Mencius. In historical reality, however, Confucianism ended up functioning as a ruling philosophy for maintaining the existing order not through law or ability but rather through communal rites and blood relations.

Laozi rigorously opposed this, preaching instead a spontaneous nature. "Spontaneous" here did not mean doing nothing: it rather signified a negation of the positive action (construction of the state system) advocated by Confucianism and the Legalist School—in short, it signaled an active attempt to deconstruct Confucianism and the Legalist School. Laozi rejected not only the centralized state but also clan society itself, calling them both artificial systems. If Confucius aimed at the restoration of the clan community, then we might call this an attempt to restore the lifestyle of the nomadic hunter-gatherer peoples. In reality, however, even Laozi's teachings ended up functioning as a kind of ruling ideology. This was because they were easily co-opted into Legalist thought, which advocated that rulers do nothing and simply leave everything up to the rule of law.

Among the Hundred Schools of Thought, the most effective and powerful in political terms were the Legalists, who built Qin into a powerful state through their advocacy of rule by law. In particular, Han Fei, who served the first Qin emperor, promoted policies that severed clan ties and created a strong centralized order by establishing a bureaucratic structure and a standing army. As soon as the first Qin emperor established the empire, he launched a ruthless suppression of Confucianism, condemning it as an anti-Legalist school of thought that supported a feudalistic (i.e., regionally decentralized) community. He launched the "burn books and bury Confucian scholars alive" campaign.

The Qin dynasty was quite short-lived, however. In the early stages of the Han dynasty that followed it, Laozi and his spontaneous nature philosophy became official doctrine. This was effective during the period of recovery for the society that had been devastated under the Qin dynasty's rule by law and terror. But the third emperor, Wu Di, sought to use Confucianism, with its grounding in the clan community, as a state ideology. Confucianism, which until this had idealized the feudal society of the Zhou dynasty and rejected the idea of a strong, centralized state, now underwent a metamorphosis, adopting the Legalist doctrine of a centralized state. Thereafter Confucianism played the role of bolstering the state order by advocating for communal rites and blood ties.

This is hardly a comprehensive accounting of Confucianism. We cannot overlook how, in the subsequent history of Confucianism, social-reformist thought grounded in the concept of benevolence would reappear—as with, for example, Wang Yangming—and give rise to various social movements. Likewise, Laozi's thought would function not just as a ruling ideology; his thought would also remain a fountain of utopianism and anarchism that rejected the very notion of ruling. Laozi's philosophy was at first known only to intellectuals, but it was popularized after he came to be regarded as the founder of Taoism. Laozi was in fact completely unrelated to the magical practices of Taoism, but his thought did become a factor when Taosim erupted in popular movements against the court. In Chinese history, the first recorded popular uprising is the Yellow Turban Rebellion near the end of the Han dynasty, a millenarian movement grounded in Taoism. It opened the path to the collapse of the empire, and in subsequent Chinese history, periods of dynastic turnover are frequently marked by the rise of religious social movements similar to the Yellow Turban Rebellion. For example, Zhu Yuanzhang, the founder of the Ming dynasty, was a leader of this kind of movement.[21]

PART THREE   THE MODERN WORLD SYSTEM

I n the preceding chapters, I considered the features of social formations in which mode of exchange B is predominant. In part III I will take up social formations in which mode of exchange C dominates. First, though, there is one issue we must consider: how did mode of exchange C become dominant? Mode of exchange C—commodity exchange—had existed since ancient times, but no matter how extensively it was practiced, it was never able to topple the social formation in which mode of exchange B was dominant. Yet somehow this did in fact occur in Europe.

Marxists have debated this as the problem of the "transition from feudalism to capitalism."[1] Paul Sweezy stresses that capitalism emerged thanks to the development of trade that preceded it—especially the influx of silver from the Americas. Maurice Dobb, on the other hand, highlights the internal collapse of feudalism. What we have here is a disagreement between those who emphasize the role of the process of circulation (Sweezy) and those who emphasize the process of production (Dobb). We cannot resolve this conflict if we solely depend on the writings of Karl Marx, because Marx offered both perspectives.

For example, he writes: "The genuine science of modern economics begins only when theoretical discussion moves from the circulation process to the production process."[2] Here Marx locates the origins of modern capitalism in manufactures—in, moreover, manufactures launched by producers (independent farmers) acting as capitalists. In other words, he locates the origins of modern capitalism in the internal collapse of feudal society. Dobb is not alone here: Marxists in general have tended to stress this aspect.

But at the same time, Marx also writes: "The circulation of commodities is the starting-point of capital. The production of commodities and their circulation in its developed form, namely trade, form the historic presuppositions under which capital arises. World trade and the world market date from the sixteenth century, and from then on the modern history of capital starts to unfold."[3] In Marx's view, this "world-embracing market" emerged in concrete terms in the fifteenth century with the linking of the international economies of the Baltic and Mediterranean regions and furthermore in the sixteenth century with the opening of intercourse that joined together

Europe, the Americas, and Asia. European capitalist development is unthinkable in the absence of a world market that brings together the hitherto isolated world-empires. Sweezy's view rests on this, and Immanuel Wallenstein's argument that the world-economy began in sixteenth-century Europe likewise follows this same line.

But neither view is able to explain why a capitalist economy emerged in Europe. In terms of the view that stresses production, before we talk about the collapse of feudalism, we need to examine why and how the specific form of feudalism found in Europe arose—it is not sufficient merely to regard it is a simple variation of the tribute state system. In terms of the view that stresses circulation, we need to explain how and why world trade and the world market began from Europe. These were of a different nature from the trade carried out under earlier world-empires. These two problems are in fact not unrelated: the world trade that began from Europe cannot be understood separately from its feudalism.

In taking up these questions, I would like to begin by distinguishing between world-empire and world-economy, following Fernand Braudel. The difference between these revolves around whether or not the state controls trade. In world-empires, state officials monopolize trade and regulate the price of foodstuffs and other goods. In contrast, a world-economy emerges when trade and local markets are integrated and there is no state control. In these terms, Wallerstein argues that the world-economy appeared in sixteenth-century Europe and proceeded to swallow up the existing world-empires around the globe, reorganizing the world into a structure of core, semiperiphery, and periphery.

Braudel, however, rejects the idea that there was a "development" from world-empire to world-economy.[4] He argues that Europe was already a world-economy before the sixteenth century—and, moreover, that world-economy was not limited to Europe. As Karl Polanyi notes, Greece and Rome also had world-economies. Greece did not adopt the sort of bureaucratic structure needed to regulate the economy, leaving matters instead up to the market. This was not because Greece was an "advanced" civilization. To the contrary, it was due to the strong persistence of the traditions of clan autonomy, as well as to a geographical location that allowed Greece to fend off external interference even as it adopted elements from the civilization of a world-empire—that is, to its location on the submargin of a world-empire.

In the same way, a world-economy emerged in western Europe not because its civilization was advanced but rather because it was located on the submargin of the Roman Empire and its successor, the Arabian world-empire. There were attempts in Europe to establish a world-empire, but these ended in failure. A centralized state never emerged, and instead there was a state of perpetual conflict among the numerous kings and feudal lords. The flip side to this was that trade and markets were left free, without state control, which resulted in the establishment of a large number of free cities. For these reasons, we cannot treat European feudalism and world-embracing commerce as if they were unrelated to one another.

Braudel compares the various world-economies and extracts a conventional tendency that they share in common: in each world-economy, there tends to be one center, a central city (world-city). In a world-empire, one city serves as the political center. But in a world-economy, being the political center does not automatically make a city the central city. To the contrary, the tendency is for the city that is at the center of trade to become politically central as well. Moreover, in world-economies the center continually shifts from one location to another.

Braudel writes, "A world-economy always has an urban centre of gravity, a city, as the logistic heart of its activity. News, merchandise, capital, credit, people, instructions, correspondence all flow into and out of the city."[5] Multiple relay cities emerge in the distance surrounding this center. Because these compete with one another, the center is never permanently fixed but is always subject to relocation. We see this, for example, in the way the world-city has shifted from Antwerp to Amsterdam to London to New York. Of course, in world-empires the center is also located in a city and sometimes sees shifts, but these are usually due to political or military factors. In a world-economy, by contrast, the political center tends to move in tandem with shifts in the central city.

In a world-empire, the spatial structure of core and periphery is primarily established in accordance to the character of political and military power. The size of an empire is determined first of all logistically (i.e., by military supply and communications lines). If one wants to not simply conquer territory but also permanently control it, there are limits to how far one can extend oneself. Second, the size of an empire is determined by the ratio between the wealth it can obtain by expanding its boundaries and the cost of the army and bureaucratic structures needed to accomplish this. A world-economy, on the other hand, has no limit, because commodity exchanges can be expanded spatially without limit. Their existence requires, however, the legal and security guarantees provided by the state. For this reason, world-economies have historically tended to been toppled or annexed by world-empires. But the modern world-economy that spread from western Europe reversed this pattern: it swallowed up the existing world-empires.

The structure of world-empires consisted of core, margin, submargin, and the out of sphere. But once we reach a situation in which a world-economy has spread to cover the entire globe, world-empires are no longer able to exist as the core. This also means that margins and submargins no longer exist. On the other hand, even in a world-economy we find a geopolitical center and periphery structure. Andre Gunder Frank was the first to point this out, calling center and periphery "metropolis" and "satellite," respectively.[6] In his view, a world-economy is a system in which the center extracts surpluses from the periphery. As a result, the development of the core leads to underdevelopment in the periphery: it's not that the periphery was undeveloped from the start, but rather that it is subjected to underdevelopment through its relations with the core. Wallerstein added the concept of the semiperiphery to this. The semiperiphery can at times join the core, but at other times the semiperiphery can fall back into the periphery. In this way, the world-economy is structured around the core, semiperiphery, and periphery.

This resembles the structure of core, submargin, and margin that Karl Wittfogel proposed for world-empires. There is, however, a decisive difference between the structures of world-empires and world-economies. In a world-empire, the core extracts surpluses from the periphery by means of violent coercion, but this becomes more and more difficult the further into the periphery one penetrates. In order to expand the territory of its empire, the core must divert its surplus into the periphery. For example, the tributary diplomatic relations of imperial China were actually reciprocal exchanges in which the countergifts offered by the emperor were greater than the tribute received. It was through this kind of gift giving that the emperor maintained his dignity and expanded the domains under his control.

Under the structure of a world-economy, however, the core extracts surpluses from the periphery not so much by direct exploitation as through simple commodity exchange. Moreover, whereas in a world-empire the periphery manufactures raw materials into products that it ships to the core, under the structure of a world-economy, it is the periphery that supplies raw materials and the core that manufactures and processes these. In this international division of labor, the manufacturing side produces greater value. The core extracts surplus value by integrating the periphery into this international division of labor.

THE MODERN WORLD SYSTEM

To sum up, in world-empires the accumulation and extraction of wealth occurs by way of an exchange of violent coercion for security—in other words, it is based on mode of exchange B. In world-economies, on the other hand, the accumulation and extraction of wealth takes place through commodity exchange—mode of exchange C. This system, which originated in Europe, quickly transformed all previously existing world systems. Before we turn to this, however, there are a couple of additional points we should note.

First, while it is a fact that during the expansion of the world market and global capitalism, the previous world-empires were rendered peripheral, this took place not in the sixteen century but rather began in the nineteenth century—with the exceptions of the Aztec (Mexico) and Incan (Peru, Bolivia) empires. Nonetheless, the overwhelming superiority that Europe has enjoyed since the nineteenth century has distorted our image of what preceded it. During the period of expansion of the European world-economy starting in the sixteenth century, Asia was no longer ruled by the ancient empires; it was neither stagnant nor in decline. Following the collapse of the great Mongolian Empire, world-empires were reconstructed across Asia, including the Qing dynasty in China, the Mughal Empire in India, and the Ottoman Empire in Turkey. Each of these enjoyed considerable economic development. Frank writes that the empires of early modern Asia, in particular China, maintained economic superiority over Europe until the end of the eighteenth century.[7] The development of the world-economy in modern Europe was achieved by using the silver obtained in the Americas to enter into trade with China and Southeast Asia. Moreover, as Joseph Needham has demonstrated, China was far more advanced in scientific technology than the West up through the sixteenth century.[8]

Second, even in regions situated on the periphery of the global world-economy, geopolitical structural differences between the core, margin, submargin, and out of sphere of the older world-empires persist. For example, whereas the margin and out-of-sphere regions of the old empires were easily colonized by the European powers, their cores and submargins were not. Japan, located in a submarginal region, rapidly adapted itself to the world-economy and eventually even joined its core, while both Russia and China, cores of old world-empires, resisted their own marginalization within the world-economy, with each attempting to reconstruct a new world system. The socialist revolutions in Russia and China should be understood in these terms. Usually, world-empires were split up into multiple ethnicities—that is, into multiple nation-states. The ability of Russia and China to avoid this fate was due to their being ruled by Marxists, who saw problems of class as more fundamental than those of ethnicity. Marxists did not intend to resurrect empires though. In Marx's words, "They do this without being aware of it."[9]

SEVEN **THE MODERN STATE**

Absolute Monarchy

Commerce and trade developed under the world-empires, but they were subject to monopoly control by the state, so that the principle of commodity exchange was unable to eclipse the other modes of exchange. A world-economy—in other words, a situation in which the principle of commodity exchange dominates over the other modes—could arise only in a region that lacked a unified, centralized state: western Europe. There political and religious power were not unified into a single entity, as was the case in the Eastern Roman Empire, the domain of the Greek Orthodox Church, or the Islamic world. Instead the region saw ongoing conflict between the church, emperors, monarchs, and feudal lords. Taking advantage of these clashes, free cities were established. Which is to say, cities existed as small states, on equal terms with monarchs and feudal lords.

The origins of the centralized state in Europe came with the absolutist-monarchy states (hereafter, absolute monarchies). These were established when kings subjugated the many feudal lords who had previously claimed equivalent status and stripped the church of its ruling authority. Several things made this possible. First among these was the invention of firearms with hitherto unprecedented destructive force. Firearms rendered obsolete previous forms of warfare and made the status of the noble-warrior meaningless. From the perspective of establishing the state's monopoly over violence, this represented a crucial step.

Another factor was the penetration of a money economy. For example, by the fourteenth century in England, feudal lords had in actual practice become a landlord class, accepting payment of land rent from the peasantry in place of feudal tribute. In their own consciousnesses they were still feudal lords though, and they continued to enjoy various feudal privileges. In this situation, the king allied with urban merchants and manufacturers to abolish the various privileges of the feudal lords and to monopolize the land tax system; moreover, the king encouraged trade in order to increase customs revenues and income taxes. The feudal lords, stripped of their power, became landlords and court aristocrats dependent on stipends distributed from the state's tax revenues. In this manner, the money economy brought about the bureaucracies and standing army that would become pillars of the absolute monarchy.

It is important to note, however, that overwhelming military power, a money economy, the subjugation of multiple tribes, and mercantilist state policies were not unique to the absolute monarchies. These attributes were found in antiquity too, in the process of formation of despotic tribute-system states. In this respect, the two systems share a number of aspects in common. As noted, in discussing the differences between feudalism and what he called "patriarchal patrimonialism" (i.e., the Asiatic state), Max Weber pointed to the existence of social-welfare policies.[1] Under feudalism, administrative functions were kept to an absolute minimum, with consideration given to the living conditions of subjects only to the extent necessary for the regime's own economic survival; by contrast, under patriarchal patrimonialism, the range of administrative concerns was maximized. On this point, Weber argues, the absolute monarchy resembled the despotic tribute-system states considerably more than it did the feudal state.

The resemblance of absolute monarchy to Asiatic despotism lies in its establishment of a centralized state apparatus. But the makeup of this apparatus was different. While the Asiatic despotic state was characterized by a social formation in which mode of exchange B was dominant, in actual practice the social formation of the absolute monarchy was one dominated by mode of exchange C. This is why the collapse of an Asiatic despotic state quickly led to the rise of another similar state, whereas the collapse of an absolute monarchy led to the emergence of bourgeois society.

On this point the absolute-monarchy state was fundamentally different from the Asiatic despotic state (world-empire). It arose in western Europe—a region that had no world-empires. Western Europe was unified under the Roman Catholic Church, but this did not entail political unification. An emperor existed in name only, being completely dependent on church support. In actual practice, the church, king, feudal lords, cities, and other entities existed in a confused state of simultaneous competition and interdependence. This was the condition from which the absolute monarchy emerged.

The absolute monarchy arose through the subjugation of the other feudal lords and cities. This is not, however, something that occurred internally within a single country. For example, the difficulties a king faces in quelling the feudal lords and others who resist his rise are due to the existence behind them of the church and the kings of other lands: civil wars instantly become foreign wars. So in order for the king to suppress the other lords and establish a monarchy, it was necessary to check the influence in his country of any external, transcendent agent. In this process the greatest obstacles were the church and the concept of an empire that the church backed.

The absolute monarchy is *absolute* in two senses. First, the monarchy was absolute in the sense that in a given realm, the monarch, who previously held a position as the first among many feudal lords, now stood in an absolute position, far above the other lords (aristocrats). Second, the monarchy was absolute in the sense that it rejected any higher-dimension structure or concept (e.g., church or emperor) standing above it. This does not mean that the monarch now stood in the position of an emperor. To the contrary, the absolute monarch deliberately rejected the position of emperor. This in itself implied recognition of the existence of other absolute monarchies. As a result, the notion of an empire that unified multiple peoples was abandoned, and a system of coexistence of multiple absolute monarchies emerged.

It was in this manner that a previously unknown type of centralized state emerged from western Europe. The sixteenth-century philosopher Jean Bodin termed this kind of absolute monarchy "sovereignty."[2] He took up sovereignty in terms of two aspects: first, externally in terms of independence from such universal authorities as the Holy Roman emperor or the pope; and second, internally, as an entity that stands above all other powers within the realm and transcends all differences of status, region, language, and religion. This duality is the duality that characterizes the absolute monarchy.

In general the state is shaped by both its interior and its relations with foreign states. For this reason, it is natural to think of sovereignty in terms of two distinct aspects, one internally and one externally oriented. But

Bodin's sovereign state grew out of the particular context of Europe. Sovereign states were formed through a process of mutual recognition. No higher entity, such as an empire, was recognized. This type of sovereign state emerged within the territory of Europe, however, and was not well suited for regions outside Europe. Why, then, did this type of state become the principle for the modern state in general?

This was due in part to the economic and military superiority of the European powers. But the adoption of the concept of the sovereign state as a general principle came about because the European powers applied this principle of the sovereign state in ruling over non-Western regions. First of all, the concept of the sovereign state itself implies that countries lacking a recognized sovereign state could therefore be ruled over by others: Europe's world conquest and imperial rule were sustained by this idea. Consequently, countries that wanted to escape from this kind of external rule had to declare themselves sovereign states and win recognition as such from the Western powers.

Second, the Western powers were incapable of directly interfering with the world empires that already existed, such as the Ottoman, Qing, and Mughal Empires. Instead, the Western powers denounced the imperial form of governance and seemed to offer liberation and sovereignty (popular self-rule) to the various peoples ruled by those empires. As a result, the old world empires collapsed and were divided up into multiple ethnic states, each of which followed the road to independence as a sovereign state. To summarize, the existence of a sovereign state inevitably leads to the creation of other sovereign states. Even if its origins were particular to European conditions, the sovereign state inevitably led to the birth of sovereign states around the globe—just as the world-economy that began in Europe likewise became global.

State and Government

The sovereign state may arise internally through a process of centralization, but its essence is as an entity that exists in relation to the outside. In the case of absolute monarchies, this was clearly evident. But this fact seemed to get overlooked in the period following the bourgeois revolutions that overthrew the absolute monarchies. For example, John Locke took the state to be a social contract entered into by the citizens, who were its sovereigns. But this view considers the state only in terms of its interior: the state is reduced to being the government that represents the people, who are the sovereigns. This view loses sight of the fact that a state exists above all in relation to other states. Furthermore, with absolute monarchies, as their mercantilist policies demonstrate, it is self-evident that we are dealing with a union of capital and state—in other words, that the state and capitalism are inseparable. After the bourgeois revolutions toppled the absolute monarchies, however, this reality was forgotten, because a split was introduced between the political and the economic. The nature of the state was misperceived in the viewpoint that emerged following the bourgeois revolutions, as well as in today's ideologies that continue to adopt that viewpoint.

It may be useful to take up Thomas Hobbes again at this point. Compared to Locke and his criticism of the absolute monarchy, Hobbes seems to have supported the absolute monarchy. But Hobbes wrote *Leviathan* in the midst of the English Puritan Revolution. In the Puritan Revolution, the overthrow of the absolute monarchy in 1648 was followed by Cromwell's dictatorship, and then, after that was toppled in 1660, a restoration of the monarchy and the establishment of constitutional monarchy with the so-called Glorious Revolution of 1688. Locke's *Two Treatises of Government* tried to provide a theoretical grounding for this. If that is so, what was Hobbes's *Leviathan* trying to provide a theoretical grounding for? His publication of the work after the fall of the absolute monarch came not because he was trying to vindicate the latter. What he was trying to defend was the sovereign as the entity capable of bringing an end to civil war.

In the era of the absolute monarch, the theory of the "divine rights of kings" was sufficient to situate the monarch as a transcendental being. But in Hobbes's view, the absolute monarchy could not be called the sovereign (Leviathan): although he had undoubtedly subjugated the aristocracy (feudal lords), these still persisted as what Montesquieu called "intermediate powers." This meant that the possibility still existed for civil war and foreign intervention. But the Puritan Revolution wiped out these intermediate powers. Accordingly, it was in the kingless republic that an absolute sovereign (Leviathan) took form. But *Leviathan* can hardly be said to advocate republican government. In Hobbes's mind, the key issue, whether in a monarchy or republic, was the existence of the sovereign and its concomitant abolition of the "state of war." This was the social contract in Hobbes's meaning. What Locke called the social contract was something that could only emerge after this.

As I've noted, Hobbes argues that the "attaining to this sovereign power is by two ways." One is a "Commonwealth by acquisition," grounded in a covenant that is "extorted by fear." The other is "Commonwealth by Institution," which arises "when men agree amongst themselves to submit to some man, or assembly of men, voluntarily, on confidence to be protected by him against all others."[3] In Hobbes's view, it is the covenant "extorted" by fear that is fundamental; the kind of covenant Locke described is only secondary.

Hobbes's view takes up the sovereign not within the interior of the state but in its relations with the exterior. If one focuses only on the interior, then the question of whether the king or the people will be sovereign seems to make a great difference. But seen from, for example, the perspective of the Irish, there was little difference between the absolute monarchy and Oliver Cromwell: no matter how the English system of government changed, the sovereign state still acted in the same manner. In Hobbes's thinking, it made no difference if the sovereign was a monarchy, aristocracy, or democracy: whether sovereign power was held by an individual or by a parliamentary body did not change its nature: "For elective kings are not sovereigns, but ministers of the sovereign; nor limited kings sovereigns, but ministers of them that have the sovereign power; nor are those provinces which are in subjection to a democracy or aristocracy of another Commonwealth demo-cratically or aristocratically governed, but monarchically."[4] For example, the Greek poleis were democracies within their interior—the sovereign power was a legislative body made up of the citizens. Yet in relation to their colo-nies or slaves, they governed monarchically.

Locke and the philosophers who arose after the bourgeois revolutions regarded each individual person as a subject, and their understanding of the "social contract" took as its point of departure these individuals (the na-tional people). But for Hobbes, all persons except for the sovereign were subjects of that sovereign. The collective national subject, that is, began with subjects subordinated to absolute sovereign. Popular sovereignty orig-inated from the absolute monarchy and cannot be understood apart from it. When the absolute monarchy is toppled, it appears as if the national people become sovereign. But the idea of sovereignty is not something that can be understood solely from within the interior of a nation. Sovereignty exists first of all in relation to the outside. As a result, even if an absolute monarchy is overthrown, there is no change in the nature of sovereignty as it exists in relation to other states.

State and Capital

The essence of the state as sovereign escapes us if we only look within the interior of the state, but that essence manifests itself at times of war. For this reason, Carl Schmitt sought to understand the sovereign in terms of "the state of exception."[5] Why does the essential nature of the state come out in war? Because the state is above all an entity existing in relation to other states. In its externally oriented aspect, the state reveals elements of itself that differ from the way it appears when viewed from within. In the theories of social contract that became mainstream thought in the wake of the bourgeois revolutions, the will of the state was believed to be the will of the people, who through elections were represented by the government. But the state is different from the government, just as the state possesses a will independent from the will of the people. This becomes plainly evident in states of exception, such as times of war.

This was always clearly visible under the absolute monarchies, as well as in states prior to the modern period. Only since the rise of the nation-state has the will of the state become invisible. Ordinarily, the people who compose the nation are not aware that the state is perpetually in a state of warfare, always in a state of military readiness. Wars appear to break out unexpectedly. In reality, though, they are anticipated, the object of long-term preparation and strategic planning. They are implemented in practice by state apparatuses—the standing army and bureaucracy. These appeared in western Europe with the absolute monarchies. What happened to the military and bureaucratic state apparatuses after the absolute monarchies were abolished by the bourgeois revolutions? Far from being abolished, they were expanded, both qualitatively and quantitatively. This was not done for the sake of the people. Even when sovereignty lies with the people, the state seeks to preserve itself for its own sake. If we take up the state only in terms of its interior, we remain blind to this reality.

The autonomy of the state and its possession of an independent will are invisible from within the interior of that state. This is because in that interior, various forces are always contending with each other, producing a tangled field of competing opinions, interests, and desires. Nonetheless, when a state confronts another state, it acts as if it possesses a single unified will. In short, when viewed from outside, the state appears as a being that exists independently from the people. This means that at the level of interstate relations, the state manifests as something estranged from the appearance it usually presents within the interior—as, in other words, something *alienated*.

Seen only from the perspective of its interior, the state does not seem particularly difficult to abolish. Both P.-J. Proudhon and the early Karl Marx understood the modern state as the self-alienation of civil society: the public nature of society was alienated into the state, while civil society became the private, bourgeois realm. In this view, if one returned the public nature to civil society, or if the class contradictions of civil society were abolished, the state would simply disappear. This way of thinking remains influential today, as seen, for example, in Jürgen Habermas's claim that the state as a form of self-alienation can be overcome by strengthening the public nature of civil society, a view that sees the state only from the perspective of its interior. But the difficulty of abolishing the state arises because it exists in relation to other states. This is most nakedly manifested in war. Of course, it is not necessary for there to be an actual outbreak of warfare—the existence of an enemy country is in itself sufficient.

Another aspect that was clearly visible under absolute monarchies but rendered ambiguous with the nation-state was capital-state—that is, the union of capital and state. Under the absolute monarchies, it was clear that capitalism was promoted by the state: the state participated as an active agent. But in the bourgeois state that emerged after the bourgeois revolutions, the state came to be regarded as an organ representing the interests of the bourgeoisie, or alternately as the site of political expression of the class interests of civil society. It was not considered to be in itself an active agent. By contrast, in the absolute monarchies, the state unambiguously showed itself to be an active agent. For example, Frederick Engels understood absolute monarchy to be a phenomenon of the period of transition from feudal to bourgeois society—it was only at times like that, he thought, that the state (absolute monarchy) played an independent, unique role. But it was in fact absolute monarchy that revealed the essential nature of capital-state and the independence of the state, aspects that were subsequently rendered invisible in bourgeois society.

The union of capital and state is particularly manifest in two aspects. First, we see it in the issuance of government bonds. Absolute monarchy used this "enchanter's wand" (Marx) to collect taxes in advance whenever it wanted.[6] At the same time, public debt became the origin of the modern banking and international credit systems.[7] Second, we see the union in protectionist state policies. The development of English industrial capital was possible thanks to protection provided by state, and it was only natural in the late-developing capitalist countries that lagged behind England that the rise of industrial capitalism would likewise rely on the state. In these cases, what was needed was an absolutist system, whether or not it was a monarchy per se. As this shows, for capitalist economies the state is not merely part of the superstructure: it is an indispensable basic component.

For example, the state carries out so-called public works that are essential to industrial capitalism, such as the development of roads and harbors. Among the tasks carried out by the state, the most important for industrial capitalism is the cultivation of an industrial proletariat. This does not simply mean the poor: it means a disciplined, industrious population, one equipped with skills that allow it to quickly adapt to a wide variety of new jobs. Members of the industrial proletariat are moreover consumers who buy products with the money they earn through wage labor—they are not self-sufficient, like farmers. Capital is unable by itself to produce this kind of industrial proletariat (labor-power commodity). The state must take on this task. In concrete terms, the state carries this out through such measures as school education and military conscription. The contribution made by the latter in training an urban proletariat outweighs even its military importance.

In absolute monarchies, the state appeared in the form of the state apparatuses of the military and bureaucracy. Following the bourgeois revolutions, bureaucratic officials came to be considered public servants who executed the will of the people as expressed and approved by parliament. Everyone knows, however, that this is not the real situation. G. W. F. Hegel, for example, writes the following about parliaments and officials: "For the highest officials within the state necessarily have a more profound and comprehensive insight into the nature of the state's institutions and needs, and are more familiar with its functions and more skilled in dealing with them, so that they *are able* to do what is best even without the Estates, just as they must continue to do what is best when the Estates are in session."[8] According to Hegel, the mission of the legislature is to obtain the consent of civil society, to engage in politics to improve civil society, and to elevate people's knowledge of and respect for the affairs of state. In other words, the legislature is not a venue that determines state policies in accord with the views of the people, but rather a venue that conveys to the people decisions made by officials in a manner so as to make it seem as if the people themselves had decided them.

We cannot simply attribute this view to Hegel's personal disregard for legislatures or to the immaturity of Prussian democracy. In today's advanced nations that are supposed to have highly developed parliamentary democracies, bureaucratic control grows stronger and stronger in reality, but it is made to appear otherwise. Parliamentary democracy is an elaborate procedure to make the people think that they have decided on proposals that are actually crafted by bureaucrats and other officials.

It was in the twentieth century, it is frequently argued, that the state began to deploy Keynesian economic interventions, as well as introduce policies designed to foster social welfare, labor, and education. And yet there has never been a time when the state did not intervene in the economy. For example, nineteenth-century liberalism was the "economic policy" of the English state, which enjoyed global hegemony both politically and economically, but that liberalism was grounded in enormous military budgets and taxation schemes designed to preserve the status quo of the system. In late-developing capitalist countries that adopted protectionist policies, such as France, Germany, and Japan, state intervention in the economy was self-evident. It was the state that caused the development of the capitalist economy, and it was the bureaucratic apparatus of the state that carried this out.

In recent years, some Marxists have viewed these seeming changes as marking a transformation of the contemporary state. But the adoption of welfare policies is hardly unique to the contemporary state, nor is it simply an obfuscation designed to mask class domination. As I have stressed repeatedly, these are phenomena that could be widely seen in both Asiatic despotism and absolute monarchies.

Moreover, in recent years many have both stressed the relative autonomy of the state and rejected the idea that power exists only in the state. This position originally derives from views espoused by Antonio Gramsci, who challenged the conventional Marxist view of the state as a violent apparatus of bourgeois class domination. He distinguished between power, grounded in violent coercion, and hegemony, which obtains the consent of the ruled. In other words, he pointed out that the state order did not solely consist of the apparatuses of violence, but also included ideological apparatuses (family, school, church, media, and so on) that caused its members to voluntarily consent to its rule. Michel Foucault further elaborated this view, arguing that individual subjects were produced via the internalization of power through discipline and that power was not a substance existing at the core but rather something ubiquitous in the form of a network.

These views remain valid as critiques of old-style Marxists who perceive state power as a violent apparatus in service of bourgeois class domination. But such views take up the state only in terms of its interior—in other words, they are blind to the aspects of the state that can only be seen in its relations with other states. The state's distinctive form of power will never be understood if we view it only from the perspective of its interior. People who take such a view tend to stress the role of hegemony in civil society and the social coercive power of the community or market economy, rather than state power. As a result, they underestimate state power and the autonomy of the state, thinking them insignificant. But the autonomy of the state only becomes visible when one grasps the state in its relations with other states.

Marx's Theory of the State

According to social-contract theory, the state is based on the voluntary will of the people. But this conflates state with government. Marxists, on the other hand, have seen the state as a tool for domination by one economic class (the bourgeoisie). In Marxists' inability to recognize the independence of the state, they resemble the social-contract theorists. Marxists believed that if class conflict were abolished, the state would wither away on its own. This view permitted the temporary seizure of state power for the purpose of abolishing the capitalist economy. But in reality, the state is in itself an independent entity: it is not and cannot be a mere means to some other end. Those who regard the state as a means are doomed to be used as a means by that state.

For example, socialist revolutions may appear to abolish the previously existing state machinery. But this immediately invites outside interference, and so in order to defend the revolution, revolutionary regimes end up having to rely on the old military and bureaucratic apparatuses. As a result, the old state machinery is not only preserved but even strengthened. Any attempt to understand the state only from the perspective of its interior will lead not to its abolition but rather to its reinvigoration. The Russian Revolution provides a good example: seen from the perspective of the state, it actually ended up preventing the dissolution of the former Russian empire into discrete nation-states and contributed to its reconstruction as a new world-empire.

Marx had penetrating insight into the nature of capitalism, but his understanding of the state was inadequate. For example, in *Capital* he argues that the total income earned by capital is distributed across three forms—profit, land rent, and wages—and that these in turn lead to the formation of the three major social classes. This essentially carries on David Ricardo's view, but with a decisive difference on one point. While Ricardo stresses the importance of taxes in his *On the Principles of Political Economy and Taxation*, Marx eliminates them from his system. For Ricardo, taxes are a levy by the state against the earnings of capital, which in a sense implicitly suggests the existence of a class (the military and bureaucracy) based on tax revenues. For this reason, the problem of taxation is the key to political economy. But Marx abstracts away the state, as well as the class formed by the military and bureaucracy.

The practical absence of the state from *Capital*, Marx's most important work, led Marxists either to neglect the problem of the state or to return to theories of the state found in Marx's works written before *Capital*. Generally speaking, for the early Marx, the state was an "imaginary community," whereas in his midperiod he considered the state primarily as an instrument of class domination. But in certain works, such as *The Eighteenth Brumaire of Louis Bonaparte* (1851), we find reflections that go beyond these rather simplistic views. This work analyzes the nightmare-like process by which Louis Bonaparte—whose only prior distinction was his status as Napoleon Bonaparte's nephew—became emperor following the 1848 revolution in France.

Here Marx does not fail to see how the state machinery (the bureaucratic apparatus) exists as a class of its own. He moreover does not fail to see the role played by various classes that do not fit into the major categories of capital, wage labor, or land rent—most notably, the small-scale farmers (small-holding peasants). His complete disregard of these in *Capital* signals his intentional bracketing them off in order to grasp in its purest form the system produced by the mode of commodity exchange. This in no way means that we can ignore the state when we look at the capitalist economy. It was acceptable provisionally to bracket the question of the state because state intervention in the economy obeys the various principles of a capitalist economy.

In general, Marxists in the past took the various political parties existing in capitalist states to be reflections of actual economic relations. In contrast, today's Marxists tend to view political structures and ideologies as being overdetermined by economic structures—that is to say, as possessing relative autonomy from economic structures. This view originally arose from the experience of fascism and the setbacks suffered by revolutions following the First World War. For example, Wilhelm Reich criticized the Marxists of his day and turned to psychoanalysis to seek the reasons for the German people's attraction to Nazism, which he located in what he called the authoritarian ideology of the family and the sexual repression that followed from it.[9] Subsequently, the Frankfurt School would also introduce psychoanalysis into its work. But if we go back to *The Eighteenth Brumaire of Louis Bonaparte* itself, there is no particular need to employ psychoanalysis, because in the work Marx comes close to anticipating Freud's *The Interpretation of Dreams*. Marx analyzed a situation that rapidly unfolded in dreamlike fashion, and in doing so, he stressed the "dream logic" driving it: not actual class interests, but rather the "dream-work" by which class unconsciousness was repressed and displaced. Freud writes:

> The dream is seen to be an abbreviated selection from the associations, a selection made, it is true, according to rules that we have not yet understood: the elements of the dream are like representatives chosen by election from a mass of people. There can be no doubt that by our technique we have got hold of something for which the dream is a substitute and in which lies the dream's psychical value, but which no longer exhibits its puzzling peculiarities, its strangeness and its confusion.[10]

Here Freud likens "dream-work" to a legislative assembly chosen by popular election. This suggests that, rather than introduce or apply psychoanalysis into Marx's analysis, we are better off doing the contrary: reading psychoanalysis from the perspective of *The Eighteenth Brumaire of Louis Bonaparte*. Marx finds the key to explicating the dreamlike incident in the assemblies chosen by popular election after the 1848 revolution. The circumstances that followed from this were all generated within this assembly (system of representation).

Outside the council lay the multiple articulations of real economic classes, while inside the council were found the multiple articulations of discourse of the various representatives. How were these related? In Marx's view, there could be no necessary connection between the representatives (discourse) and the represented (the various economic classes). This is a definitive feature of systems of representation (assemblies) chosen by popular election that are commonly found in modern states. This is precisely what made it possible for the various classes to turn their backs on their actual representatives and instead find in Louis Bonaparte their representative:

> The parliamentary party was not only dissolved into its two great factions, each of these factions was not only split within itself, but the Party of Order in parliament had fallen out with the Party of Order *outside* parliament. The spokesmen and scribes of the bourgeoisie, its platform and its press, in short, the ideologists of the bourgeoisie and the bourgeoisie itself, the representatives and the represented, were alienated from one another and no longer understood each other.[11]

Louis Bonaparte, lacking all credentials except for being Napoleon's nephew, became president and then emperor; Marx took up this dreamlike incident, to borrow Freud's words, in "its puzzling peculiarities, its strangeness and its confusion," seeing in it the *crisis* of the system of representation. One reason that Louis Bonaparte became not merely president but also emperor lay in the peasantry, a class that lacked both discourse and a representative to represent it. They saw in Bonaparte not so much their own representative as an unlimited ruling power that they could look up to—they saw him, in other words, more as emperor than as president.

But that was not the only reason Bonaparte became emperor. Marx did not forget to note the following: "This executive power with its enormous bureaucratic and military organisation; with its extensive and artificial state machinery, with a host of officials numbering half a million, besides an army of another half million, this appalling parasitic body, which enmeshes the body of French society like a net and chokes all its pores, sprang up in the days of the absolute monarchy, with the decay of the feudal system, which it helped to hasten."[12] Marx also points out the major impact of the cyclical global panic (crisis) of 1851. The bureaucracy seemed to have retreated behind the popularly elected parliament and market economy, but with this state of exception, the bureaucracy—in other words, the state—stepped back into the foreground: "Only under the second Bonaparte does the state seem to have made itself completely independent. As against civil society, the state machine has consolidated its position . . . thoroughly."[13]

Yet the state machinery was unable to directly step into the foreground under its own power. The independence of the state machinery became possible only after Bonaparte achieved autonomy as an emperor, transcending parliament. For example, Marx describes the process by which Bonaparte acquired authority by lavishly bestowing "gifts" on all classes: "Bonaparte would like to appear as the patriarchal benefactor of all classes. But he cannot give to one class without taking from another."[14] Bonaparte was merely redistributing what he had plundered, but this was perceived as a gift. As a result, he came to be represented as a supreme being who gave to all classes—as, that is, emperor. His power as emperor was established by projecting the external appearance of gift-countergift reciprocal exchanges onto what was in reality a plunder-redistribution exchange carried out by the state machinery.

This same process had already taken place during the first French Revolution. That revolution is often called a bourgeois revolution, but its real active agents were the petty producers and artisans in the cities, and power finally

THE MODERN STATE 179

ended up in the hands of Napoleon as emperor, not the bourgeoisie. In other words, it was through Napoleon that the state emerged to the forefront. In this sense, the French Revolution ended up pushing the French state, which had been driven into a crisis by the pressure of English industrial capital, into a posture of resistance. The same thing would be repeated in 1848.

Marx and Engels issued the *Communist Manifesto* on the eve of the wave of revolutions that swept across Europe, beginning in France in 1848. But Marx's prediction that the world was bound for a final struggle between the two great classes, capitalist and proletariat, completely missed the mark. The emergence of Louis Bonaparte in France and Otto von Bismarck in Prussia gave graphic evidence of the autonomous nature of the state. It is clear that Marx did not overlook this and in fact devoted considerable thought to it. Nonetheless, he continued to hold the view that, as a part of the ideological superstructure, the state would simply disappear once economic class conflict had been abolished. The consequences of this for subsequent socialism would be disastrous.

Modern Bureaucracy

If we want to understand the modern state, we need to begin not with the nation-state but with the absolute monarchy. In an absolute monarchy, the state machinery of the bureaucracy and army carry out the will of the monarch, who is sovereign. But after the bourgeois revolutions, the state was supposed to be identical to the government, which represented the will of the people, who were now sovereign. In other words, the bourgeois revolution and nation-state repressed from view the fact that the state is a subject grounded in mode of exchange B. But the notion of popular sovereignty is simply a fiction. In reality, during crisis situations, a sovereign—in other words, a powerful leader similar to an absolutist monarch—will emerge to popular acclaim. In that sense, the process by which absolute monarchy appeared in Europe is a universal one. It does not necessarily lead to a king, so long as it produces an entity capable of politically unifying the fragmented social formation. This process provides a useful reference point when we consider the measures taken by the periphery of the modern world system when it pursued independence and industrialization. The developmentalist and socialist dictatorships that appeared were equivalent to absolute monarchies.

Let me return to the question of bureaucracies. Weber emphasized their role because they represent an important problem for the modern state and capital. He regarded bureaucracy as a form of legal domination, as in fact the most rational form of authority. He identified the following defining characteristics: jurisdictions clearly defined by regulations, a hierarchical system of official ranks, appointment by contracts entered into voluntarily, promotion determined by a regularized system of rules, specialized training, and salaries paid in cash. Bureaucracy existed from the age of Asiatic states and their patrimonial bureaucracies. But those patrimonial bureaucracies had not yet broken with so-called traditional authority and were still subordinated to personal relationships with a ruler or master. This prevented them from fully realizing these characteristics. In comparison, modern bureaucracies are more rational (in the sense of instrumental rationality).

More important, modern bureaucracies exist not only in the state but also in private enterprises. Modern bureaucracy was actually established through capitalist forms of management (the division and combination of labor). In *Capital*, Marx theorizes the shift from the stage of manufactures, in which individual producers are linked together horizontally, to that of factories, which are vertically managed by capital, a shift that corresponds to the bureaucratization of private enterprises. What Marx calls the industrial proletariat are people who have been molded by this bureaucratization. By contrast, anarchism flourished in places where industrial capital was still undeveloped and workers retained the characteristics of artisans. This means that capitalist development is simultaneously bureaucratic development.

As C. Wright Mills explains, white-collar workers constitute the bureaucratic stratum of private enterprises.[15] The ratio of white-collar workers is high in advanced capitalist countries. In terms of class as defined by the economic categories of money and commodity, white-collar workers are proletariat, but in terms of status, they stand over blue-collar workers as rulers. The anguish of white-collar workers lies in the need to pass through a test akin to the Chinese civil-service examinations to acquire that status, as well as in the reality that once they do enter into service, they must sacrifice their own wills and become cogs in the organization, driven to suffering and worrying over the prospects of promotion. These problems are not general to all forms of wage labor: they are specific to bureaucracies.

In a private company, the working class is vertically divided up into such categories as managers, permanent full-time employees, and temporary part-time workers. The old theories of class conflict no longer apply. This does not mean that the conflict between capital and wage labor has been resolved in any fundamental sense. Simply, the methods of resistance used up until now, based on a view that locates class struggle only in the production process, will no longer work.

On the other hand, neoliberals (libertarians) call for dissolution of state bureaucracies through privatization or the implementation of market principles. They claim that bureaucracies are inefficient and that if the standard practices of the private sector are followed, they will produce higher efficiency and a decrease in the number of public employees. But any claim that bureaucracies can be dissolved through privatization is patently false: private enterprises are themselves already bureaucratic. The appearance of greater instrumental rationality in private enterprises is not due to their being unbureaucratic. Rather, it is because the goal of their instrumental rationality, the accumulation of capital (maximization of profits), is more clearly defined.

It is impossible to impose this kind of instrumental rationality on public officials who are engaged in a realm that does not and often cannot have a quantifiable goal such as profit. Hence, it is an error to think that bureaucracies are found only in the public sector, or that these can be abolished through privatization. Such attempts to impose instrumental rationality will not result in the dissolution of bureaucracy; instead, they will simply produce a bureaucracy characterized by an ever-more thoroughgoing instrumental rationality.

Anarcho-capitalists (libertarians) preach the privatization of all bureaucratic functions, including the police and military. But this will not lead to the abolition of bureaucracies, nor of the state. State and nation will not automatically disappear, no matter how widely the realm of mode of exchange C expands. This is because they are based on modes of exchange other than commodity exchange and because state and nation are indispensable to commodity exchange. What libertarians aim at is simply the liberation of capital from the yoke of the nation-state: that is the policy of so-called neoliberalism.

EIGHT

INDUSTRIAL CAPITAL

Merchant Capital and Industrial Capital

Merchant capitalism has existed since antiquity and has often occupied an important position in society. Nonetheless, it did not
lead to fundamental changes in social formation prior to the rise of
capitalism. In other words, mode of exchange C has existed since
antiquity, but in social formations dominated by modes of exchange A and B, mode C remained subordinate to them. A social
formation in which mode of exchange C was dominant emerged in
tandem with the rise of industrial capitalism. For this reason, the
appearance of industrial capitalism was, along with the appearance
of clan society and the appearance of the state, one of the epochal
events in world history.

   We have already located the key to this rise to dominance in the
world-economy of Europe. There the lack of a centralized state
allowed for an integration between long-distance trade and local
markets. As a result, cities appeared across Europe, and these
became free cities as a result of the balance of power among such
competing forces as the church and feudal lords. Clearly, this provided the basis for the emergence of a capitalist economy. Yet while
the expansion of trade and the expansion of cities were necessary
conditions for a capitalist economy, they were not in themselves
sufficient. For example, the production of commodities for the
world market led in eastern Europe to the rise of neoserfdom and
in Latin America to new slavery and serfdom systems. In other
words, the development of trade and cities did not necessarily
guarantee that commodity mode of exchange C would become

dominant. In order for commodity mode of exchange C to overcome the resistance of modes A and B, a transformation had to take place—but what transformation?

There is something that makes industrial capitalism different from the capitalisms that preceded it. In fact, many previous theorists have stressed the difference between industrial and merchant capital, beginning with Adam Smith. He asserted that while merchant capital earned profits by buying low and selling high, industrial capital secures its profit through increased productivity. Max Weber also saw a fundamental break between industrial capital and the merchant capitalism that had existed since ancient times, which he identified as a changed attitude toward labor. He argued that roots of industrial capitalism lay in the renunciation of the pursuit of acquisition and desire for consumption that had characterized merchant capital, as well as in the emergence of a new diligent ethos of labor.[1]

In general, those who see a fundamental break between merchant and industrial capital focus on the production process. This view has been criticized by those who take up capitalism in terms of the processes of circulation and consumption. Werner Sombart, for example, opposed Weber's views and regarded industrial capitalism as being fundamentally a further extension of merchant capitalism. He saw the moment for development of capitalism as arising not from asceticism but its opposite: from the desire for luxury. In the age of late capitalism and the consumer society, this view has been positively reevaluated.

All of these views, however, take up capitalism in terms of only one of its sides. To the best of my knowledge, only Marx has explicated capitalism in terms of both of its sides. He, after all, is the one who declared: "The genuine science of modern economics begins only when theoretical discussion moves from the circulation process to the production process."[2] Marx differed from classical political economy in that he turned his focus to the process of circulation. He began from the recognition that capitalism is produced above all by mode of exchange C. He believed that there was no fundamental difference between industrial and merchant capital: both obtained their profit through differences arising from exchange. This is why he used the formula M-C-M' to explicate the general form of capital.

Those who distinguish industrial capital from merchant capital overlook (or obfuscate) the fact that they do the same thing. It is a mistake to believe that merchant capital extracts profit through unequal exchanges. Of course, if one were to buy cheap and sell high within a single system of values, this would be an unequal exchange—more precisely, it would be a form of swindle. Moreover, while the capital on one side would gain, that on the other would lose, meaning that capital as a whole could not obtain any surplus value through this. Marx writes: "The capitalist class of a given country, taken as a whole, cannot defraud itself. However much we twist and turn, the final conclusion remains the same. If equivalents are exchanged, no surplus-value results, and if non-equivalents are exchanged, we still have no surplus value. Circulation, or the exchange of commodities, creates no value."[3]

How then is profit obtained through equal exchanges? The problem is solved when we posit circulation or commodity exchanges as taking place between different systems of value. As Marx noted, the value of one thing is determined by the system of its value relationships with all other commodities. For this reason, the same item will have different values when placed in different systems. This is how, for example, a merchant obtains surplus value, buying a thing in a location where it is cheap and selling it in a location where it is expensive, even though the exchanges in each location were for equal value. Large surplus values (margins) are produced when the two systems are spatially distant from one another—in, that is, long-distance trade. It is no easy matter, however, to travel long distances or to ferret out inexpensive goods. Accordingly, merchants who journey to distant lands are not unreasonable in regarding this profit as legitimate remuneration for their acumen and daring—just as industrial capitalists (entrepreneurs) believe that their profits come not from exploitation of workers but as legitimate remuneration for their acumen and daring.

The claim that, while industrial capital obtains its profit from the production process, merchant capital obtains it from the circulation process is simply wrong. In general, it is often said that merchant capital obtains its profits by merely acting as an intermediary in trade. Yet merchant capital also often directly engages in production. For example, Smith uses the example of the manufacture of pins to explain how the combination and division of labor leads to increased productivity. In reality, however, it was merchant capital that organized this kind of manufacture. This first appeared in the cities of Renaissance Italy and then later in Holland. Merchant capital also sought profit in increased productivity.

These manufactures could be called the primary mode of industrial capital. But as I will explain, so long as merchant capital remains dominant, industrial capital cannot get under way. Incidentally, we should note that this kind of combination and division of labor has existed since antiquity. In ancient trade increased productivity was also vital, and achieving it required the combination and division of labor. Similarly, the combination and division of labor was possible and even indispensable in slavery-based production. It is not something unique to industrial capitalism.[4]

Merchant capital obtained its margin by acting as a relay or intermediary between different systems of value. In sum, its profit came from spatial differences, which is why it mainly pursued long-distance trade. Yet this was not its only tactic. Merchant capital did not solely rely on spatial differences; it also used temporal differentiation between systems of value. For example, merchant capital would efficiently organize its own production process to increase labor productivity—in other words, to reduce the (social) labor time need to produce a commodity. It then took this product, whose production cost had dropped, and sold it at a high price in overseas markets, thereby obtaining surplus value. Acting as an intermediary is not the only way to buy low and sell high; this can also be achieved by effectively organizing one's production process. It is also true that industrial capital did not obtain its surplus value solely through technological improvements of production processes. After all, industrial capital also travels long distances in search of consumers or cheap materials and labor. As should be clear now, it is impossible to clarify the difference between merchant and industrial capital if we look only at the process of circulation or of production.

The Labor Power Commodity

Marx was not caught up by the apparent difference between merchant and industrial capital. But, in line with the classical school, he believed that industrial capital did not obtain its surplus value from the process of circulation. On the other hand, he also maintained that surplus value is essentially obtained from the process of circulation. In other words, Marx criticized both the mercantilists, who emphasized the importance of circulation, and the classical school, which emphasized the process of production. He thought that industrial capital's surplus value was not exclusively obtained from either process, circulation or production:

> Capital cannot therefore arise from circulation, and it is equally impossible for it to arise apart from circulation. It must have its origin both in circulation and not in circulation. . . . The transformation of money into capital has to be developed on the basis of the immanent laws of the exchange of commodities, in such a way that the starting-point is the

exchange of equivalents. The money-owner, who is as yet only a capitalist in larval form, must buy his commodities at their value, sell them at their value, and yet at the end of the process withdraw more value from circulation than he threw into it at the beginning. His emergence as a butterfly must, and yet must not, take place in the sphere of circulation. These are the conditions of the problem. *Hic Rhodus, hic salta!*[5]

This antinomy can only be resolved by bringing forward a special commodity: the labor power commodity. To review, the process of accumulation of value for merchant capital is money → commodity → money + α, expressed by the formula M-C-M' (M + ΔM). The accumulation of industrial capital follows the same basic pattern. But industrial capital differs from merchant capital on one point: its discovery of a commodity with unique properties. It is a commodity whose use constitutes the production process itself: labor power.

Unlike merchant capital, which simply buys and sells commodities, industrial capital sets up production facilities, buys raw materials, employs workers, and then sells the commodities produced. Here the process of accumulating value for industrial capital is given in the formula M-C ... P ... C'-M'. The difference with merchant capital arises from one element contained in C here—the labor power commodity. But if one looks only at the production process, the special qualities of this commodity will never come into view. Since merchant capital also employs wage laborers, the use of wage laborers itself does not constitute the distinguishing characteristic of industrial capital. That being the case, what kind of wage laborer is needed to make possible industrial capital—what exactly is the industrial proletariat?

Marx saw the industrial proletariat as people who were free in two senses. First, they were free to sell their own labor. This meant that they were free from various constraints that existed under feudalism. Second, they had nothing to sell other than their labor power. This meant that they were free from the means of production (land)—they did not own the means of production. These two forms of freedom are inextricably interrelated.

Let us start with the first meaning of *free*. The proletariat are neither slaves nor serfs. Whereas slaves are themselves bought and sold as commodities, with the proletariat only their labor power is sold as commodity. Moreover, this is done only through agreements freely entered into. Beyond this purchase contract (employment contract), the proletariat are not subordinated to the capitalist; they are free from extraeconomic coercion But this makes them all the more vulnerable to economic coercion. For example, in terms of the value of their labor power, they have to accept the price determined by the labor market. And in terms of the hours and kind of labor, they are forced to obey the terms of the contract. But this is true of all contracts, and it does not constitute a kind of extraeconomic coercion.

In terms of intensity of labor, however, it is not unusual for the labor of the proletariat to be more demanding than that of slaves or serfs. This is because, while a slave or serf is able to slack off when there is no direct supervision or threat of punishment, the industrial proletariat, especially when performing labor under mechanized production, are never able to evade the coercion of the labor hours under contract. Still, we should not call this kind of harsh compulsion slave-like, since it is always the result of contracts entered into by free agreement. If wages are low, this is the result of their being determined by the labor market; it is something beyond the control of the individual capitalist.

The proletariat are also different from independent farmers and guild artisans. These two groups are subordinated to their community, which makes it possible for them to achieve a certain degree of economic self-sufficiency. For example, farmers who live in a community are able to scratch out a living even if their own land is poor—they can use common lands, perform side jobs for others, and benefit from other kinds of mutual aid. But this also requires them to submit to the constraints of the community, meaning they are not free. The situation is similar for artisans. So long as they accept the terms of the apprenticeship system, their future is to a certain extent guaranteed—a form of communal constraint. On this point, the industrial proletarian is unlike the serf or the guild artisan.

But this is not the whole story. The industrial proletariat differ from slaves and serfs and other forms of wage labor in general in that they buy back the very things they themselves have produced. Wage laborers who worked in manufactures under merchant capital did not buy the products they made—primarily luxury goods intended for overseas or for the very wealthy. But industrial capital is sustained by workers who buy back the products of their own labor. Its products, moreover, primarily consist of everyday items needed by workers.

When we say that the proletariat have nothing to sell but their own labor power, it may seem that we are stressing their poverty. But what this really means is that the proletariat lack self-sufficiency in producing the necessities of life and hence must purchase them. Slaves do not buy their own necessities of life, and serfs live in self-sufficient communities. By contrast, the industrial proletariat support themselves and their families with money they obtain by selling their labor power. The emergence of the industrial proletariat is simultaneously the emergence of the consumer who buys the commodities needed for daily life. This is the most important difference between the industrial proletarian and the slave or serf.

In an industrial capitalist economy, consumption by workers cannot be separated from the process of capital accumulation: it is the way labor power is produced and reproduced. Individual consumption by members of the working class produces and reproduces the labor power that is for the capitalist the indispensable means of production: "The fact that the worker performs acts of individual consumption in his own interest, and not to please the capitalist, is something entirely irrelevant to the matter."[6]

In this way, industrial capital accumulates through the margin (surplus value) generated when industrial capital obtains the cooperation of workers by paying them wages and then having them buy back the commodities they have produced. Thanks to the existence of this unique commodity, surplus value for industrial capital is produced simultaneously in both the processes of production and circulation. This is the solution to the difficulty that Marx expressed as "*hic Rhodus, hic salta!*"[7]

The epochal nature of industrial capital lies in its establishment of a seemingly autopoietic system in which commodities produced by the labor-power commodity are then purchased by workers in order to reproduce their own labor power. This is what made it possible for the principle of commodity mode of exchange C to penetrate society across the globe. At the stage of merchant capital, it made no difference if the process of production was a slavery system, serfdom, or guild community. By contrast, precisely because it was dependent on the labor-power commodity, industrial capital needed to actively promote the spread of the principle of commodity exchange.

Let me augment my explanation of why the industrial proletariat are free in two senses. In general, the word *proletaria* carries traces of a meaning it has had since classical Rome: the word expresses the image of the poor who have lost the means of production (land) and have only their labor power to sell. But, to take up one example, it was not usually the case that farmers became wage laborers because they could no longer make a living at farming alone; rather, in most cases, they did so in order to free themselves from communal constraints. The same was true of guild artisans. Today many women who previously stayed at home are choosing to become wage laborers. This is not simply because they can no longer support themselves on their husbands' earnings alone. It is also in order to free themselves from the constraints imposed by men and family. The commodification of labor power always includes these two senses. It frees individuals—that is, it liberates them from constraints imposed by modes of exchange A and B. But individuals as bearers of the labor-power commodity then find themselves forced to submit to new constraints. They are subjected to the constant fear of losing their jobs, and in fact sometimes actually do lose them. Even so, people tend to prefer to sell their labor power rather than accept subordination to community or family.

Still, an image of poverty clings to the word *proletaria*. For example, farmers, shop owners, small-scale producers, and others who own the means of production choose to send their children off to college to make them into salaried white-collar workers, rather than have them take over the family business. In reality, this means turning their children into the proletariat, but that is not how they perceive it. Today's white-collar workers are undoubtedly wage laborers, but they never think of themselves as the proletariat. This is because a fixed idea persists that identifies the proletariat with poor people engaging in manual labor. To avoid unnecessary misunderstandings or confusion, I will refrain from using the word *proletariat* and will call these workers instead wage laborers (people who sell the labor-power commodity). The important thing is that they sell their labor power to capital, that they engage in wage labor, regardless if their standard of living is high or low.

The Self-Valorization of Industrial Capital

In the first volume of *Capital*, Marx takes up capital in its general form, not the individual kinds of capital. In fact, however, there are many different kinds and forms of industrial capital, ranging from the production of consumer goods to the production of the means of production. Moreover, the organic composition of each kind of capital differs, distributed across a range spanning from one pole, in which the ratio of constant capital is high and variable capital (labor power) low, to its opposite. In addition, the competition among capital belonging to the same category is fierce. None of this is apparent if we look only at capital in its general form. Marx took up these problems in the third volume of *Capital*, where he explored the various specific kinds of capital.

Yet there are times when we need to think of capital in general terms or in terms of total capital. I have just outlined the distinguishing characteristic of industrial capital: its system of having workers buy back the goods they have produced under capital. Naturally, this only applies to total capital and to the totality of labor that corresponds to it. For example, individual workers do not buy back the specific things they themselves have made—they buy the products of other capital, which is to say products made by other workers. Nonetheless, taken as a whole, workers do buy back the things they have produced. Moreover, workers in general buy consumer goods, not producer goods. Capital buys producer goods. Yet seen as a whole, the self-reproduction of capital consists of employing workers and then having them buy back the things they have produced.

How does this produce a difference (surplus value)? The perspective of total capital is essential for understanding surplus value: to try to explain surplus value through the various individual instances of capital will always miss the mark. For example, if one concludes that a profitable enterprise must have exploited its workers, one would also have to conclude that capitalists who ended up in bankruptcy without earning a profit were conscientious and did not exploit workers. Moreover, while it is possible for individual capitalists to obtain surplus value through unequal exchanges, this is impossible for capital taken as a whole. Marxists have proclaimed, for example, that surplus value is obtained by capital through unjust and abusive exploitation of workers. But when we view things from the perspective of total capital, it becomes clear that accumulation of capital would be impossible if this were the case. Marx says:

> Each capitalist knows that he does not confront his own worker as a producer confronts a consumer, and so he wants to restrict his consumption, i.e. his ability to exchange, his wages, as much as possible. But of course, he wants the workers of *other* capitalists to be the greatest possible consumers of *his* commodity. Yet the relationship of *each* capitalist to *his* workers is the *general relationship* of *capital and labour*, the essential relation. It is precisely this which gives rise to the illusion—true for each individual capitalist as distinct from all the others—that *apart from his own* workers, the rest of the working class confronts him not as workers, but as *consumers* and *exchangers*—as moneyspenders. . . . It is precisely this which distinguishes capital from the [feudal] relationship of domination—that the *worker* confronts the capitalist as consumer and one who posits exchange value, in the form of a *possessor of money*, of money, of a simple centre of circulation—that he becomes one of the innumerable centres of circulation, in which his specific character as worker is extinguished.[8]

All individual capitalists wish they didn't have to pay wages to their workers, but they all also desire consumers who will buy their products. Individual capitalists want all the other capitalists to pay higher wages, in other words. Likewise, individual capitalists wish they could fire their workers but would be troubled if all other companies did so, because increased unemployment means decreased consumption. Because individual capitalists pursue their own individual profits, none takes up the perspective of total capital. At times of crisis, however, the problem of total capital does manifest itself, despite the intentions of individual capitalists. It appears in the form not of an agreement between all the individual capitalists but rather as an agreement of the state. For example, in the Great Depression of the 1930s, that state acting as total capital implemented policies that none of the individual capitalists would have—this was what Keynesianism and Fordism amounted to. On the one hand, the state tried to stimulate demand through public investment. And on the other hand, corporations stimulated production and employment by raising wages.

These did not, however, amount to a modified capitalism. They only show that, when faced with a crisis, total capital in the form of the state moves into the foreground. Ultimately, when viewed from the perspective of total capital, it becomes clear that the self-valorization of capital—of, in other words, surplus value—cannot be achieved through unequal exchanges or unjust exploitation. The totality of capital must engage in an equal exchange with the totality of labor, and yet this exchange must somehow generate surplus value. Surplus value here consists of the difference between the total value paid out to workers for their labor power and the total value of the commodities they in fact produced. Where does this difference come from?

As noted, Smith, relying on the example of pin manufactures, believed that the coordination and division of labor arising when capital hires and then organizes workers resulted in levels of productivity far exceeding the sum of what individual workers could produce on their own. Smith and David Ricardo believed that individual workers had no claim to the results that were achieved when capitalists organized production through the combination and division of labor, and that the increase achieved (the profit) rightfully belonged to the capitalist who devised and implemented this organization. Ricardian socialists, however, believed that this increase represented surplus value that should return to the workers but was unjustly stolen by the capitalist. P.-J. Proudhon likewise asserted that capital did not pay for the "collective power" realized when individual laborers worked collaboratively—an instance of his assertion that "property is theft."[9]

Marx inherited these views. He called "absolute surplus value" those forms of surplus value obtained by extending working hours or by forcing people to work harder, while he called "relative surplus value" that which was obtained through technological innovation and increased productivity. The sections in *Capital* that take up absolute surplus value are better known, but it is in fact the sections on relative surplus value that are key: they reveal the true essence of industrial capital. Unlike absolute surplus value, any consideration of relative surplus value must take place at the level of total capital.

Let's look at this in terms of the value of the labor-power commodity. The value of a commodity is determined by the social-labor time required to produce it. The value of labor power, on the other hand, is the cost required to produce and reproduce it, which is in turn determined by the value of other commodities, primarily the necessities of life. If the value of those other commodities fluctuates, so too will the value of labor power. In short, the value of labor power is determined within the total system of relationships of all commodities. For this reason, the value of labor power varies by country and region, as well as historically. To take this up from another perspective, we can say that the standard for the value of labor power is determined by the productivity of labor. For example, if the wages of the workers in one country are lower than those in others, it is because the average standard of labor productivity is lower there.

To sum up, relative surplus value is generated within the value system of a single country or region by creating a new value system through technological innovation that increases productivity. A difference arises in the value of labor power between the moment when workers sell it by being hired and the moment when the products they make are sold. Industrial capital obtains its margin by carrying out exchanges (equal exchanges) across the value systems it has differentiated in this way. In that sense, it resembles merchant capital. But industrial capital encounters a difficulty unknown to merchant capital because of the way it achieves self-valorization by selling back to workers their own products. To put this in terms of Smith's example, once you've achieved a tenfold increase in production through coordination and division of labor, who is going to buy all of those pins? No matter how low the price drops, the workers aren't going to be able to buy ten times as many pins. In order for capital to generate surplus value here, it must go *outside* to find consumers to buy the pins. These locations are found in foreign markets or among newly risen laborer-consumers emerging from previously self-sufficient communities—in other words, the proletariat.

It should be clear that surplus value cannot be generated within a single value system, no matter how much productivity increases, and that under such conditions the self-valorization of capital is impossible. In order to secure the self-valorization of capital, it is not sufficient to simply raise productivity; one must also ceaselessly integrate increasing numbers of new proletarians (laborer-consumers) into the system. Marx cites as one of the necessary preconditions for industrial capital the existence of an "industrial reserve army."[10] This means newly recruited proletarians, whether from domestic rural areas or from foreign lands. This ceaseless influx of new proletarians forms the industrial reserve army. Without it, wages would rise and consumption would reach a saturation point and begin to fall, leading to a declining rate of profit for capital.

In order for the accumulation of capital to continue, it has to ceaselessly engage in the recruitment of new proletarians. Of course, they are simultaneously also new consumers. The participation of these new proletarian consumers is what makes possible the self-valorization of industrial capital. This means that industrial capital by its very nature must continuously expand in scope. Capital consists of the accumulation process M-C-M′. If capital cannot grow, it ceases to exist. Unlike merchant capital, which had only a limited surface impact on society, industrial capital by necessity has to dismember the existing community down to its deepest strata, completely reorganizing the community in order to integrate it into the commodity economy.

Origins of Industrial Capitalism

The accumulation of industrial capital is expressed by the formula M-C . . . C′-M′. The formula for merchant capital is M-C-M′ and that for usurer capital M-M′. In historical terms, the last two are older; industrial capital appeared only after they had come into existence. Marx writes that with the formation of industrial capital, merchant capital found itself displaced, confined to the commercial sector of industrial capital. The same was true for usurer capital. But the rise of industrial capital does not lead to the disappearance of merchant and usurer capital. By its nature, capital seeks surplus value through difference, not caring what kind of difference is involved. For capital, only rates of profit matter. Accordingly, where possible, capital will pursue self-valorization through commerce or finance, rather than through industrial capital, which requires investment in constant capital (fixed assets). This does not change even after industrial capital becomes the mainstay, as can be seen, for example, in the trend toward finance capital in the United States since the end of the twentieth century.

Let's consider the emergence of industrial capital. This cannot be seen simply as a shift from merchant to industrial capital. Industrial capital is not something automatically produced through the development of world markets and commodity production. For example, in the world markets of the early modern period, commodity production developed in many locations, but as I've noted, this did not necessarily lead to the appearance of industrial capital or the proletariat. Instead of leading to the destruction of the existing order, in many cases merchant capital actually preserved or even strengthened it.

As a matter of historical fact, industrial capital (capitalist production) was born in Britain. Why? Marx explains that in the shift from the feudal to the capitalist mode of production, there were two paths.[11] In the first, producers organized manufactures, while in the second the manufactures were organized by merchant capital:

> The transition from the feudal mode of production takes place in two different ways. The producer may become a merchant and capitalist, in contrast to the agricultural natural economy and the guild-bound handicraft of medieval urban industry. This is the really revolutionary way. Alternatively, however, the merchant may take direct control of production himself. But however frequently this occurs as a historical transition—for example the English clothier of the seventeenth century, who brought weavers who were formerly independent under his control, selling them their wool and buying up their cloth—it cannot bring about the overthrow of the old mode of production by itself, but rather preserves and retains it as its own precondition.[12]

According to this schema, Britain took the first path. But why and how? A famous debate took place among Marxist theorists over Marx's view of this shift from the feudal mode of production.[13] As I have discussed, the debate revolved around an opposition between those who understood capitalism from the perspective of the process of production and manufactures (represented by Maurice Dobb) and those who understood it from the perspective of the process of circulation and world markets (represented by Paul Sweezy). The former view takes its support from the manufactures that were organized by producers themselves, while the latter takes its support from the manufactures that were organized at the initiative of merchants.

Both cases existed—even in Britain. But according to adherents of the former view, the first path triumphed in Britain, and the reason was because Britain saw the earliest dissolution of the feudal mode of production. Kōhachirō Takahashi, who took Dobbs's side in the debate, argued that in any given country, the question of which of the two paths triumphs will determine the characteristics of the country's social structure in the age of capitalism. According to him, in France and England the first path triumphed, while in countries such as Germany and Japan the second path became dominant, a difference that in turn explains much of the difference in social structure between the two groups. In Japan this theory is primarily identified with Hisao Ōtsuka, Takahashi's mentor.

According to Ōtsuka, capitalism in Holland was primarily that of merchant capital, based on acting as an intermediary in the transit trade of luxury goods.[14] Britain, by contrast, pursued the path of manufactures from below, which was centered on the production of low-cost necessities of everyday life. This was carried out not in the existing cities but in new cities that sprung up around what had been agricultural villages. This means that the goods manufactured there were bought up by the laborers who had emerged from the neighboring agrarian villages. In this way, local "markets" arose across the country, markets that gradually linked together to form a domestic national market. Soon this allowed British industrial capital to drive Dutch merchant capital from the world market.

Ōtsuka argued that the rapid development of manufactures from below in Britain was due to the early collapse of feudalism there. Under this view, Britain appears to be the prototype for advanced developed countries. But in fact, this was not the case. Compared to Holland or the city-states of Italy, the development of manufactures in Britain lagged far behind. The hegemony in trade of the Italian city-states was based not simply on transit trade but also on their manufactures. The same was true for Holland in the seventeenth century. By exporting textiles from their manufactures, the merchants of Holland were able to push their way past the city-states of Italy and the Hanseatic League. Without reorganizing the process of production, merchant capital could not emerge victorious in the competition to dominate international trade. Yet Holland's manufactures did not subsequently develop into industrial capital. This was not because the roots of the feudal order were deeper in Holland than in Britain. Rather, it was because Holland had already seized hegemony in both commerce and finance. Whenever possible, capital will always prefer to pursue accumulation through merchant or finance capital rather than through riskier industrial capital. It was only natural that once Holland had seized hegemony in world trade, its capital would move into commerce and finance instead of the promotion of manufactures.

In Britain too manufactures from below organized by producers did not develop early on. Instead, what actually existed at the start were manufactures from above, which continued to make up a large percentage of the total. Mines and other large-scale manufactures were not possible without state participation. Moreover, even manufactures from below were largely dependent on merchant capital from the center. What caused the development of manufactures from below and industrial capitalism was the fact that Britain lagged behind Holland in world trade. Britain adopted mercantilist (protectionist) policies that favored domestic industries. In that sense, the British manufactures from below existed under state protection and support—a phenomenon more characteristic of late-developing nations than of advanced countries.

To reiterate, the reason Britain took the first path was not because its feudal system collapsed at a comparatively early date, but rather because Britain turned away from overseas markets. This means that the real question here is not one of manufactures from above versus manufactures from below. Instead the key issue is what markets were being targeted. Manufactures from above organized by merchant capital mainly produced luxury goods aimed at the nobility and wealthy, primarily in overseas markets. By contrast, manufactures from below concentrated on inexpensive daily necessities. Emerging not in the existing cities but around what had been agrarian villages, these manufactures set the stage for the rise of new cities. In other words, industrial capital emerged not from the existing urban artisan-guild communities or the rural agrarian communities but rather from the newly emergent industrial cities and markets. Industrial capital developed a system whereby workers recruited from neighboring agrarian villages were socially organized under capital and made to purchase the goods that they themselves had produced. During this period, Britain adopted stiff tariff barriers to protect domestic industries, in contrast to the free-trade policies pursued by Holland.

Seen in this light, it is no longer possible to accept the view that while industrial capitalism developed naturally in Britain, it emerged through state protection and encouragement in Germany and other late-developing capitalist nations. In fact, Britain followed the same pattern as those other countries. Britain did begin to advocate the doctrine of free trade in the nineteenth century, but this was because by then it had already achieved hegemony in trade, not because its market economy was somehow independent of the state. This also means that the trend since the 1930s in Britain of Keynesian state interventions into the economy did not represent an especially new tendency. After all, Germany and Japan did the same thing without any Keynesian influence. The belief that the capitalist market economy develops autonomously, outside the influence of the state, is simply mistaken.

Earlier I argued that the will of capital as a whole emerges not in the form of an agreement among all of the capitalists but rather as the will of the state. This becomes self-evident when we look at how the labor-power commodity was cultivated. We have already seen that this consists of the appearance of a proletariat who are free in two senses. It is the appearance of people who are free from (i.e., do not own) the means of production after privatization of land ownership and enclosure of the commons. But these phenomena on their own will only produce the urban vagrant. To mold people into proletariat proper, it is not sufficient merely to strip them of the means of production. The industrial proletariat consists of people who are characterized by diligence, temporal discipline, and an ability to work within systems for coordination and division of labor. This is why Weber stressed that Protestantism fostered an ethos of industriousness suited to industrial capitalism. In more universal terms, though, this ethos was actually the product of communal disciplining carried out in such institutions as schools and the military.

School education differs from the apprentice training system of craftwork artisans. For the labor-power commodity in industrial capitalism, what is needed is not specialized technical ability but rather a set of skills that are adaptable to any kind of work. The labor-power commodity needs education to provide general knowledge, such as literacy and mathematical competence. Moreover, because the self-valorization of industrial capital is based on technical innovation (increased productivity), the labor-power commodity needs, in addition to unskilled labor, to cultivate labor power capable of producing high-level scientific technology. Which is to say, it needs universities and research centers. These tasks are carried out not by individual capitalists but rather by capital as a whole—in practice, by the state.

The role of the state in cultivating labor power is especially clear when we look at late-developing capitalist states other than Britain. Largely in order to resist British capital, the state took the initiative in implementing mandatory education systems. This was largely carried out by enlightened despots or similar figures (for example, Napoleon Bonaparte or Otto von Bismarck). The same thing happened in non-Western countries that pursued rapid industrialization. Cultivation of labor power was just as important to them as the importation of industrial technology. For example, four years after Japan's Meiji Restoration, the state implemented military conscription and compulsory education. Development of industry still lagged, but through compulsory education and communal disciplining, a labor force was created that could meet the needs of capitalist production. Late-developing capitalist countries did not have the leisure of waiting for manufactures to effect a gradual transformation in the existing labor force of artisans. As this shows, state intervention was critical for the development of industrial capitalism. In turn, the state required the development of industrial capitalism to ensure its own continued existence. State and capital differ in character, yet they can only continue to exist through mutual interdependence.

The Commodification of Money

Karl Polanyi writes that in order for market economies to obtain autonomy as "self-regulating systems," labor, land, and money must become "fictitious commodities," a situation realized historically only since the end of the eighteenth century.[15] In this, the commodification of land and of labor are interlinked: the commodification of labor must be preceded by the commodification of land, in other words, by the enclosure of the commons and the privatization of land ownership. With the privatization of land ownership, the agrarian community loses its real base. Of course, even with the commodification of land, other kinds of cooperative commons necessary to the agricultural economy continue to exist, such as water supply and the natural environment. Moreover, in order to preserve these, certain limits are placed on the commodification of land. Nonetheless, by this point "community" exists only as a concept. Furthermore, the privatization of land leads not just to the dissolution of the community but also to destruction of the natural environment (ecosystem) in general, because the functioning of the agrarian community was crucial to the preservation of that environment.

The commodification of money, on the other hand, is connected to credit and finance. These originally arose in response to a fundamental difficulty encountered in commodity exchange: credit systems were established as a way to get around this difficulty. In buying and selling commodities, for example, one promises to pay the money later and hands over a promissory note. Through this credit, capital is freed up to pursue new investments. Or, if it lacks money, capital can borrow from someone, paying the money back later with interest. Through this kind of credit, commodity exchange proliferates and production expands. To put it the other way around, expansion of commodity exchange leads to an increase in usurer capital (M-M'), which treats money as a commodity.

To a certain extent, this sort of system existed in the ancient and medieval periods, and it saw further development under merchant capitalism. In fact, commercial and bank credit systems already existed by the time industrial capitalism first appeared. Moreover, merchant and usurer capital did not disappear with the rise of industrial capital; they merely reorganized themselves under its influence. Marx writes:

> The other varieties of capital which appeared previously, within past or declining conditions of social production, are not only subordinated to it and correspondingly altered in the mechanism of their functioning, but they now move only on its basis, thus live and die, stand and fall together with this basis. Money capital and commodity capital, in so far as they appear and function as bearers of their own peculiar branches of business alongside industrial capital, are now only modes of existence of the various functional forms that industrial capital constantly assumes and discards within the circulation sphere, forms which have been rendered independent and one-sidedly extended through the social division of labor.[16]

After the rise to dominance of industrial capital, merchant capital didn't become simply one branch of industrial capital. If anything, the opposite happened: merchant and usurer capital came to envelop industrial capital. From within the heart of industrial capital, forms of accumulation based on merchant and usurer capital emerged and even vied for dominance. This situation arose with the development of banks and joint-stock corporations.

Joint-stock companies began with the joint financing of long-distance trade ventures, launched for the purpose of sharing risk. They became the general practice in industrial capital for the same reason. Investment in constant capital (fixed assets) represented a substantial risk. The practice of forming joint-stock companies was adopted to avoid this: through the commodification of capital, capital itself became something that could be bought and sold on the market. With this, it became possible for the capitalist at any time to transform the real capital tied up in the production process back into monetary capital. Through this conversion into stock, capital could avoid the difficulties it otherwise encountered in the process of accumulation.

The joint-stock company encouraged the concentration of what had until then been scattered small and medium-sized capital holdings—meaning the increased socialization of labor. Marx recognized the historical significance of the joint-stock company, calling it the "the abolition of capital as private property within the confines of the capitalist mode of production itself."[17] By this, he means that the joint-stock company has abolished that entity known as "the capitalist." The "separation of ownership and control" proclaimed by Adolf Berle and Gardiner Means was a possibility inherent from the start in share capital.[18] With share capital, the capitalist becomes a stockholder, interested only in the rate of profit (rate of dividends) and disengaged from the production process. This does not mean, however, that capital has disappeared. Through the joint-stock company, capital has instead transformed from industrial capital to a kind of merchant capital: we now have capitalists who deal in the commodity of capital itself. The joint-stock company returns the capitalist to the role of speculator.

Incidentally, at the beginning of *Capital*, Marx describes a capitalist economy as an accumulation of commodities, and he records the dialectical unfolding through which commodity becomes capital. But he should have shown how the commodity included capital within itself from the beginning. If capital was already included in the commodity as the logical beginning, the development from commodity to share capital would be dialectical in the Hegelian sense. Then *Capital* could have been the narrative of the self-realization of capital-as-spirit. Of course, the joint-stock company does not finally resolve the difficulties arising from commodity exchange. To the contrary, it demonstrates the impossibility of such a resolution.

Rudolf Hilferding's *Finance Capital* made an important contribution to the development of Marxist theories of money and credit. Analyzing joint-stock companies, he explores how stock value exceeds the value of physical capital and how the issuance of new stock produces economic gain for company founders. He also argues that finance capital formed through alliances between banks and industry, the concentration of capital, and the rise of monopolistic cartels. Unlike industrial capital, finance capital is not rooted in free competition over price: it instead attempts to monopolize markets, raw materials, and labor. This theory explained late nineteenth-century imperialism in economic terms. After the world wars that this imperialism led to, a system was established for internationally regulating the movement of finance capital. But these regulations were subsequently lifted, leading to the full and unrestricted commodification of money and capital that has characterized the current wave of globalization since the 1990s.

The Commodification of Labor

The old formulas for capital accumulation (M-M' and M-C-M'), which were supposed to have receded in importance with the rise of industrial capital, have lately once again become targets for criticism. These critiques seem to presume that these represent the real essence of capitalism and that if we could only regulate them effectively, then we would finally reach a healthy capitalism. But the essence of industrial capitalism lies elsewhere: in the commodification of labor power. The commodification of land, money, and capital itself are all important factors, but the commodification of labor power is primary. Without it, commodity exchange could never have reached its full, dominant form. It is also the fundamental source for the crises of capitalism.

A capitalist economy is a system of credit. Credit was adopted as a means of sidestepping fundamental difficulties inherent to commodity exchange. For this reason, there is always a danger that credit will suddenly collapse. Credit "crises" are not accidental; they are necessary and inevitable results of exchanges involving a specific commodity: labor power. This is because, while the commodification of land, money, and capital take place within a self-regulating system—albeit an imperfect one—no such self-regulation is possible for the labor-power commodity.

I have described the rise of a kind of closed autopoietic system, in which industrial capitalism, through its purchasing of the labor-power commodity, arranges for its commodities to buy the commodities that its commodities have produced. But there is a fatal flaw in this system, one that originates in the unique character of the labor-power commodity itself: capital can acquire raw materials as commodities, and it can use these to produce other commodities, but it cannot on its own produce the commodity of labor power. Unlike other commodities, labor power is not subject to the self-regulating system of the market. One cannot simply discard it when demand falls, nor quickly produce more if shortages occur. For example, when there is a labor shortage, one can supplement the existing supply with migrant workers from abroad, but later, when they are no longer needed, they are not easily expelled. As a result, the market "price" of labor power constantly fluctuates according to supply and demand, and this in turn drives the profit rates of capital.

This unique feature of the labor power commodity makes boom-and-bust economic cycles unavoidable. In good times employment increases and wages soar, causing rates of profit to fall. But because favorable conditions lead to an overheating of credit, capital responds to the apparent presence of demand by expanding production. In the end, credit collapses and panic sets in. It becomes clear to all that there had been overproduction. The crisis and slump that follow weed out fragile companies unable to secure a profit. But the slump also causes wages and interest rates to decline, which in turn frees up capital to invest in new equipment and technology. Gradually this leads again to good times—and when that reaches its peak, the next crisis begins.

The accumulation of capital, or rise in the organic composition of capital, is achieved through this kind of business cycle. Capitalism has no other options besides this rather violent method. Seen in this light, it becomes clear that crises will not lead to the downfall of capitalism: they are actually an indispensable part of the process for capital accumulation. Even if crises of credit no longer arise in their classical form, this sort of boom-and-bust cycle will always haunt industrial capital. I should note that this explanation is based on the short-term business cycles that Marx encountered during his lifetime and which are distinct from long-term business cycles.

One other thing about crises: Marx writes that the possibility for crisis exists in the "fatal leap" undertaken in the transformation of commodity into money—in plain language, in confronting the possibility that the commodity might not sell.[19] But this represents only the formal possibility of crisis. Actual crises can occur only after the development of credit systems in a commodity economy. Credit consists of closing a deal to sell a commodity, but postponing the settling up of accounts; it is indispensable for facilitating and expanding trade. A crisis begins when something triggers the realization that the buying and selling being underwritten by credit is in fact not actually taking place. In that sense, all crises take the form of crises of credit.

The key question here is why this becomes cyclical. Economic crises existed before the rise of industrial capitalism. The global crisis that originated in Holland's "tulip mania" is a famous example. But these originated in bubbles or sudden bursts of investment and could not help explain the regular periodic crises and economic cycles that emerged beginning in the 1820s. In *Capital* Marx went a long way toward explaining these, but he only touched on the general causes of crises and did not explain why they occur cyclically. It was Kōzō Uno who demonstrated that their cyclical nature is due solely to the unique characteristics of the labor-power commodity.[20]

But why do the cycles occur at intervals of roughly a decade? Marx argues that this was because machinery used in the key textile industry had a ten-year lifespan. There is an important point here: the periodic crises and business cycles that Marx took under consideration were in a sense determined by the central role the textile industry played in production. In fact, the textile industry was labor intensive, so that wages in it tended to rise quickly, leading to a decline in profit margins within roughly ten years. This time span just happened to coincide with the average life expectancy of factory machinery.

This kind of cyclical crisis disappeared after the Panic of 1873. The Panic was the result of the development of heavy industry since the 1860s. The rate of capital investment (constant capital) increased, resulting in declining rates of profit even when labor productivity (rate of surplus value) increased. Moreover, it was not as easy to attract fresh capital investment in heavy industry as it was in the textile industry. Additionally, because the textile industry did not require as much labor power (variable capital), unemployment increased. This led to declining domestic consumption, and economic slumps became a chronic condition.

If we want to grasp the problem of economic cycles comprehensively, we have to take into consideration not only the labor-power commodity but also the commodity that is serving as the standard commodity for global capitalism. The economic cycles that Marx analyzed were short-term fluctuations, now called Juglar cycles. In contrast to these, Nikolai Kondratiev analyzed longer-term fluctuations with a cycle of around fifty or sixty years. In addition, another kind of long-term cycle has been identified that is based in long-term price fluctuations. In my view, though, cycles in industrial capitalism should be seen as problems ultimately related to the labor-power commodity. In the long term, these appear as transformations in the primary mode of production in industrial capitalism, such as the rise of the textiles industry or heavy industry. Seen from another perspective, occurrences of long-term fluctuations corresponded to changes in the world commodity (standard commodity)—from woolen fabric to cotton textiles, then to heavy industry, durable consumer goods, and so forth. Such changes in the world commodity involve transformations in level of technology and in modes of production and consumption, and hence cannot help but be accompanied by widespread social transformation.

For example, for as long as woolen fabric remained the world commodity, Britain could not surpass Holland. Holland enjoyed dominance in the woolen-fabric industry, and as a result, Holland also held hegemony in transit trade and the financial sector. But when cotton textiles began to supplant wool as the world commodity, hegemony passed from Holland to Britain— though Holland long retained hegemony in the fields of trade and finance. Britain in turn began to lag behind Germany and the United States with the shift from textiles to heavy industry, though like Holland before it, Britain maintained its hegemony in the trade and finance sectors.

I have already touched on the problems that arise at the stage of heavy industry: domestic demand recedes and economic slumps become chronic. Moreover, the products of heavy industry—railroads and shipbuilding being the classic examples—are aimed more at foreign than domestic markets. Capital is forced to seek opportunities in foreign markets, which is impossible without state support. In addition, heavy industries by their nature require massive capital investment. To achieve this, they raise capital through joint-stock companies, but this alone is insufficient; they also require state investment. This explains why Britain fell behind Germany. In this way, the state intervenes even more heavily in the economy during the heavy-industry stage than before. This is how we entered into the age we now call imperialism.

After the Great Depression of the 1930s, the world commodity shifted to durable consumer goods (for example, automobiles and consumer electronics). This led to the rise of the consumer society, characterized by mass production and mass consumption. It reached the saturation point in the 1970s, and globalization was the strategy adopted to escape from the severe recession that ensued. This meant the pursuit of new laborer-consumers. This was made possible by the collapse of the Soviet Union in 1991. World capitalism found new opportunities in the former socialist states and in regions that had been under these states' influence, areas that had previously been isolated from the world market. But this involved swallowing up enormous populations in such places as India and China, and as a result the various contradictions that had already surfaced were now aggravated to an explosive degree. Environmental destruction likewise reached critical levels.

The Limits of Industrial Capitalism

The labor-power commodity is central to the system of self-valorization for industrial capital. But limits of industrial capital also arise from its base in the labor-power commodity. First, this form of capital requires ceaseless technological innovation, because relative surplus value in industrial capitalism derives from increases in labor productivity. Second, it requires the ceaseless pursuit of inexpensive workers who are simultaneously new consumers, primarily in previously rural and peripheral regions. These two conditions are essential for capital accumulation: without them, capitalism is finished.

Smith, for example, predicted that the economic growth seen in his era was a temporary phenomenon and that the capitalist economy would soon settle into a steady state. He did not foresee the continuation of technological innovation. In a sense, though, he shows us what would happen if technological innovation were to stagnate. The question here revolves not around minor technological advances but rather the kind of technological innovation that leads to a shift in the world commodity—for example, from cotton textiles to heavy industry, and then to durable consumer goods. At present, this kind of innovation has peaked. As for the second condition, there is no longer an inexhaustible supply of potential new markets available outside the capitalist economy: these are rapidly disappearing under the forces of global deagrarianization. If, for example, India and China become fully industrialized, the result will be a steep rise in the price of the global labor-power commodity, as well as saturation and stagnation in consumption.

This overlaps with the second condition, but economic growth in industrial capitalism requires one other condition: the existence of inexhaustible nature outside the system of industrial production. This means both an inexhaustible supply of natural resources and an unlimited capacity on the part of the natural world to process the waste products of industrial production. The growth of the industrial capitalist economy up until now has been possible because nature in the above senses—human nature (labor) and natural nature (the environment)—was available in an unlimited supply. But in its present stage, industrial capitalism is rapidly approaching its limits.

This issue is connected to the relation between humans and nature. Up until now I have largely abstracted away this aspect because in fact the human-nature relation has been realized through the human-human rela-tion of modes of exchange. But the human-nature relation is of course primary. We need, however, to remain wary of ideologies that stress this and forget about human-human relations. In general, these ideologies have appeared in the form of cultural critiques, such as criticisms of in-dustrial society or of technology. Generally, they follow the pattern set by romantic critiques of modern civilization. But environmental destruction cannot be understood only in terms of human-nature relations; environ-mental destruction and the exploitation of nature are, after all, the products of a society in which humans exploit other humans. The first environmental crisis in human history occurred in the irrigated areas of Mesopotamia. In fact, all great ancient civilizations based on irrigation collapsed and un-leashed the forces of desertification. The systems (modes of exchange) for exploiting, in both the positive and negative senses of the word, humans have disrupted the processes of exchange between humans and nature (i.e., metabolism). The only hope for solving our environmental problems lies in our first superseding capital and the state.

World-Economy

I have taken up industrial capital here in terms of total capital. This is be-cause the self-valorization of capital (the production of surplus value) can-not be understood if we look only at individual capitalists. Still, up until now we have been considering industrial capital at the level of a single country. In reality, industrial capital does not limit its search for labor power, raw materials, and consumers to a single country. Industrial capital cannot exist without overseas markets. Marx also pointed out that capital-ist production in general could not exist without foreign trade. For example, the British industrial revolution, centered on the textile industry, did not arise in response only to the domestic market. The revolution represented a bid to seize international hegemony within the ongoing mercantilist competition.

Ricardo, who opposed both the mercantilism that drew its profits from overseas trade and the protectionist tariff policies that it led to, stressed that free trade would be profitable for both sides. Under his "theory of compara-tive advantage," the sectors in the industrial structure of each country with relatively high productivity—that is to say, those that could produce com-modities with relatively little labor—would focus on production for export, and through this a kind of international division of labor among nations would emerge, with each country developing its own relatively productive industrial sector. This theory of an international division is, however, a deceptive ideology. Ricardo explained it using the examples of British textiles and Portuguese wine, saying that each profited by developing its own production specialty. The actual historical result, however, was Portugal's transformation into an agricultural nation, subordinated to British industrial capital. The effect was the same as when industrial capital with its increased labor productivity comes to dominate over the agricultural sector within a single country.

Advocates of liberalism such as Smith and Ricardo opposed colonialism, on the grounds that colonization led to monopolization of trade. Nonetheless, their liberalism became the *liberal imperialism* adopted by states that had developed industrial capital. Unlike earlier empires or mercantilist states, these states had no need to exploit peripheral regions by force: they were able to obtain surplus value through free trade, a process of equal exchanges that exploited the differences between different systems of values. These differences were generated by industrial capital's relentless pursuit of increased labor productivity through technological innovation.

Compared to countries that had developed industrial capital, the raw-material-producing countries with low labor productivity had cheap labor and cheap raw materials. Accordingly, capital from the advanced countries was able to obtain surplus value not only from domestic laborers but also through equal exchanges with the periphery, exchanges involving both raw materials and migrant workers. We need to keep this issue in mind when we consider the situation of labor in the advanced countries: while workers and farmers in advanced countries are exploited by capital, this cannot compare with the situation of their counterparts in developing countries.

Ricardo's theories of comparative advantage and international division of labor are still invoked by today's neoliberal economists. The earliest objections to them were raised by Arghiri Emmanuel and Andre Gunder Frank, who argued that exchanges at world-market prices between the core and colonies inevitably became unequal exchanges profiting the core at the expense of the colony and that the effect of such unequal exchanges would be cumulative. Samir Amin would also criticize the theory of comparative advantage and international division of labor, seeking the causes for the backwardness of developing countries in the phenomena of unequal exchanges and dependency. Prior to the onset of the industrial revolution in Britain, there was no pronounced difference in economic and technological levels between Europe and the rest of the world, especially Asia.

The undeveloped state of the latter was not something existing from the start: it was produced through the rise of industrial capitalism. Broadly speaking, the assertions made by these advocates of "theories of dependency" are correct. For example, Immanuel Wallerstein writes:

> Core and periphery, then, are simply phrases to locate one crucial part of the system of surplus appropriation by the bourgeoisie. To oversimplify, capitalism is a system in which the surplus-value of the proletarian is appropriated by the bourgeois. When this proletarian is located in a different country from this bourgeois, one of the mechanisms that has affected the process of appropriation is the manipulation of controlling flows over state boundaries. This results in patterns of "uneven development" which are *summarized* in the concepts of core, semiperiphery and periphery. This is an intellectual tool to help analyse the multiple forms of class conflict in the capitalist world-economy.[21]

But there is no special "manipulation" involved in these unequal exchanges, nor any particular mystery. It only appears that way when industrial capital is regarded as being somehow of a different nature from mercantile capital. As I have argued repeatedly, whether mercantile or industrial, capital obtains surplus value from exchanges made across different systems of value. Exchanges made within each system of value are equal exchanges, but the difference between systems generates surplus value. At the stage of mercantile capital, differences between systems of value in different regions—that is, "uneven development"—originated in differences in natural conditions. The exchanges carried out by industrial capital involving industrial products, however, cause nonindustrialized countries to specialize in the production of raw materials, leading to even greater unevenness. This unevenness is then constantly reproduced.

Marx's explanations for the general tendency of the rate of profit to fall and for the increasing impoverishment of the proletariat and the emergence of two great classes have been subjected to criticism since the late nineteenth century. But, to take one example, the ability of the British working class to enjoy a measure of prosperity in defiance of Marx's law of impoverishment was due to capital's ability to obtain surplus value from overseas trade, a part of which was redistributed to British labor. The impoverishment that Marx predicted was inflicted abroad rather than domestically, and it continues to be inflicted today. To understand the problems of capitalism, we always need to grasp it not in terms of a single nation but in terms of the world-economy.

The Rise of the Nation

We have been considering how the capitalist social formation, dominated by mode of exchange C, emerged. This involved looking at changes from earlier social formations in the way the various modes of exchange were combined together. In this chapter, we will explore how, under the dominant role played by mode of exchange C, the capitalist social formation took the form of Capital-Nation-State.

The nation-state is a coupling together of two elements with different natures: nation and state. The nation-state's emergence, however, requires the previous appearance of capital-state—that is, a coupling of capital with state. This was achieved with the absolute monarchies. I have already described the situation of the social formation under absolute monarchies, in which previously dominant mode of exchange B was transformed by the impact of the emerging dominance of mode of exchange C. The nation appeared after this in the bourgeois revolutions that toppled the absolute monarchy. To put this somewhat schematically, the nation is something that appears within the social formation as an attempt to recover, through imagination, mode of exchange A and community, which is disintegrating under the rule of capital-state. The nation is formed by capital-state, but it is at the same time a form of protest and resistance to the conditions brought about by capital-state, as well as an attempt to supplement for what is lacking in capital-state.

The sensibility of the nation is grounded in blood-lineage, regional, and linguistic communities. None of these, however, possesses the secret of the nation: the nation does not form simply because of the existence of such communities. The nation appears only after the emergence of capital-state. Accordingly, we can take up the rise of the nation from two different angles: from that of the sovereign state or from that of industrial capitalism. In other words, from the perspectives of mode of exchange B or C. The nation arises as a synthesis of these two moments.

THE LEVEL OF SOVEREIGN STATE

Generally, the nation emerges through a bourgeois revolution. In England, for example, the establishment of popular sovereignty after the Glorious Revolution (1688) marks the emergence of the nation-state (commonwealth). Here state sovereignty lies with the nation (i.e., the national people). But of course this nation as sovereign (the people) did not simply exist from the start. It was formed under the now-toppled absolute monarch (sovereign), who united the people, previously fragmented into status and other groupings, by placing them all in a single, unified position as the monarch's subjects. Without this precedent established by the absolute monarchy, the nation as sovereign ("the people")could never emerge.

We see this, for example, in the Asiatic despotic states. There the toppling of one dynasty reignited struggle among the various tribes and clans and eventually led to the emergence of yet another dynasty. In order for the overturning of a despotic system to lead to the rise of the people as sovereign, there would first have to be the emergence of an absolute monarch or similar regime—an absolutist power capable of unifying multiple tribes and ethnic groups. In the underdeveloped regions of Europe, this role was played by the "enlightened" absolute monarchs, who suppressed the feudal powers and carried out political and economic modernization. In many non-European countries, the role of absolute monarch was filled by a dictator. The toppling of these dictators then led to the emergence of the people as sovereign.

The emergence of a single, unified nation, encompassing what had been multiple tribes, requires a number of negations, beginning with a rejection of the authority of any empire standing above the state. I have already described how the lack of a fully established world-empire in Europe paved the way for the emergence of a world-economy there. Yet even if no political empire existed, in a broad sense there was one entity that unified western Europe into a single world: the Roman Catholic Church, with its world language of Latin and its Roman law, which become the basis for natural

law. These were rejected by the absolute monarchs. They first of all assigned superiority to national law over the law of empire (natural law) or
church law. Second, they rejected the authority of the church. This can be
seen in its classic form in the English monarchy's confiscation of church
property. In addition, under the absolute monarchies it became standard
practice to write in the national language. In other words, with the rise of
translation from Latin into the vulgate of each nation, the written language
of each nation took shape.[1] In securing their own "absolute" status, the absolute monarchs paved the way for the existence of the nation.

I have mainly focused on western Europe, but we see the same process in
other regions. For example, in colonized areas intertribal conflicts and disparities are overcome through movements that rise up in resistance against
the ruling state. In these cases, the process of nation formation differs between countries where a state had already existed and those that never had
a state. In the former, the previous state and its civilization become the basis
for nationalist resistance to the Western rulers. In the latter, a national state
and language are established through the leverage of the colonial state apparatus. In either case, a previously nonexistent identity as nation is formed.
In that sense, the colonial state takes up the role played elsewhere by the
absolutist state, and the nation is established through the struggle to overthrow the state (i.e., through national liberation).

The tribal community is widely believed to provide the basis for the nation. In reality, however, such a community could never serve as the basis
for national identity: to the contrary, the tribal community engages in ceaseless strife and conflict with other tribes, as well as conspiracies and secret
pacts with foreign countries. In Europe it was the absolute monarchs who
suppressed the tribes to produce unity. Nations did not form in regions
where this kind of centralized power was lacking. There religious affilia-
tions that transcended individual nations retained their hold, obstructing
the unification of nations.

THE LEVEL OF INDUSTRIAL CAPITALISM

Next let's consider the nation from the perspective of mode of exchange
C—that is, of industrial capitalism. The work of Ernest Gellner is useful
here: he sought the origins of nationalism in industrial society. The distinguishing characteristics of that form of society are its "mobile division of
labour" and "sustained, frequent, and precise communication between
strangers." Modern society "provides a very prolonged and fairly thorough

training for all its recruits, insisting on certain shared qualifications: literacy, numeracy, basic work habits and social skills, familiarity with basic technical and social skills."[2]

Gellner demonstrates that nationalism emerged in tandem with the formation of the labor-power commodity under industrial capital. Under artisan-apprenticeship systems, the type of skill learned was narrowly defined, and the methods and stages of training and proficiency were rigidly fixed. Moreover, someone who was a master in one field of industry would never switch to another. But, along with the division of labor, industrial capitalism is characterized by the continual invention of new technologies that give birth to new kinds of jobs. The industrial proletariat needs to be able to respond quickly to such changes, and so what they require is not high-level proficiency in one skill but rather basic skills that can constantly be adapted to new jobs. Also needed are strict punctuality, a diligent attitude toward work, and an ability to work together with strangers. In order to work well with strangers, a shared language and culture are also necessary.

But it is neither industrial society nor industrial capital that produces this labor-power commodity: it is the modern state. The first order of business for any late-developing capitalist state is to institute military conscription and compulsory education. This means that the cultivation of nationalism cannot be separated from the cultivation of the labor-power commodity.

The Substitute for Community

These conditions are necessary to any understanding of the nation, but on their own they are insufficient. From the perspectives discussed so far, we might assume that the nation was created by the state or capital. But the nation is not simply the passive product of capital-state: it is also in itself a form of resistance to capital-state. The nation cannot be fully explained only through the processes of state unification or productive labor power, because it harbors in itself a reaction against these. In that sense, the nation is rooted in the dimension of what we might call sentiment.

The nation emerges when, following the overthrow of the absolute sovereign by a bourgeois revolution, each individual acquires freedom and equality. But these alone are not sufficient. In addition to individual freedom and equality, a sense of solidarity is also required. In the French Revolution, for example, the slogan was "Liberty, equality, fraternity." Here liberty and equality are concepts deriving from reason, but *fraternity* belongs to a dif-

ferent order: it signifies a sentiment of solidarity linking together individuals. A nation requires this kind of sentiment. Different from the love that
existed within the family or tribal community, it is a new sentiment of solidarity that arises among people who have broken away from those earlier
bonds.

Explaining the nation through sentiment may seem superficial. Some
may think it more appropriate to explain the nation in terms of its actual
bases—ethnic or linguistic communality, for example, or economic communality. Yet these forms of communality on their own do not necessarily
lead to the formation of a nation—in fact, they may even hinder it. For example, the nation may be sacrificed to the needs of tribe or religion. Accordingly, when we think about nations, we need to think of them in terms of a
kind of sentiment. This does not mean turning it into a problem of psychology. To the contrary, it means looking at *exchanges* that are cognized only
as sentiment.

As Friedrich Nietzsche pointed out, the feeling of guilt harbors within
itself an implicit exchange.[3] Of course, this is an exchange based on reciprocity—it is not a commodity exchange. In commodity exchanges, people
set aside emotions and act in a businesslike fashion. But the feeling of obligation that arises from a reciprocal exchange is something that cannot
be settled with money; in economic terms, such feeling is utterly foreign to
economic rationality. To say that the nation is manifested as sentiment is
to say that it is rooted in a mode of exchange different from those that serve
as the base for the state or capital. Nonetheless, the nation is not usually
perceived in this way.

Many Marxists have stumbled over the problem of the nation. To them
the nation is merely an ideology produced by the modern capitalist economic structure, and hence it can and should be easily dissolved through
enlightenment. In reality, however, Marxist movements that downplayed
the importance of the nation found themselves unable to resist fascism,
which rose under the banner of nationalism. Moreover, even socialist states
resorted to nationalism, to the point that armed conflicts broke out among
them.

Benedict Anderson writes that he was driven to rethink the problems
of the nation by the eruption of war between China and the USSR and
between China and Vietnam—when, that is, he was directly confronted
with this blind spot in Marxism. He came to define the nation as an "imagined community." At first glance, this seems to resemble the Marxists' view—
that the nation is a communal fantasy from which people should be awakened

through enlightenment. But one crucial difference in Anderson is that he sees the nation itself as a product of enlightenment rationality. He locates the origins of the nation in the eighteenth century, when the rise in the West of the Enlightenment and its rational worldview led to a decline in religious modes of thought. In his understanding, the nation replaces religion as that which grants individuals a sense of eternity and immortality, thereby rendering their existences meaningful:

> If the manner of a man's dying usually seems arbitrary, his mortality is inescapable. Human lives are full of such combinations of necessity and chance. We are all aware of the contingency and ineluctability of our particular genetic heritage, our gender, our life-era, our physical capabilities, our mother-tongue, and so forth. The great merit of traditional religious world-views (which naturally must be distinguished from their role in the legitimation of specific systems of domination and exploitation) has been their concern with man-in-the-cosmos, man as species being, and the contingency of life. The extraordinary survival over thousands of years of Buddhism, Christianity or Islam in dozens of different social formations attests to their imaginative response to the overwhelming burden of human suffering—disease, mutilation, grief, age, and death.[4]

Nationalism replaces religion in providing this imaginative response, according to Anderson. But what he calls the religious worldview that was undercut by Enlightenment rationality was really the worldview of the agrarian community. As was the case with Christianity or Buddhism, any universal religion originally appears as a kind of resistance against this community, but as it puts down roots in that community, it is forced to start answering to the community's needs. Universal religions ended up fusing with local religions of the agrarian community. Accordingly, the dissolution of that community meant, if anything, that universal religions were able to recover their original character. In fact, religion has continued to develop since the Enlightenment, taking the form of individualistic religion (e.g., Protestantism).

This means that we can't simply define Enlightenment rationality as a critique of religion. Enlightenment thought in the period following the English bourgeois revolution is usually associated with the thought of John Locke and his peers. But in eighteenth-century Germany and Russia, the dominant force was enlightened despotism—in other words, the absolute monarch. In order to consolidate the nation under their rule, the absolute monarchs needed Enlightenment rationality to negate external forms of authority, such as the Roman Catholic Church. In that sense, Enlightenment rationality was the ideology of the absolute monarchy, one that promoted the rise of capital-state. This inevitably resulted in the downfall of the agrarian community. If Enlightenment rationality can be understood in this way, then the romanticism that rose in reaction to the Enlightenment signified not only a criticism of capital-state but also a desire to restore the community it had destroyed, along with its principle of reciprocity. For this reason, romanticism was ambiguous in nature; it contained two sides: a nostalgic desire for a return to the past and a contemporary critique of capital-state. In general the former tendency was dominant, but in English romanticism, for example, the latter tendency was stronger, leading to the widely noted prevalence of socialists in the movement.[5]

The destruction of community at the hands of capital-state had, as Anderson indicates, enormous significance: the disappearance of the community meant the disappearance of a generational sense of time that had previously underwritten a sense of permanence. In the economy of the agrarian community, reciprocity was not limited to the living; it was assumed that reciprocal exchanges were also carried out with the dead (ancestors) and the not-yet born (descendants). The living carried out their lives while always keeping in mind their future descendants, while those descendants were in turn expected to offer gratitude to their ancestors for these considerations bestowed in advance. The collapse of the agrarian community meant the loss of this sense of immortality that individuals obtained by seeing their own existence as a link between past ancestors and future descendants. Universal religions promised immortality to individual souls but could not restore this communal temporality—that was accomplished, at least in imagined form, by the nation. The people of a nation, accordingly, include not only the living but also its past and future members. This is why nationalisms are characterized by attachments to both past and future.

Anderson views the nation as a substitute for religion, but this cannot explain the phenomenon of religious nationalism seen, for example, in Hindu nationalism in India. But if we understand the nation as a substitute for community, then we see that what appears to be religious nationalism is in fact an imaginary restoration of the vanished community. Religion in this case means not universal religion but rather the local religion of a community. Accordingly, it is not particularly puzzling to find the nation—an attempt to restore the vanished community through imagination—manifesting itself in religious forms.

We cannot understand the nation solely in terms of economic or political interest: it includes a metaphysical dimension. This does not mean, however, that unlike economy or politics, the nation exists on a spiritual plane. It means simply that the nation is based on reciprocity, a different mode of exchange from that which grounds a commodity economy. The nation is the imagined restoration of the community that was undermined by the commodity-exchange economy. The nation instills the sentiment that is lacking in capital-state. In *Elements of the Philosophy of Right*, G. W. F. Hegel calls the Hobbesian state the "state . . . *of the understanding.*"[6] By this he means that it lacks sentiment—in other words, the nation. In Hegel's thought, Capital-Nation-State is the state as envisaged by reason. To understand this more fully, let us look at the philosophical context in which the nation emerged.

The Status of Imagination

It is important to remember that late eighteenth-century Europe saw the rise not only of Anderson's "imagined communities" but also of imagination itself as a faculty attributed with special significance. In other words, the rise of the nation and the discovery in philosophy of the imagination as a mediating link between sensibility and understanding took place at the same moment. Previously in the history of philosophy, sensibility was always ranked below intellect, and imagination was similarly looked down upon as a faculty of pseudoreproduction of sense perception or, worse, arbitrary fancy. It was Immanuel Kant who first discovered the imagination as that which mediated between sensibility and understanding and as a creative faculty whose operation is prior to understanding. For example, based on his reading of Kant, the romantic poet and critic Samuel Taylor Coleridge would distinguish between fancy and imagination: imagination was something different from fancy. In this sense, when we say that the nation is an imagined community, we need to bear in mind we are dealing here with imagination, not fancy. In other words, the nation has a basis in reality and cannot simply be dissolved through enlightenment.

Historically speaking, the emergence of the sentiment of the nation occurred simultaneously with this elevation in status of imagination. In philosophy the issue was first directly problematized in the country that saw the earliest development of a capitalist industrial economy: Britain, especially Scotland. Philosophers in the early seventeenth century took up the problem of a specific kind of sentiment, the "moral sentiment" that was first broached by Francis Hutcheson. Hutcheson's student Adam Smith would also take up the question of moral sentiment, describing "sympathy" in the following terms:

> How selfish soever man may be supposed, there are evidently some principles in his nature, which interest him in the fortune of others, and render their happiness necessary to him, though he derives nothing from it except the pleasure of seeing it. Of this kind is pity or compassion, the emotion which we feel for the misery of others, when we either see it, or are made to conceive it in a very lively manner. That we often derive sorrow from the sorrow of others, is a matter of fact too obvious to require any instances to prove it. . . . By the imagination we place ourselves in [another man's] situation, we conceive ourselves enduring all the same torments, we enter as it were into his body, and become in some measure the same person with him, and thence form some idea of his sensations, and even feel something which, though weaker in degree, is not altogether unlike them.[7]

What Smith here calls "sympathy" is imagination: the ability to mentally place oneself in the position of another. There is, however, a subtle but crucial difference between this and Hutcheson's moral sentiment. For Hutcheson, moral sentiment is opposed to selfishness, but Smith's sympathy is perfectly compatible with it. If, after all, one mentally places oneself in the position of the other, one must acknowledge the selfishness of that other. As an economist, Smith believes that selfish pursuit of profit by individuals ultimately leads to the greatest welfare of the whole, and therefore he advocates a policy of laissez-faire. Smith was also, however, a moral philosopher—not just at the beginning of his career but throughout; his political economy was simply the final manifestation of his system of moral philosophy.

This doctrine of moral sentiment may seem incompatible with the doctrine of laissez-faire market principles and its affirmation of survival of the fittest. The problem is frequently posed as follows: Smith advocated laissez-faire, but also understood the evils it would inevitably give rise to, leading him to his moral philosophy. In this view, Smith is a pioneer of welfare economics. Yet Smith's advocacy of both selfishness and sympathy were in no sense contradictory. Christianity—like Buddhism and Islam—condemns selfishness and praises compassion. But Smith's sympathy is something different from compassion or pity: it is something that only emerges once selfishness is affirmed—only, that is, in a capitalist market economy.

Compassion and pity are the ethics of a society in which commodity mode of exchange C is still limited to a secondary role. Smith's sympathy is a moral sentiment or imagination that appears only after the principle of commodity exchange achieves dominance, after the principle of reciprocity has been dismantled; this sympathy could not exist in earlier social formations.

Moral Sentiment and Aesthetics

The fraternity that was proclaimed in the French Revolution is identical to what Smith called "sympathy" or "fellow feeling." As a concept, fraternity had Christian roots. However, just as Smith's sympathy differs from religious compassion and is something that arises only in a situation where selfishness is affirmed, this fraternity also bears only a superficial resemblance to its Christian counterpart. *Fraternity* in the French Revolution originated as an expression of the association of artisan workers, but over the course of the revolution, the concept was gradually absorbed into the nation. In concrete terms, *fraternity* was transformed into an expression of nationalism during the struggles against the counterrevolution and then further during Napoleon's rule.

Subsequently, fraternity would be revived by early socialism, but it always harbored a tendency toward nationalism. The most influential form of early socialism was Saint-Simonism, which called for state intervention to promote industry and address social problems. But Saint-Simonism also devolved into a form of nationalism—nationalism with a socialist hue. Napoleon III (Louis Bonaparte), for example, was a Saint-Simonist, and Otto von Bismarck in Prussia was a close friend of Ferdinand Lassalle, the closest German equivalent to Saint-Simonism. Hence the importance of P.-J. Proudhon's rejection from the start of the moment of fraternity that was so prevalent in contemporary socialism.

But in eighteenth-century Britain and France, philosophical investigations into the sentiment of sympathy and fraternity were not pursued beyond this. This development took place instead in Germany, where fraternity existed not as a political or economic problem, but rather as a topic of philosophical debate. When we read these debates today, we must not overlook the essential problems that were at stake in them.

In Germany the problem of moral sentiment emerged as the question of whether sentiments themselves included a moral or an intellectual faculty. Philosophy had previously paid little heed to sentiment: it was believed that sentiment was something that led people astray and that true understanding and morality stood in a transcendent position above it. Sensibility began to be taken more seriously with the emergence of modern science, but only in relation to sensation (sense perception): emotions were still considered inferior. Both Thomas Hobbes and Baruch Spinoza understood them to be passions that must be mastered through intellect.

The eighteenth century saw the rise of a new discourse, aesthetics, that asserted not only that emotion was what made rational cognition and moral judgment possible, but that it was a faculty that in some ways stood above understanding and reason. Today *aesthetics* primarily refers to the study of the beautiful, but originally it meant a theory of sensibility. For example, in his *Aesthetics* Alexander Baumgarten defined it as the study of sensibility, a field in which the theory of art occupied only one small part. The understanding of aesthetics as something dealing almost exclusively with the beautiful, however, arises from Baumgarten's assertion that sensibility and emotion included within themselves a rational faculty of cognition. Kant would criticize him on this point.[8]

In *Critique of Pure Reason*, Kant uses aesthetic exclusively in the sense of a theory of sensibility. Kant consistently distinguishes between sensibility and understanding—in other words, between what can be sensed and what can be thought. This distinction was crucial, because any form of speculation that did not make it—for example, the conclusion that our ability to think of something (for example, God) in and of itself proved the existence of that thing—was liable to lapse into metaphysics. In rigorously distinguishing between sensibility and understanding, Kant was criticizing not only Baumgarten's claim that sensibility included within itself a faculty of cognition, but also Hutcheson's attempt to ground morality in a moral sentiment. In Kant's thought, moral law is inherent to reason and therefore exists in neither feelings nor sensibility. If something such as moral sentiment can be said to exist, it can only be something that arises from a previous knowledge of moral law. To claim that feelings from the start include reason is to aestheticize (in terms of both sensibility and beauty) morality.

In Kant's view, sensibility and understanding are synthesized through the imagination. This means, in other words, that sensibility and understanding can be synthesized only in imagination. Kant asserts that "there are two stems of human cognition, which may perhaps arise from a common but to us unknown root, namely sensibility and understanding."[9] But he never positively demonstrates this. Even in *Critique of Judgment*, he acknowledges that it can only be suggested by the method of skepticism. The romantic philosophers who followed in Kant's wake, however, believed that sensibility and understanding were unified from the start. For example, Friedrich Schelling argued for an intuitive understanding (*intuitiver Verstand*) that transcended the duality of sense and understanding (theoretical reason), one that was a synthesis of sensibility and understanding. In other words, he posited art as the root of all cognition—an aestheticization of philosophy.

Aestheticization of the State

In standard histories of philosophy, Kant is said to have insisted on the dualism of sensibility and understanding, while the romantic school is said to have then transcended this dualism. But Kant did not simply affirm this binary. In concrete terms, the split between sensibility and understanding expresses a real split between what people think and what they really are. For example, in capitalist society everyone believes in human equality, even though they are actually unequal. In this sense, there is an actually existing split between understanding and sensibility. Works of literature are born from the attempt to transcend this split through imagination. No one would deny that such transcending of reality through literature takes place through imagination.

In the same sense, the nation is an imagined community. In the nation, the real disparities produced by the capitalist economy and the lack of freedom and equality are compensated for and resolved in imagined form. Moreover, the nation involves the imagination of a community based in reciprocity and that is distinct from the ruling apparatus of the state. The nation is thus a demand for the egalitarian and implicitly harbors a critical protest against the state and capital. At the same time, however, as the imagined resolution to contradictions generated by capital-state, the nation also shields capital-state from collapse. The nation is thus ambiguous in nature. I began my argument by asserting that what we call the nation-state must be understood instead as Capital-Nation-State. The capitalist economy (sensibility) and state (understanding) are held together by the nation (imagination). Together they form Borromean rings, in which the whole collapses if any of the three rings is removed (see figure 9.1).

The romantic philosophers, however, lost sight of the imagined status of the nation: they thought it existed as an objective reality. This arose because they rejected the dualism of sensibility and understanding. Johann Gottfried von Herder, one of Kant's disciples, was the first to attempt to super-

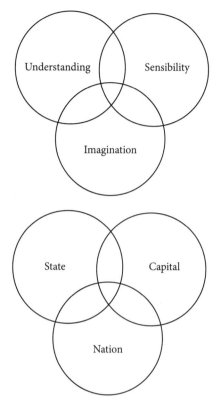

FIGURE 9.1

sede his mentor's dualism. In "Treatise on the Origin of Language" (1772), he takes up Jean-Jacques Rousseau's "Essay on the Origin of Languages," but unlike Rousseau, who saw language as based in sentiment, Herder emphasized that reason played a crucial role in the origin of language. He argued that sentiment in itself included a kind of reason.[10] For him, sensibility and understanding are from the start already synthesized. In confronting modern subjective philosophy, Herder took his point of departure from entities primarily related to sensibility: climate, language, and the folk of the linguistic community (*Volk*). In doing so, he was already rationalizing sensibility. In other words, his reason and understanding were transformed into something akin to sensibility: they were aestheticized. As a result, in his thought the reason of the state had its basis in the domain of sensibility, with such entities as climate, language, and folk. Hence, Herder's state was unlike that found in the social-contract theory of such figures as Hobbes or Locke; rather, Herder's state was based in sentiment, which is to say it was the nation.

For Johann Gottlieb Fichte, on the other hand, the core of the nation lay in language. The nation was not formed by the communality of blood lineage or region, nor by the political state, but rather by language:

> To begin with and before all things: the first, original, and truly natural boundaries of States are beyond doubt their internal boundaries. Those who speak the same language are joined to each other by a multitude of invisible bonds by nature herself, long before any human art begins; they understand each other and have the power of continuing to make themselves understood more and more clearly; they belong together and are by nature one and an inseparable whole. Such a whole, if it wishes to absorb and mingle with itself any other people of different descent and language, cannot do so without itself becoming confused, in the beginning at any rate, and violently disturbing the even progress of its culture. From this internal boundary, which is drawn by the spiritual nature of man himself, the marking of the external boundary of dwelling-place results as a consequence; and in the natural view of things it is not because men dwell between certain mountains and rivers that they are a people, but, on the contrary, men dwell together—and, if their luck has so arranged it, are protected by rivers and mountains—because they were a people already by a law of nature which is much higher.
>
>   . . . Thus was the German nation placed—sufficiently united within itself by a common language and a common way of thinking, and sharply enough severed from the other peoples—in the middle of Europe, as a wall to divide races not akin. The German nation was numerous and brave enough to protect its boundaries against any foreign attack.[11]

Fichte here clearly distinguishes the nation from the state. Whereas the state is defined by boundaries, the nation has "internal boundaries." When these internal boundaries become manifest, a truly rational state is established. It is clear, however, that in positing language as internal boundary, reason and understanding are already aestheticized, rendered into sensibility. Put the other way around, this means that the domain of sensibility has been rendered into spirit. For example, through language (especially literature) mountains and rivers are aestheticized as a specifically national landscape. Fichte continues:

> With this our immediate task is performed, which was to find the characteristic that differentiates the German from the other peoples of

Teutonic descent. The difference arose at the moment of the separation of the common stock and consists in this, that the German speaks a language which has been alive ever since it first issued from the force of nature, whereas the other Teutonic races speak a language which has movement on the surface only but is dead at the root.

... In the preceding addresses we have indicated and proven from history the characteristics of the Germans as an original people [*Urvolk*], and as a people that has the right to call itself simply *the* people, in contrast to other branches that have been torn away from it.[12]

Fichte forgets, however, how the German language was formed: through translation, such as Martin Luther's rendering of the Bible. National language is consummated at the moment its origins in translation from the written language of empire (Latin or Chinese, for example) are forgotten, and it comes to seem as if it were the direct voice of sentiment and the interior. When Herder and the other romantic philosophers began their speculations on the origins of language, national language had already attained this consummate form. The spoken languages these philosophers discovered were from the start translations of written languages (the languages of empire). In other words, the sensibility they discovered was already mediated by understanding. Earlier, I used the word *aesthetic* to describe how the romantics began from a presumption of the union of sensibility and understanding; the same could be said at the level of language.

The most complete form of German romantic philosophy arrives with Hegel. In particular, his *Philosophy of Right* was the first work to explicate the interrelationships between the capitalist economy, state, and nation. The book's argument proceeds from family to civil society to state. This represents not their historical order but rather the dialectic of their structural relationship. For example, the family that Hegel takes up at the start is not the primitive or tribal family but rather the modern nuclear family. Civil society is situated at a level above this family. This is the world of competition, in which various desires (egoisms) clash. In dealing with this level of civil society, however, Hegel incorporates not only the society of the market economy but also the state apparatus, including the police and justice system, social policies, and vocational groups. According to Hegel, this represents only the "state ... *of the understanding*": the moment of sensibility found in the nation is missing. The synthesis of the state of the understanding and the moment of sensibility only comes about in the state of reason, that is, in the nation-state. The kind of state that Hegel described did not actually exist in the Germany of his day though. In pursuing this line of thought, he took contemporary Britain as his model.

In this way, Hegel on the one hand hints that the national is based in sensibility, be it of the family or tribe, but on the other hand he also claims that the national only emerges in a higher dimension that is realized in superseding civil society (which itself had superseded family and community)—in other words, in the nation. In his logic, as in Herder's, the germ of reason is already present at the stage of sensibility, and subsequently it gradually unfolds through a process of self-realization. This means that while the nation (Volk) pertains to sensibility, it also belongs to the domain of reason, and hence it reaches its final realization in the form of the nation-state. Needless to say, this narrative has nothing to do with actual historical processes.

In *Philosophy of Right*, Hegel tried to explicate the knot formed by Capital-Nation-State. This Borromean knot cannot be grasped through a one-dimensional approach: this was why Hegel adopted the dialectical explanation outlined earlier. Advocates of statism, social democracy, and popular nationalism can all extract support for their positions from Hegel's thought, just as Hegel can also be used to critique each of these positions. This is because Hegel grasped the Borromean knot of Capital-Nation-State structurally—in his own words, he grasped it conceptually (*begreifen*). As a result, Hegel's philosophy takes on a power that is not easily denied.

Nonetheless, even in Hegel's philosophy, it is forgotten that this knot was produced in a fundamental sense by the imagination, in the form of the nation; he forgets that the nation exists only in imagination. This also explains why his philosophy was unable to foresee any possibility of superseding this knot.

The Nation-State and Imperialism

I have looked at the process of nation formation primarily in western Europe. This is because, as was the case with absolute monarchy (the sovereign state), the nation first appeared there. And just as the appearance of one sovereign state immediately gave rise to the appearance of others, the nation-state likewise proliferated to produce nation-states in other regions. The first manifestation of this came with Napoleon's conquest of Europe. Napoleon intended to transmit the ideals of the French Revolution, but as we see with Fichte, Napoleon instead paved the way for the birth of nation-states in areas occupied by France. Hannah Arendt describes this situation:

> The inner contradiction between the nation's body politic and conquest as a political device has been obvious since the failure of the Napoleonic dream. . . . The Napoleonic failure to unite Europe under the French flag was a clear indication that conquest by a nation led either to the full awakening of the conquered people's national consciousness and to consequent rebellion against the conqueror, or to tyranny. And though tyranny, because it needs no consent, may successfully rule over foreign peoples, it can stay in power only if it destroys first of all the national institutions of its own people.[13]

Arendt explains that this was because the nation-state differed from empires in that it lacked the basic principle needed for ruling over multiple ethnic peoples or states. When a nation-state comes to rule over another state or people, we have not empire but imperialism.[14] In making her case, Arendt defines the principle of empire, distinct from that of the nation-state, through the case of the Roman Empire. But this is not limited to the Roman Empire: it is the characteristic principle of empire in general.

For example, the Ottoman Empire persisted as a world empire into the twentieth century, its rule grounded in this principle of empire. The Ottoman court never attempted to convert its subjects to Islam. Its various regions were permitted to preserve their own distinct folk cultures, religions, languages, and at times even their own political structures and forms of economic activity. This sharply contrasts with the forced assimilation of citizens by the nation-state—and with the assimilation by force of other peoples under the imperialism that arises when a nation-state expands.

The dissolution of the Ottoman Empire and the independence of its various ethnic peoples was realized by the intervention of various western European states. At the time, those states asserted that they were granting independence to the various nations of the empire as sovereign states. In reality, the western European states made them independent precisely in order to dominate them economically. With this, we have left behind empire and entered into imperialism. *Imperialism* means the domination of one nation by another nation-state in the absence of the governing principle of empire. This is why the Western powers that dismantled the Ottoman Empire were immediately confronted by the reaction of Arab nationalism.[15]

"Wherever the nation-state appeared as conqueror, it aroused national consciousness and desire for sovereignty among the conquered people," writes Arendt.[16] But why did conquest by Asiatic despotisms produce empire, while conquest by nation-states led to imperialism? This problem cannot be solved if, like Arendt, we consider only the principles of political governance; the solution requires us to approach the problem from the perspective of modes of exchange.

In the case of world empires, conquest ultimately results in a system where submission and tribute payments are exchanged for security. In other words, world empires are social formations grounded in mode of exchange B. As supranational states, empires do not interfere in the internal affairs of conquered tribes or states: they do not pursue forced assimilation. This does not mean that empires never encounter resistance: as world empires seek to expand their territories, they encounter continuous tribal uprisings, frequently leading to the toppling of dynasties. But this does not lead to fundamental transformations in the society's mode of existence: when one empire falls, it is simply replaced by another.

Imperialism as the expansion of nation-states, on the other hand, has resulted in the proliferation of nation-states in many regions. This is because empire is a form of rule based in mode of exchange B, while imperialism is based in mode of exchange C. Unlike the former, the latter leads to a fundamental transformation in the social formation, as the capitalist market economy dismantles existing tribal and agrarian communities. This in turn creates the basis for the nation as an imagined community. As a result, while the rule of empire leads to tribal uprisings, the rule of imperialism gives rise to nationalism. In this way, imperialism—that is, the rule by a nation-state over other peoples—ends up creating new nation-states without ever intending to.

A nation-state is never created on a blank sheet. It is born on the ground of the already existing society. When we consider the question of nationalism outside the West, we need to pay attention to differences in this ground. Previously existing worlds are pushed into the periphery under the modern world system, but the conditions that result from this take multiple forms. These conditions differ depending on the position a given entity occupied under the previous world empire: core, margin, submargin, or out of sphere.

The outside regions of earlier empires—that is, tribal societies that had not developed states—were easily colonized under Western imperialism. This is because they were isolated from one another. In regions of this nature, the territorial divisions and state apparatus established by the colonial regime become the subsequent basis for the nation-state. For example, Indonesia is composed of many unrelated tribes, each with its own language, religion, and customs, scattered across thousands of islands, but these were unified into a single nation under Dutch rule.[17]

What was the case for the core, margin, and submargin regions of earlier world empires? The encroachment of Western powers began in marginal regions that were not fully under the control of the previous empires. In these regions, the formation of nations implies independence not only from Western imperialism but also from the previous world empire. For example, each world empire had its own shared written language and religion, akin to the role played by Latin and Christianity in western Europe. The margin is forced to make a choice about whether or not to preserve these languages and religions. In some cases independence from the older world empire is pursued through Westernization, but there are also cases in which independence from Western rule is pursued using the civilization of the old world empire. Either way, nation-states arise through the fragmentation of older world empires, even in the non-West. As for the case of the submargin, Japan and Thailand provide good examples. Because these countries were never directly subjugated in political and cultural terms to the previous world empire, they responded directly on their own to encroachments by the Western powers and thereby avoided colonization. In the case of Japan, a subsequent policy of rapid industrialization even allowed it to join the ranks of the imperialist powers.

The real question here though is the fate of the cores of the old world empires. These were economically and militarily powerful and hence were not easily colonized, but by the latter half of the nineteenth century, they faced increasing encroachment at the hands of the imperialist powers. These world empires—for example, the Ottoman or Qing Empires—attempted to remake themselves into modern states. But their efforts did not succeed because they were composed of multiple tribes and states. Only one ideology was available to them that seemed capable of implementing a highly centralized policy of industrialization while preserving the scope of the empire: Marxism, which gives priority to class over ethnicity by asserting that solving the problems of class would automatically solve the problems of ethnicity. In a sense, the socialist revolutions in Russia and China made it possible to extend the life of those older world empires.[18]

TEN **ASSOCIATIONISM**

The Critique of Religion

I have already noted that mode of exchange D appeared first in the form of universal religions and that consequently social movements have also tended to take on a religious hue. We see this not only in the ancient and medieval periods but also in modernity. For example, the first real bourgeois revolution took place in Britain with the Puritan Revolution (1642–51), which began as a social movement of classes other than the bourgeoisie and in the form of a religious movement. The role of the Levellers faction in the revolution was particularly important. Representing the class of independent commodity producers who were gradually declining in the face of the expanding capitalist economy, the Levellers resembled the anarchists of the nineteenth century. In addition, we should also keep in mind the role played by the Diggers, representing the agrarian proletariat, who clearly advocated a kind of communism and whose assertions were always couched in the language of millenarian religious ideals.

These radical factions played an important role in toppling the absolute monarchy, yet they were then quickly eliminated by the Cromwell regime. The Cromwell regime in turn was ousted in 1660 with the restoration of monarchy, and finally a constitutional monarchy was established with the so-called Glorious Revolution (1688). With this, the British bourgeois revolution can be said to have reached completion. Even so, the socialist elements that had been part of the Puritan Revolution continued to surface. For example, following the Glorious Revolution, John Bellers would propose poverty-relief measures such as a labor-based scrip system, exchange banks, and a craft-union movement, making him a forerunner to Robert Owen and P.-J. Proudhon. We should note that Bellers was a Quaker whose socialism could not be separated from his religious beliefs.

In the French Revolution (1789–99), we don't find the kind of religious hue that characterized the Puritan Revolution. In the nineteenth century, though, we still find socialist movements linked to various religious contexts. Saint-Simon's socialism, for example, was deeply colored by Christianity. It was common, moreover, for socialists to claim that Jesus was a socialist and that primitive Christianity was a form of communism.

Religious socialism remained a powerful force in the revolutions of 1848. After that, however, the link between socialism and Christianity largely disappeared. One reason for this was the fundamental changes in society that accompanied the commodification of labor power and the state-sponsored ascendancy of industrial capitalism after 1848. This rendered ineffective the religious strains of socialism that had functioned in earlier societies. Another causal factor was the appearance of Proudhon and Karl Marx.

In the 1840s, while religious socialism still prevailed, Proudhon undertook a rethinking of socialism from an entirely new perspective. He was the first to proclaim a "scientific socialism," grounding socialism not in religious concepts such as love or ethics but rather in the science of economics. In order to abolish the capitalist economy based in the labor-power commodity, he advocated reciprocal exchange relations among laborers, not equalization achieved through state redistribution. I have argued that the still-nonexistent mode of exchange D was first revealed by universal religions. But Proudhon discovered the possibility for realizing mode D within industrial capitalism itself, and he did so by looking not to religion but to actual practices of exchange—in other words, to economics.

After Proudhon, socialists tended to dismiss religion. By the end of the nineteenth century, the link between socialism and religion had disappeared—to the extent that Frederick Engels and his disciple Karl Kautsky, both of whom had advocated "scientific socialism," would eventually seek to revive the connection between socialism and religious movements.[1] But the relations between socialism and universal religion are very complicated. Mode of exchange D first appears in the form of universal religions. As a result, universal religions provide an indispensable base for socialism. Yet so long as these take the form of religions, they are inevitably absorbed into the religion-state system—this has been the fate of religions, past and present. Accordingly, the realization of socialism requires the negation of religion. But we must take care that this negation not lead to abandonment of the ethics that were first disclosed in the form of religion.

In my view, there was one thinker before Proudhon who critiqued religion while trying to extricate the ethical core of religion, mode of exchange D: Immanuel Kant. He considered the maxim that one should treat other people "always at the same time as an end and never merely as a means to an end" as a universal moral law.[2] He called the situation in which this maxim was actualized "the kingdom of ends": "In the kingdom of ends everything has a price or dignity. Whatever has a price can be replaced by something else as its equivalent; on the other hand, whatever is above all price, and therefore admits of no equivalent, has a dignity."[3]

To treat the other as an end is to treat the other as a free being, which means to respect the other's dignity—the other's singularity, that which can never have an equivalent. A free being must never treat others as if they were only means. What Kant discovered as the universal moral law was precisely the mutuality (reciprocality) of freedom—in short, mode of exchange D. That this was originally revealed by universal religions cannot be denied, but in actual practice all religions have transformed into systems of support for mode of exchange B. Kant negated religion absolutely—yet he also extricated its basic morality.

On one hand, Kant negated the church and organized religions, which had transformed into a ruling apparatus of the state or community. "Between a shaman of the Tunguses and the European prelate who rules over both church and state[,] . . . there certainly is a tremendous difference in the *style* of faith, but not in the *principle*."[4] On the other hand, Kant affirmed religion, but only its role as the discloser of universal moral law. In his view, moral law may have been disclosed by religion, but it was originally an "inner" law: moral law inhered within reason itself. Yet this is not inner; in my view, it is in fact the external mode of exchange D. Because mode D was first revealed through universal religion, it may appear to be religious in nature, but in reality it is simply the return in a higher dimension of mode of exchange A, that which has been repressed under the dominance of modes B and C. It is precisely this that made it possible for religions to become universal religions.

But why is it that the mutuality of freedom appeared in the form of an inner duty, as something compulsory? Sigmund Freud, for example, equates Kant's duty with the superego, which originates in the "father," and he argues that this superego consists of internalized social norms. But the duty to respect the mutuality of freedom is of a different nature. This does not mean we have to abandon Freud's theory. To logically explain why the mutuality of freedom persistently compels us as a duty, we must rely on what Freud called the "return of the repressed": Kant's inner duty arises from the compulsive return in consciousness of repressed mode of exchange A.

Kant's moral law is ordinarily seen only in terms of subjective morality. But it is clearly implicated in social relations. For example, the relation between capital and wage labor in a capitalist economy is formed when the capitalist treats workers solely as a means (as the labor-power commodity), thereby stripping the workers of their dignity. This suggests that Kant's moral law already implies the abolition of wage labor and capitalist economic relations.

Behind Kant's thought lay the historical situation of contemporary Germany, in particular that of Königsberg, the city where he lived. The city was previously centered on craft workers and independent commodity producers, and it was then seeing the first stirrings of capitalist production under the influence of merchant capital. Kant explored the possibility of associations of small-scale producers who resisted the domination of merchant capital. This would lead the neo-Kantian philosopher Hermann Cohen to refer to Kant as Germany's first authentic socialist.

This form of socialism was marked by its own historical limitations. Once capitalist production got under way, it would inevitably overwhelm this sort of independent producers' union, splitting it up into two poles: capital and wage labor. Nonetheless, it is clear that Kant grasped what would subsequently become the core of socialism (associationism). Socialism consists of the return of reciprocal exchange in a higher dimension. It differs from distributive justice—that is, from the amelioration of disparities in wealth through redistribution—in that it implements an exchange-based justice under which such disparities are prevented from occurring in the first place. In seeing this as a duty, Kant grasped that the return of reciprocal exchange was not simply an arbitrary desire held by some people, but rather a compulsory, compulsive idea, a kind of "return of the repressed."

I should also note that in this moral law to treat others "always at the same time as an end and never merely as a means to an end," the category of other people includes not only the living but also the dead and still unborn. For example, if I achieve economic prosperity by damaging the environment, I am sacrificing future others—I am, that is, treating them solely as means. If we understand mutual freedom in this way and put it into practice, we inevitably arrive at a critique of the capitalist economy.

It is also important to note that Kant's morality also necessarily implies abolition of the state. He believed that world history was progressing toward a cosmopolitan moral republic, what he called a "world republic." This meant the abolition of individual states. Kant asserted that war was never under any circumstances permissible: "The state of peace among men who live alongside each other is no state of nature (*status naturalis*). Rather it is a state of war which constantly threatens even if it is not actually in progress. Therefore the state of peace must be *founded*."[5]

Kant started from the same premise as Thomas Hobbes. Hobbes argued that peace was established by the sovereign state (Leviathan), but this meant only domestic peace: it did not pertain between states. By contrast, Kant was attempting to found a state of peace *between* states. The realization of this was what he called "world republic."

Kant's "perpetual peace" did not simply mean the absence of war; it meant the end of all hostilities. If the state is something that exists first of all in opposition to other states, this would mean in fact the end of the state. In other words, world republic names a society in which the various individual states have all been abolished. This is not something that can be carried out exclusively in the political realm: peace is impossible so long as economic inequality between states continues to exist. Perpetual peace can be achieved only when an exchange-based justice is realized—not just within one state but between states. Accordingly, *world republic* refers to a society that has abolished both the state and capital. In other words, the term takes into account both the state and capital; any theory that fails to include both is empty.

It is also important to note that the "kingdom of ends" and "world republic," the endpoints of Kant's world history, held the status of "Ideas." In Kant's usage, Idea implies several things. First, an Idea is a semblance (*Schein*). There are two kinds of semblances; the first appears through sensibility and therefore can be corrected by reason. The other is a kind of semblance produced by reason itself; it cannot be corrected by reason because reason itself requires this semblance. He called the latter kind of semblance a transcendental illusion.[6] For example, the semblance we have of a unified self is this kind of idea: without it, people would lapse into schizophrenia. In the same way, the belief that history unfolds with a purpose, that it is moving toward some end, is only a semblance—but its absence would lead to schizophrenia. Ultimately, people cannot help but find an end or purpose to history.

The important thing to keep in mind here is the distinction between constructive and regulative ideas, as well as that between the constructive and regulative uses of reason. To explain this distinction, Kant used the difference between mathematical proportionality and philosophical analogy. In mathematics, if three terms are given, a fourth can be determined: this is an instance of the constructive. In speculative thought, on the other hand, the fourth term cannot be derived a priori. But speculative thought provides us with an index as we search through experience for something that might serve as the fourth term. For example, if up until now things have always been a certain way, we cannot simply conclude that they will continue to be that way in the future. Yet we can proceed by supposing that they will do so; in this, we are employing the regulative use of reason. Our supposition remains only a supposition, but to proceed in accordance with this sort of index is different from simply proceeding blindly.

To put this in simple terms, we see the constructive use of reason at work in its classic form with Jacobinism (i.e., Robespierre): the violent remaking of society based on reason. By contrast, the regulative use of reason works to draw people ever closer to some index, even as that index always remains at some distance. Kant's world republic is a regulative idea: it is an index toward which people should gradually attempt to draw close. It is of course only a semblance, but because it is something we cannot do without, it has the status of a transcendental illusion. The voice of the regulative idea may be faint, but it will not cease until the idea has been realized.

World republic would be a society in which mode of exchange D has been realized. In fact, this can never be fully realized. Nonetheless, it will persist as an index toward which we gradually move. In that sense, world republic is a regulative idea. Kant, in fact, also proposed a concrete plan for actually realizing the world republic. He opposed trying from the start to establish a world government, because this would inevitably mean creating a vast world state (empire). Kant instead proposed forming a federation of nations. This meant seeking to abolish the state through an association of states. I will explore this further in the final chapter of this book.

One final comment: today many postmodernists who laugh at the notion of an Idea of history are themselves former Marxist-Leninists who once believed in a constructive Idea. Wounded by their former belief, they now reject Ideas in general and escape into various forms of cynicism or nihilism. But their assertions that socialism is simply an illusion, that it is simply another grand narrative, are of little use to people who are stuck living the wretched reality of global capitalism. Since the 1980s, postmodern intellectuals in the core of global capitalism have continued to scorn the very idea of Idea, while religious fundamentalism has rapidly gained ground in the periphery and semiperiphery because in both intent and practice it at least aims to supersede capitalism and the state. Instead of realizing a "City of God," this can only lead to rule by clerics under a theocratic state. But what right do intellectuals in advanced capitalist countries have to laugh at this?

Socialism and Statism

We can broadly differentiate socialism into two types. The first is socialism by means of the state, and the other is socialism that rejects the state (i.e., associationism). Strictly speaking, only the latter should be called socialism. The former should properly be called state socialism or welfare statism. It is often said that the socialist movement pursued the egalitarianism that the French Revolution was never able to realize. But socialism in the strict sense (associationism) is not a continuation of the French Revolution: this socialism was actually born as a rejection of that revolution.

Everyone knows the slogan of the French Revolution: "Liberty, equality, fraternity." Seen from the perspective of modes of exchange, the slogan represents a synthesis of the three modes: *liberty* refers to the market economy, *equality* to redistribution carried out by the state, and *fraternity* to the system of reciprocity. When we view the slogan in this light, the stages of the French Revolution become clear. First came the realization of liberty: the abolition of feudal privileges and restrictions. Next came the Jacobins, who proclaimed fraternity while hastily trying to implement equality. This led to the Reign of Terror and, ultimately, failure. Yet this did not mean that liberty, equality, and fraternity were abandoned. Rather, the French Revolution ended up realizing this synthesis in imaginary form.

This synthesis was effected by Napoleon Bonaparte, a military leader who won popularity through his role in the wars to defend the revolution. These were hardly revolutionary wars though—their real impact was to defend and expand the nation. Napoleon metamorphosed the fraternity of the French Revolution into a nationalism that could resist British capital. In this way, the freedom, equality, and fraternity of the French Revolution were synthesized into the Borromean knot of Capital-Nation-State. Napoleon went from being president to emperor by projecting the illusion that he was the fulfillment of the demands of all classes. In the second French Rev-

olution of 1848, Louis Bonaparte engaged in a repetition of his uncle's performance and became emperor. Yet Louis Bonaparte was in no sense an exceptional figure: he was merely the prototype for the kind of charismatic
politician who would subsequently appear everywhere, whenever Capital-
Nation-State fell into crisis.

In my view, socialism means mode of exchange D. A genuine "Freedom,
equality, fraternity" can only be realized by superseding Capital-Nation-
State. But the socialist movement that arose in the wake of the French Revolution had a different vision. Its mainstream derived from the currents of
Jacobinism—socialist movements from Saint-Simon to Louis Blanc all
shared Jacobinist tendencies. Blanc, for example, simply shuffled the slogan
"Liberty, equality, fraternity" to advocate "Equality, fraternity, liberty,"
demonstrating that his socialism was really a kind of state socialism. This is
why it could be co-opted by the government of Louis Bonaparte—himself a
Saint-Simonist.

Proudhon was the first to raise a fundamental objection to this statist
form of socialism. In the slogan "Liberty, equality, fraternity," he placed
freedom above both equality and fraternity. The significance of this becomes clear when we view it in terms of modes of exchange. It was Proudhon, after all, who first proposed that socialism should be understood from
the perspective of modes of exchange—or, in his words, "economics."

He first of all opposed the belief that equality was more important than
freedom. Because equality is realized through redistribution carried out by
the state, equality always leads to a greater or lesser extent to Jacobinism
and increased state power. Put in terms of modes of exchange, equality
sacrifices the liberty produced by mode of exchange C for a restoration of
mode of exchange B. Proudhon espied a tendency to sacrifice liberty not
only in Jacobinist revolutions but also in Rousseauian political philosophy.

Proudhon thought that Jean-Jacques Rousseau's doctrine of popular sovereignty was merely an updated version of the absolutist-monarchy state, one
that moreover concealed its own true nature. Popular sovereignty was a fiction, one that arose only when the origin of the "people" as subjects of the sovereign (the absolute monarch) was forgotten. Rousseau based his argument
on a "general will" that transcended the wills of individuals. This general will
simply meant that all individual wills were subordinated to the state. In
Rousseau's social contract, there was no place for sovereign individuals.[7]

Proudhon did not, however, completely abandon Rousseau's notion of a
social contract. Proudhon criticized Rousseau's contract for not being reciprocal, and in doing so he in a sense brought the concept of a social contract to

its ultimate logical conclusion. Proudhon's *anarchie* (anarchy) was a democracy grounded in a mutually binding (that is to say, reciprocal) contract. Anarchy is often popularly associated with chaos and disorder, but according to Proudhon, it signified order produced through self-governance.

Proudhon also refused to place fraternity above liberty. True fraternity could not exist in a form that overlapped with the bonds of the given community: it would have to transcend community and exist at the level of something like a cosmopolitan. Yet fraternity all too often ends up simply establishing a narrowly bounded community. Put in terms of modes of exchange, fraternity tends toward the formation of a nation, the return in imaginary form of mode of exchange A. The French Revolution began with "citizens," a category that transcended ethnic identity, but it ended up with the French "nation"—in other words, the revolution's fraternity turned into nationalism. In Proudhon's view, a fraternity that transcends the bonds of any given community can emerge only when liberty is made the supreme value. True fraternity and free association are only possible once individuals cut ties with their communities (in Kant's language, cosmopolitans).

This idea was given its most extreme form in Max Stirner's advocacy of the "egoist."[8] Stirner was in fact a socialist, from beginning to end, but the point he stressed was that associations could only be formed once individuals had cut ties with their communities. Otherwise, fraternity could become a dangerous trap: it could certainly lead to the establishment of associations, but these were apt to take the form of "imagined communities," with fraternity transforming into nationalism.

Seen in this way, it is clear what Proudhon aimed for in his socialism or anarchism: mode of exchange D. He did not disregard the importance of equality; he simply opposed its implementation through "distributive justice."[9] Ordinarily, "commutative justice " refers to the execution of exchange contracts. But some exchanges, while appearing to be equal, are in reality unequal exchanges. This is what leads to capital accumulation. For this reason, what Proudhon calls commutative justice can only be realized in exchange systems that do not produce exploitation in the form of surplus value. He proposed a variety of projects for establishing this sort of exchange system.

Economic Revolution and Political Revolution

Why does inequality arise in capitalist economies, which are based on exchanges carried out by mutual consent? In Proudhon's view, laborers through their combination and division of labor generate a "collective power" that exceeds the sum of their individual efforts, but they are not compensated for this; capitalists instead claim the unpaid surplus as their own property.[10] This is the source of inequality, and it is what led Proudhon to make his famous declaration that "property is theft." This is often said to be the forerunner to Marx's theory of surplus value, but in fact even before this, Ricardian socialists in England made similar assertions. In fact, Proudhon himself was to a certain extent influenced by the Ricardian socialists, as I will discuss below.

For Proudhon, socialism meant a critique of the results of the French Revolution. For example, the French Revolution produced liberty. That is to say, the revolution overthrew the previously existing class relations that were based in extraeconomic coercion. Yet this also created a new set of ruling-ruled relations, the capitalist relations of production. The capitalist made the laborer work—relying not on force, as feudal lords had with serfs, but instead on freely given consent. This did not mean that the hierarchy of ruler and ruled disappeared. The employment contract between capitalist and laborer is certainly entered into by free will. But the person who sells the commodity of labor power does not stand in a relation of equality with the capitalist who possesses money. The capitalist retains the power of management and oversight, while the wage laborer has to obey. This ruler-ruled relation is determined by who holds money and who holds commodities. In other words, the ruler-ruled relation is ultimately determined by the relation between money and commodity.

According to Proudhon, true democracy must be realized not only at the level of politics but also at the level of the economy. The French Revolution abolished the monarchy, but in economic terms it left in place a monarchy of money. The power of the capitalist has its base in this monarchy of money. Proudhon's idea for abolishing the monarchy of money was to replace money with a system of labor vouchers and credit unions. These labor vouchers would not possess the special power held by money—accordingly, they would not accrue interest. Exchanges carried out using this kind of currency would truly be reciprocal, so that there could be no "theft." If resolving economic inequality through redistribution carried out by a powerful, centralized state represents political revolution, then this vision represents economic revolution. It implements a system that avoids producing inequality in the first place.

Yet Proudhon's economic revolution did not require starting over from scratch. In reality, we are already in a capitalist economy. In it, capital employs labor, and the combination and division of labor generate a collective power that exceeds the sum of the individual laborers. While the combination and division of labor may be forms of alienation for laborers under capitalist production, they also generate a desirably high level of productivity; the key then is to abolish the condition of alienation. Proudhon argues that deep beneath the phenomenal form of society there existed a true form of society, one created by the sense of solidarity that originates in the balance of various abilities generated by social labor and in the autonomy and absolute freedom of individuals.

This line of thought resembles the theory of alienation that held sway among the Young Hegelians in 1840s Germany—who were in fact under Proudhon's influence. This is usually explained as follows: first Ludwig Feuerbach criticized the alienation in religion of human nature as species-being and called for its restoration, then the Young Hegelians, especially Moses Hess and Marx, took up this critique of religion and extended it into a critique of the state and capital. What's important to note here, though, is that even before the Young Hegelians who followed in his wake, Feuerbach was influenced by Proudhon. In other words, Feuerbach's critique of religion already included a critique of capitalism.

Feuerbach's notion of an essential species-being of humankind closely resembles Proudhon's "true society." They both signify a socialized, collective mode of production. Under capitalism this is organized by capital itself, meaning this mode appears only in alienated form—and, moreover, as something hostile and domineering to workers, as their own self-alienation. Feuerbach's aim was to overcome this self-alienation and restore the essential species-being of humankind. This is what Feuerbach meant when he referred to himself as a communist—a communism that took the form of the Proudhonists' associationism.

Feuerbach's species-being is not simply a materialist version of what G. W. F. Hegel called "Spirit." Nor, therefore, does species-being signify the kind of totality in relation to the individual that Hegel discussed. Species-being signifies instead relations between individual and individual. The concept here signifies a relationality akin to "I and Thou." "I and Thou" includes within it a kind of economic relationality—to wit, reciprocal relations of exchange. The thought of Martin Buber, for example, which revolves around the question of "I and Thou," is based on Feuerbach. It is no coincidence that he was also an advocate of cooperative-based socialism.

This was the idea of socialism that Marx inherited, taking it not only from Proudhon but also Feuerbach. Marx stuck with it throughout his life, even as he critiqued both Feuerbach and Proudhon. In other words, Marx never adopted a statist position. In the *Communist Manifesto* (1848), he argues that communism will be the realization of free associations. The fissures between Marx and Proudhon began appearing around 1846, after Proudhon rejected a proposal from Marx to combine their efforts. In a letter to Marx, Proudhon wrote:

> I have also some observations to make on this phrase of your letter: *at the moment of action.* Perhaps you still retain the opinion that no reform is at present possible without a *coup de main*, without what was formerly called a revolution and is really nothing but a shock. That opinion, which I understand, which I excuse, and would willingly discuss, having myself shared it for a long time, my most recent studies have made me abandon completely. I believe we have no need of it in order to succeed; and that consequently we should not put forward *revolutionary action* as a means of social reform, because that pretended means would simply be an appeal to force, to arbitrariness, in brief, a contradiction. I myself put the problem in this way: *to bring about the return to society, by an economic combination, of the wealth which was withdrawn from society by another economic combination.* In other words, through Political Economy to turn the theory of Property against Property in such a way as to engender what you German socialists call *community* and what I will limit myself for the moment to calling *liberty* or *equality*. But I believe that I know the means of solving this problem with only a short delay; I would therefore prefer to burn Property by a slow fire, rather than give it new strength by making a St Bartholomew's night of the proprietors.[11]

It was only after this that Marx became critical of Proudhon. While Proudhon called for an economic revolution, Marx believed that a political revolution—the seizure of political power—was necessary. But it would be incorrect to assume from this that the conflict between Marx and Proudhon amounted to a choice between political or economic revolution. Marx's assertion of the need for political revolution did not mean that he was advocating statism. He believed that, insofar as the capitalist economy is sustained by legal systems and state policies, it is necessary to bring these at least temporarily to a halt, and this requires the seizure of state power. Even Proudhon's proposed credit unions and labor-based scrip, for example, would require the backing of a legal system.

In fact, Proudhon himself would soon acknowledge that an economic revolution was impossible without a political revolution. Proudhon, who had previously dismissed political revolution as simple mob violence, ran for office under the universal suffrage realized with the February 1848 revolution and was elected to parliament. In July and August he proposed bills to the national assembly to establish exchange banks, but they were rejected both times. The Proudhon faction carried on this line following his death. In the 1871 Paris Commune, the faction ignored Marx's opposition and organized a popular uprising that seized state power. It was only after the fact that Marx came around to support this, praising it as a model for the dictatorship of the proletariat.

Marx began asserting the need to seize state power around 1848—the time he came into contact with the Blanqui faction. He endorsed Louis Blanqui's call for a dictatorship of the proletariat instituted through a revolution guided by a small vanguard secret society. But Blanqui was not a state socialist in the manner of Blanc: Blanqui basically agreed with Proudhon's views and thought that the state would disappear once economic class relations were abolished. In Blanqui's view, the vanguard (party) would not seize power; instead the revolution would begin with a mass uprising, and it would be carried out by the masses themselves. Without a small, ideologically aware vanguard (party), however, the uprising would lack a clear direction and end in failure. Hence, a vanguard needed to take a leadership role. This view does not contradict the tenets of anarchism. Proudhon too would subsequently propose that activists should be limited to members of a small elite.

Mikhail Bakunin attacked Marx for advocating statism and centralization, but in reality this was not the case. Marx believed not only that the state should be abolished but also that it could be abolished. He thought that the state would wither away if economic class relations were abolished. It was for this reason that he was willing to permit a short-lived dictatorship of the proletariat as a transitional measure. It is certainly true that Marx was not sufficiently vigilant with regard to the autonomy of the state. But this was not because he was an advocate of statism in contrast to Proudhon; rather, it was because Marx shared Proudhon's view of the state.

Labor Unions and Cooperatives

Marx criticized Proudhon's thought, which advocated resistance to capitalism from within the process of circulation. The core of industrial capitalism lay in production, and therefore the proletariat's struggle against capital must be located within the production process: this understanding has been an implacable feature of Marxism. But simply contrasting Proudhon's stress on circulation with Marx's stress on production provides only a superficial understanding.

Proudhon's idea of an economic revolution taking place within the circulation process arose in part because, in the France of his day, factory production driven by industrial capital—in other words, the industrial proletariat—hardly existed. The people who were at the time called proletariat were in fact artisans and small-scale producers whose livelihoods were under increasing pressure. In street-level struggles, they were the leading players in classical political revolutions. The economic revolution that Proudhon called for meant the organization of this proletariat from within the production process. He advocated cooperative production by artisans and small-scale producers, as well as the creation of a financial system to support them. In sum, his stress on the importance of circulation was ultimately for the sake of production.

In England, on the other hand, industrial capitalism was already highly developed, and the struggle of the industrial proletariat was organized from within the production process. This struggle was carried out primarily by labor unions. The English socialist movement likewise had its theoretical roots in classical economics—specifically David Ricardo's theories—with its focus on production. As noted, Proudhon asserted that "property is theft" because even though capital pays wages to individual workers, it does not compensate them for the surplus produced through their combination and division of labor. This line of thought was previously asserted in England by Ricardian socialists such as William Thompson, and in fact even became the basis for political praxis.[12]

Ricardian socialists believed that the total profit of any enterprise should be distributed not to the owners of the means of production but rather to those who contributed the labor. In fact, Ricardo himself made suggestions along these lines. He understood that the application of machinery, the introduction of natural science into the factory, the increased importance of tools in labor, the importation of cheap foodstuffs, and similar phenomena were instances of what Marx would call relative surplus value, and Ricardo maintained that surplus value in the form of unpaid labor was the source of profit and land rents. But Ricardo thought that because it was the capitalist who had combined the labor of the workers, the surplus thereby generated should go to that capitalist. The Ricardian socialists, by contrast, asserted that this surplus should go to the workers (i.e., the theory of the right to the whole produce of labor).

Taking their cues from this school of thought, workers banded together in a political movement to claim the unpaid portion of their labor from capitalists or, alternatively, to demand shorter hours and better working conditions. At first capital moved to suppress this, because it represented a significant threat to individual capital. The struggle of labor unions increasingly became violent class struggle. But after about 1848, when the Chartist movement reached its peak, an accommodation was reached and the demands of the working class were largely met. The workday was reduced to ten hours, for example, and wages rose and social-welfare policies were instituted. This may appear to be a defeat of capital, but in fact the opposite was true. By recognizing labor unions and acceding to their demands, capital was able to establish the method of accumulation characteristic of industrial capitalism.

Up until this point, capital had striven to pay the lowest possible wages and impose the longest possible working hours. But this was not in the interest of total capital. Let me refer back to Marx's own words: "Each capitalist knows that he does not confront his own worker as a producer confronts a consumer, and so he wants to restrict his consumption, i.e. his ability to exchange, his wages, as much as possible. But of course, he wants the workers of other capitalists to be the greatest possible consumers of his commodity."[13]

Accordingly, increased wages and improved social-welfare policies might represent losses to individual capital, but they were desirable to total capital: they expanded consumption and accelerated the accumulation of capital. This change transformed the capitalist economy. As a result of it, most members of the working class left the ranks of the poor and emerged as consumers with an increasing resemblance to the middle class. At the same time, their movement became increasingly apolitical, just as the socialist movement veered toward the kind of social democracy represented by such figures as John Stuart Mill.

These developments first appeared in Britain, but the phenomenon would be repeated wherever industrial capitalism took off. As a rule, the proletariat appears as an anticapitalist, politically radical force only at the stage in which industrial capitalism is not yet fully established. Once it is fully established, the proletariat becomes apolitical and nonrevolutionary. We see this in late nineteenth-century Germany, where Eduard Bernstein rejected the existing socialist movement and began to advocate a gradualist reformism. He claimed that Marx was anachronistic, but Marx himself was not out of touch with this situation. To the contrary, it was precisely in the face of such conditions that he wrote *Capital*.

This accounts for the difference between *Capital* and his earlier theories of capitalism. For example, in contrast to the classical economists who took up capitalism in terms of production, Marx took it up in terms of circulation: he considered capital in terms of merchant capital (M-C-M′). The definitive feature of industrial capital was its basis in a unique commodity, labor power. Industrial capital buys the labor-power commodity from its workers and then, in addition to making them work, it also makes them buy back their own products, obtaining surplus value from the difference this generated. This form of accumulation becomes possible only if workers are also consumers. How, then, can workers resist capital once this system is in place?

To answer this, we need to rethink the very nature of what a movement of resistance to capitalism is. *Capital* shows us that Marx had an extremely high degree of interest in the British cooperative movement. Cooperatives were one of two movements that emerged in response to the radical Ricardian school's theory of the right to the whole produce of labor. One was the labor unions that I have been discussing, while the other was the cooperative movement. Labor unions fought to recover the surplus value obtained by capital when it *combined* workers in the process of putting them to work. Cooperatives arose when workers themselves *associated*: when they worked together in associations with one another.[14] In associations, any profits are distributed among the workers themselves. This means that this is no longer capitalist production; the labor-power commodity no longer exists here.

Labor unions and cooperatives are both movements of resistance to capital, but they are qualitatively different. Put simply, labor unions are a form of struggle against capital taking place *within* a capitalist economy, while cooperatives are a movement that *moves away from* the capitalist system. In other words, the former is centered on production, the latter on circulation. The latter movement included labor-based scrip and credit unions, in which sense it shared much in common with Proudhon's original plan.

These two movements of resistance were closely interlinked. For example, Robert Owen was the founder of the cooperative movement and also one of the founders of the Grand National Consolidated Trades Union. The development of the cooperative movement was led by workers from Owen's faction. Because Owen's original attempt to launch a fully cooperative society had ended in failure, they adopted a different strategy, beginning on a relatively small scale with the cooperative purchase of daily necessities and moving gradually from there to expand the sphere of cooperative undertakings. They started, that is, from within the process of circulation. In 1844 they established the Rochdale Society of Equitable Pioneers, a consumers' union. Its success led to the establishment of many other consumer cooperatives based on the "Rochdale principles": (1) voluntary and open membership; (2) one-person, one-vote democratic control; (3) limits on compensation for capital invested; and (4) distribution of profits to members in proportion to their transactions with the cooperative. Numerous "producer cooperatives" (cooperative factories) were also established in the 1850s.

Marx initially took a critical stance toward Proudhon's ideas about creating noncapitalist enterprises and economic spheres outside the capitalist economy. But it is important to note that he became more sympathetic to this view in Britain, where the movement of resistance from within capitalist production had run into difficulties: the labor-union movement had already been co-opted and become merely one link in the process of capitalist accumulation. Having abandoned all possibility of abolishing the labor-power commodity, the movement was solely focused on preserving or increasing the value of labor power. In contrast, the cooperative movement still manifested a clear intention to abolish the labor-power commodity and the capitalist system.

With the exception of Titoism in the former Yugoslavia, Marxists in general have rejected or belittled producer-consumer cooperatives. Marx, however, stressed their importance. This was because cooperatives abolish the labor-power commodity. Wage labor did not exist, because in cooperatives workers themselves were the managers. Marx argued that in cooperative factories "the opposition between capital and labour is abolished."[15]

Even in cooperatives wages are not completely egalitarian, however. There are many kinds of labor, including management labor, and accordingly wage differences are inevitable. In other words, a certain degree of inequality persists. But the crucial point here is that the ruler-ruled relation grounded in the relation between money and commodity no longer exists. Workers obey their managers and directors, but not because they have been hired by those managers; workers submit to managers that they themselves have chosen. Under this system, workers are sovereign. In contrast to Rousseau's notion of popular sovereignty, which exists in name only, this constitutes real sovereignty. Relations among those who work in cooperatives are reciprocal (i.e., mutually binding). Proudhon's idea, that real democracy could be achieved not only in the political but also in the economic, was realized by the cooperatives. They put mode of exchange D into actual practice.

The difficulty arises after this. Marx praised the cooperatives and saw in them the key to abolishing the capitalist economy. But he also thought it was impossible for cooperative factories to expand to the point that they would replace capitalist enterprises. Compared to capitalist joint-stock companies, cooperative factories were much too weak and small. They were not designed to engage in competition over profits and were limited in their ability to raise capital. In fact, from the 1860s on, with the accelerated development of capitalist joint-stock corporations and in particular with the shift to heavy industry, the cooperative factories went into decline. The movement increasingly became limited to cooperatives of small-scale producers that did not engage in competition with capitalist enterprises.[16]

In this sense, Marx identified the limitations of cooperatives, just as he criticized Proudhon's credit unions and labor-based scrip. The latter was possible on a local level, where it could achieve a degree of acceptance, but it could never replace money. In the same way, cooperatives could effectively be established and achieve a degree of acceptance in areas beyond the reach of capital or as consumer cooperatives, but they would never be able to topple capitalist enterprises. No matter how desirable production carried out by workers in association may seem, it could never stand up to production organized by capital (money), based on its ability to purchase and combine the labor-power commodity.

In the wake of these criticisms by Marx, Marxists have tended to dismiss, or at best to regard as secondary, the various experiments that Proudhon proposed within the process of circulation, as well as the experimental cooperatives organized by followers of Owen. Marxists since Engels have instead tried to overcome capitalism through a strategy of nationalizing enterprises, bringing them under state ownership. Yet even as Marx pointed out the limitations of cooperatives, he also discovered within them the key to socialism. For example, Marx praised the cooperative factory movement in his address to the First International, in which Proudhon's group took the leading role: "The value of these great social experiments cannot be over-rated."[17] For Marx, socialism meant associationism, along the lines practiced by the cooperatives.

Ignoring Marx's opposition, Proudhon's followers mounted an uprising and seized state power in the Paris Commune of 1871. Marx expressed support for this after the fact, praising it as a model for the dictatorship of the proletariat:

If co-operative production is not to remain a sham and a snare; if it is to supersede the capitalist system; if united co-operative societies are to regulate national production upon a common plan, thus taking it under their own control, and putting an end to the constant anarchy and periodical convulsions which are the fatality of Capitalist production—what else, gentlemen, would it be but Communism, "possible" Communism?[18]

By contrast, Marx completely rejected Ferdinand Lassalle's "state socialism." Marx was fiercely critical of the "Gotha Program" of the German Social Democratic Party formed by the Marxists and the Lassallists, with its proposal from Lassalle to foster associations (producer cooperatives) through state power:

That the workers desire to establish the conditions for co-operative production on a social scale, and first of all on a national scale, in their own country, only means that they are working to revolutionize the present conditions of production, and it has nothing in common with the foundation of co-operative societies with state aid. But as far as the present co-operative societies are concerned, they are of value *only* insofar as they are the independent creations of the workers and not protégés either of the governments or of the bourgeois.[19]

Marx asserts that we should not rely on the state to build up cooperatives; rather, associations of cooperatives should replace the state. Yet without legal regulations and other forms of state support, producer cooperatives would inevitably lose out in competition with capitalist enterprises. Therefore, Marx concluded, it was necessary for the proletariat to seize state power. But Marx's real point of opposition to Lassalle arose from Lassalle's belief, following Hegel, that the state was grounded in reason itself; by contrast, Marx called for the abolition of the state. On this point, Marx himself was a Proudhonist. Lassalle, a close friend of Otto von Bismarck's, was the German version of a Saint-Simonist—that is to say, a state socialist.

Joint-Stock Companies and State Ownership

Marx located the key to realizing socialism—production through association—in cooperative production. At the same time, however, he also saw the limitations of this approach: its inability to expand beyond a certain level, meaning its inability to ultimately counter capitalism. In turn, Marx located the key to overcoming these limitations in the joint-stock company: "Capitalist joint-stock companies as much as cooperative factories should be viewed as transition forms from the capitalist mode of production to the associated one, simply that in the one case the opposition is abolished in a negative way, and in the other in a positive way."[20]

What does this mean? Stock companies are characterized by a split between capital and management. Shareholders have the right to receive distributions of profit in proportion to their investment, as well as the right to decide management issues by election. But they do not possess rights of ownership over the means of production: these belong to the corporation. Consequently, shareholders avoid unlimited liability for any losses suffered by the enterprise. If the company goes bankrupt, the individual shareholders lose only their investments, just as they are free at any moment to sell their shares and turn them into money capital. This structure makes it possible for stock corporations to accumulate capital and to engage in the social combination of labor on a massive scale. For cooperatives, though, expansion of this sort is very difficult. Accordingly, Marx thought that we should take existing joint-stock corporations and transform them into cooperatives—convert them, that is, to an *associated* mode of production. He declared that the stock corporation was "the most perfected form" for the purpose of "turning into communism."[21]

In the stock corporation, the capitalist withered away—at least, in the form that capitalist had taken up to this point. This meant abolishing capital only "negatively," because the categorical imperative of capital to secure a profit margin remained in place. Capital that is unable to accumulate and increase is no longer capital. Accordingly, the stock corporation does not really abolish capital, just as the republican governments that overthrew the absolute monarchies did not really abolish the state. Government based on popular sovereignty may appear to replace the state, but when push comes to shove, the state always reappears in the form of a monarch or similar charismatic leader. Likewise, capital always reappears whenever management falls into crisis.

Nonetheless, this negative abolition of capital clearly gives rise to a new and different relation between capitalist and wage laborer: it is now a relation between manager and worker. The manager is distinct from the shareholder (money capital). Likewise, the manager is not the actual owner of the physical capital: it belongs to the company (corporation). The manager is a salaried, white-collar worker, paid wages for what Marx called the "work of supervision and management," organizing and directing the workers.[22] Marx saw in this the condition of possibility for the formation of an association, in which managers and laborers win independence from shareholder (capital) control. Converting a stock company into a cooperative is a relatively simple matter: all one needs to do is take the joint-stock company that is controlled by a majority of shareholders and, following the Rochdale principles, introduce a system in which decisions are made on the one-person, one-vote principle by all members, including shareholders. No other measures are needed.[23]

This is, of course, easier said than done. If this change is implemented at the level of individual enterprises, they will quickly encounter the same difficulties that befell the producer cooperatives. Not only will they become targets for outside attacks and interference, such cooperative enterprises will be unable to compete effectively with capitalist enterprises. For example, capitalist enterprises regularly carry out restructurings and lure talented technicians with higher wages, but cooperatives are unable to act likewise—if they did, they would be cooperatives in name only. But if cooperatives stick to their principles, they either fail or end up introducing capitalist-style measures just to survive, leading to the reappearance of the very capital they were supposed to have abolished. Clearly, this kind of reform has to be implemented not through competition between individual firms but at the level of the state: it can only be realized through changes in the legal system.

In 1867 Marx wrote:

> Restricted, however, to the dwarfish forms into which individual wages slaves can elaborate it by their private efforts, the co-operative system will never transform capitalist society. To convert social production into one large and harmonious system of free and co-operative labour, *general social changes* are wanted, *changes of the general conditions of society*, never to be realised save by the transfer of the organised forces of society, viz., the state power, from capitalists and landlords to the producers themselves.[24]

Needless to say, this view did not oppose that of the Proudhonists, who had already acknowledged the difficulty of developing cooperatives or converting individual companies into cooperatives. This could only be achieved at one fell swoop, by seizing state power. As a result, Marx's views were accepted by the International Workingmen's Association (the First International), which was dominated by the Proudhon faction, and in fact the Proudhonists would put this into action during the Paris Commune.

Marx's call to seize state power only superficially resembles Lassalle's proposal to foster production cooperatives through state power. The latter calls for cooperatives organized under the state, meaning in effect state ownership of industry. As I noted, Marx rejected this idea. What was needed was not to use state power to foster cooperatives but rather to reorganize capitalist stock companies along the lines of cooperatives. Marx's stress on the need to seize state power was not for the sake of state ownership; it was for the sake of abolishing the relation between capital and wage-labor classes through the rise of cooperatives. This would in turn lead to the withering away of the state, which was grounded in class rule. Achieving this, Marx believed, would require the working class to seize control of state power—but only temporarily.

Marx stressed the transformation of corporate ownership of stock companies into communal ownership by workers instead of the nationalization of stock companies. The two approaches may seem similar but are in fact fundamentally different. For example, state ownership and capitalism are not incompatible. Proof of this can be seen even today: when large companies fall into crisis, they avoid collapse by being nationalized. Ordinarily, state-run ventures enable massive capital accumulation on a scale beyond the reach of private companies. That is why in late-developing capitalist countries, such as Japan during the Meiji period, capital-intensive industries such as steelworks began first as state-run companies and then only gradually were privatized. In that sense, the stock company represents a more advanced form than the state-run enterprise. In Marx's thinking, the stock company was "the most perfected form," and socialism meant converting this into a cooperative (communal ownership). To engage in nationalization and state ownership was to move away from socialism.

After the failure of the Paris Commune, however, Marx's theory of the cooperative was largely forgotten. This was part of a general amnesia with regard to the idea of abolishing the state through associations and cooperatives. Engels was largely responsible for this. In editing the third volume of *Capital*, Engels included comments in the text that exaggerated the degree to which Marx favorably viewed the growth of stock companies. This implicitly minimized the significance of converting them into cooperatives. Engels believed that socialism could be realized immediately by nationalizing the largest joint-stock companies. In his understanding, socialism meant transforming the capitalist economy as a whole into a planned economy. This became the original source for such later views as Vladimir

Lenin's assertion that socialism meant making the whole of society into a single factory. In subsequent Marxisms, this equation of socialism with state ownership was never questioned. This was not the product of Stalinism; to the contrary, belief in state-ownership produced Stalinism. For example, even Leon Trotsky in *The Revolution Betrayed* writes: "In order to become social, private property must . . . inevitably pass through the state stage."[25]

Of course, state ownership is one strategy for negating the capitalist economy. But it can never lead to the abolition of the labor-power commodity (i.e., wage labor). State ownership merely transforms the laborer into a public employee—that is, into a wage laborer who works for the state. The nationalization of agriculture and the introduction of collectivized farming, moreover, represent a move backward toward the agrarian community of Asiatic despotism. This is what happened in the Soviet Union and China. Nationalization and state control left state bureaucrats holding enormous power. So long as you pursue a policy of state ownership and state control, you cannot avoid bureaucratization—no matter how cautious or critical you try to be, no matter how many cultural revolutions you launch.

Simultaneous World Revolution

Marx's belief in the necessity of seizing state power did not mean that he was an advocate of statism. Rather, this belief derived from another belief that if you temporarily seize state power and abolish economic class relations, the state will then simply disappear. In this, his views were identical to Proudhon's. For this reason, Marx made common cause with the Proudhonists up until the Paris Commune. It's not widely known, but in fact Marx expressed strong opposition when the Proudhonists planned the Paris Commune uprising.[26] Rather than usurp state power, he argued, socialists should first devote themselves to rebuilding Paris and France from the chaos of defeat in war.

According to Marx, because Paris was encircled by victorious Prussia, the Commune would become a target for interference and would ultimately end in tragic defeat. This in turn would set the revolutionary movement back for decades.[27] But once the Commune was actually established, he supported it and offered words of praise. But this remained in the same vein as his previous support for producer-cooperative factories as an important experiment, even as he believed that they would inevitably lose out in competition with capital. As Marx feared, the Paris Commune was in fact crushed in just two months by the Prussian Army, at the sacrifice of count-less lives. This event spelled the end of the anarchist and classical revolutionary movements.

Marx opposed the uprising because it constituted a revolution in only one city—or, at best, in one country. He foresaw that the Commune would immediately encounter interference and obstruction from foreign states. It is impossible to abolish the state in one country while leaving it intact elsewhere. In other words, the socialist revolution cannot take place in just one country. It is possible only as a simultaneous worldwide revolution, which in turn is possible only under the "universal intercourse" produced by global capitalism. In *The German Ideology*, Marx writes:

> Furthermore, because only with this universal development of productive forces is a *universal* intercourse between men established, which on the one side produces in *all* nations simultaneously the phenomenon of the "propertyless" mass (universal competition), making each nation dependent on the revolutions of the others, and finally puts *world-historical*, empirically universal individuals in place of local ones. Without this, 1) communism could only exist as a local phenomenon; 2) the *forces* of intercourse themselves could not have developed as *universal*, hence unendurable powers: they would have remained home-bred "conditions" surrounded by superstition; and 3) each extension of intercourse would abolish local communism. Empirically, communism is only possible as the act of the dominant peoples "all at once" and simultaneously, which presupposes the universal development of productive forces and the world intercourse bound up with them.[28]

The state cannot be abolished from within. That is why Marx thought it was "only possible as the act of the dominant peoples 'all at once' and simultaneously." Note that Marx here refers to "the dominant peoples": this means the developed capitalist nations. In Marx's view, a "simultaneous world revolution" at the level of the developed nations was a necessary precondition for revolution in less-developed nations. A simultaneous world revolution at the level of Britain, France, and the other developed countries would pave the way for revolution or reform in the various countries they had colonized or were exploiting economically through the international division of labor—just as the absence of simultaneous world revolution would render the path to revolution in those countries difficult and tortuous.

Even as he limited the socialist revolution to the dominant peoples, Marx's assertion that it could only take place "'all at once' and simultaneously" shows that he was aware of the difficulties that would accompany the socialist revolution—in other words, the attempt to abolish both capital and state. A socialist revolution in only one country is impossible: the state cannot be abolished from within.

Moreover, it was not only illegal or violent revolutions that would meet interference and obstruction from other countries. Suppose, for example, that in one country a democratically elected government set out to convert its stock companies into cooperatives. This would immediately elicit a backlash, interference, and manipulation from domestic and foreign capital, as well as from other states. Merely the anticipation of such a response would already elicit strong opposition and resistance from within the country. The abolition of capitalism (wage labor) cannot be achieved in a single country. This is another way of saying that the state cannot be abolished from within: the state exists within a world system; it exists in its relations with other states.

Marx opposed the Paris Commune uprising, but he never made public his reasons for this. As a result, only his words of praise for the Commune were passed on to later generations. In particular, Lenin and Trotsky ignored Marx's initial criticism and, citing his praise of the Paris Commune, they launched the October Revolution. Marx initially opposed the uprising because he thought that it had no possibility of leading to a simultaneous world revolution. It was the Proudhonists who were determined to launch a revolution, but this was not because they were planning a revolution limited to one country. They too had a simultaneous world revolution in mind—this idea didn't belong to Marx alone. The Proudhonists and Bakunin naturally believed that they were mounting a world revolution. They began the revolution assuming that it would spread into a European world revolution. Needless to say, this was an utterly arbitrary assumption on their part.

The revolution of 1848 truly had been a world revolution. The revolutionaries of the First International established in that revolution's wake anticipated a similar simultaneous world revolution, and so it was quite understandable that they would believe in 1871 that the Paris Commune would transform into a world revolution. Marx, however, concluded that a world revolution was not possible at that moment. This was not simply by chance. The "world" needed as a precondition for simultaneous world revolution had itself undergone a fundamental transformation. Marx seems to have sensed this, though he did not leave any clear statements about it.

The notion of a simultaneous world revolution persisted, but only in the form of an empty slogan, with no attempt made to consider what its necessary preconditions might be. The important point for us to consider is this: the kind of world revolution that occurred in 1848 is no longer possible, but this does not mean that simultaneous world revolution is no longer possible. In fact, it is possible—but how? This is the problem I take up in detail in chapter 12. In the meanwhile, let us look at what happened to the vision of a simultaneous world revolution in the years after 1848.

Permanent Revolution and "Leaping Over" Stages

Beyond a doubt, the revolutions of 1848 were simultaneous and world-wide. As socialist revolutions, though, they were easily defeated. More-over, they met defeat not so much at the hands of antirevolution as of counterrevolution—that of the nation-state. This resulted in a political order that was characterized by a strong awareness of the socialist move-ment and proletarian class. I have already described this situation as it played out in Britain: the Chartist movement was defeated, but the de-mands of the working class were largely met through the implementation of various social-welfare policies. In France, after assuming the position of emperor, the Saint-Simonist Louis Bonaparte simultaneously pursued seemingly contradictory tasks: state promotion of industrial capitalism and the amelioration of labor problems. Bonaparte even supported the forma-tion of the First International. In Prussia too, after rising to power in the wake of 1848, Bismarck pursued both state-sponsored promotion of indus-trial capitalism and policies to resolve labor problems. Bismarck himself was not a socialist, but his state capitalism was in fact largely in accord with his friend Lassalle's state socialism.

In this sense, the post-1848 world took shape with socialists participating directly or indirectly in state power. In other words, this period saw the formation of Capital-Nation-State: a system, albeit still in germinal form, that featured a capitalist market economy but that also included regulations aimed at restricting the effects of unrestrained capital as well as attempts to ameliorate class conflict through redistribution of wealth and social-welfare policies. By this time, the kind of revolution that had been imagined in 1848 was already an anachronism. The Paris Commune marked its last burst of glory and was not a harbinger of the future.

By 1880 Engels came to believe that the revolutions of 1848 were anach-ronistic and that the situation of England now presented the possibility for a true socialist revolution. In 1886, three years after Marx's death, Engels wrote: "Surely, at such a moment, the voice ought to be heard of a man

[Marx] whose whole theory is the result of a lifelong study of the economic history and condition of England, and whom that study led to the conclusion that, at least in Europe, England is the only country where the inevitable social revolution might be effected entirely by peaceful and legal means."[29] In the 1890s, with the German Social Democratic Party making great strides in parliamentary elections, Engels came to believe that Germany was also ripe with the same conditions. In other words, he came to believe that socialist reforms were possible in the developed countries through parliamentary democracy. But the reason Engels saw the possibility for this kind of reform in England was that the Capital-Nation-State system had been established there; he could not see that this system could never be superseded by the very reforms that it had made possible.

Engels's position in his last years came very close to social democracy. Following Engels's death, his anointed successor, Bernstein, would reject as unrealistic the Marxist theories of socialist revolution that had appeared since 1848. Kautsky would criticize this as revisionism, and yet there was little practical difference in position between the two. Both advocated pursuing a socialist revolution through democratic parliamentary means, with the state regulating capitalism and redistributing wealth. If Bernstein called for a kind of welfare state system, then Kautsky advocated a brand of social democracy.

But this line of thought is only possible in a situation where Capital-Nation-State has already been established. This has two important implications: first, that the Capital-Nation-State system could never be superseded through reforms of this nature, and, second, that because each Capital-Nation-State exists in competition with the others in a world system, if the existence of any is threatened, then social democracy is immediately discarded. When Germany plunged into the First World War, to cite a real instance, both Bernstein and Kautsky switched sides to support the nation. This made the collapse of the Second International inevitable, bringing to an end the international socialist movement in the developed capitalist nations.

In the developed capitalist countries, it was clear that the previous forms of revolutionary movement were no longer viable. Yet the Marxists who confronted this problem tended not to tackle it directly and instead turned to revolutions in the periphery, where classic revolutionary movements and class struggle were still possible. This tendency was initially seen with the first Russian revolution (1905), which arose as a result of the Russo-Japanese War (1904–5). Based on this experience, Trotsky and Rosa Luxemburg each began revising the generally held view in Marxism that a socialist revolution was possible only in the most highly developed stages of capitalism.

To take up the case of Luxemburg first, as a native of Poland, a part of the Russian Empire, she experienced the first Russian revolution and after it began to think about a theory of revolution on the periphery. Moreover, theorizing that capital accumulation in the core (developed countries) depended on the exploitation of the periphery (developing countries), she began to think of revolution in the periphery not as something that would follow the lead of revolutions in the developed countries but rather as a way to strike a blow against capital accumulation in the developed countries. In a sense, this meant using Marx's thought to challenge Marx. Trotsky, on the other hand, developed the theory of permanent revolution from the work of the early Marx and used it in an attempt to provide a theoretical basis for socialist revolution in developing countries.

As of 1848, Marx approved of Blanqui's notions of an uprising led by a small vanguard party and the dictatorship of the proletariat. He believed, moreover, that in the Germany of his day, in which industrial capitalism was undeveloped and a bourgeois democratic revolution had yet to take place, what was needed was a bourgeois revolution, but that it should not stop there: a dictatorship of the proletariat should follow, which would in a single blow carry matters forward into a socialist revolution. This was his theory of permanent revolution. Just two years later, however, Marx would reject this:

> I have always defied the momentary opinions of the proletariat. We are devoted to a party which, most fortunately for it, cannot yet come to power. If the proletariat were to come to power the measures it would introduce would be petty-bourgeois and not directly proletarian. Our party can come to power only when the conditions allow it to put *its own* views into practice. Louis Blanc is the best instance of what happens when you come to power prematurely. In France, moreover, it isn't the proletariat alone that gains power but the peasants and the petty bourgeois as well, and it will have to carry out not its, but *their* measures. The Paris Commune shows that one need not be in the government to accomplish something.[30]

After this, Marx would become extremely cautious about the idea of leaping over historical stages. This is clear in his letter to Vera Zasulich. In spite of this, Trotsky would dredge up the idea of permanent revolution that Marx himself had rejected. Trotsky thought that revolution would occur in those regions most severely manifesting the contradictions of global capitalism, and that in those regions a socialist revolution that leapt over stages of development was possible. This is certainly adopted from Marx, but in reality it actually mounts a challenge to Marx's own conclusions. Lenin followed Trotsky's influence on this issue.

The Russian Revolution broke out in February 1917, when the signs of Russia's defeat in the First World War had become obvious. As a result, the imperial government was toppled and a parliament established, and at the same time worker and farmer councils (soviets) began to spring up spontaneously. This dual authority system, with parliament and the councils, continued for a time. In both levels, however, the mainstream was formed by the Menshevik wing of the Social-Democratic Labour Party and the Socialist Revolutionary Party, while the Bolshevik wing of the Social-Democratic Labour Party constituted a minority faction. In October, however, Trotsky and Lenin ignored the fierce opposition of the other members of the Bolshevik Central Committee (with the exception of Joseph Stalin) and mounted a coup d'état under the slogan "All power to the soviets." In actual practice, this meant not only shutting down parliament but also expelling members of other factions from the soviets. After this the councils functioned in name only, and dictatorship by the Bolsheviks began. At the time they anticipated that a world revolution would break out across Europe in Russia's wake, but of course this did not happen. Far from it: the Bolsheviks instead met immediate interference and military incursion from abroad. The need to defend the revolution from foreign interference in turn required them to reconstruct a powerful state apparatus. A despotic ruling structure quickly solidified, combining party and state bureaucrats.

Theoretical legitimation for the coup d'état came from the doctrine of permanent revolution and the claim that one could directly advance into socialism by leaping over historical stages. The outcome of these events is all too well-known. Trotsky would later call the system that arose after Stalin's rise to power a betrayal of the revolution, but it was in fact the logical outcome of the October Revolution. In that sense, the October Revolution itself was already a betrayal of the revolution.

By and large, all of the attempts to challenge Marx's own rejection of permanent revolution, all of the attempts to leap over historical stages, ended in failure—including Mao Zedong's. In the end, it was impossible to leap over stages. In the revolutions of the twentieth century (all of which took place in developing countries), the socialists who seized power all ended up falling into the same pattern of playing the role that should have been played by the bourgeoisie—or, more accurately, by the absolute monarchy.

In Europe the absolute monarchies created the identity of the nation by suppressing the feudal aristocracies and uniting the people as subjects of the monarch. Moreover, through the destruction and exploitation of the older agrarian community, the absolute monarchies put in place the base for a capitalist economy. Marx called this process "primitive accumulation." The bourgeoisie who overthrew the absolute monarchy in violent revolutions subsequently built the capitalist economy on this base that was constructed by their predecessors.

By contrast, nearly all regions where the development of industrial capitalism lagged fell under colonial rule: they lacked sovereignty. Tribal conflicts persisted, and a shared sense of identity as nation never appeared. The Western powers skillfully manipulated this fragmented situation to pursue their agenda of colonization. Moreover, these regions were characterized by the existence of self-sufficient agrarian communities. In such a situation, who could carry out the task of unifying the nation, overturning the previously existing feudal order, and pursuing the path of industrialization? The landowning class and the comprador capitalists were by and large satisfied with the status quo. In this situation, only the socialists were capable of agitating for ethnic independence and social reform. Accordingly, in these areas the socialists had to carry out the role played elsewhere by the absolute monarchy or bourgeois revolution.[31]

As Marx noted, these tasks do not properly belong to socialists. But in countries on the periphery, socialists are the only ones able to carry them out. It was only natural that socialists would take them on, and in fact they deserve credit for it. But we need to remain critical of anyone who gives the name *socialism* to these tasks. Doing so does irreparable harm to the idea of socialism—harm that ultimately derives from the problematic concepts of permanent revolution and leaping over historical stages.

The Problem of Fascism

In trying to master capitalism by means of the state, Marxists fell into a trap laid by the state. I've already provided an extensive explanation of this, but here I would like to address one additional stumbling block that this involves: the problem of the nation. In the *Communist Manifesto*, published just before the outbreak of the 1848 revolutions, Marx and Engels express their expectation that, because the proletariat has no fatherland, world revolution would arise as a decisive battle between two great classes, the bourgeoisie and the proletariat, transcending national boundaries. In reality, the opposite happened: issues of nation and ethnicity became increasingly important, taking their place alongside issues of class.

Marxists believed that the nation was part of the ideological superstructure and that it would therefore disappear once class structure was abolished. But this is not what happened. The nation functioned autonomously, independent of the state—just as it continues to function today. As I've already argued, the nation is the imaginative return of community or reciprocal mode of exchange A. It is egalitarian in nature. As a result, there is an often-confusing resemblance between nationalist and socialist (associationist) movements.

For example, in movements of national liberation directed against colonial rule, socialism often fuses with nationalism. This is because the capital in colonized countries is comprador or dependent capital, meaning that only socialists are prepared to pursue nationalism. As a result, socialism and nationalism are sometimes unavoidably equated in such situations. It really becomes a problem elsewhere—when nationalism takes on the guise of socialism in developed industrial capitalist states. This is what we call fascism. Fascism is National Socialism, as seen in the official name of the Nazi Party (the National Socialist German Workers' Party). It is, in other words, an attempt to transcend capital and the state through the nation. It is hostile to both capitalism and Marxism. But it is impossible to supersede capitalism and the state through the nation. National Socialism created an imagined community that appeared to transcend capital and state. The powerful attraction held by fascism in many countries arose from the vision it offered of a dream world—really, a nightmare world—in which all contradictions were overcome in the here and now.

The collapse of Marxist movements in the face of fascism in so many places came about because they regarded the nation as merely superstructural. Ernst Bloch, confronting the reality of Marxist impotence in the face of Nazism, argued that unlike Marxism, Nazism was able to summon up and mobilize various elements from the past that had been repressed under capitalist rationality.[32] This means that Nazism was able to make use of the nation as the imaginary return of mode of exchange A. This seemed to promise socialism—in other words, mode of exchange D.

This also helps explain why so many anarchists were won over to fascism. Italy's Fascists, for example, were under the influence of the anarchist theorist Georges Sorel. Benito Mussolini was originally a leader of the Socialist Party, breaking with it only after its initial opposition to participation in the First World War. Even then he did not abandon the cause of rebelling against capital and the state. In his view, capital and the state were to be superseded by the nation. In this sense, Italian fascism was really a corrupted form of anarchism.

In the case of German Nazism, a number of elements were involved. These included the Sturmabteilung storm troopers, an anarchist faction who opposed capital and the bureaucratic state. They too believed that National Socialism could overcome capital and the state through the nation. This was what attracted Martin Heidegger to the Nazis: he rejected the Nazis only after the purge of the Sturmabteilung. It wasn't so much that he abandoned the Nazis as it was that the Nazis abandoned National Socialism.

Likewise, in Japanese fascism one of the most influential thinkers in the 1930s was Seikyō Gondō. He advocated an antistate, anticapitalist philosophy, calling for the restoration of *shashoku*, a version of the agrarian community. The symbol of this was supposed to be the emperor—meaning not the absolute monarchy that had ruled since Meiji but the chiefdom that prevailed in ancient Japanese society before the rise of the state. It is interesting to note that Gondō enjoyed wide support among anarchists, who believed that the emperor represented the only possibility for a stateless society. Here again we see an affinity between fascism and anarchism.

This affinity arises because of the resemblance between nationalism and socialism (associationism). This is easily understood when we look at them in terms of modes of exchange. Both respond to the reality of class division and alienation in the capitalist economy by attempting to imaginarily restore mode of exchange A. They differ only in how they would effect this restoration. Previously, I pointed out how universal religion arose in the form of an unconscious, compulsory "return of the repressed," rather than a conscious, nostalgic restoration of the past. We can draw the same distinction with regard to nationalism and socialism. Nationalism is nostalgic, a proactive attempt to restore past ways of life. By contrast, even as associationism seeks to restore the past form of mode of exchange A, it is not about restoring the past. Associationism is about creating the future anew. This is why associationism seeks to transform the status quo, while nationalism generally ends up affirming it.

Late in his life, Marx received a query from Zasulich, a Narodnik activist from Russia. Under the influence of Bakunin, the Narodniks celebrated the Russian agrarian community, seeing in it a living communism. But would the Russian agrarian community directly evolve into the communism of the future, or did it first have to undergo a process of dissolution under the pressure of capitalist privatization? That was the question Zasulich raised. Marx's response was a long time in coming, because at that very moment he was reading Lewis H. Morgan's *Ancient Society*, which was forcing him to rethink his position.

Originally, Marx envisioned the future communal society (association) as the restoration in a higher dimension of primitive communism. In fact, this was not unique to Marx—it was a view widely shared among socialists in general. The idea of restoring gesellschaft by overlaying it onto gemeinschaft—to use Ferdinand Tönnies's terms—is based on romantic thought. But the mature Marx rejected this romantic tendency. The position he adopted in his last years, regarding socialism as the restoration in a higher dimension of community, did not come from a romantic outlook. The motivation for it seems to have come rather from his reading of Morgan's *Ancient Society*. Morgan identified clan society not only with egalitarianism but also with independent, autonomous individuals: it was based in a warrior-farmer community. In his view, ancient Greek democracy inherited this. Accordingly, the clan community that Marx took as the model for what should be restored was one never subordinated to a higher-order collective. In other words, Marx took as his model the aspects in clan society that had been carried over from nomadic society.

The existing mir communes in Russia were not this sort of community. Fully subordinated to the despotic state, they were not simply a more highly evolved form of clan society. Instead they were originally established after the Mongol invasion of 1236, under the Kipchak Khanate's indirect rule during the 250 years of the "Tatar Yoke"—in other words, under an Asiatic despotic state. Marx pointed this out.[33] These agrarian communities no longer possessed the spirit of independence that had characterized the warrior-farmer community. Their members were submissive toward and dependent on higher authorities. In fact, they worshipped the czar (the monarch and the royal family). For these reasons, the cooperative society (association) of the future could never arise from these agrarian communes. If anything, reliance on them would result in a socialism that resembled Asiatic despotism.

Accordingly, if the question was whether the communes in Russia could directly evolve into the association of the future, the answer was no. This did not mean, however, that they would necessarily pass through a stage of collapse under the impact of privatization. Even as the penetration of the capitalist economy undermined the agrarian community, people's attitude of subservience toward the state would not likely change. The atomized masses could hardly form an association: they would only seek a new czar. For this reason, what was needed was to generate an association-like autonomy in the agrarian community, distinct from that produced by the rise of capitalism. Marx therefore responded no to Zasulich's query, but at the same time he did not believe what she suggested was completely impossible: "This commune is the fulcrum of social regeneration in Russia, but in order that it may function as such, it would first be necessary to eliminate the deleterious influences which are assailing it from all sides, and then ensure for it the normal conditions of spontaneous development."[34] Marx took this up in more concrete terms elsewhere:

> Now the question is: can the Russian *obshchina* [agrarian community], a form of primeval common ownership of land, even if greatly undermined, pass directly to the higher form of communist common ownership? Or must it, conversely, first pass through the same process of dissolution as constitutes the historical development of the West?
>
> The only answer possible today is this: If the Russian Revolution becomes the signal for a proletarian revolution in the West, so that the two complement each other, the present Russian common ownership of land may serve as the starting point for communist development.[35]

Marx here is outlining a vision of the simultaneous world revolution: this revolution cannot occur in a single country. This example is suggestive when we view today's struggles by indigenous peoples around the world against the destructive intrusions of global capitalism. In them, the power to resist capital and the state comes less from the socialist Idea than from the practices of reciprocal exchange, the sense of a shared environment, and communal traditions. But if we ask whether this kind of movement can itself directly lead to a socialist formation (i.e., mode of exchange D), the answer will likely have to be the same one that Marx gave: that would only be possible with the aid and support that a socialist reform in the developed countries could provide.

Welfare Statism

Since 1990 the Left in the developed nations has completely abandoned the kind of revolution that it previously sought. Accepting the role of the market economy, the Left now advocates addressing the various contradictions it produces through public consensus achieved through democratic means and redistribution. In other words, the Left has settled into the position of advocating welfare-state policies and democratic socialism. But this also implies affirming the existence of the Capital-Nation-State framework and abandoning any attempt to move beyond it. This is the situation that Frances Fukuyama called "the end of history." In fact, this is no different from the position Bernstein adopted a century earlier. I say this not to celebrate Bernstein's prescience, but rather to point out that we still lack any fundamental critique of his position.

Welfare statism was adopted reluctantly by the advanced capitalist nations as part of the effort to counter Soviet-style socialism. But one thinker emerged in the midst of this who is worth noting for his attempts to construct an active theoretical grounding for welfare statism: John Rawls. Relying on an a priori morality of "justice," he tried to provide a theoretical basis for redistribution of wealth as a response to economic disparity:

> Justice is the first virtue of social institutions, as truth is of systems of thought. A theory however elegant and economical must be rejected or revised if it is untrue; likewise laws and institutions no matter how efficient and well-arranged must be reformed or abolished if they are unjust. Each person possesses an inviolability founded on justice that even the welfare of society as a whole cannot override. For this reason justice denies that the loss of freedom for some is made right by a greater good shared by others. It does not allow that the sacrifice imposed on a few are outweighed by the larger sum of advantages enjoyed by many.[36]

Rawls believed that his method of starting from the principle of an a priori justice was Kantian. In one sense, he is correct—but only if we ignore a crucial difference. For Kant, justice meant the moral imperative to treat people "always at the same time as an end and never merely as a means to an end." Accordingly, a capitalist economy that rendered this impossible could never for Kant constitute justice. By contrast, for Rawls, justice means at most redistributive justice. In other words, his concept of justice leaves the mechanism that produces inequality untouched and instead relies on the government to adjust its outcomes. Kant's justice, however, would demand the abolition of the capitalist economy that gave birth to those disparities in the first place.

Kant was critical of the British school of empirical morality. This school appeared in two forms: utilitarianism, which maintained that good lies in happiness and that happiness derives from economic wealth, and the form represented by Adam Smith, which sought morality in a moral sentiment such as sympathy. Kant criticized both schools and instead sought morality in freedom. Freedom means to be self-causative (spontaneous and autonomous). Profit, happiness, moral sentiment, and the like are all matters of sensibility and therefore are determined by natural causality; nothing based in them can be freedom.

Another crucial point here: this freedom cannot be obtained by sacrificing the freedom of others. This led to what Kant regarded as a transcendental moral law (categorical imperative): the idea that one must never treat others only as a means but always at the same time as an end (i.e., a free being). We can think of this as an insistence on the mutuality (or reciprocity) of freedom. Kant's ethics have been widely regarded as subjective. But Kant himself was clearly aware that this mutuality of freedom could not be separated from the problem of actual economic relations with others. A society grounded in reciprocal exchange is the inevitable result of Kantian morality; Proudhon was the first to point this out clearly.

In the English-speaking world, Kant's thought was largely rejected as a kind of subjective ethics, and the utilitarianism that he criticized instead became dominant. Utilitarianism roughly equates good with economic benefit, that is, with profit. In other words, it reduces ethics to economics. It may appear that Rawls introduced a Kantian ethics into this cultural domain, but that is not the case: Rawls's notions of good and equality achieved through distribution leave untouched the capitalist economy, which is the ultimate basis for utilitarianism. These notions include no consideration of the mutuality of freedom and for that reason can hardly be called Kantian.

The intimate connections between Kant's morality and the critique of capitalism have been largely ignored. In the same way, the moral dimensions of Marx's socialism have also been generally overlooked. The young Marx wrote: "The criticism of religion ends with the teaching that *man is the highest being for man*, hence with the *categorical imperative to overthrow all relations* in which man is a debased, enslaved, forsaken, despicable being."[37] More than a criticism of religion, this suggests that religion will not disappear until the mutuality of freedom has been realized. Accordingly, (economic) criticism of actual society must replace the criticism of religion. Throughout his life, Marx never abandoned this position. The Kantian roots of this categorical imperative to realize the mutuality of freedom are clear.

PART FOUR **THE PRESENT AND THE FUTURE**

ELEVEN **THE STAGES OF GLOBAL CAPITALISM AND REPETITION**

The Historical Stages of Capitalism

Up until now, I have taken up state, capital, and nation separately. They do not, however, exist independently of one another. I dealt with them separately only in order to clarify the characteristics of each. As I have already mentioned, in *Capital* Karl Marx bracketed off the state. For example, he divided the return on capital into three types—profit, land rent, and wages—and indicated that these in turn form three great classes. This was a view he inherited from David Ricardo, but while Ricardo's *On the Principles of Political Economy and Taxation* stressed the importance of taxation, as the book's title shows, Marx entirely abstracted taxation from his considerations. In other words, he abstracted away the class formed by the state—the army and bureaucracy.

This was a methodological choice. In fact, in *The Eighteenth Brumaire of Louis Napoleon*, Marx does not overlook the existence of the state system (the bureaucratic apparatus) as a kind of class, nor does he fail to see the role played by various classes that do not fall into the three categories of capital, wage labor, and land rent—most notably, small-scale farmers (the yeomanry). The total absence of these from *Capital* signifies his intentional bracketing of them in order to grasp in pure form the system produced by commodity exchange as a mode. Political economy as practiced by such figures as Adam Smith or Ricardo primarily dealt with the economy of the polis or nation. By contrast, the subtitle of Marx's *Capital, A Critique of Political Economy*, signifies his intent to examine capitalism beyond the framework of the polis.

At first glance, it may appear that he takes Britain as the model for capitalist development—and that he has abstracted away the world outside Britain. Yet Marx's focus was always on global capitalism. Shouldn't he have included other countries in his considerations and tried to theorize the totality that they composed in sum? But the world-economy (global capitalism) is not simply the sum of the various national economies. Marx took the British economy as his object because Britain at the time was the hegemonic power in the global economy. The remaining countries were not elided from his thought: through their relations of trade, they were internalized to the economy of Britain, which was advocating the principle of free trade. Marx took the British economy as his primary object, but he rejected the political-economy approach and instead treated the British economy as a world-economy.

Naturally, we can identify a significant gap between the world depicted in *Capital* and the actual economies of various countries. In actual capitalist social formations, capitalist production and the market economy do not completely blanket everything. Other modes of exchange and relations of production continue to exist. This was true even in the nineteenth-century Britain that Marx took as his model—and, it should go without saying, in late-developing capitalist countries as well. Even in Britain, with its economic policies based in classical liberalism, the existence of the state was crucial for capitalism. This was all the more so for late-developing nations: as the examples of France, Germany, and Japan show, it was the state that actively fostered industrial capitalism. Moreover, even if we confine ourselves to the case of Britain, the gap between the world depicted in *Capital* and the actual economy became especially pronounced in the age of imperialism. Imperialism arose out of the capitalist economy, yet this in itself does not suffice to explain imperialism. Understanding imperialism requires us to see how the state acted as an active agent, not simply as part of the ideological superstructure.

These disconnects between *Capital* and actual political economy were a source of vexation for Marxists. As a result, there were some people who saw *Capital* as a historical work that needed to be further "developed"—which for some meant, in short, to abandon it. I am particularly interested in the work of Kōzō Uno, who stressed the continuing importance of *Capital* even as he tried to resolve these disconnects. Uno thought that Marx in *Capital* had posited "pure capitalism."[1] Pure capitalism did not actually exist in Britain—nor would it ever exist in the future. But with its liberalism and its relative abstraction of the state, the capitalism of Britain in Marx's day can be regarded as approximating a state of pure capitalism, so it provided an opportunity for understanding what the mechanisms of pure capitalism might be. Still, for Uno pure capitalism remained a theoretical question. He believed that *Capital* provided a theory of how, if all other factors were bracketed, a capitalist economy would function when commodity exchange achieved full penetration. Accordingly, so long as a capitalist economy continued to exist, *Capital* would retain theoretical validity and require no particular modifications.

This is how Uno saw *Capital*, but he also thought that in actual social formations, which encompass a wide range of factors, the state intervenes in the economy through economic policies and that these produce the historical stages of capitalism—mercantilism, liberalism, and imperialism, according to Uno. In addition, he believed that a new stage had emerged following the First World War and the Russian Revolution, one qualitatively different from that of imperialism. In this stage, the state adopted socialist or Keynesian economic policies. This is what is generally called late capitalism, but it can also be called Fordism or welfare statism. Robert Albritton, who has adopted Uno's theory, calls this stage consumerism.[2]

In my view, these various stages can also be identified by changes in the key currency, or what can be called the *world commodity*: the wool industry in the stage of mercantilism, the cotton textile industry in liberalism, heavy industries in imperialism, and durable consumer goods (automobiles and electronics) in the stage of late capitalism. The stage of late capitalism has been replaced by a new stage since the 1980s, one in which information serves as the world commodity. Below I will return to the question of what we might call this new stage.

Developmental stage theories such as this were quite common among Marxists. They focused on how the economic base or developments in the forces of production transformed the ideological superstructure of politics and culture. From that perspective it seemed that, since merchant capital required state protection, mercantilist policies were necessary, while industrial capital did not require such measures and thus led to the adoption of policies based on classical liberalism. At the stage of imperialism, in turn, capital was exported abroad and therefore state military intervention became necessary. In this way, the political was always determined by the economic. According to this view, these sorts of changes were produced by transformations in the capitalist economy itself, and to understand them we need to engage in a further theoretical "development" of Marx's *Capital*.

But Uno's theory of historical stages is different. He examined the developmental stages of capitalism in terms of the economic policies of the state. In doing so, he brought the state, which had been bracketed off in *Capital*, back into the picture. Moreover, he did so without altering the basic principles of pure capitalism that were theorized in *Capital*. This perspective of grasping the developmental stages of capitalism in terms of economic policy reintroduced the state as an active agent, independent of capital: the state was no longer simply determined by changes in the capitalist economy.

For example, at the stage of mercantilism, the state was not concealed in the background, hiding behind merchants; to the contrary, it was the leading force in trade. This tendency dated back to the age of the ancient empires, when long-distance trade was carried out by the state itself. What was the case at the stage of classical liberalism? Here too the state was hardly inactive: England's liberalism was backed by its naval power that dominated the seven seas. Liberalism is the policy adopted by a state that has achieved economic and military dominance. To counter this, other states adopt protectionist (mercantilist) policies and attempt to foster and strengthen their own industrial capital; failure to do so means being colonized. The state stands most clearly in the foreground at the stage of imperialism, as well as in fascism and welfare-state capitalism. The actual history of the capitalist economy cannot be grasped if we abstract away the dimension of the state. Uno, however, was careful to speak only from the position of an economist and generally refrained from making overt statements about the role of the state. As a result, his theory of stages ended up being largely absorbed into the existing debates over historical stages.

The historian Immanuel Wallerstein, on the other hand, took up the questions of mercantilism, liberalism, and imperialism as problems of hegemony in the modern world system (global capitalism); he too brought the state back in as an active agent. In his view, liberalism is in general the policy of a hegemonic state and therefore is not limited to the period of the mid-nineteenth century. In fact, liberalism has appeared in other ages as well. In Wallerstein's understanding, though, there have been only three hegemonic states in the modern world-economy: Holland, Britain, and the United States.

As a hegemonic state, Holland adopted the policies of liberalism. During this period (from the late sixteenth century to the mid-seventeenth century), Britain maintained mercantilist (protectionist) policies. And in political terms, Holland was a republic, not an absolute monarchy, making it considerably more liberal than Britain. For example, its capital of Amsterdam was an exceptional city in the Europe of its day, providing refuge to the exiled René Descartes and John Locke and offering a safe haven to Baruch Spinoza—a phenomenon reminiscent of Marx's exile to London during the age of British hegemony. Wallerstein notes that "generations of Scotsmen went to the Netherlands for their university education. This is another link in the chain that explains the Scottish Enlightenment of the late eighteenth century, itself a crucial factor in the British industrial surge forward."[3]

Wallerstein argues that changeovers in hegemony follow a pattern: "Marked superiority in agro-industrial productive efficiency leads to dominance of the spheres of commercial distribution of world trade, with correlative profits accruing both from being the entrepôt of much of world trade and from controlling the 'invisibles'—transport, communications, and insurance. Commercial primacy leads in turn to control of the financial sectors of banking (exchange, deposit, and credit) and of investment (direct and portfolio)."[4] In this way, the state secures its hegemony first in the manufacturing sector, then in commerce, and finally in the financial sector. Moreover, "It follows that there is probably only a short moment in time when a given core power can manifest *simultaneously* productive, commercial, and financial superiority *over all other core powers*."[5] In other words, hegemony is fleeting: its decay begins as soon as it is established. At the same time, however, it is possible to maintain hegemony in the commercial and financial sectors even after losing it in the sphere of production.

Giovanni Arrighi has raised a number of objections to Wallerstein's formulation of the modern world system.[6] First, he argues that even before Holland, Genoa functioned as a hegemonic state. Moreover, he maintains that Genoa, Holland, Britain, and the United States each repeated a process by which an expansion in production was transformed into a financial expansion. Second, while Wallerstein seeks the basis for this transformation in Kondratiev long waves, Arrighi argues that both Kondratiev long waves and Fernand Braudel's "long duration" are based on long-term price fluctuations and therefore are applicable even to precapitalist periods, meaning that they are inadequate for grasping phenomena unique to the system of capital accumulation (the self-valorization of capital).

In discussing the mechanisms of capital accumulation, Arrighi takes up the two formulas that Marx developed in *Capital*: the M-C-M' of merchant capital and the M-M' of interest-bearing capital. When capital accumulates through investment in trade or manufacturing, it follows the first formula, but in cases where this does not provide a sufficient rate of profit, it turns to the second. This is the secret behind the repeated process by which hege-monic countries pursue expansion in production during their ascendancy, but financial expansion during their period of decline. But Arrighi does not see the modern world system in terms of the competitive coexistence of multiple forms of capital or multiple states. As a result, while Wallerstein posits the state as an active agent, Arrighi reduces the state to the dimen-sion of economic processes. This doesn't solve our crucial problem: under-standing how capital and the state form a double-headed being.

In the latter half of the eighteenth century, even after its manufacturing industry had been surpassed by that of Britain, Holland still retained hege-mony in the spheres of circulation and finance. Britain's complete superior-ity was achieved only in the nineteenth century, in the period of Uno's stage of liberalism. But liberalism is the policy of a hegemonic state. If we call the period of British hegemony in global capitalism the stage of liberalism, the same name should also apply to the age of Holland's hegemony. Mercantil-ism, on the other hand, refers to the period in which no state had achieved hegemony—in other words, the period after Holland had lost its hegemonic status and Britain and France battled one another to become its successor. The stage of imperialism after 1870 followed a similar pattern: Britain lost its hegemony in manufacturing, while the United States, Germany, Japan, and other countries begin fighting to become its successor. In this way, the stages of mercantilism and imperialism resemble one another. I will refer to them both as imperialistic. The various stages of global capitalism are shown in table 6.

From this we can see that the different stages of global capitalism arise as changes in the nature of the union between capital and the state and that these moreover unfold not as a linear development but as a cyclical process. For example, what I call mercantilism (1750–1810) in table 6 is not simply the economic policy pursued by England or the economic stage corre-sponding to it; rather, it refers to the transitional period between Holland's liberalism and England's liberalism—to the imperialistic stage of Holland's decline and England's and France's fierce struggle to replace Holland. Simi-larly, the period of imperialism beginning in 1870 was not simply character-ized by finance capital and the export of capital; it was also the age in which Germany, the United States, and Japan emerged as powers amid the decline of previously hegemonic Britain. The wars of imperialism were fought by the newly rising powers as they struggled to redistribute the territories that Britain, France, and Holland had acquired during the age of mercantilism. In this way, the stages of global capitalism unfold as a linear development

TABLE 6 The World-Historical Stages of Capitalism

	1750–1810	1810–1870	1870–1930	1930–1990	1990–
Global Capitalism	Mercantilism	Liberalism	Imperialism	Late capitalism	Neoliberalism
Hegemonic State		Britain		United States	
Economic Policy	Imperialistic	Liberalism	Imperialistic	Liberalism	Imperialistic
Capital	Merchant capital	Industrial capital	Finance capital	State-monopoly capital	Multinational capital
World Commodity	Textiles	Light industry	Heavy industry	Durable consumer goods	Information
State	Absolute monarchy	Nation-state	Imperialism	Welfare state	Regionalism

driven by increasing productivity and as an ongoing cyclical alternation between liberalist and imperialistic stages.

Repetition in Capital and State

In order to understand the stages of the modern world system (capital and the state) and their cyclical nature, we need to examine not only the form of repetition particular to capitalism but also that found in the state. As for the former, I have already touched upon the long business cycle, and so here I will focus on the form of repetition particular to the state. In *Eighteenth Brumaire of Louis Bonaparte*, Marx provides useful insights on this, beginning with the famous opening passage: "Hegel remarks somewhere that all facts and personages of great importance in world history occur, as it were, twice. He forgot to add: the first time as tragedy, the second as farce."[7] Marx here stresses that the process by which Louis Bonaparte was named emperor during the 1848 revolution was a repetition of the process by which Napoleon Bonaparte became emperor sixty years earlier in the first French Revolution. But this was not the only repetition involved: the first French Revolution itself followed a pattern borrowed from ancient Roman history. In that sense, these were instances of repetition as *re-presentation*.

But this type of repetition does not arise simply because people borrow patterns from the past. In other words, this form of repetition is not just a problem of representation. Representation can produce repetition only when there is a structural resemblance between present and past—only, that is, when a structure of repetition unique to the state exists, one that transcends the consciousness of individual persons. In fact, G. W. F. Hegel wrote something to this effect in his *The Philosophy of History*: "By repetition that which at first appeared merely a matter of chance and contingency, becomes a real and ratified existence."[8] As an instance of a world-historical individual, Hegel takes up the case of Julius Caesar, assassinated as he was about to become emperor. Caesar attempted to become emperor at a time when the Roman city-state had expanded to a point where the principles of republican government had lost their ability to function; his murder came at the hands of Brutus and others who were attempting to preserve the republic. It was only after the murder of Caesar, though, that people came to accept the unavoidable reality of the empire (emperor). While Caesar himself never became emperor, his name became the common noun designating emperors (Caesar, czar, and so on).

When Marx wrote that "Hegel remarks somewhere . . ." he may have forgotten passages such as this. But in *Eighteenth Brumaire of Louis Bonaparte*, Marx certainly depicts the situation that arises when a city-state expands to become an empire. The repetition of Caesar's fate reveals with precision the structures involved in the formation and preservation of the state in general, not simply that of Rome. In the French Revolution, the king was murdered, and then, from the midst of the republican government that followed, an emperor appeared, cheered on by the masses. This is exactly what Sigmund Freud called the "return of the repressed." Of course, the emperor is in one sense the return of the murdered king, but he is no longer merely king. An emperor, after all, corresponds to an empire, which transcends the scope of a city-state (polis) or nation-state.

Napoleon opposed British industrial capitalism and called for European unity. In the face of Britain's maritime empire, it was imperative for him to create an empire on the continent capable of blockading Britain. In that sense, there was a logic behind his need to take on the title of emperor. On these points, Louis Bonaparte resembled his uncle: the nephew pursued a policy of state-sponsored heavy industrialization to counter Britain, and at the same time, as a socialist (a follower of Saint-Simon) he instituted social policies with the aim of permanently resolving class conflict. He was thus simultaneously the despotic ruler of the state and the representative of the people—that is, he was caesar (emperor). Of course, as Marx notes, there was a gap between what people thought they were doing and what they actually were doing.

It should be clear that Marx was concerned here with the state's own structure of repetition. In the *Eighteenth Brumaire of Louis Bonaparte*, Marx did not overlook how the global panic of 1851 drove the bourgeoisie of France to desire strong leadership in the form of Louis Bonaparte's regime. In reading this work, we need to pay special attention to how he perceived the state as an active agent, one with its own structure of historical repetition.

In fact, Napoleon was unable to realize his empire. The empire he built through conquest lacked the sort of governing principle needed to sustain an empire. As I have already argued, an empire that forms through the expansion of a nation-state has to become imperialistic in nature. Napoleon's conquest of Europe signified both the export of the French Revolution and an attempt to form a European union capable of standing up to British industrial capitalism. What the conquest actually achieved though was the awakening of nationalism in Germany and elsewhere. This was the first instance of a phenomenon that Hannah Arendt identified: the imperialist expansion of one nation-state leading to the creation of other new nation-states.[9] By the twentieth century, imperialism had created nation-states around the world in this manner.

Why is it impossible for the expansion of a nation-state to result in empire? It is because the nation-state's precursor, the absolutist centralized state, was born precisely as a negation of the principles of empire. Not just in Europe but everywhere, basically the same process was followed as nation-states appeared through the negation and fragmenting of previous world empires. The absolutist state did not have to take the specific form of a monarchy: in fact, such cases seem rather unusual. It was more common for the absolutist state to appear in the form of a dictatorship, whether developmentalist or socialist. As this indicates, the nation-state emerges in the form of a unit within the world-economy. It is a historical construct, and an unstable one at that. We also need to realize, however, that the nation-state cannot easily be dismantled and, moreover, that if it is too hastily dismantled, it will simply be replaced by a religious or lineage-based community.

Nonetheless, it is also clear that the nation-state is not the final unit sitting at the end of history. The modern nation-state emerged out of the negation and fragmentation of earlier world empires, but this means that it will always harbor an impulse to return to its old world empire and to the cultural and religious communality that existed under it. In such cases, if a single country takes the lead in trying to restore empire, the result can only be imperialism: Germany's Third Reich and Japan's Greater East Asia Co-prosperity Sphere are instances. Yet the impetus to return to empire does not disappear, even when imperialism is rejected. This is the form of repetition specific to the dimension of the state—though it is of course inseparable from the movement of global capitalism. For that reason, to understand it we need a viewpoint that can comprehend both capital and the state as active subjects.

Since 1990

Since 1990 we have entered a new stage, one in which the collapse of the Soviet Union led to intensified globalization of capitalism under overwhelming U.S. superiority. We also call this the stage of neoliberalism, and the United States is often regarded as resurrecting the liberalism of the nineteenth-century British Empire. In reality, however, the period since 1990 has been less liberal than imperialistic. In other words, we are now in a stage where, despite appearances, the previously hegemonic power is in decline and, with the absence of a clear successor, other countries have entered into a fierce struggle to become the next hegemonic power.

The period of U.S. liberalism that most resembled nineteenth-century England (the British Empire) actually occurred during the Cold War (1930–90). During this period, the Soviet Union seemed to be a powerful rival to the United States, although in reality, it never posed a real threat to global capitalism. Under the Cold-War order of the United States and the Soviet Union, the developed capitalist countries were able to cooperate, taking the Soviet bloc as their common enemy. Brought to ruin by the Second World War, the developed capitalist states succeeded in pursuing economic development with the help of U.S. aid and by relying on their access to the U.S. market.

As a result though, Japan and Germany began to catch up with the United States in the manufacturing sector. The production and consumption of durable consumer goods (automobiles and consumer electronics), the world commodity of this period, reached a saturation point. The collapse of U.S. hegemony became apparent with the 1971 suspension of the convertibility of the dollar to gold. But even as the United States saw its manufacturing sector decline, it still enjoyed hegemony in the financial and commerce sectors (related to oil, grain, and other raw materials and energy sources). The country also retained overwhelming military superiority. Still, we must not let these external appearances fool us into thinking that the United States remains the same hegemonic state it was before.

The United States has already abandoned liberalism in one other important aspect. According to Wallerstein, "the period leading up to the dominance of a hegemonic power seem to favor the intrastate form."[10] Both Holland and Britain during the period in which they were hegemonic—during, that is, their liberalism period—were domestically characterized by robust social-welfare systems. The United States similarly implemented domestic social-welfare and worker-protection policies from the 1930s as part of its effort to counter the Soviet Union. In that sense, the Cold-War formation can be said to have helped produce liberalism in the United States.

The United States began to abandon this liberalism in the 1980s, as symbolized by the Reagan doctrine of cutting back on social welfare and reducing taxes and regulations on capital—the program that we now call neoliberalism. As should be clear, this is quite different from the liberalism of nineteenth-century Britain; neoliberalism resembles instead the imperialism that became dominant from the 1880s: the United States had lost its hegemony in the manufacturing sector, thereby setting off a struggle to see who would become the new hegemonic power. The Soviet menace was a threat in name only; if anything, the presence of the Soviet Union helped check the outbreak of struggle among the capitalist states. The situation that has emerged since 1990 and the collapse of the Soviet Union is often called globalization, but it is better understood as an imperialistic struggle for hegemony, one that now involves even Russia—the former Soviet Union.

During this period people spoke about neoliberalism, not imperialism. But the real situation was identical to that of imperialism. For example, Vladimir Lenin identified the export of capital as one of the distinguishing historical characteristics of the stage of imperialism. This refers to capital that, facing saturated domestic markets and hence an inability to achieve self-valorization at home, moved overseas in search of new markets. At the same time, the great powers intervened militarily abroad in order to protect their overseas capital. But we should not let this military aspect distract us from seeing the real essence of imperialism: globalization.

This export of capital then causes major transformations in domestic politics, because it leads to cuts in employment and benefits for workers in the home country. In Britain this tendency became particularly evident after 1870, in tandem with the shift to imperialism. Arendt argues that the imperialism of this period is what politically liberated the bourgeoisie:

> The central inner-European event of the imperialist period was the political emancipation of the bourgeoisie, which up to then had been the first class in history to achieve economic pre-eminence without aspiring to political rule. The bourgeoisie had developed within, and together with, the nation-state, which almost by definition ruled over and beyond a class-divided society. Even when the bourgeoisie had already established itself as the ruling class, it had left all political decisions to the state. Only when the nation-state proved unfit to be the framework for the further growth of capitalist economy did the latent fight between state and society become openly a struggle for power.[11]

This political emancipation of the bourgeoisie meant that capital was emancipated from the constraints of the nation. At the same time, the state was emancipated from its need to consider the nation. In other words, state-capital was freed from the egalitarian demands that characterized the nation. The livelihoods of the national people were necessarily sacrificed in the name of international competitiveness. In this sense, the ideologies of neoliberalism closely resemble those of imperialism. The ruling ideology of the age of imperialism was a survival-of-the-fittest social Darwinism, which is today being recycled in new forms under neoliberalism. We no longer hesitate to sort people into winners and losers or question the way free competition ranks people into distinct categories: management, regular full-time employees, temporary part-time workers, and the unemployed.

Imperialism emerged as a result of capital sacrificing the nation, but with the First World War, imperialism began to falter. This was due in large measure to the socialist revolution in Russia, which threatened to spread across the globe. In order to contain this, a counterrevolution was launched in the other imperialist states. The fascism (National Socialism) that arose in Italy, Germany, and Japan marked a revolution that aimed to supersede capital and state through the nation. Britain and the United States, on the other hand, enacted social-democratic or welfare-state policies. It was no longer possible to ignore the egalitarian principle of the nation. This was true not only with regard to one's own country but also with regard to people in colonized lands—it was no longer possible to ignore nationalist demands for self-determination. As a result, even though the reality remained imperialistic, it became common everywhere to at least feign opposition to imperialism.

In the 1930s, different blocs formed: fascism (Germany, Japan, Italy), welfare-state capitalism (Britain, United States), and socialism (Soviet Union). The conflicts among these eventually resulted in the Second World War, and the fascist camp was defeated. In the postwar world, the victorious United States and Soviet Union established the Cold-War regime. As I've already noted, however, the reality here was a system in which the United States was hegemonic; its global dominance had been clear since the 1930s. Accordingly, the world that arose with the decline of the United States was not the world that had existed prior to the Second World War; it resembled instead the world of the 1870s, the period of British decline.

The post-1990 age of neoliberalism and the post-1870 age of imperialism resemble each other in another way: just as in the 1870s the old world empires (the Russian, Qing, Mughal, and Ottoman Empires) stubbornly held on in the face of pressure from Western imperialism, in the period since the 1990s, these same powers have revived to become new empires.

The Empire of Capital

In the 1991 Gulf War, the United States enjoyed absolute military hegemony, but it went into action only after receiving the support of the United Nations. Antonio Negri and Michael Hardt saw in this U.S. maneuvering something that resembled the Roman Empire: "The importance of the Gulf War derives rather from the fact that it presented the USA as the only power able to manage international justice *not as a function of its own national motives but in the name of global right.*"[12]

Certainly at this time the United States attempted to act in concert with UN mandates and international law. The claim, however, that the United States was not imperialist and was carrying out a political mode based on law was refuted ten years later in the Iraq War: far from obtaining the United Nation's backing, the United States openly flouted it, pursuing a course of unilateralism. Negri and Hardt did not persist in the view that the United States resembled the Roman Empire. We should also note that, in their view, "Empire" is something that exists nowhere.

> The capitalist market is one machine that has always run counter to any division between inside and outside. It is thwarted by barriers and exclusions; it thrives instead by including always more within it sphere. Profit can be generated only through contact, engagement, interchange, and commerce. The realization of the world market would constitute the point of arrival of this tendency. In its ideal form there is no outside to the world market: the entire globe is its domain. We might thus use the form of the world market as a model for understanding imperial sovereignty. . . . In this smooth space of Empire, there is no *place* of power—it is both everywhere and nowhere. Empire is an *ou-topia*, or really a *non-place.*[13]

What Negri and Hardt call "Empire" is more a world market, but insofar as it is sustained by force, they regard the United States as Empire. The problem with this view is that it rests on the mistaken perception that the United States remains the hegemonic state. In this their view resembles that of Marx during the period of British hegemony. In the *Communist Manifesto* (1848), Marx predicted that under the conditions of "intercourse in every direction, universal inter-dependence of nations," differences of nationality or state would soon be erased.[14]

In the same way, Negri and Hardt predict that under Empire (world market), the nation-state will lose its real significance and that the "multitude" will rise up against it. This multitude seems to be a multifaceted collective that includes not only laborers but also minorities, migrants, and indigenous peoples: a kind of unruly masses. But this all resembles the perception that Marx had in the 1840s, his prophecy that the world would come to a decisive battle between the two great classes, the capitalists and proletariat. Negri and Hardt in fact stress that Marx's proletariat is not limited to the narrow meaning of the working class and that it resembles their multitude.

Negri and Hardt say that they take the concept of multitude from Spinoza, but this relies on a somewhat forced misreading. Multitude was in fact originally used by Thomas Hobbes, for whom it signified a mass of individuals living in a natural condition. These people individually cede their sovereignty to the state and in doing so escape the condition of the multitude to become citizens or national subjects. Spinoza was basically of the same mind on this point. He differed from Hobbes only in that Spinoza acknowledged a wider sphere of natural rights that need not be ceded to the state; he neither affirmed the multitude nor placed his hopes in it.

Negri and Hardt's thought is actually closer to that of P.-J. Proudhon's idea of a true form of society that lies deep beneath the surface, the site of a pluralistic and creative democracy. Which is to say, it is a kind of anarchism. This is clear even though they do not mention Proudhon and only cite Spinoza and Marx. It was under the influence of Proudhon that Marx posited a civil society existing at the base, one that transcended national divisions. He outlined a vision in which the overcoming of the proletariat's self-alienation and the realization of absolute democracy at this level would lead to the global abolition of the state and capital. If we simply substitute *multitude* here for *proletariat*, we arrive at Negri and Hardt's position. In sum, instead of calling for a simultaneous world revolution by the proletariat, they call for one by the multitude.

Wallerstein ranks the revolution of 1968 alongside the world revolution of 1848. If we accept this, we might regard Negri and Hardt's position as deriving from the vision that motivated the world revolution not only of 1848 but also of 1968, which was a reawakening of the former. But this all rests on a fundamental misunderstanding of the historical stages of capitalism. The 1848 revolution took place in the period when Britain held absolute hegemony. Similarly, the 1968 revolution occurred in a period when the United States was hegemonic. What did these revolutions bring about? The revolution of 1848 did not erase national and state differences; far from it— it led to state capitalism in France and Germany, to the economic decline of Britain, and ultimately to the age of imperialism. We can say roughly the same thing about 1968: the decline of U.S. hegemony, symbolized by the suspension of the dollar's direct convertibility to gold, dates from this period.

The Next Hegemonic State

No matter how completely capitalism penetrates the globe, the state will not disappear: it is based on its own principle, not that of commodity exchange. For example, liberals in nineteenth-century England trumpeted their "cheap government," but in reality Britain's liberal imperialism was supported by massive military power and the world's highest taxation— as is the case with today's U.S. neoliberalism. Libertarians and anarcho-capitalists believe that capitalism will dismantle the state, but this is impossible. Contrary to Negri and Hardt's assertions, the situation that has unfolded since 1990 has not been the establishment of a U.S. "Empire," but rather the emergence of multiple Empires. This period of conflict among multiple empires is precisely what I have called an imperialistic period.

Ellen M. Wood has criticized Negri and Hardt, noting quite correctly that "the state is more essential than ever to capital, even, or especially, in its global form. The political form of globalization is not a global state but a global system of multiple states, and the new imperialism that takes its specific shape from the complex and contradictory relationship between capital's expansive economic power and the more limited reach of the extra-economic force that sustains it."[15]

Theorists of the European Union have claimed that it represents an overcoming of the modern sovereign state, but if the nation-state was compelled into existence by the modern world system, the same is true for regional communities. In order to compete with the United States, Japan, and others, the various nations of Europe have created a European community, ceding economic and military sovereignty to a higher-order structure. But this can hardly be called the abolition of the modern state: what it marks instead is the banding together of several states to form a supranational state under the pressure of global capitalism (the world market).

This kind of supranational state is hardly new. Its precursors include the Third Reich envisioned by Germany and the Greater East Asia Co-prosperity Sphere planned by Japan in the 1930s as attempts to counter the economic bloc created by the alliance of Britain, the United States, and France. These continental economic zones were represented as transcending the modern world system, that is, capitalism and the nation-state. In western Europe, the vision of creating a European league has existed since before Napoleon, conceptually based on the cultural identity that existed under the older empires. Yet the attempts to implement this always end up as imperialism, whether by France or Germany. Today, in establishing the European Union, the people of Europe have not forgotten this past. They are clearly trying to bring into existence an empire that is not imperialist, but this can only result in a supranational state that remains within the sway of the global economy.

We also need to note the emergence of Empire in other regions. The former world empires that were situated on the periphery of the modern world system—China, India, the Islamic world, Russia, and so on—have begun to reemerge. In each region, because the nation-state emerged from the splitting up of former world empires, there is a still-raw past that includes not only a shared identity as a civilization but also a history of fragmentation and antagonism. That each state has as a nation bracketed off these memories of the past and formed a community that significantly restricts its own sovereignty shows how keenly they feel the pressure of contemporary global capitalism. Ernst Renan described how crucial historical forgetting was to the formation of Nation.[16] The same is true for the establishment of the supranational state: it too is an imagined community or an invented community. It would be naive to look here for the possibility of superseding Capital-Nation-State.

Will a new hegemonic state emerge out of this struggle among empires? In the past an imperialistic situation persisted for about sixty years, followed by the rise of a new hegemonic power. Yet we are now unable to predict the future with any confidence. That China and India will emerge as economic powers is beyond doubt, and they will certainly enter into conflict with the already-existing economic powers. Yet it seems unlikely that a new hegemonic power will emerge from this. First, for a single state to achieve hegemony requires something more than simple economic supremacy. Second, the development of China and India harbors the possibility of bringing global capitalism to an end.

The historical repetition that I have described involved both capital accumulation and the state. Taking up capital accumulation first, Marx used the formula M-C-M′ to represent the process of accumulation for industrial capital. This formula indicates that capital is only capital so long as it is able to expand through its process of self-valorization; if this becomes impossible, it is no longer capital. As I argued, the growth of industrial capitalism required three preconditions: first, that nature supply unlimited resources from outside the industrial structure; second, that human nature be available in an unlimited supply outside the capitalist economy; and, third, that technological innovation continue without limit. These three conditions have been rapidly disappearing since 1990.

In terms of the first condition, the enormous scale of industrial development in China and India has resulted in depletion of natural resources and accelerating environmental destruction. In terms of the second, more than half of the world's agrarian population lives in China and India. Once these are exhausted, no major sources for creating new proletarian consumers will remain. These two conditions will make it impossible for global capital to expand itself through self-valorization.

The end of capital does not mean the end of human production or exchanges: noncapitalist forms of production and exchange remain possible. But for capital and the state, this represents a fatal situation. The state will undoubtedly go to great lengths in attempting to preserve the possibility of capital accumulation. In this situation, the world in which commodity exchange (mode of exchange C) is predominant will regress to a world based on plunder and violent appropriation carried out by the state. In other words, the most likely result of a general crisis of capitalism is war. This provides yet another reminder that any understanding of the capitalist economy must also take the state into consideration.

Countermovements against Capital

When we reflect on the characteristics of the state and industrial capital, we see that struggles against capitalism until now have been characterized by major weaknesses. First, they attempted to counter capital by means of the state. This is certainly possible, but it results in excessive state power. Moreover, in order to maintain the state, it eventually becomes necessary to summon capitalism back up again. This was the fate of the socialist revolutions of the twentieth century. We need to remain vigilant in our awareness that the state is an autonomous entity. If the abolition of capitalism is not at the same time an abolition of the state, it will be meaningless.

Another weakness came from socialist movements basing themselves in worker struggles at the site of production. Looking at nineteenth-century socialist movements, we see that they initially placed great importance on the process of circulation—as with, for example, Robert Owen and P.-J. Proudhon. They thought that workers should resist capital by creating their own forms of currency and credit, finally abolishing wage labor through associations (producer cooperatives) of laborers. But at this time there were still many independent, small-scale producers in which workers retained the characteristics of artisans. As the reorganization of labor by industrial capital got under way, Marx pointed out that such movements were unable to counter capitalism because of these fatal limitations. With the exception of Britain, however, industrial capitalism remained undeveloped, and Proudhonist movements were predominant.

It is also true that as industrial capitalism developed, socialist movements came to base themselves in the site of production—that is, in the struggles of organized labor. The turning point came with the 1871 Paris Commune. For example, after this anarchists faded from the scene, with some of them turning to terrorism, but they subsequently came back with a new focus. They now preached a syndicalism based in labor unions, one that sought to realize the socialist revolution through the general strike. In the socialist movements that arose after the Paris Commune, the Marxists were not alone in giving priority to struggle at the site of production

At the same time, struggle at the site of production met with its own particular difficulties. In situations characterized by undeveloped industrial capital and an absence of labor unions, conflict between capital and labor takes a violent form: class conflict here is not simply economic; it is also political. These struggles ultimately result, however, in the legalization and expansion of labor unions, as the struggles between labor and management take on a purely economic character and become in effect one link in the labor market. As a result, any possibility for a revolutionary movement that would seek to abolish wage labor disappears. This tendency becomes more pronounced as industrial capitalism develops and deepens. This makes it increasingly impossible to hope for a working-class revolutionary movement in the advanced capitalist countries.

In this situation, as Vladimir Lenin would assert, the working class is closed off in a kind of natural consciousness, necessitating an external intervention by a Marxist vanguard party in order to get it to rise up in class struggle. Georg Lukács rephrased this idea in the vocabulary of philosophy. He asserted that the working class had fallen prey to a reified consciousness and therefore a vanguard party of intellectuals was needed to awaken them to class consciousness and political struggle.[1] The trouble is, the more industrial capitalism develops, the more difficult this becomes.

During the initial stages of industrial capitalism, capital exploited laborers under brutal working conditions, and workers truly were wage slaves. The struggles of workers against capital at this stage resembled slave and serf revolts. But the relationship between capital and wage labor is qualitatively different from that between master and slave or lord and serf. Industrial capitalism resembles the latter only at the stage where mode of exchange C (commodity exchange) has yet to completely penetrate and reorganize the social formation. At this stage, wage labor is hard to distinguish from semi-feudal or slave labor. This situation can still be found today on the peripheral underside of global capitalism, where political struggles still resemble classical class conflict or slave revolts. But we should not look to such places to find the essence of industrial capitalism; moreover, toppling the social order in them will not lead to the superseding of capitalism.

Industrial capital is a system for obtaining surplus value entirely through the principles of commodity exchange. Older concepts of class struggle are utterly ineffective against it. This does not mean, however, that class struggle has ended: so long as the conflicts arising from the relations between capital and wage labor are not abolished, class struggle will continue. The ineffectiveness of the old concept of class struggle comes from its being centered on the process of production. In other words, it comes from the lack of a perspective capable of seeing the definitive features of industrial capital in the totality of its processes of accumulation.

In a capitalist society, commodity mode of exchange C is dominant, yet this comes in varying degrees. For example, in the initial stages, industrial production develops but traditional communal ways of life persist in rural areas. As industrial capitalism advances, mode of exchange C gradually permeates into areas previously under the domain of the family, community, or state. But this process always remains incomplete: even in the heart of capitalist enterprises, for example, we find the persistence of strong traces of communal elements—of mode of exchange A.

As industrial capital develops, however, mode of exchange C penetrates deeply into all domains. In the stage of so-called neoliberalism that has arisen since 1990, we see this to a particularly dramatic degree. We see the increasing penetration of capitalism not only in the former socialist bloc or developing countries but also within the advanced capitalist nations. There we see the intensified penetration of capitalism into fields that were previously relatively impervious to the capitalist economy, such as social welfare, medicine, and universities. Mode of exchange C now permeates not only the processes of production but also the very basis of human (labor-power) reproduction. What kind of resistance to capital is possible in this situation? None—if we limit ourselves to the production process. But resistance is not impossible from a perspective that grasps the process of accumulation of capital as a totality.

Let us consider once more the process of accumulation of capital. In general, capital is often equated with money, but in Marx's view, capital signifies the totality of processes of transformation that can be expressed as M-C-M'. For example, the physical plant of production constitutes invariable capital, while contract workers constitute variable capital. These transformations are the means by which capital achieves self-valorization. Workers are just as subject to transformation as is capital: they are transformed as their position vis-à-vis capital changes. The encounter between laborer and capitalist unfolds in three phases: first, workers sell their labor as a commodity to the capitalist; second, they engage in the labor contracted for; and, third, workers take up the role of consumers and buy back the goods that they have produced.

In the first phase, the employment contract is based on mutual consent. Its conditions are fundamentally determined by the labor market and involve no extraeconomic compulsion. For this reason, a wage laborer is unlike a slave or serf. But in the second phase, workers are subject to the dictates of capital: they have to carry out the terms of the employment contract. To see the working class in terms of the site of production is to focus on this second phase. Here the wage laborer clearly resembles a slave. Hence, Ricardian socialists called the wage laborer a wage slave.

In this second phase, it is still possible for workers to resist capital, and in fact they have often done so, demanding higher wages, shorter hours, and better working conditions. In such cases, however, the relation between capital and workers has simply returned to the first phase: this represents nothing more than an improvement in the terms of the employment contract. For this reason, the labor-union movement, which initially resembles a slave revolt, is quickly accepted by the capitalist and transformed into a regular part of the system. Capital does more than accept labor unions; it actually requires them: the labor market takes shape from the results of labor-union struggles.

But even after labor unions are made a regular part of the system, workers in the second phase are still forced to carry out the terms of their contract with capital: they still have to obey the dictates of capital. Up until now, Marxists have placed their hopes for worker uprisings in this second phase. Previously, labor unions engaging in struggle within this phase have at times appeared to be revolutionary. This is sometimes true even now, depending on location. But in so far as these unions legally constitute a regular part of the existing system, their struggles at the site of production will always return to the question of improving the terms of the employment contract. In other words, they will not go beyond being economic struggles. As a result, Marxists such as Lukács came to the conclusion that it was necessary find some other way to get workers to engage in *political* struggle at the site of production.

Once the labor movement is legalized, however, it becomes almost impossible for the working classes to engage in struggle that is both universal and political at the site of production. To begin with, if they do so, they risk being fired. Moreover, at the site of production, workers are apt to adopt the same position as capital. Each capitalist exists in competition with other capitalists and with overseas capital as well. If an enterprise loses out in that competition, it goes bankrupt and its workers lose their jobs. Accordingly, at the site of production, workers to a certain extent share the interests of management. For this reason, we can hardly expect them to engage in a universal class struggle that transcends particular interests. Faced with this, Marxists take up the task of awakening workers from their "reified consciousness" so that they will embrace true class consciousness. But in the developed countries, this proves ineffective. Marxists' focus then turns either to the capitalist periphery, where the labor movement remains a vital force within the site of production, or to political struggles outside the labor movement proper, such as those involving gender or minority issues. This in turn gives rise to a tendency to undervalue the struggles of the working classes themselves.

When we consider the working class, however, we should focus on the third phase. The process of accumulation for industrial capital differs from that of other forms of wealth in its system of not only hiring laborers to work but also making them buy back the products of their own labor. The decisive difference between laborers and slaves or serfs lies in this third phase rather than in the first. A slave produces but never takes up the position of consumer. A serf likewise is self-sufficient and hence completely unrelated to industrial capital.

The working classes have generally been thought of only in terms of poverty. As a result, when their activity as consumers became impossible to ignore, people began to speak of a "consumer society" or "mass society," as if some fundamental change were taking place. But in reality, the proletariat of industrial capital originally appeared in the form of new consumers. In other words, it was only when workers simultaneously functioned as consumers buying back the products of their own labor that industrial capitalism was able to achieve autonomy as a self-reproducing system. If we consider only the second phase, the struggle between capital and the working class will appear analogous to the struggle between slaves and their masters. But in the third phase, a new and previously unknown form of struggle becomes possible.

Let me reiterate the words of Marx I previously quoted: "It is precisely this which distinguishes capital from the [feudal] relationship of domination—that the *worker* confronts the capitalist as consumer and one who posits exchange value, in the form of a *possessor of money*, of money, of a simple centre of circulation—that he becomes one of the innumerable centres of circulation, in which his specific character as worker is extinguished."[2] By now it should be clear that this means that while workers may be subjected to a kind of servitude within production processes, as consumers they occupy a different position. Within the processes of circulation, it is capital that finds itself placed in a relation of servitude to worker-consumers. If workers decide to resist capital, they should do so not from the site where this is difficult, but rather from the site where they enjoy a dominant position vis-à-vis capital.

Within the site of production, workers share the same consciousness as managers, making it difficult for them to see beyond that particular interest. For example, if an enterprise engages in practices that are socially harmful, we cannot expect its workers to take the lead in protesting against it. Within the site of production, it is difficult for workers to adopt a universal point of view. By contrast, when they occupy the positions of consumer and local resident, people are more sensitive to, for example, environmental problems and hence more likely to see things from a cosmopolitan perspective. In sum, the third phase offers the best opportunity for the working classes to acquire a universal class consciousness.

This understanding of industrial capitalism should lead us to rethink countermovements against capitalism. For example, many people say that the core of social movements has passed from workers to consumers and citizens. Yet with the exception of those few people who make their living from unearned income (rentiers), every consumer and citizen is also a wage laborer in some form or another. Consumers are simply members of the proletariat who have stepped into the site of circulation. This means that consumer movements are also proletariat movements and should be conducted as such. We should not regard citizen movements or those involving gender or minority issues as being separate from working-class movements.

Within the site of production, capital is able to control the proletariat and even compel its members into active cooperation. This makes resistance there extremely difficult. Previous revolutionary movements have called for political strikes by the proletariat, but these have always failed. Within the process of circulation, however, capital is unable to control the proletariat: capital has the power to force people to work, but not to make them buy. The primary form of struggle by the proletariat in the circulation process is the boycott. Capital has no effective means for countering this nonviolent, legal form of struggle.

Because Marx criticized Proudhon, Marxists have tended to belittle resistance movements based within the processes of circulation. Yet this is precisely where the working class is best able to actively resist capital as a free subject. There it is able to adopt a universal perspective, to see and criticize the various excesses committed by capital in its pursuit of profits and demand a halt to them. Moreover, this is also where possibilities exist for creating a noncapitalist economy—concretely speaking, through consumer-producer cooperatives and local currencies and credit systems.

Since Marx pointed out their shortcomings, producer cooperatives and local-currency schemes—that is movements to transcend the capitalist social formation from within—have rarely been taken seriously. Yet even if they are unable to immediately transcend capitalism, the creation of an economic sphere beyond capitalism is crucial. It gives people a foreshadowing of what it might mean to transcend capitalism.

I have already noted that if the primary means of resistance to capital in the production process is the strike, then its equivalent in the circulation process is the boycott. There are, in fact, two kinds of boycotts. In the first, one refuses to buy, while in the second, one refuses to sell the labor commodity. But in order for these to succeed, the necessary conditions must be created—that is, a noncapitalist economic sphere must be created.

When capital can no longer pursue self-valorization, it stops being capital. Accordingly, sooner or later we will reach the point where rates of profit go into general decline, and when that happens, capitalism will come to an end. This will lead at first to a general social crisis. At that time, however, the existence of a broad, well-established noncapitalist economy will aid in the absorption of this blow and help us move beyond capitalism.

The emphasis on production to the neglect of circulation has undercut movements attempting to counter the processes of capital accumulation. To correct this, we need at a very fundamental level to rethink the history of social formations from the perspective not of modes of production but rather modes of exchange.

Countermovements against the State

The capitalist economy is primarily formed through overseas trade, just as the economy of any given country exists within a world-economy. For this reason, the socialist revolution cannot succeed if it is limited to a single country. If by chance the revolution should occur in one country, it would immediately encounter interference and sanctions from other countries. Any socialism that did not elicit this sort of interference would be closer to welfare-state capitalism than to actual socialism: it would present no threat to either state or capital. On the other hand, a socialist revolution that really aimed to abolish capital and state would inevitably face interference and sanctions. A successful revolution that wants to preserve itself has only one option: to transform itself into a powerful state. In other words, it is impossible to abolish the state from within a single country.

The state can only be abolished from within, and yet at the same time it cannot be abolished from within. Marx was not troubled by this antinomy, because it was self-evident to him that the socialist revolution was "only possible as the act of the dominant peoples 'all at once' and simultaneously."[3] The 1848 "world revolution" had shown this. Mikhail Bakunin held the same view: "An isolated workers' association, local or national, even in one of the greatest European nations, can never triumph, and . . . victory can only be achieved by a union of all the national and international associations into a single universal association."[4]

How then will the next simultaneous world revolution be possible? It is not something that will simply break out one day, simultaneously in all parts of the world, without our having to do anything. Without an alliance among revolutionary movements around the world established beforehand, simultaneous world revolution is impossible. This is why Marx and Bakunin, among others, organized the First International in 1863: it was supposed to provide the foundation for a simultaneous world revolution.

It is difficult, however, to unite movements from various countries whose industrial capitalism and modern state exist at different stages of development. The First International included a mixture of activists, some from regions where the immediate goal was socialism, and others from places such as Italy, where the primary task was national unification. Moreover, the First International included a split between the Marx and Bakunin factions, one that went beyond a simple opposition between authoritarianism and anarchism, because behind the split lurked the different social realities faced by the various countries.

For example, workers from Switzerland were anarchists and supported Bakunin. These were, however, mostly watchmakers, artisans whose position derived in part from the pressure they felt from mechanized high-volume production in Germany and the United States. In Germany, on the other hand, industrial workers favored organizational movements, which were anathema to anarchists. For these reasons, the split between the Marx and Bakunin factions was linked to nationalist conflicts. Bakunin, for example, accused Marx of being a Pan-Germanist Prussian spy, while Marx responded by linking Bakunin to the Pan-Slavism of the Russian Empire. This split between the Marx and Bakunin factions led to the dissolution of the First International in 1876. But this should not be understood as simply a result of a split between Marxism and anarchism.

The Second International, established in 1889, primarily comprised German Marxists. But it too was undermined by enormous differences among the various countries and increasingly bitter internal conflicts based on nationalism. As a result, when the First World War broke out in 1914, the socialist parties in each country switched over to supporting national participation in the war. This demonstrates that even when socialist movements from various nations are united in an association, as soon as the state actually launches into war, the movements are unable to resist the pressures of nationalism. Benito Mussolini, the leader of the Italian Socialist Party, for example, turned to fascism at this time.

In February 1917, in the midst of the First World War, the Russian Revolution broke out. After it, a dual power system was set up including a parliament and worker-farmer councils (soviets). The Bolsheviks were a minority faction on both levels. In October Vladimir Lenin and Leon Trotsky brushed aside the opposition of the Bolshevik party leadership to shut down parliament through a military coup d'état and gradually monopolize power by excluding opposing factions from the soviets as well. At this point, Lenin and Trotsky are said to have anticipated a world revolution, starting with a revolution in Germany. But this was an unlikely prospect.

The failure of a German revolution to follow in succession after Russia was entirely predictable: the forceful implementation of the October Revolution radically intensified the vigilance and resistance toward socialist revolution in other countries, above all Germany. Moreover, the October Revolution was—for example, in the aid given to help Lenin return home from exile—in important ways supported by the German state, which hoped for a revolution that would cause the Russian Empire to drop out of the war. The October Revolution actually aided German imperialism and set back the possibility of a socialist revolution. Under such conditions, it was foolish to hope for a simultaneous world revolution.

With the intention of fostering world revolution, Lenin and Trotsky established the Third International (Comintern) in 1919. But this bore only a superficial resemblance to simultaneous world revolution. In the previous

Internationals, despite differences in relative influence due to differences in the scale of their movements and in their theoretical positions, the revolutionary movements of various countries met as equals. But in the Third International, as the only member to have seized state power, the Soviet Communist Party enjoyed a position of overwhelming dominance. The movements from other countries followed the directives of the Soviet Communist Party and lent their support to the Soviet state. As a result, the international communist movement acquired a degree of real power hitherto unseen. This was because Soviet support made it possible for socialist revolutions around the world to avoid direct interference from the capitalist powers. But this also meant that those revolutionary movements were subordinated to the Soviet Union, subsumed into its world-empire-like system.

But the Idea of a simultaneous world revolution did not end there. For example, Trotsky launched the Fourth International in an attempt to organize a movement that was both anticapitalist and anti-Stalinist. But this was never able to achieve effectiveness. Subsequently, Mao Zedong can be said to have proposed a simultaneous revolution of the Third World against the so-called First World (capitalism) and Second World (Soviet bloc). This too, however, was short-lived. In 1990 the Soviet bloc—in other words, the Second World—collapsed, and this meant also the collapse of the Third World. Its sense of a shared identity was lost, and it fragmented into a number of supranational states (empires): the Islamic world, China, India, and so forth.

Did the vision of a simultaneous world revolution disappear with this? Certainly not. In a sense, 1968 was a simultaneous world revolution. It arose unexpectedly and, seen from the perspective of political power, ended in failure, yet seen from the perspective of what Immanuel Wallerstein calls "antisystemic movements," 1968 had a tremendous impact.[5] On this point, it resembles the revolution of 1848. In fact, 1968 was in many ways a reawakening of the outcome of the 1848 European revolution. For example, 1968 saw the rehabilitation of the early Marx, Proudhon, Max Stirner, and Charles Fourier. What was the fate of the vision of simultaneous world revolution after this? Since 1990 it has served as a summons to reawaken the world revolution of 1968—really, of 1848—as seen, for example, in Antonio Negri and Michael Hardt's notion of a simultaneous worldwide revolt by the "multitude"—a multitude that is equivalent to the proletariat of 1848.[6] To wit, the people who were called the proletariat in the 1848 uprisings shouldn't be thought of as industrial workers: they were in fact the multitude.

In that sense, the notion of a simultaneous world revolution still persists today. But it is never clearly analyzed, which is precisely why it functions as a myth. If we want to avoid repeating the failures of the past, we need to subject the notion to a detailed analysis. To reiterate, simultaneous world revolution is sought by movements that seek to abolish the state from within. But the movements in different countries are characterized by large disparities in terms of their interests and goals. In particular, the deep fissure between global North and South lingers—now taking on the guise of a religious conflict. A transnational movement will always fall prey to internal splits arising due to conflicts between states, no matter how closely its members band together. The emergence of a socialist government in one or more countries may make it possible to avoid this kind of schism, but would only lead to a different kind of schism—that between movements that hold state power and those that don't. For this reason, any attempt to build a global union of countermovements that arise within separate countries is destined to end in failure.

Kant's "Perpetual Peace"

When we think about simultaneous world revolution, Immanuel Kant is our best resource. Of course, Kant was not thinking in terms of a socialist revolution: what he had in mind was a Rousseauian bourgeois revolution. He also realized the difficulties inherent in it. If a bourgeois revolution aims not just at political liberty but also economic equality, it will invite interference not only from within its own country but from surrounding absolutist monarchies. Accordingly, the bourgeois revolution could not be a revolution confined to a single country. Kant writes:

> *The problem of establishing a perfect civil constitution is dependent upon the problem of a law-governed **external relation between states** and cannot be solved without having first solved the latter.* What good does it do to work on establishing a law-governed civil constitution among individuals, that is, to organize a *commonwealth*? The same unsociability that had compelled human beings to pursue this commonwealth also is the reason that every commonwealth, in its external relations, that is, as a state among states, exists in unrestricted freedom and consequently that

states must expect the same ills from other states that threatened individuals and compelled them to enter into a law-governed civil condition.[7]

"A perfect civil constitution" here refers to the state as an association formed through a Rousseauian social contract. Such a civil constitution's establishment depends on relations with other states—specifically, with surrounding absolutist monarchies. Without somehow preventing armed intervention by other states, a bourgeois revolution in a single state is impossible. For this reason, Kant added that such states must reach the point "where, on the one hand internally, through an optimal organization of the civil constitution, and on the other hand externally, through a common agreement and legislation, a condition is established that, similar to a civil commonwealth, can maintain itself *automatically*."[8] In sum, the idea of a federation of nations was originally conceived precisely for the sake of realizing a true bourgeois revolution.

In fact, the French Revolution produced a civil constitution, but it was immediately subjected to interference and obstruction at the hands of the surrounding absolute monarchies. This led to a distortion of the democratic revolution. Maximilien de Robespierre's Reign of Terror was in large measure amplified by this terror from outside. In 1792 the Legislative Assembly launched a war to defend the revolution. But at the same moment, the state as association was transformed into an authoritarian state. As a result, the distinction between the war to defend the revolution and the war to export the revolution became hazy—which is to say, it became difficult to distinguish the war to export the revolution from a conventional war of conquest. Kant published his "Toward a Perpetual Peace" in the period when Napoleon Bonaparte had begun to make a name for himself in the wars to defend the revolution. After this, the world war now known as the Napoleonic Wars broke out across Europe.

But if we look again at the passages I quoted, it is clear that Kant had already to a certain extent anticipated this situation. The frustration of the bourgeois revolution in a single country resulted in world war. It was at this point that Kant published "Toward a Perpetual Peace." Consequently, Kant's notion of a federation of nations has been read somewhat simplistically as a proposal for the sake of peace—it has been read, that is, primarily within the lineage of pacifism that begins from Saint-Pierre's "perpetual peace." But Kant's perpetual peace does not simply mean peace as the absence of war; it means peace as "the end to all hostilities."[9] This can only mean that the state no longer exists; in other words, perpetual peace signifies the abolition of the state. This is clear when we look back at the proposal Kant made prior to the French Revolution for a federation of nations for the sake of the coming bourgeois revolution.

Kant's refusal to admit the possibility of revolution in a single country was not only due to the way that revolution invited interference from other countries. Kant from the start gave the name "Kingdom of Ends" to the society that had realized the moral law of always treating others not solely as means but also always as ends. This necessarily refers to a situation in which capitalism has been abolished. Yet this Kingdom of Ends could never exist within a single country. Even if one country should manage to realize a perfect civil constitution within, it would still be based on treating other countries solely as means (i.e., exploitation) and therefore could not qualify as the Kingdom of Ends. The Kingdom of Ends cannot be thought of in terms of a single country; it can only be realized as a "World Republic." Kant argues that the World Republic was the Idea toward which human history should strive: "*A philosophical attempt to describe the universal history of the world according to a plan of nature that aims at the perfect civil union of the human species must be considered to be possible and even to promote this intention of nature.*"[10]

Kant's "Toward a Perpetual Peace" has generally been regarded as proposing a practical plan for realizing this Idea of a World Republic. In that sense, some have said that the text represents Kant taking a step back from the ideal and making a compromise with reality. For example, Kant writes:

> As concerns the relations among states, according to reason there can be no other way for them to emerge from the lawless condition, which contains only war, than for them to relinquish, just as do individual human beings, their wild (lawless) freedom, to accustom themselves to public binding laws, and to thereby form a *state of peoples* (*civitas gentium*), which, continually expanding, would ultimately comprise all of the peoples of the world. But since they do not, according to their conception of international right, want the positive idea of a *world republic* at all (thus rejecting *in hypothesi* what is right *in thesi*), only the *negative* surrogate of a lasting and continually expanding *federation* that prevents war can curb the inclination to hostility and defiance of the law, though there is the constant threat of its breaking loose again.[11]

But Kant called for a federation of nations not simply because it was a realistic, "negative surrogate." From the start, he believed that the road to a World

Republic lay not with a *"state of peoples"* but rather with a federation of nations. Here we find something fundamentally different from Thomas Hobbes and from the line of thought that developed from him. Kant, of course, begins from the same premise as Hobbes, namely the "state of nature": "The state of nature (*status naturalis*) is not a state of peace among human beings who live next to one another but a state of war, that is, if not always an outbreak of hostilities, then at least the constant threat of such hostilities. Hence the state of peace must be *established*."[12] Kant differs from Hobbes in how he proposes to establish this state of peace.

For Hobbes, the existence of the sovereign (i.e., the state) who monopolizes violence signifies the establishment of the state of peace. In the relations between states, however, a state of nature continues. The existence of the state was in itself sufficient, and Hobbes never considered its abolition. If, however, we attempt in the same manner to overcome the state of nature existing between states, it is self-evident that we would need to propose a new sovereign, a world state. What Kant calls "a state of peoples" refers to this. But Kant opposed this. It could certainly lead to peace as the absence of war, but it could never lead to *perpetual peace*. For Kant, a state of peace could only be established through the abolition of the state. A state of peoples or a world state, after all, would still be a state.

Kant and Hegel

We need to think about how it might be possible to create a federation of nations, one without a world state (empire) acting as ultimate sovereign, that would obey international law or the "Law of Peoples."[13] From a Hobbesian perspective, this is impossible: just as was the case domestically, a state of peace becomes possible only when the various countries enter into a social contract under a sovereign who monopolizes power. Without this, a federation of nations would lack the means to punish violations of international law. G. W. F. Hegel also took this view, criticizing Kant on this point:

> Kant's idea was that eternal peace should be secured by an alliance of states. This alliance should settle every dispute, make impossible the resort to arms for a decision, and be recognized by every state. This idea assumes that states are in accord, an agreement which, strengthened though it might be by moral, religious, and other considerations, nevertheless always rested on the private sovereign will, and was therefore liable to be disturbed by the element of contingency.[14]

In Hegel's view, the functioning of international law requires a state with the power to punish countries that commit violations, meaning that there cannot be peace in the absence of a hegemonic state. Moreover, Hegel does not see war itself as something automatically to be rejected. In his view, world history is a courtroom in which states pursue disputes with one another. The world-historical idea is realized through this process. As we see with Napoleon, for example, the world-historical idea is realized through the will to power of a single sovereign or state. This is what Hegel called the "cunning of reason."[15]

But Kant's idealism did not, as Hegel claimed, arise from a naive point of view. Albeit in a different sense from Hegel, Kant held the same view as Hobbes: the essence of humanity (human nature) lay in unsociable sociability, which Kant believed could not be eliminated. Common wisdom pits Kant in contrast to Hobbes on this point, but this is a shallow understanding. Kant's proposal for a federation of nations as the basis for perpetual peace arose from his clear recognition of the difficulty of doing away with the fundamentally violent nature of the state. He did not think that this meant we should abandon the regulative idea of a world republic, but rather that we should try to approach it gradually. The federation of nations was to be the first step in this process.

Additionally, while Kant proposed a federation of states, he never believed that this would be realized through human reason or morality. Instead he believed that a federation of states would be brought about by human unsociable sociability—that is, by war. In contrast to Hegel's cunning of reason, this is sometimes called the "cunning of nature": what Kant described here was to be realized precisely through the cunning of nature. At the end of the nineteenth century, the age of imperialism was dominated by Hegelian-style thought; the struggle for hegemony among the great powers was interpreted as signifying a struggle to become the world-historical state. The result was the First World War. On the other hand, together with the rise of imperialism, the end of the nineteenth century also saw a revival of Kant's theory of a federation of nations. This was actually realized to a limited extent with the establishment of the League of Nations after the First World War. This came about as an expression not so much of Kantian ideals as of what he called humanity's unsociable sociability, demonstrated on an unprecedented scale in the First World War.

The League of Nations remained ineffective due to the failure of the United States, its original sponsor, to ratify its charter, and it was ultimately unable to prevent the Second World War. But that war resulted in the

creation of the United Nations. In other words, Kant's proposal was realized through two world wars—through, that is, the cunning of nature. The
United Nations was established after the Second World War with due re-
flection on the failings of the League of Nations, yet the United Nations
also remained ineffective. The United Nations has been criticized as being
nothing more than a means by which powerful states pursue their own
ends; since it lacks an independent military, it has no choice but to rely on
powerful states and their militaries. Criticisms of the United Nations
always come back in the end to Hegel's criticism of Kant: the attempt to resolve international disputes through the United Nations is dismissed as
Kantian idealism. Of course, the United Nations really is weak—but if we
simply jeer at it and dismiss it, what will the result be? Another world war.
And this will in turn result in the formation of yet another international
federation. Kant's thought conceals a realism much crueler than even
Hegel's.

A federation of nations is unable to suppress conflicts or wars between
states, because it will not grant recognition to a state capable of mobilizing
sufficient force. But according to Kant, the wars that will arise as a result
will only strengthen the federation. The suppression of war will come about
not because one state has surpassed all others to become hegemonic. Only
a federation of nations established as a result of wars can accomplish this.
On this point, the thought of Sigmund Freud in his later years is suggestive.
The early Freud sought the superego in prohibitions "from above" issued by
parent or society, but after he encountered cases of combat fatigue and war
neurosis in the First World War, he revised his position. He now saw the
superego as externally directed aggressiveness redirected inward toward
the self. For example, those raised by easygoing parents often become the
bearers of a strong sense of morality. What Kant called humanity's unsociable sociability is similar to what Freud called aggressiveness. Seen in this
way, we can understand how outbursts of aggressiveness can transform into
a force for restraining aggression.[16]

This discussion of Kant and Hegel may sound dated, but in fact it directly touches on present-day actualities. We see this, for example, in the
conflict between unilateralism and multilateralism surrounding the 2003
Iraq War, a conflict between the United States, acting independently of the
United Nations, and Europe, which stressed the need to act with UN autho-
rization. In the midst of this, Robert Kagan, a representative intellectual of
the neoconservative school, argued that whereas the United States with its
military might was grounded in a Hobbesian worldview of a war of all

against all, the militarily inferior Europe stressed economic power and non-military means (soft power), basing itself on Kant's worldview and the pursuit of the ideal of perpetual peace. But according to Kagan, the state of perpetual peace à la Kant that Europe desired could only be realized after security had been achieved through military force (hard power) based on the Hobbesian worldview of the United States.[17]

But the theoretical grounding of U.S. unilateralism comes less from Hobbes than Hegel: its advocates believed that the war would lead to the realization of a world-historical idea. That Idea was liberal democracy, according to the neoconservative ideologue Francis Fukuyama, who in fact quoted Hegel directly. To argue that the United States took a unilateralist line only because it was pursuing its own interests and hegemony does not change matters: under Hegelian logic, it is America's pursuit of its own particular will that will finally lead to the realization of the universal Idea. This is precisely what Hegel called the cunning of reason. In that sense, the United States is the world-historical state.

By contrast, Negri and Hardt describe this conflict in the following terms: "Most of the contemporary discussions about geopolitics pose a choice between two strategies for maintaining global order: unilateralism or multilateralism."[18] Here unilateralism means the position of the United States, which "began to redefine the boundaries of the former enemy and organize a single network of control over the world."[19] Multilateralism refers to the position of the United Nations or of Europe, which criticized the United States. Negri and Hardt reject both positions: "The multitude will have to rise to the challenge and develop a new framework for the democratic constitution of the world."[20] They continue, "When the multitude is finally able to rule itself, democracy becomes possible."[21]

If Europe's position was Kantian and America's Hegelian, then Negri and Hardt's position would have to be called Marxist (albeit, that of the 1848 Marx). Their position that because the various states represent the self-alienation of the multitude, they will be abolished when the multitude is able to rule itself clearly derives from the early Marx—more precisely, from the anarchism of Proudhon. In this light, their "new framework for the democratic constitution of the world" is akin to the International Working-men's Association (the First International), jointly formed by the Proudhon and Marx factions. But Negri and Hardt never consider why simultaneous world revolutions since the nineteenth century have all ended in failure.

We have seen how the historical situation that has emerged since 1990 has involved a repetition of the classical philosophy of Kant, Hegel, and

Marx. Accordingly, to rethink these figures is to touch on problems integral to the reality of today's world. But we have to reject the common view that believes that Kant was superseded by Hegel, and Hegel in turn by Marx. We need instead to reread Kant from the perspective of understanding how local communes and countermovements against capital and the state can avoid splintering and falling into mutual conflict. A federation of nations: this is where Kant saw the possibility for "a new framework for the democratic constitution of the world."

The Gift and Perpetual Peace

Kant located the way to perpetual peace not in a world state but in a federation of nations. This means that Kant rejected Hobbes's view, which sought to create a state of peace through a transcendent, Leviathan-like power. This is not how Kant is generally understood though—he has been criticized, for example, on the grounds that a powerful world state could emerge out of this federation of nations. The origins of this lie in Kant's failure to clearly demonstrate the possibility of creating peace without relying on Hobbesian principles. Accordingly, our task here is to clarify this from the perspective of modes of exchange.

According to Hobbes, a state of peace was established through a covenant with the sovereign "extorted by fear"—in other words, through mode of exchange B. What was Kant's position? In "Toward a Perpetual Peace," for example, Kant sees the development of commerce as a condition for peace: the development of dense relations of trade between states will render war impossible. This is partially true. But mode of exchange C is dependent on state regulation—in other words, on mode of exchange B. For this reason, mode C can never bring about the complete abolition of mode of exchange B. In reality, the development of mode of exchange C—that is, the development of industrial capitalism—gave rise to a new kind of conflict and war, of a different nature than those that had previously existed: the imperialistic world war.

At present, war between the developed countries is generally avoided, probably for the reasons that Kant spelled out. Yet a crisis situation involving deep hostility and warfare still exists between the developed countries and the developing countries economically subordinated to the developed countries and the late-developing countries now in a position to compete with the developed countries—in other words, between North and South. Even as this takes the guise of a religious conflict, it is fundamentally economic and political in nature. This antagonism cannot be subdued through military pressure. A true resolution of this hostility is only possible through the elimination of economic disparities between states—and of the capitalist formation that reproduces such disparities.

Any number of efforts have been made to eliminate economic disparities between countries. For example, advanced countries provide economic aid to developing countries. This is regarded as a kind of redistributive justice. But in reality, this aid serves to generate further accumulation of capital in the advanced countries. In this, the aid resembles the case of domestic social-welfare policies within those countries: in both cases, redistribution simply functions as another link in the process of capitalist accumulation. Far from eliminating inequality, redistributive justice actually proliferates inequality. It also has the result of legitimating and strengthening the state power responsible for carrying out this redistribution. Ultimately, it perpetuates the state of war between North and South.

In his last major work, *The Law of Peoples*, John Rawls locates justice between states in the realization of economic equality. He describes this as a self-critical development of the notion of justice in a single country that he had written about in such earlier essays as "Justice as Fairness." Yet Rawls here continues to consider justice only in terms of redistributive justice. For that reason, just as distributive justice within a single country always ends up in a kind of welfare-state capitalism, distributive justice between states requires a push to strengthen the entities that would carry out redistribution. In the end, this means redistribution carried out by economically powerful countries, meaning in practice either world empire or imperialism.

Kant's justice, however, was not distributive justice: it was justice based in exchange. It did not mean the amelioration of economic disparity through redistribution; it was to be realized through the abolition of the system of exchange that gave birth to those disparities in the first place. Of course, it had to exist not only domestically within countries but also between nations as well. In sum, Kant's justice could only be achieved through a new world system. How could this be realized? So long as we think of power only in terms of military or economic power, we will end up taking the same road as Hobbes.

There is an important hint to be had from the example of the tribal confederations that existed before the rise of the state. Confederations of tribes were headed by neither a king nor an all-powerful chief. Previously, I discussed these "societies against the state." Here, though, I would like to reconsider them for what they might tell us about how to overcome the state of war between nations without resorting to a sovereign that stands above the various states. Tribal confederations were sustained by mode of exchange A—by the principle of reciprocity. They were sustained, in other words, not by military or economic power but by the power of the gift. This likewise served as the guarantor of the equality and mutual autonomy of the member tribes.

A federation of nations in the sense that Kant intended is of course different from a tribal confederation. The base for the former lies in a world-economy developed on a global scale—on, that is, the generalization of mode of exchange C. A federation of nations represents the restoration of mode of exchange A on top of this. We have up until now thought about this primarily at the level of a single country. But as I have repeatedly stressed, this cannot be realized within a single country. It can only be realized at the level of relations between states—in other words, through the creation of a new world system. This would be something that goes beyond the previously existing world systems—the world-empire or the world-economy (the modern world system). It can only be a world republic. It marks the return of the mini-world system in a higher dimension.

We have already looked at the return in a higher dimension of the principle of reciprocity in terms of consumer-producer cooperatives. Now we need to consider this in terms of relations between states. The only principle that can ground the establishment of a federation of nations as a new world system is the reciprocity of the gift. Any resemblance between this and today's overseas aid is only apparent. For example, what would be given under this are not products but the technical knowledge (intellectual property) needed to carry out production. Voluntary disarmament to abolish weapons that pose a threat to others would be another kind of gift here. These kinds of gifts would undermine the real bases of both capital and state in the developed countries.

We should not assume that this would lead to disorder. The gift operates as a power stronger than even military or economic power. The universal rule of law is sustained not by violence but by the power of the gift. The world republic will be established in this way. Those who would dismiss this as a kind of unrealistic dream are the ones who are being foolish. Even Carl Schmitt, a consistent advocate of the most severe form of a Hobbesian worldview, saw the sole possibility for the extinction of the state in the spread of consumer-producer cooperatives:

Were a world state to embrace the entire globe and humanity, then it would be no political entity and could only loosely be called a state. If, in fact, all humanity and the entire world were to become a unified entity . . . [and should] that interest group also want to become cultural, ideological, or otherwise more ambitious, and yet remain strictly nonpolitical, then it would be a neutral consumer or producer co-operative moving between the poles of ethics and economics. It would know neither state nor kingdom nor empire, neither republic nor monarchy, neither aristocracy nor democracy, neither protection nor obedience, and would altogether lose its political character.[22]

What Schmitt here calls a world state is identical to what Kant called a world republic. In Schmitt's thinking, if we follow Hobbes's view, the abolition of the state is impossible. This does not mean, however, that the state cannot be abolished. It suggests rather that it is possible only through a principle of exchange different from that which formed the basis of Hobbes's understanding.

The Federation of Nations as World System

Just as Kant predicted, the United Nations was born as the result of two world wars. But today's United Nations is far from being a new world system; it is merely a venue where states vie for hegemony. Yet the United Nations is also a system established on the basis of enormous human sacrifice. For all its inadequacies, the future of the human species is unthinkable without it.

Most criticism aimed at the United Nations relates to the Security Council, the World Bank, and the International Monetary Fund. But today's United Nations is not limited to these entities. It is in fact an enormous, complex federation that might best be called the UN system. Its activities cover three primary domains: (1) military affairs, (2) economic affairs, and (3) medical, cultural, and environmental issues. Unlike the first two domains, the third domain has many historical precedents that date back to before the League of Nations or United Nations.

For example, the World Health Organization is an international organization that began in the nineteenth century that has linked up with the United Nations. In other words, leaving aside the first and second domains, the UN system was not deliberately planned; it instead took shape as entities that initially arose as separate international associations and then later merged with the United Nations. These will continue to appear with the expansion of world intercourse. Moreover, in the third domain, there is no rigid distinction between national (state-based) and non-national entities. As can be seen, for example, in the way NGOs participate as delegates alongside nations at world environmental meetings, these already transcend the nation. In that sense, the UN system is already something more than a simple united nations.

The situation is different in the first and second domains, because they are closely related to the state and capital. They have a determinative impact on today's United Nations. In other words, modes of exchange B and C continue to determine today's United Nations. If the same sort of characteristics found in the third domain were to be realized in the first and second domains, we would in effect have a new world system. But this will not simply happen as a kind of natural outgrowth of the expansion of world intercourse: it will no doubt face resistance from the state and capital.

Transforming the United Nations into a new world system will require a countermovement against the state and capital arising in each country. Only changes at the level of individual countries can lead to a transformation of the United Nations. At the same time, the opposite is also true: only a reform of the United Nations can make possible an effective union of national countermovements around the world. Countermovements based in individual countries are always in danger of being fragmented by the state and capital. There is no reason to expect that they will somehow naturally link together across national borders, that a simultaneous world revolution will somehow spontaneously be generated. Even if a global alliance (a new International) is created, it will not have the power to counter the various states; there is, after all, no reason to expect that what hitherto has been impossible will become possible to achieve.

Usually, a simultaneous world revolution is narrated through the image of simultaneous uprisings carried out by local national resistance movements in their own home countries. But this could never happen, nor is it necessary. Suppose, for example, one country has a revolution that ends with the country making a gift of its military sovereignty to the United Nations. This would of course be a revolution in a single nation.[23] But it wouldn't necessarily result in external interference or international isolation. No weapon can resist the power of the gift. It has the power to attract the support of many states and to fundamentally change the structure of the United Nations. For these reasons, such a revolution in one country could in fact lead to simultaneous world revolution.

This kind of revolution may seem an unrealistic possibility. But without a global movement for such a revolution, we are almost certainly headed for world war. In fact, that still remains the likeliest outcome. But this doesn't demand pessimism: as Kant believed, a world war will only lead to the implementation of a more effective federation of nations. This will not happen automatically, however: it will only come about if there are local countermovements against the state and capital in all the countries of the world.

The realization of a world system grounded in the principle of reciprocity—a world republic—will not be easy. Modes of exchange A, B, and C will remain stubborn presences. In other words, the nation, state, and capital will all persist. No matter how highly developed the forces of production (the relation of humans and nature) become, it will be impossible to completely eliminate the forms of existence produced by these modes of exchange—in other words, by relations between humans.[24] Yet so long as they exist, so too will mode of exchange D. No matter how it is denied or repressed, it will always return. That is the very nature of what Kant called a regulative Idea.

ACKNOWLEDGMENTS

Some of the chapters in this book are based on pieces I have previously published, in particular my book *Toward a World Republic: Superseding Capital-Nation-State*, where I first outlined the arguments made here.[1] I subsequently published a series of articles under the title "Notes for *Toward a World Republic*."[2] I also revised and expanded *Toward a World Republic* in the process of preparing overseas editions of the book. In addition, I published in English earlier versions of some of the material presented here, including "Beyond Capital-Nation-State" (in *Rethinking Marxism* 20, no. 4 [2008]), "World Intercourse: A Transcritical Reading of Kant and Freud" (in *UMBR(a)* [2007]), and "Revolution and Repetition" (in *UMBR(a)* [2008]).

I also discussed problems dealt with in this book in public lectures that I delivered between 2006 and 2009 in the United States (University of Massachusetts, Amherst; University of Chicago; Stanford University; State University of New York, Buffalo; and Loyola University), Canada (University of Toronto), England (Tate-Britain and Middlesex University), China (Tsinghua University), Croatia, Slovenia (University of Ljubljana), Turkey (Istanbul Bilgi University), and Mexico (Universidad Nacional Autónoma de México), among others. I learned much from the discussions on those occasions. In particular, my travels to China, Turkey, and Mexico gave me the experience of seeing parts of the "structure of world history" in action. Along the way, the argument presented here was refined and developed through a series of public presentations, as I made a number of subtle but important adjustments and revisions. This book represents what I expect to be its final version.

During the eight years I worked on this book, I received help from a number of people, both at home and abroad. I would first of all like to express my gratitude to those who organized the above events. I am indebted to Michael Bourdaghs, Indra Levy, and Lynne Karatani for their help in preparing English translations. Yoshimichi Takase, Shūji Takazawa, Tetsurō Maruyama, and Kiyoshi Kojima have been constant sources of encouragement. Without their help, I doubt I could have carried through with this work, and I am grateful to them all.

NOTES

PREFACE

1. Francis Fukuyama seems to have studied Alexandre Kojève under Fukuyama's teacher, Allan Bloom. But Kojève's position differed from theirs. For him, the concept of "the end of history" did not have a single fixed meaning; it underwent major historical transformations. What sort of society would arise at the end of history? At first Kojève believed it would be communism. But he subsequently located the end of history in the American (animal) way of life and then in the Japanese way of life (snobbism). See Alexandre Kojève, *Introduction to the Reading of Hegel: Lectures on the Phenomenology of Spirit*, trans. James H. Nichols Jr. (Ithaca, NY: Cornell University Press, 1969).

2. Kojin Karatani, *Transcritique: On Kant and Marx*, trans. Sabu Kohso (Cambridge, MA: MIT Press, 2003), 281.

3. On Kant's distinction between illusion and transcendental illusion, and between regulative idea and constructive idea, see the section on "Nature and Freedom" in chapter 3 of Karatani, *Transcritique*, 112–30.

4. Ernst Bloch, *The Principle of Hope*, vol. 1, trans. Neville Plaice, Stephen Plaice, and Paul Knight (Cambridge, MA: MIT Press, 1986), 5–6.

5. Karl Marx and Frederick Engels, *The German Ideology*, in Marx and Engels, *Collected Works*, vol. 5 (New York: International Publishers, 1975), 49.

6. Immanuel Kant, *Grounding for the Metaphysics of Morals*, 3rd ed., trans. James W. Ellington (Indianapolis, IN: Hackett, 1993), 36.

7. Marx and Engels, *The German Ideology*, 49.

INTRODUCTION. ON MODES OF EXCHANGE

1. Karl Marx, "Preface" to *A Contribution to the Critique of Political Economy*, in Karl Marx and Frederick Engels, *Collected Works*, vol. 29 (New York: International Publishers, 1975), 262–64.

2. While Louis Althusser emphasized that the economic base is determinative "in the last instance," in reality this was for the purpose of instigating a Maoist form of political praxis that leapt over the economic instance.

3. Marshall Sahlins, *Stone Age Economics*, 2nd ed. (New York: Routledge, 2003).

4. I am not the first person to raise doubts about the concepts of mode of production or economic base structure. This was a trend within postmodernism. For example, Jean Baudrillard in *The Mirror of Production* argued that Marx's "production" amounted to the projection back onto precapitalist societies of a concept derived from capitalist societies. The Marxist critique, "by pretending to illuminate earlier societies in the light of the present structure of the capitalist economy, . . . fails to see that, abolishing their difference, it projects onto them the spectral light of political economy." Jean Baudrillard, *The Mirror of Production*, trans. Mark Poster (New York: Telos Press, 1975), 66. His conclusions here were motivated by Mauss and Georges Bataille's views on archaic societies. This is because the concept of mode of production cannot be applied to those societies. From this, Baudrillard ultimately rejected any view that took the economic domain as constituting the "last instance." This led him to reject Marxism. But in my view, insofar as we can call exchange "economic" in the broad sense, we can call all fundamental modes of exchange "economic," and in that sense we can speak of them as constituting the so-called economic base. What Baudrillard calls "symbolic exchange" is nothing other than reciprocal mode of exchange A. For this reason, in the case of archaic societies, we can call this the "economic" base. A capitalist economy, on the other hand, is sustained by the commodity mode of exchange C. Baudrillard did not take these differences into consideration. In negating the supremacy of production, he brought forth the supremacy of consumption. But this was only compatible with phenomena of the consumer society that became so prominent at that time. Baudrillard accused Marx of projecting a capitalist economy onto archaic societies, but those since Bataille who have stressed the importance of consumption are equally guilty of projecting a Keynesian capitalist economy onto archaic societies. They do not see the totality of the capitalist economy but instead focus only on one limited aspect of it, the phenomenon of the consumer society.

5. Karl Marx, *Capital: A Critique of Political Economy*, vol. 1, trans. Ben Fowkes (Harmondsworth, UK: Penguin Books, 1976), 182.

6. Karl Polanyi, *The Livelihood of Man* (New York: Academic Press, 1977).

7. Polanyi takes up the example of eighteenth-century Dahomey and argues that it had an economy of reciprocity and redistribution that was of a different nature from a capitalist market economy. Karl Polanyi, *Dahomey and the Slave Trade: An Analysis of an Archaic Economy* (Seattle: University of Washington Press, 1966). But when we look at the process of development of the Kingdom of Dahomey that he describes in detail, we realize that this explanation is absurd. This kingdom developed after the beginning of the American slave system and sugarcane plantations. Dahomey supplied the slaves for this, buying firearms from the West in return; with these it repeatedly invaded surrounding countries and tribes, selling the slaves it thereby obtained, and as a result it rapidly expanded into a kingdom. Far from being a primitive society, the Kingdom of Dahomey took form within the modern global market. Here is how Hegel describes Dahomey in his *The Philosophy of History*: "In Dahomey, when they are thus displeased, the custom is to send parrots' eggs to the King, as a sign of dissatisfaction with his

government. Sometimes also a deputation is sent, which intimates to him, that the burden of government must have been very troublesome to him, and that he had better rest a little. The King then thanks his subjects, goes into his apartments, and has himself strangled by the women." G. W. F. Hegel, *The Philosophy of History*, trans. J. Sibree (New York: Dover, 1956), 97. If this is true, it means simply that even Dahomey was not all that different from a chiefdom: the king did not hold absolute power. Most likely, this means that Dahomey was a society based not so much on market-economy principles as on reciprocity and redistribution, as Polanyi stresses. Hegel also writes, "Another characteristic fact in reference to the Negroes is Slavery. Negroes are enslaved by Europeans and sold to America. Bad as this may be, their lot in their own land is even worse, since there a slavery quite as absolute exists; for it is the essential principle of slavery, that man has not yet attained a consciousness of his freedom, and consequently sinks down to a mere Thing—an object of no value" (96). Hegel claims that the reason Europeans enslaved Africans is that the latter had no "consciousness of freedom" and hence did not reject slavery. We cannot but be disturbed by Hegel's failure to question whether the Europeans who imposed the slavery system on the Africans themselves really had any "consciousness of freedom." It is also, however, a fact that the African slavery system was "produced" by Africans themselves. Unlike Hegel, Polanyi shows no interest in this: he is content merely to praise Dahomey for having been a state that carried out a reciprocal redistribution domestically. This ignores the fact that Dahomey functioned as a "state" in relation to its exterior; it overlooks how a state is always a state in relation to other states. If one overlooks this characteristic of the state—if one looks only at the interior of a state—one falls into the error of painting it over as a system of redistribution.

8. Carl Schmitt, *The Concept of the Political*, trans. George Schwab (Chicago: University of Chicago Press, 1996), 26.

9. According to Schmitt, "Hobbes designated this . . . as the true purpose of his *Leviathan*, to instill in man once again 'the mutual relation between Protection and Obedience'; human nature as well as divine right demands its inviolable observation." Schmitt, *The Concept of the Political*, 52. But this means that "the political" exists not so much in "the mutual relation between Protection and Obedience" as in a certain kind of "exchange."

10. Hannah Arendt, *Crises of the Republic* (New York: Harcourt, Brace and World, 1972), 231. Moreover, the anthropologist David Graeber points out that contemporary forms of "council" are rooted in systems that have existed since primitive society. When he attended meetings of the Direct Action Network in New York, he noticed that the process used closely resembled the councils he had observed during two years of fieldwork in the Madagascar highlands. David Graeber, *Fragments of an Anarchist Anthropology* (Chicago: Prickly Paradigm Press, 2004), 86.

11. Marcel Mauss, *The Gift: Forms and Function of Exchange in Archaic Societies*, trans. W. D. Halls (London: Routledge, 2002), 95.

12. Mauss, *The Gift*, 49.

13. Thomas Hobbes, *Leviathan: With Selected Variants from the Latin Edition of 1668*, ed. Edwin Curley (Indianapolis: Hackett, 1994), 86.

14. Marx, *Capital*, vol. 1, 159.

15. Karl Marx and Frederick Engels, *The German Ideology*, in Marx and Engels, *Collected Works*, vol. 5 (New York: International Publishers, 1976), 85, 66, 50, 84.

16. Moses Hess, "On the Essence of Money," trans. Julius Kovesi, in Julius Kovesi, *Values and Evaluations* (New York: Peter Lang, 1998), 185.

17. "The human productive powers had first to be developed, the human essence evolved. At first there were merely raw individuals, simple elements of mankind, who had either not yet come into mutual contact and drew their sustenance and bodily needs directly from the earth as plants do, or had made only such contact with each other as to join forces in the brutish warfare of animals. Hence the first form of product-exchange, of intercourse, could only be murder-for-gain, the first form of human activity the labour of the slave. On this basis of historic right, as yet uncontested, no organised exchange could take shape, and only a bartering of products was possible—which was what in fact occurred. The laws that rest on this historical basis have merely regulated murder-for-gain and slavery, have merely erected into a rule or principle what at first occurred by chance, without consciousness or will. Past history till now is no more than a history of the regulation, justification, execution and universalisation of murder-for-gain and slavery. We shall show in what follows how we have at last reached the point where we all, without exception and at every moment, traffic in our activities, our productive powers, our potentialities and our very selves; how the cannibalism, mutual murder and slavery with which human history started have been elevated into a principle—and how out of this general exploitation and universal vassalism the organic community can first be born." Hess, "On the Essence of Money," 188.

18. This view of the earth as a heat engine is based on the work of the physicist Atsushi Tsuchida, who took up the theory of entropy in terms of an open stationary system. See Atsushi Tsuchida, *Netsugaku gairon: Seimei kankyō o fukumu kaihōkei no netsuriron* (Tokyo: Asakura Shoten, 1992).

19. Marx himself, however, did not overlook the waste products that accompany the production process. For example, he writes about waste products in this passage: "As the capitalist mode of production extends, so also does the utilization of the refuse left behind by production and consumption. Under the heading of production we have the waste products of industry and agriculture, under that of consumption we have both the excrement produced by man's natural metabolism and the form in which useless articles survive after use has been made of them. Refuse of production is, therefore, in the chemical industry, the by-product which gets lost if production is only on a small scale; in the production of machinery, the heap of iron filings that appears to be waste but is then used again as raw material for iron production, etc. The natural human waste products, remains of clothing in the form of rags, etc. are the refuse of consumption. The latter are of the greatest importance for agriculture. But there is a colossal wastage in the capitalist economy in proportion to their actual use. In London, for example, they can do nothing better with the excrement produced by $4\frac{1}{2}$ million people than pollute the Thames with it, at monstrous expense." Karl Marx, *Capital:*

A Critique of Political Economy, vol. 3, trans. David Fernbach (Harmondsworth, UK: Penguin Books, 1976), 195.

20. There are some Marxists, however, who focus on ecological issues. For example, the Marxist economist Yoshirō Tamanoi frequently focused on the problem of "ecology" in Marx and, based on the theories of Tsuchida, conceived of a new kind of economics. See Yoshirō Tamanoi, *Ekonomii to ekorogii* (Tokyo: Mizusu Shobō, 1978). For an explication of Marx's ecological awareness, see John Bellamy Foster, *Marx's Ecology: Materialism and Nature* (New York: Monthly Review Press, 2000).

21. Marx, *Capital*, vol. 1, 637.

22. Marx, *Capital*, vol. 1, 638.

23. Marx, *Capital*, vol. 3, 216.

24. Karl Marx, "Critique of the Gotha Programme," in Karl Marx and Frederick Engels, *Collected Works*, vol. 24 (New York: International Publishers, 1975), 81.

25. Karl Marx, "Forms Preceding Capitalist Production," in Karl Marx and Frederick Engels, *Collected Works*, vol. 28 (New York: International Publishers, 1976), 399–439.

26. These five modes are more than adequate for classifying social formations. Samir Amin proposed two additional social formations, the trade-based social formation seen in various Arab countries and the social formation based on the "simple petty-commodity" mode of production seen in seventeenth-century Britain. But the former really belongs to the "Asiatic social formation," while the latter is simply an early stage in the development of the "capitalist social formation." Samir Amin, *Unequal Development: An Essay on the Social Formations of Peripheral Capitalism* (New York: Monthly Review Press, 1976).

27. Wallerstein does not consider the mini-systems (or what Chase-Dunn calls "very small systems") that precede the rise of the state to be world systems. But Chase-Dunn asserts that these too are world systems. This is because "world" is not dependent on scale. Chase-Dunn goes on to formally classify world systems into very small systems, world-empires, and world-economies. Christopher Chase-Dunn and Thomas D. Hall, *Rise and Demise: Comparing World Systems* (Boulder, CO: Westview Press, 1997). This approach clarifies the characteristics of each, but it is unable to explain how mini-systems, world-empires, and world-economies exist and transform in a state of interrelationship. To explain this problem requires the perspective of modes of exchange.

28. Fernand Braudel, *The Wheels of Commerce*, vol. 2, *Civilization and Capitalism, 15th–18th Centuries*, trans. Siân Reynolds (New York: Harper and Row, 1983).

29. Karl A. Wittfogel, *Oriental Despotism: A Comparative Study of Total Power* (New Haven, CT: Yale University Press, 1957).

30. Montesquieu, *The Spirit of Laws*, trans. Anne M. Cohler, Basia C. Miller, Harold Stone (Cambridge, UK: Cambridge University Press, 1989).

PART I. MINI WORLD SYSTEMS

1. See, for example, V. Gordon Childe, *Man Makes Himself* (New York: New American Library, 1951).

2. Alain Testart, *Les chasseurs-cueilleurs, ou: L'origine des inégalités* (Paris: Société d'ethnographie, 1982). English translation by Bourdaghs.

3. The Neolithic Revolution (Agricultural Revolution) took place some ten thousand years ago, and rapid social transformations have continued ever since. It appears as if the previously leisurely pace of human development had suddenly accelerated. Given this, people have sought the causes for this change. But we should understand that this sudden development occurred not because something new was added to the mix but rather because that which hitherto had held this development in check was removed. Recent archeology has demonstrated through DNA analysis that *Homo sapiens* first appeared some two hundred thousand years ago in Africa and that about sixty thousand years ago several hundred of them left Africa and began to migrate across the globe. Following this the human race was scattered geographically, with hardly any contact between regions, so that each developed independently. But the human body and brain had largely reached their mature form by the time of the departure from Africa, so there was little genetic evolution after this. Furthermore, humans possessed common cultural capital, such as language and writing, the production of tools, the use of fire and cooking, the technical skill to produce clothing and ornaments, and shipbuilding techniques. For this reason, although humans subsequently followed various forms of development, they had at their root common elements. According to the archeologist Colin Renfrew, the real puzzle is why it took so long for the human race, equipped with a high degree of intellectual ability, to reach the Agricultural Revolution. Colin Renfrew, *Prehistory: The Making of the Human Mind* (London: Weidenfeld and Nicolson, 2007). My belief is that this was because *Homo sapiens* were trying to preserve the lifestyle of a nomadic people. Even after they inevitably adopted fixed settlements, they tried to preserve in clan society the conditions that had existed at the nomadic stage. In comparison to this, the Agricultural Revolution can hardly be called a great development. It was simply the result of opening the Pandora's box that they had labored so hard to keep closed.

CHAPTER 1. THE SEDENTARY REVOLUTION

1. Marshall Sahlins, *Stone Age Economics*, 2nd ed. (New York: Routledge, 2003), 94.

2. Our inability to distinguish in clan societies between pooling within a household and reciprocity is, in a sense, similar to the way today's families carry out pooling while thinking of it in terms of reciprocity or commodity exchange.

3. Sahlins, *Stone Age Economics*, 193–95.

4. Bronislaw Malinowski, *Argonauts of the Western Pacific: An Account of Native Enterprise and Adventure in the Archipelagoes of Melanesian New Guinea* (London: Routledge, 1922).

5. Pierre Clastres, *Archeology of Violence*, trans. Jeanine Herman (Los Angeles: Semiotext(e), 2010).

6. Sahlins, *Stone Age Economics*, 170.

7. Alain Testart, *Les chasseurs-cueilleurs, ou: L'origine des inégalités* (Paris: Société d'ethnographie, 1982), 48–49; English translation by Bourdaghs.

NOTES TO PAGES 42–51   **317**

8. On the difficulties that arise with fixed settlement, I have learned much from Masaki Nishida, *Jinruishi no naka no teijū kakumei* (Tokyo: Kōdansha, 2007).

9. Maurice Bloch, *Marxism and Anthropology* (Oxford: Oxford University Press, 1983), 77.

10. Nishida proposed the "sedentary revolution" in his *Jinruishi no naka no teijū kakumei.*

11. Claude Lévi-Strauss, *The Elementary Structures of Kinship* (Boston: Beacon, 1969), 67.

12. Sahlins, *Stone Age Economics*, 171–83.

13. Karl Marx, "Marx's Excerpts from Lewis Henry Morgan *Ancient Society*," in Lawrence Krader, ed., *The Ethnological Notebooks of Karl Marx*, 2nd ed. (Assen, Netherlands: Van Gorcum, 1974), 162. Italics in original dropped here.

14. The avoidance of incest among anthropoids has been demonstrated by primatologists at Kyoto University, including Masao Kawai and Jun'ichirō Itani.

15. Emile Durkheim, *Incest: The Nature and Origin of the Taboo*, trans. Albert Ellis (New York: Lyle Stuart, 1963).

16. Lévi-Strauss thought that kinship structure was formed by the giving away of "daughters" by the household or clan. But Maurice Godelier argues that this is an arbitrary conclusion resulting from bias, pointing out many instances where boys are given away. What is important here, however, is not gender difference, but identity as a structure. Maurice Godelier, *The Enigma of the Gift*, trans. Nora Scott (Chicago: University of Chicago Press, 1999).

17. Lévi-Strauss, *Elementary Structures of Kinship*, 65.

CHAPTER 2. THE GIFT AND MAGIC

1. Claude Lévi-Strauss, *Introduction to the Work of Marcel Mauss*, trans. Felicity Baker (London: Routledge and Kegan Paul, 1987), 48–49, 55.

2. Maurice Godelier, *The Enigma of the Gift*, trans. Nora Scott (Chicago: University of Chicago Press, 1999), 71.

3. Godelier argues that Mauss's hau—the way that in gift giving only the right to use is handed over, not the right to own, and that therefore the hau in the gift-object wants to return to its original location—signifies that the gift-object continues to belong to the donor. In this case the right of ownership belongs to the community. But Godelier's understanding, in which the community's right of ownership adheres to the object in the form of hau, is not completely opposed to Mauss's view. After all, Mauss from the time of his early studies of magic stressed that magic (what the primitive peoples of Oceania call *mana*) was a social power, and even earlier his uncle Durkheim had stressed that property rights were social and that in primitive societies these had been manifested in a religious form. For example, Durkheim sees religious taboo lying at the root of property rights. In taboo, an object is avoided because it is seen as sacred, as belonging to the realm of the divine. Without this deification of things, ownership cannot arise. In these cases, the sacred is thought to dwell within the thing itself: "The quality that makes property an object of respect and inviolable—a quality which in effect makes it property—is not communicated by men to the domain; it is not an

318 NOTES TO PAGES 51-53

attribute which has been inherent in men and from them has devolved on things. It is
in things that the quality originally resided, and it is from things that it has risen
towards men. The things were inviolate in themselves by virtue of sacred concepts, and
it is this derived inviolability that has passed into the hands of men, after a long process
of being diminished, tempered and canalised." Emile Durkheim, *Professional Ethics
and Civic Morality*, trans. Cornelia Brookfield (Westport, CT: Greenwood Press, 1983),
157–58. To say that property right originated not in people but in things is to say that it
began as "communal ownership." This is not how people thought about it though; they
took objects of communal ownership to be either owned by the gods or to have divine
spirits dwelling within the object. Thus, the donor community's right of ownership
adheres to the gift-object in the form of hau. The community that accepts the gift is in a
sense possessed by this spirit, which poses a threat even more powerful than human
violence. The gift recipient is rendered unable to attack the donor.

4. Jirō Tanaka notes that the Bushmen people of the Kalahari Desert practice little
magic. For example, their magic spell to bring forth rain is used only when conditions
for rain already seem promising: "Their knowledge of nature is surprisingly rich and
accurate. The explanations they employ for natural phenomena are inevitably
unscientific, but the kind of magical elements seen in many other 'primitive peoples'
are exceedingly rare in their world, and their outlook is permeated with a highly
rational way of thinking." Jirō Tanaka, *Sabaku no karyūdo: Jinrui shigen no sugata o
motomete* (Tokyo: Chūkō Shinsho, 1978), 127; English translation by Bourdaghs.

5. Freud explained the development from animism to religion as follows: "If we may
regard the existence among primitive races of the omnipotence of thoughts as evidence
in favour of narcissism, we are encouraged to attempt a comparison between the
phases in the development of men's view of the universe and the stages of an individual's libidinal development. The animistic phase would correspond to narcissism both
chronologically and in its content; the religious phase would correspond to the stage of
object-choice of which the characteristic is a child's attachment to his parents; while
the scientific phase would have an exact counterpart in the stage at which an individual
has reached maturity, has renounced the pleasure principle, adjusted himself to reality
and turned to the external world for the object of his desires." Sigmund Freud, *Totem
and Taboo and Other Works*, trans. James Strachey, in *The Standard Edition of the
Complete Works of Sigmund Freud*, vol. 13 (London: The Hogarth Press and the
Institute of Psycho-analysis, 1955), 90.

6. Claude Lévi-Strauss, *Elementary Structures of Kinship* (Boston: Beacon Press,
1969), 92.

7. Martin Buber, *I and Thou*, trans. Ronald Gregor Smith (New York: Scribner, 1958), 4.

8. Buber, *I and Thou*, 97–98.

9. Mauss describes the relation between magic and science: "This treasury of ideas,
amassed by magic, was a capital store which science for a long time exploited. Magic
served science and magicians served scholars. In primitive societies, sorcerers are the
only people who have the leisure to make observations on nature, to reflect and dream
about these matters. They do so as part of their profession. . . . In the lower strata of
civilization, magicians are scholars and scholars are magicians." He also notes: "We

feel justified in saying that medicine, pharmacy, alchemy and astrology all developed within the discipline of magic, around a kernel of discoveries which were purely technical and as basic as possible. . . . Magic is linked to science in the same way as it is linked to technology. It is not only a practical art, it is also a storehouse of ideas." Marcel Mauss, *A General Theory of Magic*, trans. Robert Brain (New York: Norton, 1975), 143–44, 142–43.

10. Sigmund Freud, *Moses and Monotheism: An Outline of Psycho-Analysis and Other Works*, trans. James Strachey, in *The Standard Edition of the Complete Works of Sigmund Freud*, vol. 23 (London: The Hogarth Press and the Institute of Psycho-analysis, 1964), 131.

11. Freud describes the return of the repressed in the following terms: "It is worth specially stressing the fact that each portion which returns from oblivion asserts itself with peculiar force, exercises an incomparably powerful influence on people in the mass, and raises an irresistible claim to truth against which logical objections remain powerless: a kind of *'credo quia absurdum.'*" Moreover, "We have learnt from the psycho-analysis of individuals that their earliest impressions, received at a time when the child was scarcely yet capable of speaking, produce at some time or another effects of a compulsive character without themselves being consciously remembered. We believe we have a right to make the same assumption about the earliest experiences of the whole of humanity." Freud, *Moses and Monotheism*, 85, 129–30.

PART II. WORLD-EMPIRE

1. Karl Marx, *Capital: A Critique of Political Economy*, vol. 1, trans. Ben Fowkes (Harmondsworth, UK: Penguin Books, 1976), 452–91.

2. Marshall Sahlins, *Stone Age Economics*, 2nd ed. (New York: Routledge, 2004), 94.

3. Karl A. Wittfogel, *Oriental Despotism: A Comparative Study of Total Power* (New Haven: Yale University Press, 1957), 27–29.

4. See Lewis Mumford, *Technics and Human Development*, vol. 1, *The Myth of the Machine* (New York: Harcourt, Brace and World, 1967).

5. The difficulty of making nomadic people adopt fixed settlements can be seen in the examples of Russia and China, where even after the emergence of a strong state power it was not possible to force nomadic peoples to adopt sedentary settlement. Another example can be seen in resistance offered by craft workers in late eighteenth-century England when mechanized production began in the textile industry. This led to the use of women and children in the factories. These artisans in a sense resembled the hunter-gatherer peoples. They despised routinized, mechanical work and frequently drifted from one workplace to another in nomadic fashion. It was not easy to compel this sort of artisan to submit to mechanized labor: it required both coercion and discipline (education). In many cases, these were provided by state policies of compulsory education and military conscription.

CHAPTER 3. THE STATE

1. Jane Jacobs, *The Economy of Cities* (New York: Vintage, 1970).

2. Beyond the examples of the so-called four great civilizations of the world, we see the same pattern in the completely unrelated civilizations of the Americas, which

began with fishing at river mouths and then with trading carried out by boat. The Huaca Prieta and Aspero ruins in the coastal areas of the Andes show the first stages in the development of what would become the Inca Empire. Archaeological surveys show that these began as fixed settlements adopted for the sake of fishing, and that crop cultivation subsequently began there as a natural development. Here too we can presume a process that led from the establishment of proto-city-states to the establishment of states through expansion of trade and war, and finally to the rise of empire. The same is true for Teotihuacan in the highlands of Mexico: it originally emerged as a proto-city-state located at a vital position along trade routes linking coastal regions.

3. Max Weber, *The City*, trans. Don Martindale and Gertrud Neuwirth (Glencoe, IL: Free Press, 1958).

4. Jean-Jacques Rousseau, *Discourse on Inequality*, trans. G. D. H. Cole (Whitefish, MT: Kessinger Publishing, 2004), 54.

5. The contract that brings about what Hobbes calls a commonwealth is of a different nature from those that arise after it: "It is true that in a commonwealth once instituted or acquired, promises proceeding from fear of death or violence are no covenants, nor obliging, when the thing promised is contrary to the laws; but the reason is not, because it was made upon fear, but because he that promiseth hath no right in the thing promised." Thomas Hobbes, *Leviathan: With Selected Variants from the Latin Edition of 1668*, ed. Edwin Curley (Indianapolis, IN: Hackett Publishing, 1994), 127–28. "Covenants extorted by fear" precede what we ordinarily call a contract. In Hobbes's words, "covenants, being but words and breath, have no force to oblige, contain, constrain, or protect any man, but what it has from the public sword" (112).

6. Hobbes, *Leviathan*, 86.

7. Hobbes, *Leviathan*, 109–10.

8. Hobbes, *Leviathan*, 131.

9. Christopher Gill, Norman Postlethwaite, and Richard Seaford, *Reciprocity in Ancient Greece* (New York: Oxford University Press, 1998).

10. Frederick Engels, *The Origin of the Family, Private Property and the State*, in Karl Marx and Frederick Engels, *Collected Works*, vol. 26 (New York: International Publishers, 1975), 251.

11. Rousseau, *Discourse on Inequality*, 53.

12. Karl Marx, *Capital*, vol. 1, *A Critical Analysis of Capitalist Production*, trans. Ben Fowkes (Harmondsworth, UK: Penguin Books, 1976), 479.

13. John Maynard Keynes, *The General Theory of Employment, Interest and Money* (New York: Palgrave Macmillan, 2007).

14. Yasuhiro Ōtsuki in his *Teikoku to jizen: Bizantsu* (Tokyo: Sōbunsha, 2005) points out that the Eastern Roman Empire (Byzantine) was unlike western Europe in that it was a kind of welfare state.

15. Max Weber, *Economy and Society*, vol. 3, trans. Ephraim Fischoff (New York: Bedminster Press, 1968), 1106–7.

16. With regard to the agricultural community, in China the sort of community that Marx found in India did not exist. The existence of the clans that are characteristic of Chinese society down to the present day is not the result of some unbroken blood lineage stretching back to the primitive community. The clans (*bang*) arose with the maturing of the bureaucratic system based on civil-service examinations, and were associations formed out of resistance by the ordinary people, separate from the village communities that were organized from above as administrative units. For this reason, if we look at Chinese history it becomes clear that the so-called eternally unchanging Asiatic community is a fiction. What remains permanently is instead the state bureaucratic apparatus. The famous Russian mir communities were also organized under the rule of the Mongols. They are the products of the despotic state, not vice versa.

17. Weber, *Economy and Society*, vol. 3, 971–72.

18. Karl A. Wittfogel, *Oriental Despotism: A Comparative Study of Total Power* (New Haven, CT: Yale University Press, 1957).

19. Michael Mann criticizes Wittfogel's theory, which explicates the origins of the Asiatic despotic state by way of hydraulic agriculture: "In short, there was no necessary connection in the ancient world between hydraulic agriculture and despotism, even in the three apparently favorable areas of China, Egypt, and Sumer." Michael Mann, *The Sources of Social Power*, vol. 1, *A History of Power from the Beginning to A.D. 1760* (Cambridge, UK: Cambridge University Press, 1986), 97.

20. See, for example, Karl A. Wittfogel, "The Marxist View of Russian Society and Revolution," *World Politics* 12:4 (July 1960), 487–508.

21. Weber, *Economy and Society*, vol. 3, 967.

22. Weber, *Economy and Society*, vol. 3, 963–94.

23. The system of civil-service examinations and rule was also adopted by neighboring countries (Korea, Vietnam). The Koryŏ dynasty established the exam system and civil-service rule in the tenth century. In Japan, despite the full importation of various Chinese systems, the bureaucratic system alone failed to take root, and a warrior culture was preserved at its base.

CHAPTER 4. WORLD MONEY

1. Karl Marx, *Capital: A Critique of Political Economy*, vol. 1, trans. Ben Fowkes (Harmondsworth, UK: Penguin Books, 1976), 178.

2. Karl Marx, *Capital: A Critique of Political Economy*, vol. 3, trans. David Fernbach (Harmondsworth, UK: Penguin Books, 1976), 728.

3. Marx, "Preface to the First German Edition," *Capital*, vol. 1, 90.

4. Marx, *Capital*, vol. 1, 167.

5. Marx, *Capital*, vol. 1, 139–40.

6. Marx, *Capital*, vol. 1, 154–77.

7. Marx, *Capital*, vol. 1, 187.

8. Marx, *Capital*, vol. 1, 159.

9. Marx, *Capital*, vol. 1, 149 n. 22.

10. Marx, *Capital*, vol. 1, 138–62.

11. Marx, *Capital*, vol. 1, 183.

12. Karl Marx, *A Contribution to the Critique of Political Economy*, in Karl Marx and Frederick Engels, *Collected Works*, vol. 29 (New York: International Publishers, 1975), 385.

13. Karl Marx, "The Commodity," English translation of the first-edition German version of chapter 1 of *Capital*, vol. 1, trans. Albert Dragstedt, in Albert Dragstedt, *Value: Studies by Karl Marx* (New Park Publications, London, 1976), available at the Marxists Internet Archive, http://www.marxists.org/archive/marx/works/1867-c1/commodity.htm.

14. Karl Polanyi, *The Livelihood of Man* (New York: Academic Press, 1977), 99.

15. The error in the view that sees money as arising due to state backing is evident from the limits on the ability of the state to force its money to circulate. State fiat alone cannot cause money to be accepted domestically. Moreover, a currency that is not accepted abroad will stop being accepted at home For example, even in a powerful state like the USSR, toward the end of its rule its currency (the ruble) was no longer accepted even domestically. In its place tobacco (Marlboros) functioned as money.

16. My argument here is based on Katsuyoshi Yamada, *Kahei no Chūgoku kodai shi* (Tokyo: Asahi Shinbunsha, 2000).

17. One view rejects Marx's taking up money from the perspective of commodities and argues that it is instead grounded in mutual credit. Marx called money "the joint contribution of the whole world of commodities," but according to this view, mutual credit can be seen as the joint contribution of the whole world of people or the joint contribution of the whole world of states. In other words, this view maintains there is no need for money to be a commodity (gold); whatever the various states agree on and support will become the world money. This view has grown more influential since the 1970s, as the dollar continued to function as the global key currency even after it was no longer backed with gold. But the gold standard for the dollar was suspended precisely to prevent the outflow of gold, which in itself demonstrates that the dollar is in fact supported by gold. Even today, gold persists as the tacit world money used for settling up international accounts. Of course, the age of the dollar as world money (reserve currency) will not continue for long. Having said that, this does not mean that we can expect a return to the gold standard. The world money will likely be the "commodity basket": not just gold and silver but also rare metals, oil, grain, and so on. These are instances of commodity money; for any money to circulate globally, it must itself possess use value.

18. Polanyi, *The Livelihood of Man*, 98.

19. Any currency that does not in itself possess use value cannot become world money. An exception to this can be found in the paper money that was promulgated by the Mongol Empire. This money arose not from state power but rather from the mutual credit extended among the Mongolian ruling community that covered a wide area. This was a reciprocal power. It is also what made the Mongolian empire possible on a scale not seen before or since.

20. Marx, *Capital*, vol. 1, 228.

21. Since Georg Lukács, there has been an ongoing debate among Marxists about whether the relations of production take the form of relations between things or whether class relations are concealed within the simple exchange (contract) relation—in other words, the theory of reification. But this fails to see that under industrial capitalism, the relations between people are organized by the exchange relationship between money and commodity. This view bases itself on mode of production and regards modes of exchange as mere surface phenomena. For example, according to the theory of reification, the master-slave relation of production lies concealed underneath the money-commodity relation as the actual base. For this reason, it takes countermovements or workers against capital to be similar to slave rebellions.

22. Aristotle, *Politics*, trans. Benjamin Jowett (New York: Random House, 1943), 68.

23. Aristotle, *Politics*, 68.

24. Marx, *Capital*, vol. 1, 231.

25. Marx, *Capital*, vol. 1, 254–55.

26. Marcel Mauss, *The Gift: The Form and Reason for Exchange in Archaic Societies*, trans. W. D. Hall (London: Routledge, 2002), 47.

27. Marx, *Capital*, vol. 1, 176.

28. Marx, *Capital*, vol. 3, 516.

29. Marx, *Capital*, vol. 3, 733.

30. Marx, *Capital*, vol. 3, 728.

31. Polanyi, *The Livelihood of Man*, 84.

32. Marx, *Capital*, vol. 3, 731.

33. Aristotle, *Politics*, 71.

34. Babylon's Code of Hammurabi includes provisions covering the lending of money, collection of debts, compensation for damages, and buying and selling slaves. These were all for the purpose of regulating the usurers who had already appeared on the scene.

35. In medieval Europe Christianity banned the charging of interest, and interest-bearing financial transactions were left in the hands of Jews. But the Jews also banned usury among their own people. Under the "double ethic," in which different ethical standards are applied within and without the community, a money economy can never become the general rule.

36. See, for example, Karl Polanyi, "Marketless Trading in Hammurabi's Time," in *Trade and Markets in the Early Empires*, ed. Karl Polanyi, Conrad M. Arensberg, and Harry Pearson (Free Press, New York, 1957), 12–25.

37. Herodotus, *The Histories*, trans. George Rawlinson (London: J. M. Dent, 1992), 83.

CHAPTER 5. WORLD EMPIRES

1. Karl A. Wittfogel, *Oriental Despotism: A Comparative Study of Total Power* (New Haven, CT: Yale University Press, 1957).

2. On this point, the Russian and Chinese Revolutions can be seen as attempts to restore the old world-empires. Wittfogel argues that the Russian and Chinese Revolutions were built on the foundations of the Asiatic despotic states and for that reason ended up reproducing Asiatic despotism. But he overlooks the fact that Russia

and China were world-empires—meaning that multiple communities and states were unified under them. If bourgeois revolutions had taken place there, these older world-empires would almost certainly have fractured into multiple nation-states. At this time, Marxism, with its stress on the primacy of class, provided the sole ideology capable of modernizing and restoring the old world-empires without breaking them up into multiple nation-states. The socialist revolutions in Russia and China established within the world-economy (global capitalism) a world system that rejected that world-economy—an economic sphere grounded in not-for-profit exchanges.

3. The Chinese court experienced continuous intervention from nomadic tribes. For example, the Han, Song, and Ming dynasties are often regarded as dynasties that arose through Han rebellions against rule by nomadic peoples. Yet the Han dynasty up until the time of Emperor Wu was practically a vassal state of the nomadic Xiongnu people, the founding of the Song dynasty was dependent on the deployment of the military might of nomadic peoples, and the military forces of the Ming dynasty included many Mongol units. In sum, the imperial courts of China were established, either directly or through indirect support, by nomadic peoples. In China, the legitimacy of dynasties was judged not by ethnicity but rather according to whether political unification brought about stability, peace, and prosperity. For example, the Qing dynasty was founded by external conquerors, but it was regarded as legitimate because it secured political unification and expanded the realm of the empire.

4. Lewis Henry Morgan, *Ancient Society* (New Brunswick, NJ: Transaction Publishers, 2000), 105.

5. Marx noted that Greece preserved the various clan-period systems even as it attained a high degree of civilization, explaining that "[only the] unsettled condition [and] incessant warfare [of the] tribes (Attic), from their settlement in Attica [through the time of] Solon [made it possible to maintain for so long the old gentile organization.] . . . [By the time of] Solon[,] Athenians already a civilized people, had been so for 2 centuries; [extensive] development of useful arts, commerce at sea became a national interest, advancement of agriculture [and] manufacture, commencement of written composition in verse; [but their] institutions of government still gentile, of the type of the Later Period of Barbarism." Lawrence Krader, *The Ethnological Notebooks of Karl Marx: Studies of Morgan, Phear, Maine, Lubbock*, 2nd ed. (Assen, Netherlands: Van Gorcum, 1974), 213–14; modified, with German phrases translated by Bourdaghs. While this may more or less apply to the case of Athens, it does not apply to that of Ionia.

6. According to one theory, it was the reform of Phoenician writing and the creation of a phonetic writing system (the alphabet) that anyone could master that brought about Greek democracy. It is certainly true that in Egypt and China, considerable time and ability were required to master the writing system. But to say that democracy arose because there was phonetic writing is to invert cause and effect. When there is a bureaucratic system, it is not in the interest of that system for the masses to acquire writing. For example, in Egypt there was a form of written language used by the masses, but the official class, which wanted to preserve its monopoly over information and knowledge, continued to use cuneiform and other difficult-to-master writing

systems. Accordingly, the adoption and development of phonetic writing in Greece occurred because its bureaucratic structure was undeveloped. This in turn was due to the practice of leaving economic matters in the hands of market forces rather than subjecting these matters to bureaucratic control.

7. Hannah Arendt, *On Revolution* (London: Penguin, 1963), 30.

8. The polis of Athens began as a federation of tribes, segmented into the following strata: family (*oikos*), above which came *genos* (clan), and then *phratry* (brotherhood, kinfolk), and *phyle* (tribe). Athens included four different tribes.

9. Arendt, *On Revolution*.

10. Benedict Anderson, *Imagined Communities: Reflections on the Origins and Spread of Nationalism*, 2nd ed. (London: Verso, 2006).

11. The natural philosophy of Ionia was developed by people who did not look down on craft and manual labor, unlike the Athenians. The same can be said about Herodotus's *The Histories*, trans. George Rawlinson (London: J. M. Dent, 1992). He included in it a wide variety of marginal tribes, beginning with Persia, without falling into a Greco-centric bias, adopting instead an attitude remarkably similar to that of today's anthropologists. As Mariko Sakurai points out, Herodotus's stance differed sharply from that of the Athenian historian Thucydides. Sakurai, *Herodotosu to Toukyudidesu* (Tokyo: Yamakawa Shuppan, 2006). As for Hippocrates, his Hippocratic oath, with its pledges to provide medical treatment without injustice to all, free or slave, and to protect the privacy of the patient, remains to this day the standard for medical practitioners.

12. Plato, "Apology," in *Plato: Six Great Dialogues*, trans. Benjamin Jewett (Mineola, NY: Dover Publications, 2007), 14.

13. Hannah Arendt, *The Principles of Totalitarianism* (New York: Houghton Mifflin Harcourt, 1973), 125–27.

14. Max Weber, *The Agrarian Sociology of Ancient Civilizations*, trans. R. I. Frank (Atlantic Highlands, NJ: Humanities Press, 1976).

15. Samir Amin, *Eurocentrism*, trans. Russell Moore (New York: Monthly Review Press, 1989).

16. Thomas Hobbes, *Leviathan: With Selected Variants from the Latin Edition of 1668*, ed. Edwin Curley (Indianapolis, IN: Hackett Publishing, 1994), 86.

17. One reason the church was stronger than emperors and feudal lords in western Europe was that, as Caesar points out in *The Gallic Wars*, originally among the Celts the priestly class outranked the military class, a situation that Christianity used to its advantage when it began proselytizing.

18. It is sometimes said that feudalism existed in China during the Zhou dynasty. But what existed there was a system in which the king ruled the lands and peoples by appointing for each a single powerful family or retainer as its feudal lord. It was a ruling system based on family lineages, with no reciprocal relationships among warriors. It was opposed to the concept of the county and prefecture system, which was put into effect by the first Qin dynasty emperor. Confucius held up Zhou feudalism as an ideal because he believed it ruled not through "armed force" or law, but rather through "rites and music."

19. Karl A. Wittfogel, *Oriental Despotism: A Comparative Study of Total Power* (New Haven, CT: Yale University Press, 1957).

20. Marc Bloch, *Feudal Society*, vol. 2, *Social Classes and Political Organization*, trans. L. A. Manyon (Chicago: University of Chicago Press, 1964), 382.

21. Feudalism in Japan must be understood not just from the perspective of the ruling class of warriors but also from that of the ruled classes. While there were communal property and communal bonds such as typically accompany rice cultivation, the peasants of Japan beginning from the fourteenth century acquired de facto private ownership over land. For example, the Taikō cadastral survey launched in 1582 was carried out for the sake of ensuring state tax receipts (annual payments), but it had the effect of reconfirming the private landed property of the peasantry. Moreover, in the sixteenth century, autonomous cities such as Sakai and Kyoto came into being. These were repressed under the Tokugawa regime from the seventeenth century on, but this repression was not total. Even after it the cultural activities of the *chōnin* (literally, "townspeople," bourgeoisie) would continue. In that sense, the Japanese social formation can be said to have been feudal and not Asiatic. This in no way contradicts the reality that Japan was always under the influence of the Asiatic empire-civilization. For example, although the laws and organs of the ancient ritsuryō state had become empty shells, they were never formally abolished. They were even revived by the Meiji Restoration under the policies of building a centralized state— carried out under the slogan "restoration of imperial rule."

22. Samir Amin in *Eurocentrism*, trans. Russell Moore (New York: Monthly Review Press, 1989), expresses skepticism toward the idea of an unbroken Western history stretching from ancient Greece to the present day. This view requires the repression of the reality that modern Europe could not have come into being without the existence of medieval Arabic civilization, and also that the supposed birthplace of ancient Greece was in fact on the periphery of a highly developed country: Egypt. The two great strands of Western thought—the "poiesis" philosophy of Plato and Aristotle and the monotheistic creator of Judaism—both originated in Egypt. In Amin's view, in an empire such as Egypt, because these two strands already took fully developed form, they became rigid and stagnant, whereas in a peripheral region such as the states on the undeveloped coast of the Greek peninsula, their culture could be developed freely and flexibly. Moreover, Amin sees similarity in the relationship between Egypt and Greece and those between the Roman Empire and its western European periphery, between the western European continental empires and the island nation England on their periphery, and between China and the island nation of Japan on its periphery. Amin argues that capitalism developed from these peripheral states in which systems were not yet fully developed. In these peripheral states, particularly those located in island nations, there was no need to expend energy simply to maintain territorial integrity. Moreover, no matter what they chose to import from outside, they could process it pragmatically and creatively, unconstrained by the force of traditional norms. This is a remarkably perceptive observation, but as should be clear, Wittfogel had already pointed the way with his concept of submargin. Amin's failure to acknowledge this seems unfair.

CHAPTER 6. UNIVERSAL RELIGIONS

1. See chapter 2 in Max Weber, *The Sociology of Religion*, trans. Ephraim Fischoff (Boston: Beacon Press, 1963).

2. Weber, *The Sociology of Religion*, 25.

3. Weber, *The Sociology of Religion*, 27.

4. Friedrich Nietzsche, *On the Genealogy of Morals*, trans. Douglas Smith (Oxford: Oxford University Press, 1996), 44, 51, 52.

5. Ortwin Hessler, *Formen des Asylrechts und ihre Verbreitung bei den heidnischen Germanen* (Frankfurt: V. Klostermann, 1954).

6. "But throughout Mesopotamia and Arabia, however, it was not rain that was the creator of the harvest, but artificial irrigation alone. In Mesopotamia, irrigation was the sole source of the absolute power of the monarch, who derived his income by compelling his conquered subjects to build canals and cities adjoining them, just as the regulation of the Nile was the source of the Egyptian monarch's strength. In the desert and semiarid regions of the Near East this control of irrigation waters was indeed one source of the conception of a god who had created the earth and man out of nothing and not merely fashioned them, as was believed elsewhere." Weber, *Sociology of Religion*, 57.

7. Nietzsche, *On the Genealogy of Morals*, 70.

8. Weber, *The Sociology of Religion*, 24.

9. In Egypt the earliest pharaonic court was a confederation of tribes (a federated monarchy), and the pharaoh was merely one relatively powerful chief among others. As the monarch became more powerful and established a centralized state structure, there arose the concept of the "divine king," which regarded pharaohs as incarnations of gods. But during the Fourth dynasty, worship of the sun god Ra gained popularity. This clearly signified the decline of the monarchy. Pharaohs were no longer "god kings": they became only entities that performed the role of gods. A revival in the power of the monarchy came with the founding of a new monarchy. Egypt, which had until then been confined to the region bordering on the Nile, now became an empire whose domain extended to Asia. The traditional structures and religion were no longer adequate to this situation. It was at this time that Akhenaten's Amarna reform was launched, a religious reformation that established the sun god as the sole, absolute deity. During Akhenaten's reign, Egypt lost its Asian territories. His successor, Tutankhamen, abolished the reforms, erasing all traces of their existence.

10. Karl Marx, *Capital: A Critique of Political Economy*, vol. 1, trans. Ben Fowkes (Harmondsworth, UK: Penguin Books, 1976), 229–30.

11. Frances MacDonald Cornford, *From Religion to Philosophy: A Study in the Origins of Western Speculation* (Princeton, NJ: Princeton University Press, 1991).

12. Confucius, "Zi Han," in Confucius, *Confucian Analects, the Great Learning and the Doctrine of the Mean*, trans. James Legge (New York: Dover, 1971), 221.

13. Weber, *The Sociology of Religion*, 16.

14. Weber introduced the theory that around the time of the court of Solomon, *Egypt* was a byword for a despotic tributary state, so that the "exodus from Egypt" symbolized an escape from the situation of passage toward an Egyptian-style

despotism. See Max Weber, *The Agrarian Sociology of Ancient Civilizations*, trans. R. I. Frank (Atlantic Highlands, NJ: Humanities Press, 1976), 142.

15. Ernst Bloch, *The Principle of Hope*, vol. 1, trans. Neville Plaice, Stephen Plaice, and Paul Knight (Cambridge, MA: MIT Press, 1986), 114–15.

16. There is a common perception that Judaism does not engage in proselytizing because it is the religion of a single ethnic people. But Judaism is a universal religion. According to Shlomo Sand, the increase in the population of Jews in the Roman Empire, Africa, and Russia was due to an increase in the number of converts to Judaism. A Jewish person is first of all an adherent of the Jewish faith. According to Sand, the notion of a Jewish ethnicity or race was an "invention" of late nineteenth-century Jewish nationalism (Zionism) in response to the pressures of rising European nationalisms. See Shlomo Sand, *The Invention of the Jewish People*, trans. Yael Lotan (London: Verso, 2010).

17. All biblical quotations use *New English Bible*.

18. Frederick Engels, *The Peasant War in Germany*, in Karl Marx and Frederick Engels, *Collected Works*, vol. 10 (New York: International Publishers, 1978), 422.

19. We can find another example of this in the Alevi of Turkey. This was a heresy arising in the Sunni denomination that maintained that mediators such as prophets and clergy were unnecessary to achieve the sought-for mystical union with God; the Alevi also rejected mosques and various precepts, including abstinence from alcohol and the requirement for women to wear veils. The Alevi formed a reciprocal (communistic) community and generated democratic social movements. Despite their minority status, the Alevi were highly influential. The separation of church and state in today's Turkey is said to derive more from the Alevi than from Westernization.

20. Shinran, quoted in Yuien, *Tannishō: Passages Deploring Deviations of Faith*, trans. Bandō Shōjun and Harold Stewart (Berkeley, CA: Numata Center for Buddhist Translation and Research, 1996), 5.

21. Mao Zedong in the Chinese Revolution was inspired more by the history of religious popular revolts, such as that of the founder of the Ming dynasty, than by Marxist literature.

PART III. THE MODERN WORLD SYSTEM

1. Paul Sweezy, Maurice Dobb, Christopher Hill, Georges Lefebvre, Kohachiro Takahashi, Giuliano Procacci, John Merrington, Eric Hobsbawm, *The Transition from Feudalism to Capitalism* (London: NLB, 1976).

2. Karl Marx, *Capital: A Critique of Political Economy*, vol. 3, trans. David Fernbach (Harmondsworth, UK: Penguin Books, 1976), 455.

3. Karl Marx, *Capital: A Critique of Political Economy*, vol. 1, trans. Ben Fowkes (Harmondsworth, UK: Penguin Books, 1976), 247.

4. Citing the version of Marx who stressed the process of circulation, Braudel criticizes Wallerstein: "I do not share Immanuel Wallerstein's fascination with the sixteenth century. Is the problem that perplexes him not in the end the same one that was raised by Marx? . . . I am therefore in agreement with the Marx who wrote (though

he later went back on this) that European capitalism—indeed he even says capitalist *production*—began in thirteenth-century Italy." Fernand Braudel, *Civilization and Capitalism, 15th–18th Century*, vol. 3, *The Perspective of the World* (Berkeley: University of California Press, 1982), 57.

5. Braudel, *Civilization and Capitalism, 15th–18th Century*, vol. 3, 27.

6. See, for example, Andre Gunder Frank, "The Development of Underdevelopment," *Monthly Review* 18:4 (September 1966), 17–31.

7. Andre Gunder Frank, *ReOrient: Global Economy in the Asian Age* (Berkeley: University of California Press, 1998).

8. Needham writes: "Apart from the great ideas and systems of the Greeks, between the first and fifteenth centuries the Chinese, who experienced no 'dark ages,' were generally much in advance of Europe; and not until the scientific revolution of the late Renaissance did Europe draw rapidly ahead. Before that time, however, the West had been profoundly affected not only in its technical processes but in its very social structures and changes by discoveries and inventions emanating from China and East Asia. Not only the three which Lord Bacon listed (printing, gunpowder and the magnetic compass) but a hundred others—mechanical clockwork, the casting of iron, stirrups and efficient horse-harness, the Cardan suspension and the Pascal triangle, segmental-arch bridges and pound-locks on canals, the stern-post rudder, fore-and-aft sailing, quantitative cartography—all had their effects, sometimes earth-shaking effects, upon a Europe more socially unstable." Joseph Needham, *The Grand Titration: Science and Society in East and West* (London: Allen and Unwin, 1969), 11.

9. Marx, *Capital*, vol. 1, 166.

CHAPTER 7. THE MODERN STATE

1. Max Weber, *Economy and Society*, trans. Ephraim Fischoff, vol. 1 (New York: Bedminster Press, 1968), 1086, 1102–4.

2. Jean Bodin, *On Sovereignty*, trans. Julian H. Franklin (Cambridge, UK: Cambridge University Press, 1992).

3. Thomas Hobbes, *Leviathan: With Selected Variants from the Latin Edition of 1668*, ed. Edwin Curley (Indianapolis, IN: Hackett, 1994), 86, 109–10.

4. Hobbes, *Leviathan*, 123.

5. Carl Schmitt, *Political Theology: Four Chapters on the Concept of Sovereignty*, trans. George Schwab (Chicago: University of Chicago Press, 2005).

6. Karl Marx, *Capital: A Critique of Political Economy*, vol. 1, trans. Ben Fowkes (Harmondsworth, UK: Penguin Books, 1976), 919.

7. Karl Marx, *Capital*, vol. 1, 919–20.

8. G. W. F. Hegel, *Elements of the Philosophy of Right*, trans. H. B. Nisbet (Cambridge, UK: Cambridge University Press, 1991), 340.

9. Wilhelm Reich, *The Mass Psychology of Fascism*, trans. Vincent Carfagno (New York: Farrar, Strauss and Giroux, 1970).

10. Sigmund Freud, *New Introductory Lectures on Psycho-analysis*, trans. James Strachey (New York: Norton, 1965), 14.

11. Karl Marx, *The Eighteenth Brumaire of Louis Bonaparte*, in Karl Marx and Frederick Engels, *Collected Works*, vol. 11 (New York: International Publishers, 1979), 169–70.

12. Marx, *The Eighteenth Brumaire of Louis Bonaparte*, 185.

13. Marx, *The Eighteenth Brumaire of Louis Bonaparte*, 186.

14. Marx, *The Eighteenth Brumaire of Louis Bonaparte*, 195.

15. C. Wright Mills, *White Collar: The American Middle Class* (New York: Oxford University Press, 2002).

CHAPTER 8. INDUSTRIAL CAPITAL

1. Max Weber, *The Protestant Ethic and the Spirit of Capitalism*, trans. Peter Baehr and Gordon C. Wells (New York: Penguin, 2002).

2. Karl Marx, *Capital: A Critique of Political Economy*, vol. 3, trans. David Fernbach (Harmondsworth, UK: Penguin Books, 1976), 455.

3. Karl Marx, *Capital: A Critique of Political Economy*, vol. 1, trans. Ben Fowkes (Harmondsworth, UK: Penguin Books, 1976), 266.

4. Early modern manufactures dramatically accelerated the development of techniques for the combination and division of labor. This does not mean, however, that there weren't increases in productivity due to the combination and division of labor in ancient times. For example, Polanyi argues that exchange rates were fixed in ancient trade. But this means only that there was almost no change in the (social) labor hours required to manufacture the product. In most cases, the products of each region were prescribed by natural conditions, meaning there was almost no variation. Nonetheless, in reality there was change, albeit at a slow pace. The state, which administered or monopolized trade, would sometimes open new mines, develop new products or weapons, and introduce new technologies such as metal working. As a result, improvements in production technology led to the overcoming of natural limitations and produced changes, albeit gradual ones, between the value systems of different regions. The manufactures of early modern Europe should be seen as an extension of this process.

5. Marx, *Capital*, vol. 1, 268–69.

6. Marx, *Capital*, vol. 1, 718.

7. *Hic Rhodus, hic salta!* literally means "here is Rhodes, jump here!" and figuratively means "show me how it's done right here and now."

8. Karl Marx, *Grundrisse, Section Two: The Circulation Process of Capital*, in Karl Marx and Frederick Engels, *Collected Works*, vol. 28 (New York: International Publishers, 1986), 346–49.

9. P.-J. Proudhon, *Proudhon: What is Property?* Cambridge, UK: Cambridge University Press, 1994.

10. Marx, *Capital*, vol. 1, 781–93.

11. Elsewhere in *Capital* Marx writes that there was a threefold transition in the shift from the feudal to the capitalist mode of production: "First, the merchant becomes an industrialist directly; this is the case with crafts that are founded on trade, such as those in the luxury industries, where the merchants import both raw materials and

workers from abroad, as they were imported into Italy from Constantinople in the fifteenth century. Second, the merchant makes the small masters into his middlemen, or even buys directly from the independent producer; he leaves him nominally independent and leaves his mode of production unchanged. Third, the industrialist becomes a merchant and produces directly on a large scale for the market." Marx, *Capital*, vol. 3, 454. But according to Marx, the first and the second transitions tend to preserve the old mode of production. Therefore, in broad terms, this threefold distinction is really a twofold distinction between the first and the second, on the one hand, and the third.

12. Marx, *Capital*, vol. 3, 452.

13. Paul Sweezy, Maurice Dobb, Christopher Hill, Georges Lefebvre, Kohachiro Takahashi, Giuliano Procacci, John Merrington, Eric Hobsbawm, *The Transition from Feudalism to Capitalism* (London: NLB, 1976).

14. See Hisao Ōtsuka, "Shihonshugi shakai no keisei," in Hisao Ōtsuka, *Ōtsuka Hisao chosakushū*, vol. 5 (Tokyo: Iwanami shoten, 1969).

15. Karl Polanyi, *The Great Transformation: The Political and Economic Origins of Our Time* (Boston: Beacon, 2001), 71–80.

16. Karl Marx, *Capital*, vol. 2, *A Critique of Political Economy*, trans. David Fernbach (Harmondsworth, UK: Penguin Books, 1978), 136.

17. Marx, *Capital*, vol. 3, 567.

18. Adolph A. Berle and Gardiner C. Means, *The Modern Corporation and Private Property* (New Brunswick, NJ: Transaction Publishers, 1991).

19. Marx, *Capital*, vol. 1, 200.

20. Kōzō Uno, "Kyōkōron," in Kōzō Uno, *Uno Kōzō chosakushū*, vol. 5 (Tokyo: Iwanami shoten, 1974). An English translation of this work by Ken Kawashima is forthcoming.

21. Étienne Balibar and Immanuel Wallerstein, *Race, Nation, Class: Ambiguous Identities* (London: Verso, 1991), 123–24.

CHAPTER 9. NATION

1. Luther's translation of the Bible is a representative instance of this. Luther's reformation is usually thought of in terms of religion, but in fact it was significant in multiple registers. His resistance to the Roman Catholic Church took the direct form of a rejection of indulgences, which at the same time meant a challenge to the church's economic dominance. In that sense, Luther's reformation also implied independence for the various tribal states that had been subordinated to this "empire" and promoted the rise of sovereign states that stood above imperial and church laws and peasant movements that sought liberation from the various feudal systems. We must also not forget that Luther's translation of the Bible into the vulgate (High German) had another significance as well: it not only brought the Bible closer to the masses and thereby spread religious reform but it also served as the womb for what would become standard German. Of course, he did not undertake these for the purpose of establishing a nation; nonetheless, in effect, they set in place what would become the foundation of the nation.

2. Ernest Gellner, *Nations and Nationalism* (Ithaca, NY: Cornell University Press, 1983), 34, 28.

3. Friedrich Nietzsche, *On the Genealogy of Morals*, trans. Douglas Smith (Oxford: Oxford University Press, 1996), 44.

4. Benedict Anderson, *Imagined Communities: Reflections on the Origins and Spread of Nationalism*, 2nd ed. (London: Verso, 2006), 10.

5. For example, the poet Percy Bysshe Shelley worshipped the anarchist William Godwin and even married his daughter Mary (the author of *Frankenstein*). This tradition would continue through the nineteenth century with such figures as John Ruskin and William Morris. Morris, founder of the Arts and Crafts movement, was one of the first British Marxists, but his Marxism was of a different nature from that of subsequent democratic socialism or Leninism, and was closer to associationism (i.e., anarchism). Given the tradition described here, this is hardly surprising.

6. G. W. F. Hegel, *Elements of the Philosophy of Right*, trans. H. B. Nisbet (Cambridge, UK: Cambridge University Press, 1991), 221.

7. Adam Smith, *The Theory of Moral Sentiments*, ed. D. D. Raphael and A. L. Macfie (Indianapolis, IN: Liberty Fund, 1984), 9.

8. "The Germans are the only ones who now employ the word 'aesthetics' to designate that which others call the critique of taste. The ground for this is a failed hope, held by the excellent analyst Baumgarten, of bringing the critical estimation of the beautiful under principles of reason, and elevating its rules to a science. But this effort is futile. For the putative rules or criteria are merely empirical as far as their sources are concerned, and can therefore never serve as *a priori* rules according to which our judgment of taste must be directed, rather the latter constitutes the genuine touchstone of the correctness of the former. For this reason it is advisable again to desist from the use of this term and to save it for that doctrine which is true science (whereby one would come closer to the languages and the senses of the ancients, among whom the division of cognition into *aisthētá kai noētá* [sensed or thought] was very well known." Immanuel Kant, *Critique of Pure Reason*, trans. and ed. Paul Guyer and Allen W. Wood (Cambridge, UK: Cambridge University Press, 1998), 156.

9. Kant, *Critique of Pure Reason*, 152.

10. Herder writes: "If, that is to say, reason is no compartmentalized, separately effective force but an orientation of all forces that is distinctive to his species, *then the human being must have it in the first condition in which he is a human being.* . . . If in its first condition the soul has nothing positive of reason in it, how will this become real even in millions of succeeding conditions? . . . But the most sensuous condition of the human being was still human, and hence awareness was still effective in that condition, only in a less marked degree." Johann Gottfried von Herder, "Treatise on the Origin of Language," in *Philosophical Writings* (New York: Cambridge University Press, 2002), 85–87.

11. Johann Gottlieb Fichte, *Addresses to the German Nation*, trans. R. F. Jones and G. H. Turnbull (Chicago: Open Court, 1922), 223–24.

12. Fichte, *Addresses to the German Nation*, 68, 108.

13. Hannah Arendt, *The Origins of Totalitarianism* (San Diego, CA: Harcourt Brace, 1976), 128.

14. "Conquest as well as empire building had fallen into disrepute for very good reasons. They had been carried out successfully only by governments which, like the Roman Republic, were based primarily on law, so that conquest could be followed by integration of the most heterogeneous peoples by imposing upon them a common law. The nation-state, however, based upon a homogeneous population's active consent to its government (*"le plébiscite de tous le jours"* [Renan's "daily referendum"]), lacked such a unifying principle and would, in the case of conquest, have to assimilate rather than to integrate, to enforce consent rather than justice, that is, to degenerate into tyranny." Arendt, *Origins of Totalitarianism*, 125.

15. Threatened with encroachment by western Europe and Russia, the Ottoman Empire labored to form its empire into a nation-state, but this ultimately resulted in its division into multiple nations. At the same time as Ottoman society sought Westernization, it also sought in Islam a principle for resistance against this. Today's dominant Islamism is largely a product of this period.

16. Arendt, *Origins of Totalitarianism*, 127.

17. Benedict Anderson notes that the Indonesian people and even the Indonesian language were formed through Dutch rule and through the resistance movements that rose up against it. *Imagined Communities*, 182.

18. The old world empires were preserved through Marxist revolutions, but as of 1990 they had fragmented into multiple nation-states—with the exception of China. Why was China exempt from this fate? Unlike the other world empires, the Chinese empire since the Qin dynasty possessed the principle of preserving continuity through changes in dynasty. In practice, the legitimacy of a dynasty was judged on its ability to produce stability, peace, and prosperity through unification. The Qing dynasty of Manchurian rulers was seen as legitimate because it fulfilled these conditions. For example, Sun Yat-sen proclaimed the establishment of a new ethnic state of the Han people, but withdrew this following the 1911 revolution. Even having toppled the Qing dynasty and established a modern state, it would be impossible to acquire legitimacy if China splintered into multiple nation-states. Sun Yat-sen began advocating the idea of the nation, which he saw as different from ethnicity. This represented an attempt to transform the whole empire into a nation-state. This was finally realized not by Sun, but by Mao Zedong. The Chinese Communist Party in principle inherited the expanded domain that the Qing dynasty had realized, as well as its policies toward minority peoples. In that sense, the Communist Party's rule enjoyed legitimacy because it had preserved China as an empire. The reason China, unlike the Soviet Union, was able to avoid fragmentation after 1990 was not because its Communist Party's rule was so powerful but rather because its empire was already a nation-state. This all derived from the unique qualities of empire in China.

CHAPTER 10. ASSOCIATIONISM
1. Karl Kautsky's *Foundations of Christianity: A Study in Christian Origins* (New York: Monthly Review Press, 1972) and *Communism in Central Europe in the Time of the*

Reformation (New York: Russell and Russell, 1959) both locate the origins of socialist movements in Christianity.

2. Immanuel Kant, *Grounding for the Metaphysics of Morals* (1785) 3rd ed., trans. James W. Ellington (Indianapolis, IN: Hackett, 1993), 36.

3. Immanuel Kant, *Grounding for the Metaphysics of Morals*, 3rd ed., trans. James W. Ellington (Indianapolis, IN: Hackett, 1993), 40. Kant understood kingdom as follows: "By 'kingdom' I understand a systematic union of different rational beings through common laws" (39).

4. Immanuel Kant, "Religion within the Boundaries of Mere Reason," in Immanuel Kant, *Religion and Rational Theology*, trans. Allen W. Wood and George Di Giovanni (Cambridge, UK: Cambridge University Press, 1996), 195.

5. Immanuel Kant, "To Eternal Peace," trans. Carl J. Friedrich, in Immanuel Kant, *Basic Writings of Kant*, ed. Allen W. Wood (New York: Modern Library, 2001), 440.

6. Immanuel Kant, *Critique of Pure Reason*, trans. and ed. Paul Guyer and Allen W. Wood (Cambridge, UK: Cambridge University Press, 1998), 384–86.

7. P.-J. Proudhon, *General Idea of the Revolution in the Nineteenth Century*, trans. John Beverley Robinson (Mineola, NY: Dover, 2003).

8. See, for example, Max Stirner, *Stirner: The Ego and its Own* (Cambridge, UK: Cambridge University Press, 1995).

9. See, for example, Proudhon, *General Idea of the Revolution in the Nineteenth Century*, 112.

10. See, for example, Proudhon, *General Idea of the Revolution in the Nineteenth Century*, 277.

11. P.-J. Proudhon, letter to Karl Marx, May 17, 1846, in *The Anarchist Reader*, ed. George Woodcock (Hassocks, UK: Harvester, 1977), 138–40.

12. William Thompson, *Labour Rewarded: The Claims of Labour and Capital Conciliated* (London: Hunt and Clarke, 1827).

13. Karl Marx, *Grundrisse*, in Karl Marx and Frederick Engels, *Collected Works*, vol. 28 (New York: International Publishers, 1986), 346.

14. Motonobu Hironishi in *Shihonron no goyaku* (Tokyo: Seiyūsha, 1966) points out that Marx uses the word *combine* (*kombinieren*) in discussing the combination and division of labor organized by capital, and the word *associate* (*assozieren*) when discussing spontaneous, autonomous actions by workers—as well as the failure of Japanese translations of Marx to maintain this distinction, thereby giving rise to confusion.

15. Karl Marx, *Capital: A Critique of Political Economy*, vol. 3, trans. David Fernbach (Harmondsworth, UK: Penguin Books, 1976), 571.

16. Cooperatives are unable to compete with capitalist enterprises. The same is true for the sort of worker-managed enterprises that John Stuart Mill proposed in chapter 7, volume 1 of his *Principles of Political Economy*, 2 volumes (London: Longmans, Green, Reader and Dyer, 1871). He predicted that workers would be happy to work in such an enterprise even if wages were low, allowing them to achieve higher productivity and to successfully compete with and ultimately replace capitalist firms. But there are no instances of this having ever actually happened.

17. Karl Marx, *Inaugural Address of the Working Men's International Association*, in Karl Marx and Frederick Engels, *Collected Works*, vol. 20 (New York: International Publishers, 1985), 11.

18. Karl Marx, "The Third Address," in *The Civil War in France*, in Karl Marx and Frederick Engels, *Collected Works*, vol. 22 (New York: International Publishers, 1986), 335.

19. Karl Marx, *Critique of the Gotha Programme, Part III*, in Karl Marx and Frederick Engels, *Collected Works*, vol. 24 (New York: International Publishers, 1989), 93.

20. Marx, *Capital*, vol. 3, 572.

21. In a letter to Engels dated April 2, 1858, Marx describes *"share capital* as the most perfected form (turning into communism)." Karl Marx and Frederick Engels, *Collected Works*, vol. 40 (New York: International Publishers, 1983), 298.

22. Marx, *Capital*, vol. 3, 507.

23. On this point, I've learned a great deal from Hironishi's *Shihonron no goyaku*. But I don't think it is possible to transform capitalist corporations into cooperatives without seizing state power—without, that is, reforming the legal system. This does not mean nationalization. When we think about transforming capitalist corporations into cooperatives under the existing legal system, it only means introducing profit-sharing models or employee stock-ownership systems, as Hironishi proposes. Such measures cannot, however, abolish capitalism or wage labor. Rather, they are instituted to preserve the existence of capital. For example, employee stock-owner systems are sometimes used as measures to fend off hostile takeovers and at other times as a device for lifting employee morale and productivity. Louis Kelso's Employee Stock Ownership Plan is an example.

24. Karl Marx, article 5, "Cooperative Labour," *Instructions for the Delegates of the Provisional General Council: The Different Questions*, in Karl Marx and Frederick Engels, *Collected Works*, vol. 20 (New York: International Publishers, 1985), 190.

25. Leon Trotsky, *The Revolution Betrayed* (Delhi: Aakar Books, 2006), 224.

26. See, for example, Karl Marx, "Second Address of the General Council of the International Working Men's Association on the Franco-Prussian War," in Karl Marx and Frederick Engels, *Collected Works*, vol. 22 (New York: International Publishers, 1992), 263–70.

27. Ten years after the Paris Commune, Marx would write: "You may, perhaps, refer me to the Paris Commune but, aside from the fact that this was merely an uprising of one city in exceptional circumstances, the majority of the Commune was in no sense socialist, nor could it have been. With a modicum of common sense, it could, however, have obtained the utmost that was then obtainable—a compromise with Versailles beneficial to the people as a whole." Karl Marx, letter to Ferdinand Domela Nieuwenhuis, 22 February 1881, in Karl Marx and Frederick Engels, *Collected Works*, vol. 46 (New York: International Publishers, 1992), 65–67.

28. Karl Marx, *The German Ideology*, in Karl Marx and Frederick Engels, *Collected Works*, vol. 5 (New York: International Publishers, 1976), 49.

29. Frederick Engels, preface to the 1886 English edition of *Capital*, in Karl Marx and Frederick Engels, *Collected Works*, vol. 35 (New York: International Publishers, 1996), 35–36.

30. Karl Marx comment recorded in "Meeting of the Central Authority, September 15, 1850," Karl Marx and Frederick Engels, *Collected Works*, vol. 10 (New York: International Publishers, 1978), 628–29.

31. For example, we can say that the dictatorship of Mao Zedong in China played the same role as the absolute monarchies in Europe: it unified the people previously scattered among various regions, ethnicities, and status groups into a single people and thereby led to the formation of a unified subject as Nation. Of course, this was not what Mao Zedong had intended to accomplish.

32. Ernst Bloch, *Heritage of Our Times*, trans. Neville Plaice and Stephen Plaice (Cambridge, UK: Polity Press, 1991).

33. In his response to Zasulich, Marx writes: "There is one characteristic of the 'agricultural commune' in Russia which afflicts it with weakness, hostile in every sense. That is its isolation, the lack of connexion between the life of one commune and that of the others, this *localised microcosm* which is not encountered everywhere as an immanent characteristic of this type but which, wherever it is found, has caused a more or less centralised despotism to arise on top of the communes. The federation of Russian republics of the North proves that this isolation, which seems to have been originally imposed by the vast expanse of the territory, was largely consolidated by the political destinies which Russia had to suffer after the Mongol invasion." Karl Marx, "First Draft of Letter to Vera Zasulich," in Karl Marx and Frederick Engels, *Collected Works*, vol. 24 (New York: International Publishers, 1989), 353.

34. Karl Marx, "Letter to Vera Zasulich" (March 8, 1881), in Karl Marx and Frederick Engels, *Collected Works*, vol. 46 (New York: International Publishers, 1992), 72.

35. Karl Marx and Frederick Engels, "Preface to the Second Russian Edition of the Manifesto of the Communist Party," in Karl Marx and Frederick Engels, *Collected Works*, vol. 24 (New York: International Publishers, 1989), 426.

36. John Rawls, *A Theory of Justice*, rev. ed. (Cambridge, MA: Harvard University Press, 1999), 3.

37. Karl Marx, "Introduction," in *A Contribution to the Critique of Hegel's Philosophy of Right*, in Karl Marx and Frederick Engels, *Collected Works*, vol. 3 (New York: International Publishers, 2005), 182.

CHAPTER 11. THE STAGES OF GLOBAL CAPITALISM AND REPETITION

1. Kōzō Uno, *Principles of Political Economy: Theory of a Purely Capitalist Society*, trans. Thomas T. Sekine (Brighton, UK: Harvester, 1980).

2. Robert Albritton and Thomas T. Sekine, *A Japanese Approach to Stages of Capitalist Development: Unoist Variations* (New York: St. Martin's Press, 1995).

3. Immanuel Wallerstein, *The Modern World System II: Mercantilism and the Consolidation of the European World-Economy, 1600–1750* (Berkeley: University of California Press, 2011), 66.

4. Wallerstein, *The Modern World System II*, 38.

5. Wallerstein, *The Modern World System II*, 39.

6. Giovanni Arrighi, *The Long Twentieth Century* (London: Verso, 1994).

7. Karl Marx, *The Eighteenth Brumaire of Louis Bonaparte*, in Karl Marx and Frederick Engels, *Collected Works*, vol. 11 (New York: International Publishers, 1979), 103.

8. G. W. F. Hegel, *The Philosophy of History*, trans. J. Sibree (New York: Dover, 1956), 313.

9. Hannah Arendt, *The Origins of Totalitarianism* (San Diego, CA: Harcourt Brace, 1976).

10. Wallerstein, *The Modern World System II*, 70.

11. Arendt, *The Origins of Totalitarianism*, 123.

12. Michael Hardt and Antonio Negri, *Empire* (Cambridge, MA: Harvard University Press, 2000), 180.

13. Hardt and Negri, *Empire*, 190.

14. Karl Marx and Frederick Engels, *Communist Manifesto*, in Karl Marx and Frederick Engels, *Collected Works*, vol. 6 (New York: International Publishers, 1976), 488.

15. Ellen M. Wood, *Empire of Capital* (London: Verso, 2005), 5–6.

16. Ernest Renan, "What Is a Nation?," trans. Martin Thom, in *Nation and Narration*, ed. Homi K. Bhabha (London: Routledge, 1990), 8–22.

CHAPTER 12. TOWARD A WORLD REPUBLIC

1. Georg Lukács discusses "the correct class consciousness of the proletariat together with its organized form, the Communist Party," in *History and Class Consciousness: Studies in Marxist Dialectics*, trans. Rodney Livingstone (Cambridge, MA: MIT Press, 1972), 75.

2. Karl Marx, "Circulation Process of Capital," notebook IV, *Grundrisse*, in Karl Marx and Frederick Engels, *Collected Works*, vol. 28 (New York: International Publishers, 1986), 349.

3. Karl Marx, *The German Ideology*, in Karl Marx and Frederick Engels, *Collected Works*, vol. 5 (New York: International Publishers, 1976), 49.

4. Mikhail Bakunin, "The Policy of the International," in Mikhail Bakunin, *Bakunin on Anarchism*, ed. Sam Dolgoff (Montreal: Black Rose Books, 2002), 162.

5. See, for example, Immanuel Wallterstein, "1968, Revolution in the World-System: Theses and Queries," *Theory and Society* 18:4 (July 1989), 431–49.

6. Michael Hardt and Antonio Negri, *Multitude: War and Democracy in the Age of Empire* (New York: Penguin, 2004).

7. Immanuel Kant, "Idea for a Universal History from a Cosmopolitan Perspective" (seventh proposition), in Immanuel Kant, *Toward a Perpetual Peace and Other Writings on Politics, Peace, and History*, ed. Pauline Kleingeld and trans. David L. Colclasure (New Haven, CT: Yale University Press, 2006), 9–10.

8. Kant, "Idea for a Universal History from a Cosmopolitan Perspective," 11.

9. Immanuel Kant, "Toward a Perpetual Peace: A Philosophical Sketch," in Kant, *Toward a Perpetual Peace and Other Writings on Politics, Peace, and History*, 68.

10. Kant, "Idea for a Universal History from a Cosmopolitan Perspective" (ninth proposition), 14.

11. Kant, "Toward a Perpetual Peace," 81.

12. Kant, "Toward a Perpetual Peace," 72–73.

13. John Rawls, *The Law of Peoples* (Cambridge, MA: Harvard University Press, 2001).

14. G. W. F. Hegel, *Philosophy of Right*, trans. S. W. Dyde (London: George Bell, 1896), 338.

15. G. W. F. Hegel, *The Philosophy of History*, trans. J. Sibree (New York: Dover, 1956), 33.

16. On this point, please refer to my essay "Shi to nashonarizumu" (Death and nationalism), in Kojin Karatani, *Teihon Karatani Kōjin shū 4: Nēshon to bigaku* (Tokyo: Iwanami shoten, 2004).

17. Robert Kagan, *Of Paradise and Power: America and Europe in the New World Order* (New York: Vintage, 2004), 3, 37, 57–58, 73.

18. Michael Hardt and Antonio Negri, *Multitude: War and Democracy in the Age of Empire* (New York: Penguin, 2004), 312.

19. Hardt and Negri, *Multitude*, 316.

20. Hardt and Negri, *Multitude*, 324.

21. Hardt and Negri, *Multitude*, 340.

22. Karl Schmitt, *The Concept of the Political*, trans. George Schwab (Chicago: University of Chicago Press, 1996), 57.

23. For example, Japan's postwar constitution includes Article 9, which renounces the right to engage in warfare. Accordingly, all that is needed is to actually put this into practice. In reality, however, while the article remains in place, it has been reinterpreted as permitting the present situation in which Japan possesses a large military and vast stockpiles of armaments. Actually putting Article 9 into practice would therefore require a revolution.

24. World history will not end with the rise of a world republic. There could, for example, be reversions to the forms of society in which modes of exchange B or C are dominant. Even under these, however, the impulse toward mode of exchange D will never disappear.

ACKNOWLEDGMENTS

1. Kojin Karatani, *Sekai kyōwakoku e: Shihon=Nēshon=Kokka o koeru* (Tokyo: Iwanami shoten, 2006).

2. Kojin Karatani, "*Sekai kyōwakoku e* ni kansuru nōto," serialized in the quarterly journal *at* (published by Ōta shuppan) from 2006 to 2009.

BIBLIOGRAPHY

Albritton, Robert, and Thomas T. Sekine. *A Japanese Approach to Stages of Capitalist Development: Unoist Variations*. New York: St. Martin's Press, 1995.

Amin, Samir. *Eurocentrism*. Trans. Russell Moore. New York: Monthly Review Press, 1989.

———. *Unequal Development: An Essay on the Social Formations of Peripheral Capitalism*. New York: Monthly Review Press, 1976.

Anderson, Benedict. *Imagined Communities: Reflections on the Origins and Spread of Nationalism*. 2nd ed. London: Verso, 2006.

Arendt, Hannah. *Crises of the Republic*. New York: Harcourt, Brace and World, 1972.

———. *On Revolution*. London: Penguin, 1963.

———. *The Origins of Totalitarianism*. San Diego, CA: Harcourt Brace, 1976.

———. *The Principles of Totalitarianism*. New York: Houghton Mifflin Harcourt, 1973.

Aristotle. *Politics*. Trans. Benjamin Jowett. New York: Random House, 1943.

Arrighi, Giovanni. *The Long Twentieth Century*. London: Verso, 1994.

Bakunin, Mikhail. *Bakunin on Anarchism*. Ed. Sam Dolgoff. Montreal: Black Rose Books, 2002.

Balibar, Etienne, and Immanuel Wallerstein. *Race, Nation, Class: Ambiguous Identities*. London: Verso, 1991.

Baudrillard, Jean. *The Mirror of Production*. Trans. Mark Poster. New York: Telos Press, 1975.

Berle, Adolph A., and Gardiner C. Means. *The Modern Corporation and Private Property*. New Brunswick, NJ: Transaction Publishers, 1991.

Bloch, Ernst. *Heritage of Our Times*. Trans. Neville Plaice and Stephen Plaice. Cambridge, UK: Polity Press, 1991.

———. *The Principle of Hope*. Vol. 1. Trans. Neville Plaice, Stephen Plaice, and Paul Knight. Cambridge, MA: MIT Press, 1986.

Bloch, Marc. *Feudal Society*. Vol. 2, *Social Classes and Political Organization*. Trans. L.A. Manyon. Chicago: University of Chicago Press, 1964.

Bloch, Maurice. *Marxism and Anthropology*. Oxford: Oxford University Press, 1983.

Bodin, Jean. *On Sovereignty.* Trans. Julian H. Franklin. Cambridge, UK: Cambridge University Press, 1992.

Braudel, Fernand. *Civilization and Capitalism, 15th–18th Centuries.* 3 vols. Trans. Siân Reynolds. New York: Harper and Row, 1982–84.

Buber, Martin. *I and Thou.* Trans. Ronald Gregor Smith. New York: Scribner, 1958.

Chase-Dunn, Christopher, and Thomas D. Hall. *Rise and Demise: Comparing World Systems.* Boulder, CO: Westview Press, 1997.

Childe, V. Gordon. *Man Makes Himself.* New York: New American Library, 1951.

Clastres, Pierre. *Archeology of Violence.* Trans. Jeanine Herman. Los Angeles: Semiotext(e), 2010.

Confucius. *Confucian Analects, the Great Learning and the Doctrine of the Mean.* Trans. James Legge. New York: Dover, 1971.

Cornford, Frances MacDonald. *From Religion to Philosophy: A Study in the Origins of Western Speculation.* Princeton, NJ: Princeton University Press, 1991.

Durkheim, Emile. *Incest: The Nature and Origin of the Taboo.* Trans. Albert Ellis. New York: Lyle Stuart, 1963.

———. *Professional Ethics and Civic Morality.* Trans. Cornelia Brookfield. Westport, CT: Greenwood Press, 1983.

Fichte, Johann Gottlieb. *Addresses to the German Nation.* Trans. R. F. Jones and G. H. Turnbull. Chicago: Open Court, 1922.

Foster, John Bellamy. *Marx's Ecology: Materialism and Nature.* New York: Monthly Review Press, 2000.

Frank, Andre Gunder. "The Development of Underdevelopment." *Monthly Review* 18:4 (September 1966): 17–31.

———. *ReOrient: Global Economy in the Asian Age.* Berkeley: University of California Press, 1998.

Freud, Sigmund. *New Introductory Lectures on Psycho-analysis.* Trans. James Strachey. New York: Norton, 1965.

———. *The Standard Edition of the Complete Works of Sigmund Freud.* 24 vols. London: Hogarth Press and the Institute of Psycho-analysis, 1955–74.

Gellner, Ernest. *Nations and Nationalism.* Ithaca, NY: Cornell University Press, 1983.

Gill, Christopher, Norman Postlethwaite, and Richard Seaford. *Reciprocity in Ancient Greece.* New York: Oxford University Press, 1998.

Godelier, Maurice. *The Enigma of the Gift.* Trans. Nora Scott. Chicago: University of Chicago Press, 1999.

Graeber, David. *Fragments of an Anarchist Anthropology.* Chicago: Prickly Paradigm Press, 2004.

Hardt, Michael, and Antonio Negri. *Empire.* Cambridge, MA: Harvard University Press, 2000.

———. *Multitude: War and Democracy in the Age of Empire.* New York: Penguin, 2004.

Hegel, G. W. F. *Elements of the Philosophy of Right.* Trans. H. B. Nisbet. Cambridge, UK: Cambridge University Press, 1991.

———. *The Philosophy of History.* Trans. J. Sibree. New York: Dover, 1956.

———. *Philosophy of Right.* Trans. S. W. Dyde. London: George Bell, 1896.

Herder, Johann Gottfried von. *Philosophical Writings*. New York: Cambridge University Press, 2002.

Herodotus. *The Histories*. Trans. George Rawlinson. London: J. M. Dent, 1992.

Hess, Moses. "On the Essence of Money." Trans. Julius Kovesi. In Julius Kovesi, *Values and Evaluations: Essays on Ethics and Ideology*. Ed. Alan Tapper, 183–207. New York: Peter Lang, 1998.

Hessler, Ortwin. *Formen des Asylrechts und ihre Verbreitung bei den heidnischen Germanen*. Frankfurt: V. Klostermann, 1954.

Hilferding, Rudolf. *Finance Capital: A Study of the Latest Phase of Capitalist Development*. London: Routledge, 2006.

Hironishi, Motonobu. *Shihonron no goyaku*. Tokyo: Seiyūsha, 1966.

Hobbes, Thomas. *Leviathan: With Selected Variants from the Latin Edition of 1668*. Ed. Edwin Curley. Indianapolis, IN: Hackett, 1994.

Jacobs, Jane. *The Economy of Cities*. New York: Vintage, 1970.

Kagan, Robert. *Of Paradise and Power: America and Europe in the New World Order*. New York: Vintage, 2004.

Kant, Immanuel. *Basic Writings of Kant*. Ed. Allen W. Wood. New York: Modern Library, 2001.

———. *Critique of Pure Reason*. Trans. and ed. Paul Guyer and Allen W. Wood. Cambridge, UK: Cambridge University Press, 1998.

———. *Grounding for the Metaphysics of Morals*. 3rd ed. Trans. James W. Ellington. Indianapolis, IN: Hackett, 1993.

———. *Religion and Rational Theology*. Trans. Allen W. Wood and George Di Giovanni. Cambridge, UK: Cambridge University Press, 1996.

———. *Toward a Perpetual Peace and Other Writings on Politics, Peace, and History*. Ed. Pauline Kleingeld and trans. David L. Colclasure. New Haven, CT: Yale University Press, 2006.

Karatani, Kojin. *Sekai kyōwakoku e: Shihon=Nēshon=Kokka o koeru*. Tokyo: Iwanami shoten, 2006.

———. *Teihon Karatani Kōjin shū 4: Nēshon to bigaku*. Tokyo: Iwanami shoten, 2004.

———. *Transcritique: On Kant and Marx*. Trans. Sabu Kohso. Cambridge, MA: MIT Press, 2003.

Kautsky, Karl. *Communism in Central Europe in the Time of the Reformation*. New York: Russell and Russell, 1959.

———. *Foundations of Christianity: A Study in Christian Origins*. New York: Monthly Review Press, 1972.

Keynes, John Maynard. *The General Theory of Employment, Interest and Money*. New York: Palgrave Macmillan, 2007.

Kojève, Alexandre. *Introduction to the Reading of Hegel: Lectures on the Phenomenology of Spirit*. Trans. James H. Nichols Jr. Ithaca, NY: Cornell University Press, 1969.

Krader, Lawrence. *The Ethnological Notebooks of Karl Marx: Studies of Morgan, Phear, Maine, Lubbock*. 2nd ed. Assen, Netherlands: Van Gorcum, 1974.

Lévi-Strauss, Claude. *The Elementary Structures of Kinship*. Boston: Beacon, 1969.

———. *Introduction to the Work of Marcel Mauss.* Trans. Felicity Baker. London: Routledge and Kegan Paul, 1987.

Lukács, Georg. *History and Class Consciousness: Studies in Marxist Dialectics.* Trans. Rodney Livingstone. Cambridge, MA: MIT Press, 1972.

Malinowski, Bronislaw. *Argonauts of the Western Pacific: An Account of Native Enterprise and Adventure in the Archipelagoes of Melanesian New Guinea.* London: Routledge, 1922.

Mann, Michael. *The Sources of Social Power.* Vol. 1, *A History of Power from the Beginning to A.D. 1760.* Cambridge, UK: Cambridge University Press, 1986.

Marx, Karl. *Capital: A Critique of Political Economy.* Vol. 1. Trans. Ben Fowkes. Harmondsworth, UK: Penguin Books, 1976.

———. *Capital: A Critique of Political Economy.* Vol. 2. Trans. David Fernbach. Harmondsworth, UK: Penguin Books, 1978.

———. *Capital: A Critique of Political Economy.* Vol. 3. Trans. David Fernbach. Harmondsworth, UK: Penguin Books, 1976.

Marx, Karl, and Frederick Engels. *Collected Works.* 50 vols. New York: International Publishers, 1975–2004.

Mauss, Marcel. *A General Theory of Magic.* Trans. Robert Brain. New York: Norton, 1975.

———. *The Gift: Forms and Function of Exchange in Archaic Societies.* Trans. W. D. Halls. London: Routledge, 2002.

Mill, John Stuart. *Principles of Political Economy.* 2 volumes. London: Longmans, Green, Reader and Dyer, 1871.

Mills, C. Wright. *White Collar: The American Middle Class.* New York: Oxford University Press, 2002.

Montesquieu. *The Spirit of Laws* Trans. Anne M. Cohler, Basia C. Miller, Harold Stone. Cambridge, UK: Cambridge University Press, 1989.

Morgan, Lewis Henry. *Ancient Society.* New Brunswick, NJ: Transaction Publishers, 2000.

Mumford, Lewis. *Technics and Human Development.* Vol. 1, *The Myth of the Machine.* New York: Harcourt, Brace and World, 1967.

Needham, Joseph. *The Grand Titration: Science and Society in East and West.* London: Allen and Unwin, 1969.

Nietzsche, Friedrich. *On the Genealogy of Morals.* Trans. Douglas Smith. Oxford: Oxford University Press, 1996.

Nishida, Masaki. *Jinruishi no naka no teijū kakumei.* Tokyo: Kōdansha, 2007.

Ōtsuka, Hisao. "Shihonshugi shakai no keisei." In Hisao Ōtsuka, *Ōtsuka Hisao chosakushū,* vol. 5, 3–24. Tokyo: Iwanami shoten, 1969.

Ōtsuki, Yasuhiro. *Teikoku to jizen: Bizantsu.* Tokyo: Sōbunsha, 2005.

Plato. *Plato: Six Great Dialogues.* Trans. Benjamin Jewett. Mineola, NY: Dover, 2007.

Polanyi, Karl. *Dahomey and the Slave Trade: An Analysis of an Archaic Economy.* Seattle: University of Washington Press, 1966.

———. *The Great Transformation: The Political and Economic Origins of Our Time.* Boston: Beacon, 2001.

——. *The Livelihood of Man*. New York: Academic Press, 1977.

——. "Marketless Trading in Hammurabi's Time." In *Trade and Markets in the Early Empires*. Ed. Karl Polanyi, Conrad M. Arensberg, and Harry Pearson, 12–25. New York: Free Press, 1957.

Proudhon, P.-J., *General Idea of the Revolution in the Nineteenth Century*. Trans. John Beverley Robinson. Mineola, NY: Dover, 2003.

——. Letter to Karl Marx, May 17, 1846. In *The Anarchist Reader*. Ed. George Woodcock, 138–40. Hassocks, UK: Harvester, 1977.

——. *Proudhon: What is Property?* Cambridge, UK: Cambridge University Press, 1994.

Rawls, John. *The Law of Peoples*. Cambridge, MA: Harvard University Press, 2001.

——. *A Theory of Justice*. Rev. ed. Cambridge, MA: Harvard University Press, 1999.

Reich, Wilhelm. *The Mass Psychology of Fascism*. Trans. Vincent Carfagno. New York: Farrar, Strauss and Giroux, 1970.

Renan, Ernest. "What Is a Nation?" Trans. Martin Thom. In *Nation and Narration*. Ed. Homi K. Bhabha, 8–22. London: Routledge, 1990.

Renfrew, Colin. *Prehistory: The Making of the Human Mind*. London: Weidenfeld and Nicolson, 2007.

Ricardo, David. *On the Principles of Political Economy and Taxation*. New York: Dover, 2004.

Rousseau, Jean-Jacques. *Discourse on Inequality*. Trans. G. D. H. Cole. Whitefish, MT: Kessinger Publishing, 2004.

Sahlins, Marshall. *Stone Age Economics*. 2nd ed. New York: Routledge, 2003.

Sakurai, Mariko. *Herodotosu to Toukyudidesu*. Tokyo: Yamakawa Shuppan, 2006.

Sand, Shlomo. *The Invention of the Jewish People*. Trans. Yael Lotan. London: Verso, 2010.

Schmitt, Carl. *The Concept of the Political*. Trans. George Schwab. Chicago: University of Chicago Press, 1996.

——. *Political Theology: Four Chapters on the Concept of Sovereignty*. Chicago: University of Chicago Press, 2005.

Smith, Adam. *The Theory of Moral Sentiments*. Ed. D. D. Raphael and A. L. Macfie. Indianapolis, IN: Liberty Fund, 1984.

Stirner, Max. *Stirner: The Ego and Its Own*. Cambridge, UK: Cambridge University Press, 1995.

Sweezy, Paul, Maurice Dobb, Christopher Hill, Georges Lefebvre, Kohachiro Takahashi, Giuliano Procacci, John Merrington, Eric Hobsbawm. *The Transition from Feudalism to Capitalism*. London: NLB, 1976.

Tamanoi, Yoshirō. *Ekonomii to ekorogii*. Tokyo: Mizusu Shobō, 1978.

Tanaka, Jirō. *Sabaku no karyūdo: Jinrui shigen no sugata o motomete*. Tokyo: Chūkō Shinsho, 1978.

Testart, Alain. *Les chasseurs-cueilleurs, ou: L'origine des inégalités*. Paris: Société d'ethnographie, 1982.

Thompson, William. *Labour Rewarded: The Claims of Labour and Capital Conciliated*. London: Hunt and Clarke, 1827.

Trotsky, Leon. *The Revolution Betrayed*. Delhi: Aakar Books, 2006.

Tsuchida, Atsushi. *Netsugaku gairon: Seimei kankyō o fukumu kaihōkei no netsuriron.* Tokyo: Asakura Shoten, 1992.

Uno, Kōzō. "Kyōkōron." In Kōzō Uno, *Uno Kōzō chosakushū*, vol. 5, 3–172. Tokyo: Iwanami shoten, 1974.

———. *Principles of Political Economy: Theory of a Purely Capitalist Society*. Trans. Thomas T. Sekine. Brighton, UK: Harvester, 1980.

Wallerstein, Immanuel. *The Modern World System II: Mercantilism and the Consolidation of the European World-Economy, 1600–1750*. Berkeley: University of California Press, 2011.

———. "1968, Revolution in the World-System: Theses and Queries." *Theory and Society* 18:4 (July 1989): 431–49.

Weber, Max. *The Agrarian Sociology of Ancient Civilizations*. Trans. R. I. Frank. Atlantic Highlands, NJ: Humanities Press, 1976.

———. *The City*. Trans. Don Martindale and Gertrud Neuwirth. Glencoe, IL: Free Press, 1958.

———. *Economy and Society*. Trans. Ephraim Fischoff. 3 vols. New York: Bedminster Press, 1968.

———. *The Protestant Ethic and the Spirit of Capitalism*. Trans. Peter Baehr and Gordon C. Wells. New York: Penguin, 2002.

———. *The Sociology of Religion*. Trans. Ephraim Fischoff. Boston: Beacon Press, 1963.

Wittfogel, Karl A. "The Marxist View of Russian Society and Revolution." *World Politics* 12:4 (July 1960), 487–508.

———. *Oriental Despotism: A Comparative Study of Total Power*. New Haven, CT: Yale University Press, 1957.

Wood, Ellen M. *Empire of Capital*. London: Verso, 2005.

Yamada, Katsuyoshi. *Kahei no Chūgoku kodai shi*. Tokyo: Asahi Shinbunsha, 2000.

Yuien. *Tannishō: Passages Deploring Deviations of Faith*. Trans. Bandō Shōjun and Harold Stewart. Berkeley, CA: Numata Center for Buddhist Translation and Research, 1996.

INDEX

absolute monarchy, 73, 88, 165–69, 171, 209–12, 214, 224, 235, 257, 276, 296; and bureaucracy, 26, 124, 166, 173, 179; and mode of exchange B, 26; as welfare state, 76–77, 174

aesthetics, 219–21, 223

agriculture, 18, 20, 21, 63–64; and fixed settlement, 33, 44; revolution, 59–61

Akhenaten, 132–33, 140

Albritton, Robert, 269

Alevi, 328n19

Alexander the Great, 23, 109, 118

Althusser, Louis, 311n2

Amin, Samir, 23, 122, 207, 315n26, 326n22

anarchism, 9, 156, 180, 236, 281, 286, 292–93, 301

Anderson, Benedict, 27, 116, 213–15, 216

animism, 52–54, 61, 129

Arendt, Hannah, 8–9, 113–14, 118, 225–26, 276, 278

Ashoka the Great, 153

Aristotle, 94, 99–100, 101, 117, 119, 152, 326n22

Arrighi, Giovanni, 271–72

Asiatic despotic state, 23, 62, 73–74, 76–80, 104, 106, 110, 124, 138, 147, 166, 174, 180, 210, 226, 250, 260

Asiatic mode of production, 4, 73

Asiatic social formation, 20–23, 75–76

associationism, 9, 234, 245, 258–59

associations, 16, 18, 143, 231, 243, 246–47, 260

Assyria, 75, 79, 139

asylum, 130

Athens, 102, 111, 113–18

Atkinson, James, 55

Aztecs, 26, 163

Babylon, 69, 75, 91, 96, 138, 139, 142, 323n34

Bachofen, Jakob, 44

Bakunin, Mikhail, 240, 252, 259, 292–93

base (economic), ix

Baudrillard, Jean, 312n4

Baumgarten, Alexander, 219

Bellers, John, 228–29

Berle, Adolf, 200

Bernstein, Eduard, 242, 254

Bismarck, Otto von, 179, 198, 218, 246, 253

Blanc, Louis, 235, 255

Blanqui, Louis, 240, 255

Bloch, Ernst, xviii, 142, 258

Bloch, Marc, 125, 126

Bloch, Morris, 44–45

Bodin, Jean, 167–68

bourgeoisie, 26, 123, 278

bourgeois revolution, 26, 123, 124, 168–72, 178, 209, 210, 212, 214, 228, 257, 278, 296–97

boycott, 291

Braudel, Fernand, 23, 88, 125, 160–61

Britain: and bourgeois revolution, 210, 214, 228–29, 254, 270, 277; and feudalism, 123; and imperialism, 278; and industrial capital, 172, 174, 194–98, 204, 206–7, 241–42, 275; and money economy, 166; as nation-state, 224; as submargin, 126; and world-economy, 268